Folens

Learning Centre

essential ICT

for AQA

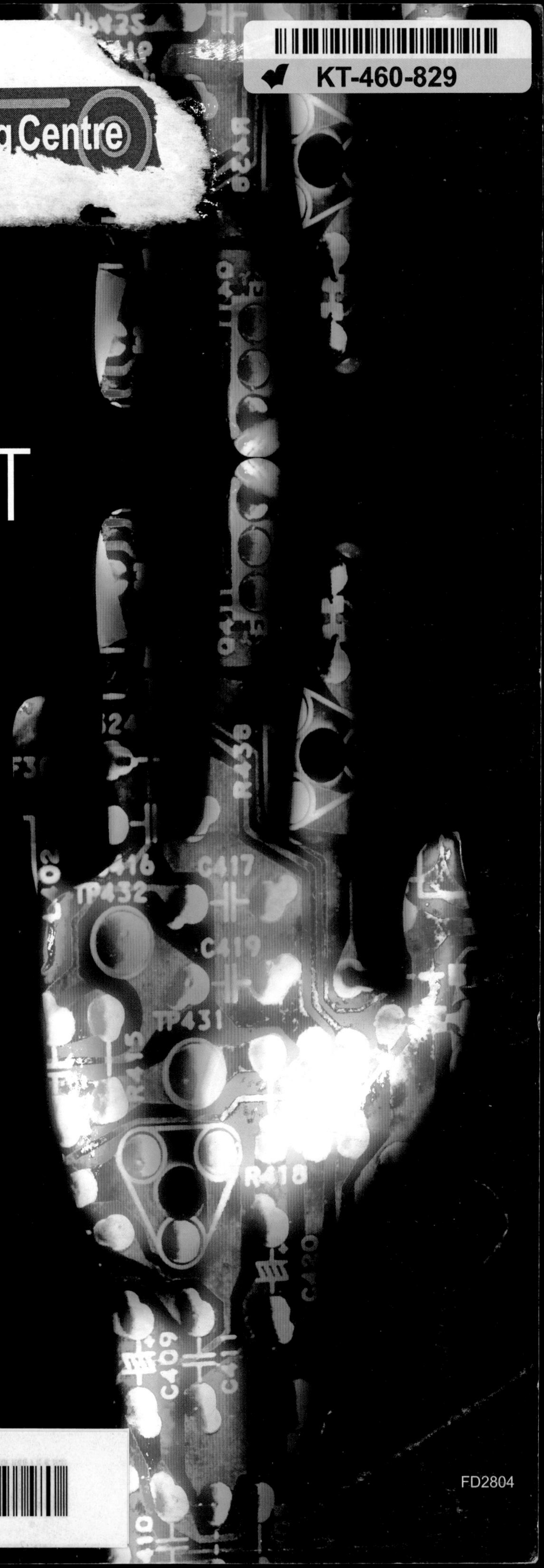

AS Level | Stephen Doyle

FD2804

Stephen Doyle hereby asserts his moral right to be identified as the author of this work in accordance with the Copyright, Designs and Patents Act 1988.

Editor:	Geoff Tuttle
Concept design:	Patricia Briggs
Layout artist:	GreenGate Publishing Services
Illustrations:	GreenGate Publishing Services
Cover design:	Jump To! www.jumpto.co.uk
Cover image:	Courtesy of Chris Harvey/Fotolia.com

First published 2008 by Folens Limited.

Every effort has been made to contact copyright holders of material used in this publication. If any copyright holder has been overlooked, we should be pleased to make any necessary arrangements.

British Library Cataloguing in Publication Data. A catalogue record for this publication is available from the British Library.

ISBN 978-1-85008-280-4

Contents

Unit 1
Practical Problem Solving in the Digital World

Unit 2
Living in the Digital World

Introduction to the AS Units

There are two units for the AS Information and Communication Technology:

Unit 1 Practical Problem Solving in the Digital World INFO1
Unit 2 Living in the Digital World INFO2

Unit 1: Practical Problem Solving in the Digital World INFO1

In this unit you will gain practical skills in using a whole range of hardware, software and communications technology for solving a wide range of practical problems. You will learn the transferable skills, knowledge and understanding needed to work on the solutions to a range of problems.

Assessment for Unit 1

Question paper with answers written in an answer booklet which is externally marked by AQA.
Two sections to the paper:

- Section A – short answer questions.
- Section B – three or more structured questions which require discursive answers. These answers will require argument/ reason.
- All the questions in both Section A and Section B are compulsory.
- Duration of paper – 1½ hours.
- 50% of the total AS marks.
- 25% of the total A-level marks.

Unit 2: Living in the Digital World INFO2

In this unit you will learn about the wider picture of the use of ICT. You will learn the theory in using ICT and look at the issues which the use of ICT creates. As you progress through the unit, you will be building up a specialist vocabulary and be able to understand the concepts involved in the study of ICT. As ICT moves forward at a fast pace, you will be looking at the latest developments in ICT and the issues this creates.

Unit 1: Practical Problem Solving in the Digital World INFO1

Range of software and problems

You will be using a range of applications software to cover the processing of text, images, numbers and sound.

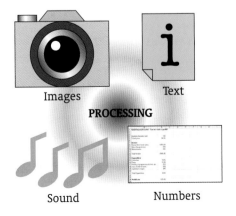

Images Text
PROCESSING
Sound Numbers

What skills I am expected to develop in this unit?

You are expected to develop the following skills:

- analysing
- designing
- implementing
- testing
- evaluating systems.

In order to demonstrate these skills you will need to address several problems which have ICT solutions. You will be able to negotiate with your teacher/ lecturer, the type of problems you will work on, so that you work on a suitable problem that will give sufficient scope to develop the above skills.

Typical problems with ICT solutions that you could develop include:

- an electronic photo album
- a rolling multimedia presentation for a school open day

- a website for a local nursery
- organising a blog for a local councillor
- producing invoices for a small business
- an interactive multimedia display for a tourist information centre.

How is my work assessed?

Although you are expected to complete one or two pieces of work to demonstrate that you have developed the skills, you are actually tested for this module by an examination. These pieces of work are referred to as sample work.

In the examination you will be asked about the work you should have done as part of your sample work. The better your sample work, the more likely you will be able to answer questions about it in the examination.

In the examination you will be asked to repeat a process that you have completed as part of the project – for example, in the project you may have been asked to identify suitable software in order to solve a problem, and in the examination you might be asked a question on how you might identify suitable software.

You could also be asked a question on what you actually did for part of your sample work.

You will be asked questions that will test your practical experience in identifying methods of solution, and the design, implementation, testing and evaluation of actual solutions to problems based on a range of applications software. These questions will relate to the processing of all the different types of data (e.g., text, numbers, sound and images).

What happens to the sample work?

You must keep the sample work and bring it with you to the examination. Here you will use information contained in the sample work to help you answer the questions in the examination.

You also have to give the sample work in along with your question paper/answer booklet.

Is there a limit on the sample work?

Yes there is and the limit is between 10 and 20 pages, so there is a requirement for the sample work to be:

- succinct (i.e., to the point, without any padding)
- clearly laid out
- legible to the examiner.

Organisation of the sample work

You will be required to have a Candidate Record Form as the first page of the sample work and this will need to be signed by you and your teacher. This form, as well as giving identification details, will also authenticate the work as being your own.

You must have page numbers on your sample work and these must go consecutively from start to finish. Page numbers are essential as you will need to say in some of the examination questions for Unit 1 on which page in your sample

work a particular section appears. Without the page numbers the examiner will not have time to search for the section of your work you are referring to.

Choosing a suitable problem

If you ask around, most people who use ICT have a problem they would like to solve using ICT if they had the time. Try to gather several problems and assess with your teacher which problem or problems (you are allowed to submit two) will give you the right scope. Choosing the right kind of problem is essential in order to be able to produce sample work that will enable you to answer questions about it in the examination.

Tips about choosing an ICT problem

Read through the part of the specification that outlines sample work so that you fully understand what you need to produce before selecting your problem.

Some problems make it difficult to get evidence. If you cannot find a problem that allows you to provide evidence in all the sections, you may need to change the problem or do two different types of problem.

Make sure you use a real client with a real problem.

The organisation of Unit 1

It is up to your teacher to work through appropriate material with you that will develop your problem solving skills and eventually give you sample material that you can take into the examination with you.

Unit 1 is divided into the following topics:

1 Health and safety in relation to the use of ICT systems
2 Analysis
3 Design of solutions
4 Selection and use of input devices and input media
5 Selection and use of storage requirements, media and devices
6 Selection and use of output methods, media and devices
7 Selection and use of appropriate software

8 Implementation of ICT-related solutions
9 Testing of ICT-related solutions
10 Evaluation of ICT-related solutions

1. Health and safety in relation to the use of ICT systems

Any ICT system that is developed must take into account health and safety legislation.

When a new system is developed it often involves the purchase of new hardware and software as well as office equipment such as chairs, desks, etc. There are regulations covering hardware, software and office equipment and these are covered in a separate section in this book.

In your sample work, you will need to mention how any new system meets health and safety requirements. It is important to note that software needs to be easy to use, as difficult and frustrating to use software causes stress to users. This is why the user interface (i.e., the way the user interacts with the system) needs to be appropriate for the user.

2. Analysis

Analysis of a system involves collecting information about the problem that needs solving. In order to develop the best solution to a problem, it is necessary to collect information from the person who wants the system developed.

Analysis involves:

- problem identification
- producing a list of the client's requirements
- interpreting lists of requirements as input, processing and output for ICT solutions.

Problem identification

Start off with a problem – this should be identified by a client who wants a problem solved using ICT, e.g. we need to create a website to attract customers, or we need an interactive presentation to show off our goods at an exhibition.

This involves a clear statement of the problem the client wants you to solve. Usually this will just be a short paragraph outlining:

1. What the problem you are going to solve is.
2. Who needs the solution to the problem (i.e., who the client is).
3. Who will be using the solution you have developed (i.e., who the user is).
4. An identification of what the user's skills are.
5. Details of any further intended audience.

Note that the person who asks for the solution (i.e., the client) may not be the same person who uses the solution. The client may ask for a website to be produced that will be used by anyone who is interested in their products or services.

Example of a client's problem

The manager of a tourist information office, who is the client, would like an interactive multimedia display to be used by tourists visiting the city.

The idea is that the tourists are presented with a list of the main attractions and they can then select one for further information, such as opening times, admission prices, maps to get there, what is there, and so on.

Although many tourists are ICT literate, some older tourists who will want to access the information do not have these skills, so the system needs to be very easy to use.

A list of the client's requirements

Here you will consult the client and identify the following:

- what the solution is to produce (i.e., what the final outputs need to be)
- how the solution is to work.

This is best outlined as a list of bulleted points.

An interpretation of the list of requirements in terms of input, processing and output

The previous list will have identified:

- the format that the output needs to be in
- the data which needs to be input to produce the required output
- what processing is needed to turn the input into output.

In this section you write a list of:

- items of data input into the system
- the various processes that need to be performed on the input data
- a list of the information which is produced as the output.

3. Design of solutions

By this stage you will have collected enough information about the problem to be able to start on the solution to the problem. As problems are so different (e.g., you could be developing an interactive presentation or a customer database), their solutions will be different. Usually there will be a variety of different ways of solving a problem and a variety of different software to choose from.

Selection of design tools and techniques and their application to identified problems

You will need to choose the software that will allow you to develop the solution to the ICT problem. Sometimes you will have to choose from different software and pick the one that best suits the problem. An example of this might be a simple database which could be developed using spreadsheet software or by using database management software.

Depending on your choice of software, you will then have to explain the techniques you used in order to solve the ICT problem. In this section you will need to design data capture forms if these are appropriate. If you are developing a solution for capturing music and/or images, then you will need to describe how data is captured for use in your system.

Design of data entry into the ICT system

Here you need to describe the methods you intend to use in your solution to ensure the accuracy of data entry. You will need to use the following checks if they are appropriate:

- verification checks
- validation checks.

With all the checks you need to consider how errors could occur during data entry and then make sure that possible errors can be reduced using a whole range of error checks.

Design of processes

In this section, you need to describe the various processes that are performed on the input data to produce the output.

The types of processes you describe will depend on the nature of the solution. For example, if you are developing a spreadsheet, you will need to describe the calculations you performed on the data or any logic expressions used.

Design of output of information

Here you need to describe how you designed the results from the solution. You will need to explain whether these results appeared on the screen or as a printout or in some other format (e.g., sound in a podcast).

In the case of information on screen or as a printout, the information needs to be presented in a suitable sequence.

Designs needed to be used by other people

Sometimes you can develop the solution to an ICT problem and need to use another person for the implementation.

4. Selection and use of input devices and input media

There are many different input devices that can be used to input data into an ICT system. In this section you need to choose the most appropriate input device to input the data into your ICT solution. In some cases a direct method of input could be used, so in these cases you will need to describe the input media being used to input the data into the solution. An example of this might be the input of photographs to form a picture library from data in the form of a memory card from a digital camera. Other examples could be music stored on a pen drive. You need to describe:

- what input device you intend to use
- what input media you intend to use (if applicable)

- an explanation of why the input device or media is suitable.

5. Selection and use of storage requirements, media and devices

You need to describe:

- what storage devices you intend to use (NB there will always be more than one)
- what storage media is used, for each of the storage devices
- justification of your reasons for choosing the storage devices and media.

6. Selection and use of output methods, media and devices

There are many different types of output from an ICT system. In many cases the output will be in the form of text and still images, but output can be in the form of sound, video, animation, etc. Each of these types of output will need a different method of producing the output.

You will need to consider the output methods most suitable for the solution to the ICT problem and then you will need to justify your choice. It may be the case that several output methods are used and you need to justify each one. In your justification you need to consider what output methods there are that would be suitable and then state with reasons which ones you chose.

7. Selection and use of appropriate software

Before deciding which software to use you will have to find out what software is available. You will need to consult with your teacher/lecturer on this. You may be tempted to use software you have at home that the school/college does not have. Be careful about this. You will not be able to simply load this software onto the school/college computers as the software will not be properly licensed. Another problem is that your teacher/lecturer may not have the expertise in using the software and be unable to give you the help you require.

There are two main groups of software:

- systems software
- applications software.

You will need to specify both types of software for your ICT solution.

In this section of the sample work you will need to describe:

- the software that was available
- the software you chose for the ICT solution
- justification of your choices of software for each problem.

8. Implementation of ICT-related solutions

In this section you need to describe how you have used the following to solve your ICT problems:

- hardware
- software
- communications technologies.

9. Testing of ICT-related solutions

ICT solutions have to be thoroughly tested. It should never be assumed that they are producing the correct output. It is very easy to make a mistake in the design that will lead to incorrect results being produced.

In this section you will need to describe the following aspects relating to a test plan:

- test plans including a range of test data
- identification of the expected outcomes (i.e., what the test data should produce)
- tests to check that the client's requirements have been met.

In this section you need to describe how you used the test plan to test your ICT solution by describing the following:

- testing evidence that is cross-referenced to the test plan
- testing that is clearly annotated to show an understanding of the testing process
- interpreting the results of tests and showing what was done to correct any problems with the solution
- a check against the list of client requirements to make sure that the ICT solution meets them all
- a description of the results of the testing which can be used as evidence in the evaluation of the solution.

10. Evaluation of ICT-related solutions

In this section you need to describe your solution to the client's problem.

Here are some questions you need to answer for the evaluation:

- Does the solution do what it was supposed to do – does the solution meet all the requirements as agreed with the client?
- Does it do it how it was supposed to do it?
- Is the solution an effective one? Is it the best solution or has it been compromised in any way?
- If the solution isn't as effective as it could be, what is wrong with it and how might it be corrected to be an effective solution?

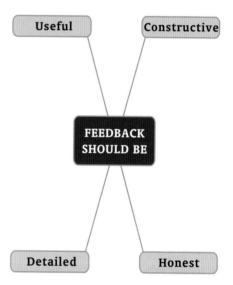

You could include in your evaluation comments that users or your client have made about your solution. Do not make these up – they should be honest accurate comments.

Feedback from clients and users is good to include in your evaluation.

Here are some comments from a client:

- I think you would be better allowing the user to switch off the sound. The music playing was a real distraction and besides I hate Rap music.
- I was able to enter ridiculous data into the spreadsheet and it was accepted and subsequently processed.
- Some of the links did not work. I found this annoying and my customers will too.

Unit 2: Living in the Digital World INFO2

In this unit you will learn about the wider picture of the use of ICT. You will learn the theory in using ICT and look at the issues which the use of ICT creates. As you progress through the unit, you will be building up a specialist vocabulary and be able to understand the concepts involved in the study of ICT. As ICT moves forward at a fast pace, you will be looking at the latest developments in ICT and the issues this creates.

Assessment for Unit 2

Question paper with answers written in an answer booklet which is externally marked by AQA.

Two sections to the paper:

- Section A – short answer questions.
- Section B – three or more structured questions which require discursive answers. These answers will require argument/reason.
- All the questions in both Section A and Section B are compulsory.
- Duration of paper – 1½ hours.
- 50% of the total AS marks.
- 25% of the total A-level marks.

The organisation of Unit 2

Unit 2 looks at the use of ICT by themselves and others and also looks at the issues arising from the use of ICT for individuals, society and organisations.

Unit 2 is divided up into the following topics:

1 An ICT system and its components
2 Data and information
3 People and ICT systems
4 Transfer of data in ICT systems
5 Safety and security of data in ICT systems
6 Backup and recovery
7 What ICT can provide
8 Factors affecting the use of ICT
9 The consequences of the use of ICT

1. An ICT system and its components

Here you will be looking at the definitions of terms such as ICT and system and also at the components of ICT systems. You will learn that ICT systems do not just consist of hardware and software but also consist of people, data, procedures and information.

2. Data and information

There is a subtle difference between the terms data and information and you need to be able to define and use these two terms correctly. Here you will learn the definitions and be able to use them to describe ICT systems. You will learn about the forms which data can take and the difference between coding and encoding data.

The result of processing data is information and you will learn about the factors that affect the quality of information.

3. People and ICT systems

ICT systems are designed for and used by people and they are commissioned for a purpose. In this topic you will look at the characteristics of the people whose use ICT, such as age, experience, etc., and look at how it is possible to take these factors into consideration when designing ICT systems. You will then look at the way users interact with ICT systems by looking at the different types of user interface.

There are many different jobs available to ICT professionals and in this topic you will be looking at the names of these jobs, what the jobs entail and what particular skills are needed for the job. As many of the jobs in ICT involve working as part of a team, you will learn about the characteristics that make such teams effective.

4. Transfer of data in ICT systems

This topic looks at technologies that enable data to be transferred from one place to another. You will be looking at the elements of an ICT network and how each part of the network works with the other parts.

There is a difference between the terms the World Wide Web and the Internet and here you will learn what this difference is. You will also look at the uses of communication technologies and also the reasons why standards are needed in order for such technologies to work.

5. Safety and security of data in ICT systems

This topic looks at the need to protect data in ICT systems and the types of threat that such systems face. You will look at the difference between internal and external threats and the difference between malpractice and crime.

The measures that can be taken to protect all parts of ICT systems will be looked at as well as the legislation that covers ICT.

6. Backup and recovery

Everyone who uses ICT needs to be able to backup and recover their files in the event of them being lost and this topic looks at how this is done.

It also looks at why, in organisations, one person should be given responsibility for the taking of backup copies and the reasons why, with some ICT systems, continuity of service is essential at any cost.

7. What ICT can provide

This topic looks at the facilities that ICT can provide and also the limitations in what ICT can be used for and in the information that it produces.

The topic also looks at the different types of processing: batch, interactive and transaction and the uses for which each is appropriate.

8. Factors affecting the use of ICT

This topic looks at how the use of ICT is influenced by cultural, economic, environmental, ethical, legal and social factors.

9. The consequences of the use of ICT

This topic looks at the consequences of the use of ICT for individuals and then for society as a whole.

Introduction to the features in the student book

The philosophy behind the student book

This student book has been based on extensive research from schools and colleges on the different ways ICT is taught and this book has been developed with all the findings in mind. As this is a new specification, many students and teachers/lecturers will be finding their way and the aim of the book is to provide a depth of coverage for all the material for Units 1 and 2. This book covers all the material for the AS level in ICT.

This book should be used by the teacher/lecturer in conjunction with the teacher support materials. Of course this book can be used stand-alone, but if you are a teacher then there are many resources in the teacher support materials to help your students succeed and maximise their marks. The Teacher Support CD-ROM contains the following non-digital resources: Answers to the Questions, Activities and Case studies and also provides additional Questions and Case studies.

The Teacher Support CD-ROM also includes a wealth of digital materials such as PowerPoint presentations, multiple choice questions, interviews, webquests, missing word tasks, voting exercises and free text tasks. These will all help your students consolidate their understanding of the topics.

The structure of the student book

The AQA AS-level consists of two units with each unit being divided into topics. In this book each topic has been further divided up into spreads. This allows division of each topic into bite-size easily digested chunks of material. For consistency and to make the student book easy to use, all topics are structured in the same way.

Topic spreads

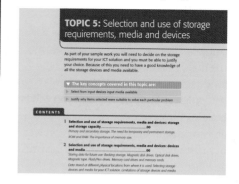

The first page of each topic consists of an introduction to the material in the topic and includes the following features:

Topic introduction: just a couple of paragraphs introducing students to the subject matter in the topic.

Key concepts: this lists the key concepts covered in the topic. These key concepts are identical to those in the AS AQA specification.

Contents: the contents lists the spreads used to cover the topic and each spread covers key concepts.

Cartoons: relevant cartoons drawn by the cartoonist Randy Glasbergen add a bit of humour and fun to the topics.

Introduction: introduces the content on the spreads.

You will find out: this tells you what you will learn from the content of the spreads.

The content: what you need to learn is presented in the content and this material has been written to give you the essential information in order to answer examination questions.

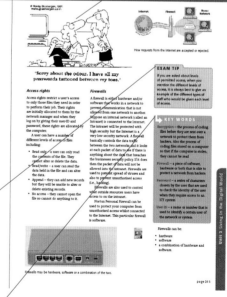

Diagrams and photographs: brings the topic to life with relevant and carefully researched images.

Exam tips: useful tips based on the problems that students have when they answer questions on the topics.

Key words: these are specialist terms used in the content spreads and it is important that you not only remember these words, but you can use them with confidence when describing aspects of ICT systems. There is also a glossary at the back of the book which can be used for reference.

Questions, Activities and Case study spreads

These are usually included at the end of the content spreads and are used to consolidate learning. There are some occasions where Activities or Questions are included within the content spreads. Each block of questions covers a certain number of pages and most of the time this will be a double page spread. This allows you to look at the spreads and then practise the questions. The answers to all the questions are available in the teacher support materials, which are available separately on CD-ROM and complement the student text.

▶ Questions 1 | pp. 168–169

1 Many ICT systems are used to process personal information about individuals. Many people say that such systems erode privacy.
   (a) Explain the meaning of the term 'privacy'. **(2 marks)**
   (b) Give **three** items of personal information which a bank or building society would hold about you. **(3 marks)**
   (c) Give **three** items of personal information that you would not want to be disclosed to others and for each item give a reason why you would not want this information disclosed. **(6 marks)**
   (d) Name the Act which governs the way organisations must deal with personal information. **(1 mark)**
2 Protection of your privacy is essential if you bank or shop on-line.
   (a) Give the names of **three** different pieces of personal information you would need to supply in order to complete an on-line purchase. **(3 marks)**
   (b) Give **one** item of personal information (that you would not want others to know) that you need to supply in order to complete an on-line purchase. **(1 mark)**
   (c) Give **one** method by which the item of personal information in your answer to (b) can be kept private. **(1 mark)**

▶ Activity 2 Creating a mind map on threats

For this activity you have to create a mind map which covers the broad subject of 'threats to an ICT system'.
   You can use mind mapping software, such as Inspiration, for this task or if you do not have the software then you can draw the mind map on paper.
   You can use the following list of threats to start you off:
   · viruses
   · Trojans
   · worms
   · spyware
   · adware
   · spam
   · abuse by staff (accidental or deliberate)
   · hacking
   · fire
   · theft
   · natural disasters
   · faulty hardware or software
If your teacher lets you, you can work in small groups which will allow you to work collaboratively and bounce ideas off one another.

▶ Case study 3 | pp. 182–183

Big Brother is watching you!

A Big Brother database is being planned by the government which will hold large amounts of data about each one of us that can be used by government departments as well as some private organisations.
   The trouble is that many government departments have data about us which is untrue or out-of-date. The idea is that government departments would be able to share the data that has been collected. This would help individuals such as the family member who needed to contact the different government departments to sort out the affairs of someone who had just died. With the new database only the one set of data about a person is held so it would only be necessary to contact one of the departments to update the details.

One problem that the government would have is that the law would need to be changed regarding the sharing of information.
   As the data contained on such a database would be very personal, the use of the database would need to be carefully monitored. Each time someone used the database the details of who accessed it and why the information was needed would be recorded. This in itself would add a huge amount to the data being stored. For example, if a building society needed to check on someone's identity before they decided to give them a mortgage, then the details of the mortgage application would also be recorded.
   With this information added, the government have access to huge amounts of information and can build up a picture of a person's life.

1 (a) Give the name of the Act that would have to be changed in order for the transfer of personal data to be allowed. **(1 mark)**
   (b) (i) Which of the eight principles would be contravened if the database went ahead? **(1 mark)**
       (ii) Describe the principle which is being contravened. **(2 marks)**

2 (a) Describe what is meant by the term privacy. **(2 marks)**
   (b) Give **one** way that could be used to make sure that the data in the database is not out-of-date. **(1 mark)**
   (c) Describe, with a reason, why it is more efficient to hold personal details in one huge database compared to lots of separate smaller databases. **(2 marks)**

3 People are worried that their right to privacy is being eroded with the development of this database.
   (a) Give **two** reasons why a person's privacy could be eroded by this database. **(2 marks)**
   (b) Describe **one** benefit to the government in sharing the data in the database between departments. **(1 mark)**
   (c) Give **one** advantage to a private company in being able to use some of the data contained in the database. **(1 mark)**

Questions: are included at the end of each topic and refer to the content in the spreads and are clearly labelled so that you can either do them after each double-page spread or all in one go at the end of the topic. The questions are designed to be similar to AS examination questions and have marks to give students the opportunity to understand how answers are marked.

The answers to the questions are included in the Teacher Support CD-ROM.

Activities: offer interesting things for you to do which will help add to and reinforce the material in the spreads.

Case studies: real-life case studies are included that relate directly to the material in the topic. Case studies give a context in which you can answer the examination questions. Often examination questions on ICT ask not only for a definition or explanation but also an example. Case studies build up your knowledge of how the theory you learn about is used in practice.

Case study questions: will give you practice at answering questions which relate to real-life situations. The questions have been carefully constructed to be similar to the examination questions you could be asked and relate directly to the case study and other material contained in the content spreads.

If your teacher has the Teacher Support CD-ROM, they will have the answers to these case study questions.

Exam support

Worked example: is an important feature because it gives you an insight into how the examination questions are marked. At AS level you can have the knowledge but still fail to get a good mark because you have failed to communicate what you know effectively. It is essential that you understand just what is expected of you when answering questions at AS level.

Student answers: you can see an examination question which has been answered by two different students. For each student answer there is a corresponding Examiner's comment.

Examiner's comment: offers you an insight into how examiners mark student answers. The main thing here is to be able to see the mistakes that some students make and ensure that you do not make similar mistakes. By analysing the way answers are marked you will soon be able to get more marks for the questions that you answer by not making common mistakes.

Examiner's answer: offers some of the many possible answers and an indication of how the marks are distributed between the answers. It should be borne in mind that there are many possible correct answers to some questions and that any mark scheme relies on the experience of the markers to interpret the mark scheme and to give credit for answers that do not appear in the mark scheme.

Summary mind maps

Mind maps are great fun to produce and a very good way of revising. They are included here to summarise the material contained in the topic. Sometimes there will be only one mind map and other times there will be several – it all depends on how the material in the topic is broken down.

As well as using these mind maps to help you revise, you should produce your own.

Why not produce them using the computer. There are many good pieces of mind mapping software.

Worked example 1

1 A health and fitness club would like to offer past members who have let their membership lapse, special deals to rejoin the club. They use data they collected five years ago to decide what special deals and promotions should be offered.
   (a) Explain why the data from five years ago might not be suitable to decide on the offers made to past members today. **(2 marks)**
   (b) Explain the effect on the health club if they used this data from five years ago. **(2 marks)**

Student answer 1

1 (a) Data from five years ago would be out of date. For example, they could have changed address so they would not hear about the offers.
   (b) The health club would lose money and they could be prosecuted.

Examiner's comment

1 (a) A fairly simple question if it had been read carefully. This student has answered a completely different question such as 'what are the consequences of using out-of-date data'. This answer does not answer the question – it needs to refer to the data being used to make a decision. **(0 marks out of 2)**
   (b) There are two marks here so at least two points are needed.
   General statements, such as 'lose money' without saying why, gain no marks.
   Again 'could be prosecuted' is too general to being given credit, without giving the reason why. **(0 marks out of 2)**

Student answer 2

1 (a) The data would no longer be accurate. Their circumstances could have changed and they may have a family and not have time to attend a health club.
   (b) The response rate for the offer would be low and not justify the time, effort and cost of letters sent out.

Examiner's comment

1 (a) There are two marks here. You are safer explaining two separate points rather than give a fuller description of a single point.
   This student should have given two points or made it clearer that the two points made are distinctly different. **(1 mark out of 2)**
   (b) Again there are two marks and one point is given.
   Answer is correct but two separate answers should have been given. **(1 mark out of 2)**

Examiner's answers

1 (a) One mark each for two of the following:
   Market conditions may have changed from five years ago, e.g. there may be more competition.
   People's tastes change so what attracted them five years ago might not attract them today.
   People will be five years older so could have more demands on their time, e.g. families.
   (b) One mark each for two of the following:
   They may waste time and money offering deals no-one wants.
   The price offered may be wrong owing to the competition being cheaper thus losing money.
   They would be in violation of the Data Protection Act 1998 for keeping data for longer than necessary and for processing out-of-date data.

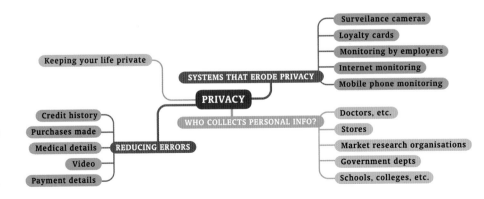

TOPIC 1: Health and safety in relation to the use of ICT systems

In this topic you will need to understand the current health and safety problems associated with working using ICT systems. You will need to understand the nature of the health problems, how they are caused and how the risks from them can be reduced with correct working practices or properly designed equipment.

You will learn about the legislation that applies to working with ICT systems and what responsibilities employers have when introducing new hardware and software in the workplace.

▼ The key concepts covered in this topic are:

▷ Understand the need for current health and safety legislation that relates to the use of ICT systems.

▷ Understand the application of current health and safety regulations that relate to the use of ICT systems.

▷ Understand how health and safety guidelines cover the design and introduction of new software.

CONTENTS

EHWLC LEARNING CENTRE
EALING GREEN

Unit 1 Practical Problem Solving in the Digital World

The need for current health and safety legislation

Introduction

Using computer equipment is a safe occupation but there are a number of health problems which can pose a hazard to users. In this section you will be looking at what these health problems are and how it is possible to prevent them.

The health problems

The main health problems that may occur when working with ICT systems are:

- Back ache
- Repetitive strain injury (RSI)
- Eye strain
- Stress.

Back ache

Back ache is mainly caused by sitting with incorrect posture. Slouching in a chair whilst using the computer can lead to back problems. Sitting awkwardly at a desk is another cause.

To help prevent back problems:

- Use an adjustable chair (NB in workplaces this is a legal requirement but you need to ensure that the chair you use at home is adjustable).
- Always check the adjustment of the chair to make sure it is suitable for your height. Use a foot support called a footrest if necessary.
- Sit up straight on the chair with you feet flat on the floor.
- Make sure the screen is lined up and tilted at an appropriate angle.

Using a chair like this is essential to avoid health problems

Repetitive strain injury (RSI)

Repetitive strain injury (RSI), sometimes called ULD (upper limb disorder), causes aches and pain in hands, wrists, arms and neck. Usually the symptoms do not last but they can be persistent and eventually disabling.

RSI can be prevented by good workstation design and good working practices.

To help prevent RSI:

- adjust your chair to the correct seating position for you
- make sure there is enough space to work comfortably
- use a document holder
- use an ergonomic keyboard/mouse
- use a wrist rest
- keep your wrists straight when keying in
- position the mouse so that it can be used keeping the wrist straight
- learn how to type properly – two-finger typing has been found to be much worse for RSI.

If you slouch in your chair, you may end up with back ache.

Eye strain

Eye strain causes blurred vision and headaches. It is caused by using the screen for long periods, glare on the screen, dirt on the screen and working without the best lighting conditions.

To avoid eye strain:

- keep the screen clean so it is easy to make out the characters on the screen
- use appropriate lighting (fluorescent tubes with diffusers) and blinds to avoid glare which can cause headaches
- take regular breaks to avoid stress and give your eyes a rest
- have regular eye-tests (NB if you use a screen in your work, then your employer is required by law to pay for regular eye-tests and glasses if they are needed)
- ensure you are not sitting too near the screen, to avoid the possible risks of radiation.

Stress

Using ICT systems can be stressful, especially when things go wrong.

The people who produce ICT systems for others to use (e.g., websites, databases, on-line ordering systems, etc.) have a responsibility to us all to make them simple to use.

Stress can come from:

- the pace of work (e.g., too much to do in too little time)
- worry about using the new technology – older people feel they cannot cope
- software that is frustrating to use because it has not been designed properly
- losing work, problems with viruses and technical problems.

GLASBERGEN

'It's an ergonomic ankle support designed to help you be more productive.'

Stress is often caused by too much work to do in too little time.

EXAM TIP

It is always best to err on the side of caution by adding more information to an answer than you think you might need. For example, if you are asked to state a health problem, do not just write a one-word answer (unless it says in the question that a one-word answer is acceptable). Write a short sentence such as 'back ache caused by slouching in a chair whilst surfing the Internet'.

Stress caused by unreasonable workloads is a problem for many employees.

The application of current health and safety regulations

Introduction

Because of the problems identified in the previous section, the health and safety regulations were applied to the use of ICT equipment in the workplace. The Act in force which applies to the use of ICT equipment is called the Health and Safety at Work Act 1974.

Health and safety legislation

Under the Health and Safety at Work Act 1974, employers have a duty to minimise risks to employees in the workplace. Employees need to have a safe place to work and have a safe system of work.

The Health and Safety at Work Act 1974 is fairly general and more specific regulations covering the use of computer equipment are contained in the Health and Safety (Display Screen Equipment) Regulations 1992.

The regulations made it law for employers to take certain measures to protect the health and safety of their employees who use ICT equipment.

The Health and Safety Executive (HSE) are the government department responsible for health and safety in the workplace. Part of their job is to promote good health and safety practice in the workplace and they produce many leaflets (both on-line and paper) to this effect.

Computer screens

Computer screens should:

- tilt and swivel
- be at an appropriate height for the user
- display a stable image with no flickering
- have brightness and contrast control
- be free from reflections
- be of an appropriate size for the software application being run (e.g., CAD (computer aided design) needs a large screen because there is so much displayed on the screen at one time).

Appropriate training

There should be training of employees so that they:

- know how to make adjustments to the screen (i.e., alter the brightness and contrast)
- understand the need for taking regular breaks
- adjust the size of text and other screen elements so that they can be read easily
- understand the importance of keeping the screen clean.

Chairs

There is a tendency to slouch in chairs when using computers and especially when surfing the Internet. This should be avoided because prolonged slouching will almost certainly lead to back problems in the future. Chairs should be:

- adjustable in height so that the feet can be placed flat on the floor. If this is not possible because a person is short, then a footrest should be provided
- have seat backs which provide proper back support (i.e., they should have adjustable height and tilt)
- have five feet with castors for stability and to ensure that it is easy for the chair to be moved closer and further away from the desk.

Desks or workstations

Desks or workstations should:

- be big enough for computer equipment and paperwork
- have a matt surface to reduce glare.

Keyboards

The keyboard design we are used to has evolved from the development of the typewriter. If a keyboard were to be designed today, from an ergonomic point of view, the keys would not be arranged in this way.

There have been many attempts at putting the keys in different orders but getting users to use them has been difficult.

This ergonomic keyboard separates the keys completely.

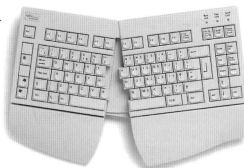

This keyboard isn't broken. It is one of many ergonomic keyboard designs.

▶ Activity: Workstation health and safety

The diagram below shows a user sitting at a workstation. This user is adopting good practice.

Label this diagram with as many examples of good practice as you can spot. You should be looking for a minimum of 7.

© 1998 Randy Glasbergen.

If the QWERTY keyboard were arranged ergonomically, it would have this arrangement of keys. This arrangement reduces the finger travel distance for keystrokes which helps reduce RSI.

Research sites

The Health and Safety Executive is the government department responsible for publicising and enforcing health and safely legislation. Their site can be found at: *http://hse.gov.uk*

The TUC's site offers useful advice on RSI: *http://www.tuc.org.uk/h_and_s/tuc-7697-f0.cfm%20*

'Suspending your keyboard from the ceiling forces you to sit up straight, thus reducing fatigue.'

GLASBERGEN

Health and safety guidelines covering the design and introduction of new software

▼ **You will find out**

▶ About the problems with software that can cause stress in users

▶ About how software can be designed so that it does not cause stress in users

Introduction

The health and safety guidelines cover the design and introduction of new software as this is frequently a source of stress amongst employees. Employees are often given little input into the design of software, even though they may be using it for long periods each day. Software that is poorly designed or frustrating to use causes employee stress. In this section you will be looking at what can be done to minimise the problems.

Making software less stressful to use

Software can be designed ergonomically so that it is easier and less stressful to use.

Software designers can make software less stressful to use by ensuring:

- that software is bug free and does not cause the computer to freeze or crash, sometimes resulting in the user losing work
- that fonts and font sizes are chosen carefully to make text easier to read
- that information is displayed in a logical order on the screen –

important items are displayed at the top left of the screen
- that the software is intuitive so that it behaves in a way users would expect it to behave
- help screens tell the user what to do in a way they understand and do not leave the user more frustrated
- methods which minimise the amount a user has to key in should be used in order to reduce the likelihood of RSI
- any music or any animations can be switched off or skipped past by the user
- shortcuts should be used wherever possible to minimise mouse clicks.

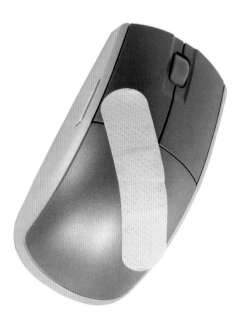

Other things can be done to make the use of software less stressful

There are other things apart from the correct design of software that will help make the use of ICT systems less stressful. These include:

- having a help-desk to help with user problems
- training users fully in all the ICT systems they use
- a procedure of logging problems as they arise so that they can be corrected.

How software can be designed so that it does not cause stress in users

Software design is not simply about getting the software to complete a task. When designing the software it is very important to remember that people will be using it on a day-to-day basis. Here are some of the things that should be considered:

- Ensure that the order of material on each screen is logical and that the important items always come first.
- Ensure that all software is thoroughly tested so that it does not crash.
- Software should be tested by users so that any frustrating user-identified problems can be eliminated.
- Try to minimise the mouse movements needed to make selections to save a user time and to reduce RSI. Use drop-down menus where possible.
- Keep consistency from one screen to the next, which will make the software easier to learn.
- Put items such as buttons, menus, etc., on the screen where users would expect them.
- Help screens should be written simply. This should be tested by novice users.

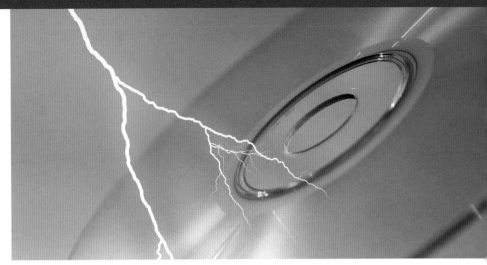

Losing data is a major cause of stress.

Chatting to a usability engineer

Amy Hawkes is a usability engineer whose job is simply to eliminate problems in software that makes users grit their teeth. She improves all those confusing messages, eliminates links that don't work, and makes menus less confusing.

Amy explains: 'It is my job to make users' jobs easier and less stressful. For example, it should not take six steps to do something that could take three.'

She goes on to say: 'As part of the training for my job I have to understand how people learn and remember. I also trained to understand layouts of the screens and the psychology of colours.'

In order to increase the efficiency of users, Amy looks at users to see what they are likely to want to do next after completing a task. The idea is to increase the efficiency of the user.

Amy uses real users to see if she was right. Amy says: 'I do this by making paper prototypes of the design. I then use graphics software to create a model of what the screens, icons and menus will look like.'

Amy explains: 'I then ask the user to point to the icons they need to do the work on the paper. Depending on which icon they use, I can then quickly give them another piece of paper. I can get a feel for the design of the solution by doing this.'

Not knowing what is happening is a major cause of stress.

Questions and Case studies

▶ Questions 1 pp. 2–3

1 The use of ICT systems has been associated with a number of health problems.
   (a) State **three** health problems that have been associated with the prolonged use of ICT systems. (3 marks)
   (b) In order to avoid computer-related health problems certain preventative actions can be taken. Describe **six** such preventative actions that can be taken to alleviate the health problems you have identified in part (a). (6 marks)

2 An employee who spends much of their time at a keyboard typing in orders at high speed is worried about RSI.
   (a) What do the initials RSI stand for? (1 mark)
   (b) Give **one** of the symptoms of RSI. (1 mark)
   (c) Write down **two** precautions that the employee can take to minimise the chance of contracting RSI. (2 marks)

▶ Questions 2 pp. 4–5

1 A person employed in a telephone ordering department works for long periods typing order details into a computer using a keyboard. To ensure the health and safety of the employee, state, with reasons:
   (a) **Two** design features that the chair, the employee sits on, should have to minimise health problems. (2 marks)
   (b) **Two** design features that the screen, the employee uses, should have to minimise health problems. (2 marks)

2 (a) Give the name of the health and safety regulations which cover working with display screens. (1 mark)
   (b) The regulations lay down certain steps which employers must follow to protect their workers when they are working with computer equipment.
      (i) Give **two** features that a display screen must have when being used in the workplace. (2 marks)
      (ii) Give **two** features a workstation must have when being used in the workplace. (2 marks)

▶ Questions 3 pp. 6–7

1 Poorly designed software can cause stress amongst employees. For example, the text on the screen may be too small for the user to read properly. Describe **three** other features in the design of a software package that could cause stress in a user. (6 marks)
2 You are designing an ICT system for use by others. Describe **two** things that can be done to check that the user interface is not frustrating to use. (2 marks)

3 Using ICT systems can result in user stress. Employers could be sued if they cause bad health owing to poor working practices. Describe **one** working practice that could result in a stress problem when working with ICT systems. (2 marks)

► Case study 1 | pp. 2–5

Computers 'could disable children'

Children use computers early on and this could put them at risk of permanent injury.

The problems include neck and back ache as well as numbness and tingling in the fingers caused by RSI.

A doctor worried about the problem said: 'this is the first generation of children who have used computers since early childhood while their muscles and bones are developing'.

One child complained of severe pain in their neck and back which gets worse after prolonged sessions on the computer. They complained that: 'no matter which way you sit or lie, you just cannot get comfortable'.

Some lawyers have suggested that schools need to train children to use computers in a safe way in order to avoid legal action from pupils and their parents. They also need to check workstations for problems.

1. You have been asked by the headteacher of a primary school to look at the workstations and ICT equipment in order to identify any issues that could give rise to health problems.
Describe **four** things you would look for and for each one give a reason why it is important. (4 marks)

2. (a) Give the meaning of the abbreviation RSI. (1 mark)
   (b) RSI can be caused by computers. Describe **two** things that a user might do which would make them more susceptible to RSI. (4 marks)

3. The Health and Safety (Display Screen Equipment) Regulations 1992 only apply to the workplace and do not apply to students/pupils in schools and colleges but they do apply to staff.
Give one reason why the regulations do not apply to pupils/students attending schools and colleges. (1 mark)

► Case study 2 | pp. 2–8

Is working in an office making you ill?

Working in an office could be making you ill. The way you work in an office affects your general well-being.

Back pain is a big problem with office workers with many people unable to work with it and others having to take long periods off sick with it. Health and safety advisors say that they are amazed at the chairs people who work with computers have to sit on. They say that a good chair should fit you individually and should be adjustable, have five feet and should be able to move freely.

'Repetitive strain injury (RSI) is a real problem' says the safety advisor and to prevent the problem 'you need to support your wrists with wrist rests which the employer should provide'.

Eye strain is caused by long periods staring at a computer screen. Reflection from windows and lights can cause headaches as it makes text more difficult to read.

Rising stress levels are also worrying and so much so that it has become the largest health and safety problem.

1. (a) Give the meaning of the initials RSI. (1 mark)
   (b) Give **two** precautions a user can take in order to reduce the likelihood of them contracting RSI through the use of ICT equipment. (2 marks)

2. Eye strain can cause headaches. Eye strain can be caused by glare on screens. Describe **two** things that can be done to eliminate the glare on computer screens. (4 marks)

3. Stress has been identified in the article as a major health problem. Give **one** thing that an employer can do in order to reduce employee stress when working with ICT systems. (2 marks)

Exam support

Worked example 1

1 Health problems can be caused by poorly designed workstations.

State **three** features of a well designed workstation and for each feature state the health problem that could be reduced. **(6 marks)**

Student answer 1

1 Make sure that the seat is comfortable so user is relaxed.

Use blinds on the windows to reduce glare which can cause eye strain.

Do not leave trailing wires which people could trip on and injure themselves.

Have a dull desk surface to reduce glare.

Examiner's comment

1 The question refers specifically to the workstation and not the entire room.

The chair answer is relevant but not appropriate. A settee is comfortable and gives a relaxed sitting position yet would be inappropriate for use with a workstation.

The blinds and trailing wires answers refer to the room rather than the workstation so there are no marks for the first three answers.

The last answer is ok for the feature but glare gives rise to a health problem and there is no mention of what this is (i.e. eye strain). A feature and the health risk the feature reduces is needed for two marks. **(1 mark out of 6)**

Student answer 2

1 There needs to be sufficient desk space to rest hands which will reduce the likelihood of the user contracting repetitive strain injury (RSI).

The user could use an ergonomic mouse or keyboard which will reduce the likelihood of contracting RSI.

The screen should be adjustable so that neck strain is reduced.

An adjustable chair with five points should be used so that the user adopts the correct posture which will reduce future back ache.

Examiner's comment

1 This student has clearly identified a feature of a workstation and also clearly stated the health problem that the feature is likely to reduce. This is a perfect answer and gains full marks. **(6 marks out of 6)**

Examiner's answers

1 One mark for the feature and one mark for how the feature reduces the health risk. Note that the answer must be relevant to a workstation.
   - Sufficient desk space (1) to rest hands will reduce the likelihood of RSI (1).
   - Using footrests (1) if the person is short will reduce back ache (1).
   - Use a tiltable/adjustable screen (1) to reduce neck strain (1).
   - Use a screen with a matt surface (1) to reduce eye strain due to glare (1).
   - Use an ergonomic keyboard (1) to help reduce the likelihood of RSI (1).
   - Matt surface on the desk (1) reduces glare and hence eye strain (1).
   - Use an adjustable chair (1) which will reduce back ache (1).

Worked example 2

2 Software needs to be designed to be 'user friendly' in order to prevent health problems to users. For example, a software developer can design software having the function of clear error messages that will allow users to identify what is wrong and how to correct it thus reducing user frustration and stress.

   Give **four** other functions that a software developer can provide in the software that will help prevent the health problem of user stress when using an ICT system. **(8 marks)**

Student answer 1

2 Choose a large font so that the text can be easily read.
  Choose a font colour and a background colour that make the text easy to see.
  Help is provided in easy to understand terms so that a user does not get stuck using the software which will increase their stress.
  Use autosaving facilities so that if the computer is turned off by mistake or the power is switched off, the user has most of their work saved thus reducing the stress of losing a lot of work.

Student answer 2

2 Reducing the amount users have to type in by using drop-down lists, which will reduce the amount of typing users have to do, which will reduce the likelihood of contracting RSI.
  Ensuring that the forms used on the screen match up with the paper forms being used to hold the data for input, which will reduce user frustration and reduce stress.
  Messages on the screen after a set time to tell the user to take a break, which will reduce eye strain and fatigue.
  Use short cut keys so that experienced users can use keys rather than menus, which will reduce the stress in using the software.

Examiner's comment

2 Here the question asked for a function of the software rather than simple features. A function of the software is the way that it performs. The first two answers about fonts and colours are really simple features rather than functions. Also there is no mention of the health problem and how the function helps prevent the health problem. There are no marks for the first two answers.

   The next two answers are much better. Both answers give a function of the software and they also identify the health problem and how the function prevents it. So, full marks for each of these answers. **(4 marks out of 8)**

Examiner's comment

2 All the answers refer to the functions of the software. The functions described all do something. Also how the function helps reduce the health risk is clearly stated. This is a very good answer. **(8 marks out of 8)**

Examiner's answers

2 One mark for the function of the software (note must be a function and not a simple feature) and one mark for how the function prevents the health problem.

  • Messages on the screen after a set time to tell the user to take a break (1) which will reduce eye strain and fatigue (1).
  • Use short cut keys (1) so that experienced users can use keys rather than menus, which will reduce the stress in using the software (1).
  • Suitable validation checks (1) during entry ensure that problems caused by processing incorrect data do not cause stress (1).
  • Use drop-down lists (1) rather than type in data, which will reduce the likelihood of RSI (1).
  • Use help screens (1), which will reduce stress when users get stuck (1).

Summary mind maps

The need for current health and safety legislation

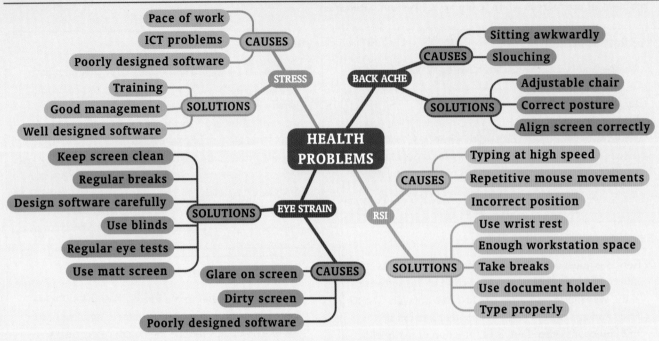

The application of current health and safety regulations

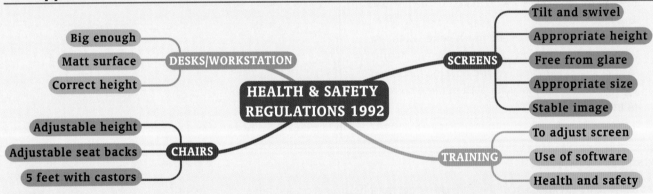

Health and safety guidelines covering the design and introduction of new software

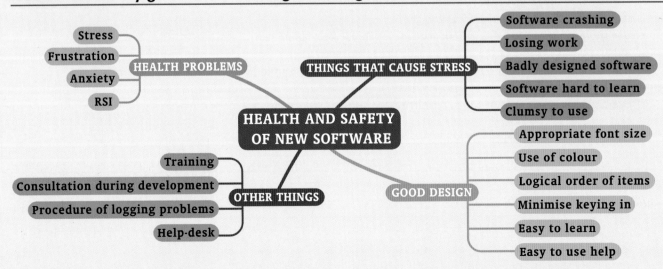

TOPIC 2: Analysis

In this topic you will learn about how to choose a suitable problem or set of problems that you need to produce solutions for. Before you start this topic, make sure you have read, understood and digested the material in the Unit Introduction.

This unit gives detail on the overall material you need to produce as part of the sample work.

▼ The key concepts covered in this topic are:

▷ Problem identification

▷ Produce a list of the client's requirements

▷ Interpret lists of requirements as input, processing and output for ICT solutions

CONTENTS

What is analysis?

▼ You will find out

▶ About how to analyse a user defined ICT problem

▶ About the difference between a client, user and audience

▶ About how to produce and interpret client requirements

Introduction

The analysis stage in solving an ICT problem involves meeting with a user to discuss the problem that they wish you to solve. At this meeting and subsequent meetings you need to fully understand the nature of the problem and the requirements of the user. During analysis you will need to collect facts about the inputs, processing and outputs for the new system.

Problem identification

Choosing the right kind of problem or problems is essential if you want to get a good mark for this unit. You need to have a problem or problems that will allow you to develop a solution or solutions that allow you to produce sample work which covers all the topics in this unit.

Before you start thinking about a problem you must make sure that you have experience in using a range of different software. This will allow you to see what software you can use for the problem or problems. Without the knowledge and skills developed using a whole range of software you will be limited in the problems you can solve and you will probably not get as good a mark.

Steps to follow

1 Describe clearly and in detail what the problem is you are going to solve. You do not have to say here how you are going to solve the problem.
2 Identify who needs the solution to the problem. The person identifying the problem and asking for a solution is called the client. Give some information as to the context in which the client needs the solution (e.g., the client is retired and lives off the income from stocks and shares that they have, and they would like to see the value of their portfolio on a particular day).

3 Identify who will use the solution. Note that the person who asks for the solution (i.e., the client) may not always be the user of the system. For example, a person may ask you to develop a website to market their business. The people who use the website will be anyone who is interested in their products or services. The client could be the owner or manager of the business and the user could be an employee of the business.
4 Word-process all of the above under the following headings which can form part of your sample work for the ICT solution to the problem.
Description of the problem
Identification of the client (i.e., the person who needs the solution to the problem)
Identification of the user (i.e., the person who will use the solution to the problem)
Identification of any audience for the solution (i.e., people who will simply view the solution and will not alter it in any way)

What is a client?

The client is the person who needs the solution to an ICT problem which they have identified. The client could be the owner of a business or a manager or they could be anyone who has a problem that needs an ICT solution.

EXAM TIP

Make use of your teacher/lecturer. Always discuss with them the one or more problems you intend to solve. Your teacher will have a good idea if you have chosen any unsuitable ones. It is much better to identify unsuitable problems at the start rather than work on them and then find they are unsuitable.

What is a user?

A user is a person who makes active use of an ICT solution to solve an ICT problem. Active use means that they alter the input and produce the output to use in some way. In some cases the client and the user can be the same person. In many cases they will be different. For example, a client may ask for a solution to a problem that will be used by their employees (i.e., the users).

In summary, a user will:

- actively use the solution
- alter the input
- update content
- use the output in some way.

Analysis – breaking a problem down so that it is easier to understand and solve. Analysis of problems that have an ICT solution involves understanding the inputs, processes and outputs

What is an audience?

An audience for an ICT solution will only view the content. They will not supply inputs or change content in any way. For example, an audience would simply browse a website or view a multimedia presentation.

Considering the skills of the user

In producing an ICT solution to a problem, you need to take account of the skills of the users. Here are some of the things you will need to consider:

- Members of the public have variable ICT skills, so if your solution is aimed at this group, you will need to make sure that your solution is capable of being used by this wide group.
- If your user is an employee of an organisation, they can be trained to use the ICT solution.

Be aware of the following when creating your solution:

- age of users
- ICT skills of users
- language level used
- the type of user interface.

Producing a list of the client's requirements

Ask the client (i.e., the person you are producing the solution for) to clearly state what they want from the solution to the problem. In particular, you need to know what information needs to be output.

Arrange a meeting with your client in order to find out their requirements for the solution. Here are some tips to help produce a list of client requirements:

- First find out a little about their business or interests.
- Talk generally about what they want you to do for them.
- Try to limit the scope of the problem – you need to be able to solve the problem – do not be too ambitious.
- Go away and think about whether using your skills, you will be able to produce a solution.
- Think about what they told you.
- Write down some questions you would need answering and arrange another meeting with your client.
- Inform your client that you only have a limited amount of time to solve the problem and that this will limit the complexity of the problem you can solve.
- Agree on what the ICT solution must do.

When you have done all the above, produce a list of the client's requirements and get them to check through each one of them with you. This is what you will be producing, so it is important that it is correct and agreed by both parties.

Make sure you document this by word-processing it and adding it to the sample work for assessment in the exam.

Interpreting the list of requirements

Once the list of requirements has been produced and the client has agreed with them, the next step is to identify to which of the following each requirement belongs:

- Input
- Processing
- Output.

You will find it is easier to work from the output as these are the results or answers the client wants from the system. ICT solutions can be so different – the output from a financial model is different to the output from an organised collection of photographs.

Output – what information is needed in what format?

Process – what processing needs to be done on the input data in order to produce the output as specified by the user?

Input – in order for the system to produce the required output, what input data will be needed and where will it come from and how will it get into the ICT system?

In the documentation for this section, you will need to show:

- items of data input into the system
- the various processes that need to be performed on the input data
- a list of the information that is produced as the output.

Questions

▶ Questions 1 | pp. 14–15

1 (a) Explain by giving an example, the difference between a client for an ICT solution and a user of an ICT solution. (2 marks)

(b) Explain how the user of a solution to an ICT problem differs from an audience for the solution. (2 marks)

2 You are developing a spreadsheet solution in the form of a financial model for a client who is just starting a new business.

(a) Before starting on the solution you need to know about who will use the ICT solution. Give **one** reason why this is important. (1 mark)

(b) Give **two** ways in which it would be possible to find out about the skills that a user has in using software such as spreadsheet software. (2 marks)

Checklist for analysis

It is important that you have documented the analysis part of your sample work.

The following table will help you check off that you have completed and documented the analysis part correctly.

Heading	Sub-heading				
Problem identification					
	Description of problem				
	Details of client, user and audience (if applicable)				
	Assessment of skills of user				
Client requirements					
	What the solution has to produce				
	How the solution is to work				
Requirements in terms of input, processing and output					
	Output requirements				
	Input requirements				
Processing required					

Once the above has been agreed and checked with the client, you can word-process the document with the above headings and sub-headings. Ensure that:

- All headings and sub-headings stand out clearly – you will have to refer to these sections in the examination so you don't want to waste time trying to find them.
- All the pages are suitably numbered, as you may need to refer to the page number in the examination.

Exam support

Worked example 1

1 Answer this question using the sample work that you have brought into the examination with you.

Problem identification

(a) (i) Explain the difference between a client and a user. (2 marks)

(ii) Explain the difference between a user of a solution and an audience for a solution. (2 marks)

(b) (i) Copy out **one of the requirements that you have included.** (1 mark)

Restate this requirement as:

(ii) Input (2 marks)

(iii) Processing (2 marks)

(iv) Output for your ICT solution. (2 marks)

Student answer 1

1 (a) (i) A client is someone who owns a business and a user is a person who uses the computer.

(ii) A user will use the solution that has been produced.
An audience will just view what has been produced.

(b) (i) A table is produced showing the price a share was bought for and the share price today obtained automatically from the Internet.

(ii) Input – the number of each share owned is entered.

(iii) Processing – the number of each share held is multiplied by the current price.

(iv) Output – a screen display shows all the information the client has asked for.

Examiner's comment

Part (a) (i) Gains no marks. You do not have to own a business to be a client for a solution and 'a user is a person who uses a computer is a statement of the obvious and gains no marks. The main point they should have made is that a user is actively supplying input and producing and using the output in some way.

Part (a) (ii) The definition of 'user' needs to be more specific, so no marks here.

The definition of audience needs further clarification by giving an example or mentioning that there is no alteration of input or content so no marks here.

Part (b) (i) This is a clear indication of part of what the solution should do so one mark here.

Part (b) (ii) Input – There are two marks allocated. The data the student suggests is relevant to the requirement and it has been broken down to single input so two marks here.

Part (b) (iii) Processing – There are two marks allocated. The processing the student suggests is relevant to the requirement and it has been broken down in enough detail (i.e., the calculation has been identified) so two marks here.

Part (b) (iv) Output – There are two marks allocated. The student has mentioned the output method but only one mark here. **(6 marks out of 11)**

Exam support continued

Student answer 2

Please note that the student has embarked on a different ICT problem to that produced by student 1.
This student has produced a multimedia quiz using PowerPoint software for testing health and safety knowledge for people who use ICT in the workplace.

1 (a) (i) A client is someone who has identified a problem and has asked for it to be solved using ICT and a user is a person who will actively use the solution developed and will change the content.

   (ii) A user will use the solution by altering the content of the multimedia quiz I have developed.
        An audience will just view the multimedia quiz – they will not alter any questions.

   (b) (i) The multimedia quiz must give feedback and tell the person whether they have answered the question correctly or not.

   (ii) Input – An answer A, B, C or D is entered via the keyboard.

   (iii) Processing – A link is provided if the correct letter is keyed in and a different link is provided if the incorrect letter is pressed. These links take you to different slides, one for the correct and the other for the incorrect answer.

   (iv) Output – Two screens – one saying well done you have supplied the correct answer and the other saying they were wrong and giving them information about the correct answer.

Examiner's answers

1 (a) (i) Two marks allocated as follows:
A client is a person who has asked for an ICT problem to be solved (1) whereas the user is the person who makes use of the ICT solution to solve the problem and supplies inputs and produces the output (1).

   (ii) Two marks allocated as follows:
A user actively uses the solution to solve a problem and will supply the inputs to the system and make use of the output from the system (1). An audience for an ICT solution will only view the content and will not alter inputs or change content in any way (e.g., browse a website, look at a multimedia presentation, etc.) (1).

   (b) (i) One mark for a requirement being stated (NB the requirement must be what the solution should do or produce).

   (ii) Input – two marks. One mark for each of the following:
The data being supplied must be relevant to the requirement stated in (b)(i) – it must not be a general requirement (1).
The data should be broken down into single inputs (1).

   (iii) Processing – two marks. One mark for each of the following:

Examiner's comment

Part (a) (i) This is a clear definition so full marks.
Part (a) (ii) This is clear – they have identified that the user alters the content and they have put their answer into a context (i.e., their quiz) so two marks.
Part (b) (i) This is a clear requirement for the quiz – it explains clearly what part of the quiz should be capable of doing. One mark.
Part (b) (ii) The input is clearly stated and refers to the user requirement. Two marks for this.
Part (b) (iii) This is processing because a decision is made on the basis of the input to show one of two screens and the process is in sufficient detail for a design to be produced. This gains two marks.
Part (b) (iv) The method of output is stated (i.e., using two screens) and it is clear what each screen would contain. This gains both marks. **(11 marks out of 11)**

The process must be identified and must be relevant to the requirement stated in (b) (i) (1).
The process is stated in enough detail so that a design can be produced (1).

   (iv) Output – two marks. One mark for each of the following:
Information that applies to the stated requirement in part (b) (i) (1).
The method of output is stated (1).
The format of the output is stated (1).
The order of the output is stated (1).

Worked example 2

2 Answer this question using the sample work that you have brought into the examination with you.

Analysis

(a) (i) When developing an ICT solution a developer will often start from the output or results and then work out the input and processing that is needed. Give one reason why this is. **(2 marks)**
(ii) Explain the meaning of the term 'analysis'. **(2 marks)**
(iii) Explain one process your ICT solution does in order to turn the input data into output information. **(2 marks)**

Student answer 1

This student has produced a simple website for a teacher/lecturer who offers private tuition after school and at weekends.

2 (a) (i) The output is important so it needs to be done first.
(ii) Analysis is the stage where you look at the problem and break it down into steps so that you can go away and design a solution.
(iii) It takes the data in the form of content such as text, images (still and video) and combines it by arranging it on a series of webpages. Hyperlinks are then used to link the pages together.

Examiner's comment

2 (a) (i) No marks for this answer as they have not added anything to what was given in the question.
(ii) One mark for saying that the problem is broken down into parts. No marks for the last part, because it does not say why it is easier to go away and design a solution.
(iii) This is a website so the processing is the arrangement of the content on the webpage. One mark for this part of the question and one mark for the explanation of hyperlinks. **(3 marks out of 6)**

Student answer 2

This student has produced a break-even analysis for a person who is going to grow pond-plants and sell them by mail order and by using the Internet auction site eBay.

2 (a) (i) The output are the results and are what the client wants to get out of the ICT solution. We need to see exactly what they want output, so we can see what data has to be input and also to work out how the input will be processed.
(ii) Analysis breaks the problem down into parts so the developer can understand the problem and work out what needs to be done to solve it. Analysis involves producing a list of requirements and then breaking these down into input, processes and output.
(iii) The user enters the costs that vary, such as the costs of compost, pots, packing, postage, etc., and the costs which stay more constant, such as wages, fuel costs, rent, etc. These are all inputs to the model.

Examiner's comment

2 (a) (i) This is a good answer and is worth two marks.
(ii) Three main points have been included which each add correctly to the definition of the term analysis so both marks are awarded.
(iii) Good explanation of the inputs to a break-even model. Two marks here. **(6 marks out of 6)**

Examiner's answers

2 (a) (i) Two marks:
The output is the results (1) or what the client wants from the solution (1).
By specifying the output the developer can determine the inputs needed to produce the output (1).
They can work out what processing is needed to turn the input into output (1).

(ii) Two marks from:
Breaking down a problem so that it is easier to understand and solve (1).
Ensuring that you identify and understand the client's requirements (1).
Writing a list of the client's requirements (1).
Determining the input, processing and output needed from the client's requirements (1).
(iii) One mark for a description of an item or items of input data and one mark for a reason or further explanation as to why this data is input.

Summary mind map

What is analysis?

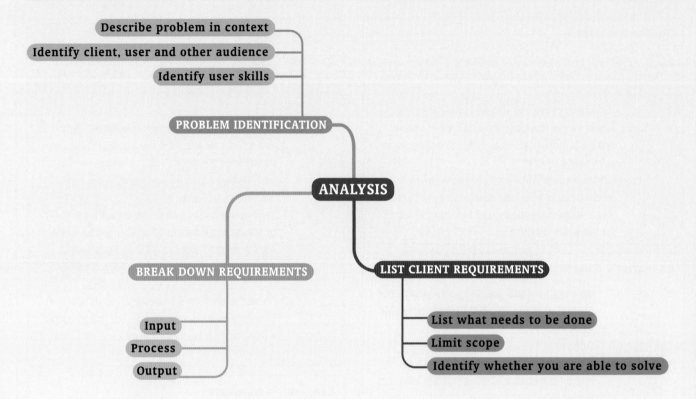

TOPIC 3: Design of solutions

In this topic you will carry on from the analysis stage and use the information gained to set about designing a solution to the ICT problem. You will select the design tools (i.e., the software used for the solution) and then apply them to the problem. You will then proceed to design the way the input data gets into the computer for processing. The design of the processes and the design of the output of information will then be carried out. If there are designs that need to be used by other people, then these will be produced.

▼ The key concepts covered in this topic are:

▶ Select design tools and techniques and apply them to identified problems

▶ Design of data entry into ICT systems

▶ Design of processes

▶ Design of output of information

▶ Designs needed to be used by other people

CONTENTS

EHWLC LEARNING CENTRE
EALING GREEN

Select design tools and techniques and apply them to identified problems

▼ **You will find out**

▶ About what design tools are

▶ About how to choose the most appropriate design tools for an ICT solution

▶ About what design techniques are

▶ About how to choose design techniques

Introduction

Once a problem has been identified it is necessary to solve it using one or more pieces of software (called design tools) and a variety of techniques (called design techniques).

Because problems can be so different, the software tools and techniques needed will vary from problem to problem.

What are design/ICT tools?

Design tools are the software you use to provide a solution to a problem using ICT.

In many cases you will need to use more than one piece of software to solve a particular problem. For example, you may decide to produce a website and also need to use some word-processing software and image editing software to prepare material for inclusion in the website as well as the website design software.

It is important to realise that even if you are using one item of applications software, you will be using two items of software because the applications software will not run without systems software.

Choosing design/ICT tools

Some tools are better than others. For example, if you wanted to saw a piece of wood in two, an electric saw would be better than a manual saw.

Choosing the best software tool is no different. Many pieces of software can be used for more than one job.

For example, a simple newsletter can be produced using word-processing software but specialist desktop publishing software might be better.

The most appropriate software tools for the task will depend on:

- The tools that are available.
- Your experience at using the various tools. For example, there may be better software for doing the job but you may not have the time to learn how to use it.
- Whether the piece of software will work with the other pieces of software that you also need to use. For example, certain applications software will only work with a particular make of systems software.

What are design/ICT techniques?

Design techniques are the ways you use the design/ICT tools to solve problems.

What documentation do I need to produce?

In this section you need to describe what you plan to do and how you will use the chosen software to solve the problem.

Ways of capturing data

In order for data to be processed it needs to be in a form that the computer can use. Data capture is the term for the various methods by which data can be entered into the computer so that it can be processed. The most common way to capture data is to use the keyboard, but this is not appropriate in many instances. For example, how do you capture a piece of music using a keyboard or obtain a digital version of an old photograph?

The choice of data capture method depends on the type of ICT problem you are solving.

Data supplied using paper forms

Data from the outside world is often obtained from forms or by speaking to a person over the telephone. These forms, called data entry forms, need to contain the data that has to be input. Examples of such forms include:

- application forms
- forms for supplying change of details (e.g., contact details, name, employer, etc.)
- filled-in questionnaires
- order forms
- requests for further information
- booking forms.

Remember that depending on the volume of data, it may be better to look at automatic data entry methods.

Data supplied from websites

Data can be obtained from websites. Sometimes this data, in the form of text, images, video and audio, is simply copied but it is also possible to provide a link back to the website. This means that if the data changes in the website, the changes can also be made in the ICT solution. For example, you could have a link to a website which contains constantly changing share prices. By providing a link to the data on the website, the data used by the ICT solution can be kept constantly up-to-date.

Data supplied from other systems

The information output from one system can be used as input to a different system. For example, attendance from your school's information system can be used to produce a comparison with other schools in the area and the national average and the results presented graphically using spreadsheet software.

Podcasts

Creating a podcast is easy – all you need is a computer, a microphone, some software and an Internet connection.

Podcasts are very popular due to the huge number of audio listening devices such as the iPhone, iPod or MP3 players. A podcast is an audio file that is created in MP3 file format which means it can be read using all audio players. This audio file is recorded using special audio software and is then edited and saved in MP3 file format.

A simple free program that can be used for audio recording and editing is called Audacity and can be downloaded from the website at http://www.audacity.co.uk/

The MP3 file is then uploaded with an RSS (really simple syndication) file to the server you use or one of the podcasting hosting services. You can then access your audio file and download it to your computer or portable media device such as an iPod. Podcasts are ideal for:

- making your own radio programmes
- helping you and others revise while on the move
- promoting a new product or service
- providing news of events.

To avoid you having to keep looking to see if there is a new MP3 file on the website, you can subscribe to a podcast using podcast software. The software is then informed by RSS when a new episode is produced and it is downloaded automatically. The RSS feeder software can be downloaded and saved onto your computer but there is also some browser software that can be used on-line.

The steps in making a podcast:

1. Plan the content of your podcast. Produce a script if it helps.
2. Check that you have a microphone connected to the computer.
3. Load the audio software such as Audacity and record the podcast.
4. Save the podcast in MP3 file format.
5. Upload the podcast to the server or podcast hosting service.
6. Create the podcast feed.

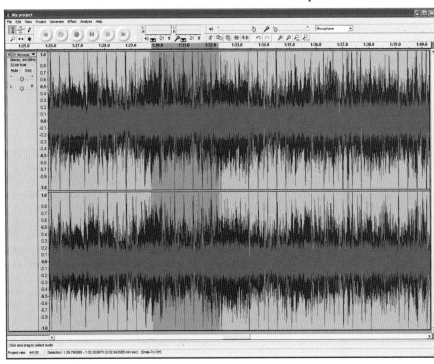

Design of data entry: problems with errors

Introduction

The processing of incorrect data can produce ridiculous and embarrassing output. Errors can take time and effort to sort out and can be distressing to any people affected by incorrect personal data. When an ICT system is developed, it is essential that error checking is incorporated into the design. In this section you will be covering the types of error that can occur and how error checking techniques can increase the accuracy of data entry.

Problems with inaccurate data

The processing of accurate data is essential for any ICT system. Errors in data can cause all sorts of problems such as:

- incorrect decisions being made resulting in loss of money
- goods being sent to the wrong address
- having to spend time sorting out mistakes
- loss of goodwill
- loss of trust
- being prosecuted under the Data Protection Act 1998 for not keeping personal data accurate.

It is essential that techniques are built into any data entry method so that errors can be reduced, or in some cases eliminated.

The validity and correctness of data

For a piece of data to be valid, it has to obey certain rules. For example, if a field has been set for the entry of a number, and a letter is entered instead, then the letter is not a valid piece of data for that field. As you can set fields in databases to accept only certain types of data, this would be spotted by the database and the piece of data would not be accepted.

If the surname 'James' was entered incorrectly as 'Jones' then it would be accepted into the database, as 'Jones' is as much a piece of valid data as 'James'. Both pieces of data are valid yet one is incorrect. You can see that there is a difference between the correctness and validity of data.

Reducing errors using validation and verification techniques

During the entering of data into ICT systems all sorts of errors can occur. To prevent the processing of data containing errors, two methods are used:

- verification
- validation.

Verification

Verification means checking that the data being entered into the ICT system perfectly matches the source of the data. For example, if details from an order form were being typed in using a keyboard, then when the user has finished, the data on the form on the screen will be identical to that on the paper form (i.e., the data source). There are two methods of verification:

- proof reading
- double entry of data.

Proof reading involves one user carefully reading what they have typed in and comparing it with what is on the data source (order forms, application forms, invoices, etc.) for any errors, which can then be corrected.

In **double entry of data**, two people use the same data source to enter the details into the ICT system and only if the two sets of data are identical, will

they be accepted for processing. The disadvantage of this is that the cost of data entry is doubled.

On-line entry of data

As e-commerce takes over, more and more people are involved in data entry. This reduces the costs because organisations get you and I to key in the data and it also reduces the errors because people are more careful when keying in personal and financial information about themselves.

Types of error which can occur during data entry

The commonest errors during data entry using a keyboard can be put into two groups:

- transcription errors
- transposition errors.

Transcription errors

Transcription involves the transferring of data (written or printed on a form) to the computer usually by keying it in. Transcription can also involve typing what a person says into the computer. Unfortunately human operators who have to key in the data are faced with a number of problems, namely:

- Problems with understanding speech – the person not speaking clearly enough into the phone.
- A caller not spelling out unusual words or names – the person doing the keying in, guesses the spelling.
- Poor handwriting – the source document (application form, order form, payment slip, etc.) has writing on it which cannot be read.
- Misinterpretation – the person keying in misinterprets information on the form or what was said over the phone.
- Typing mistakes – the keyboard operator reads or hears the right information but makes a mistake when typing it in.

Transposition errors

Transposition errors are easy to make when typing at high speed and involve the accidental swapping around of characters. Examples of transposition errors include typing in:

- 'fro' instead of 'for'
- the account number 100065 instead of the correct account number 100056
- the flight number AB376 instead of BA376.

It has been estimated that around 70% of keyboarding errors are transposition errors. Transposition errors can be spotted during the proof reading process and it is also possible to spot some of them by using spellcheckers.

Important numbers such as account numbers, employee numbers, VAT numbers, National Insurance numbers, etc., make use of check digits which enable checking on the accuracy of the input of these numbers.

Verifying and validating content

If you are developing a multimedia ICT solution to a client problem, there are many ways of checking content so that the final solution is accurate and fit for purpose. Content means the material you are putting on the website, presentation, etc., such as text, images (photographs, cartoons, line drawings, sketches), video, sound, etc.

During the development of multimedia products it is necessary to check the content or the arrangement of the content by:

- Checking the accuracy of any content supplied. Any factual information included should be checked.
- Checking the readability of the content based on the characteristics of the user/audience such as age, ICT experience, etc.
- Spellchecking – there is nothing worse than clients, users or audiences spotting spelling mistakes. Use the spellchecking feature of the software tools to make sure that these do not occur.
- Grammar checking – correct grammar is essential and so use the grammar checking feature of the software tools to check this automatically. You should also allow others to read through the content to check that it makes sense.
- Checking all the content is present – it is easy to leave out a bit of text or an image. Proof reading by yourself or others will be able to spot this.
- Ensuring that there is no duplication of content – one common mistake is to say the same thing twice. Proof reading will be able to spot this.
- Checking consistency of layout – webpages or slides with similar content should have a consistent design. Again this can be spotted and corrected by proof reading.
- Checking images – images should be checked to make sure they are the correct size and of an appropriate resolution.
- Checking that the font and font size are appropriate for the characteristics of the user and/or audience.
- Checking that images are suitable for the text.

Data entry using a keyboard is fine for small volumes of data.

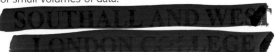
> **KEY WORDS**
>
> **Transcription error** – error made when typing data in using a document as the source of the data
>
> **Transposition error** – error made when characters are swapped around so they are in the wrong order
>
> **Verification** – checks that the data being typed in matches exactly the data on the document used to supply the information
>
> **Validation** – the process which ensures that data accepted for processing is sensible and reasonable

Design of data entry: validation

▼ You will find out

▶ About how validation is used

▶ About the various validation checks that can be used

▶ About the types of checks used during batch processing

Introduction

There are a number of validation checks that can be used to validate data being entered into an ICT system. The more validation in place, the less likely ridiculous data is to be processed.

Validation

Validation is a check performed by a computer program during data entry. Validation is the process which ensures that data accepted for processing is sensible and reasonable. Validation is performed by the computer program being used and consists of a series of checks called **validation checks**.

When a developer develops a solution to an ICT problem, they must create checks to lessen the likelihood of the user entering incorrect information. This is done by restricting the user as to what they can enter, or checking that the data obeys certain rules.

Validation checks

Validation checks are used to restrict the user as to the data they can enter. There are many different validation checks each with their own special use including:

- Data type checks – these check if the data being entered is the same type as the data type specified for the field. This would check to make sure that only numbers are entered into fields specified as numeric.
- Presence checks – some database fields have to be filled in, whilst others can be left empty. A presence check would check to make sure that data had been entered into a field. Unless the user fills in data for these fields, the data will not be processed.
- Length checks – checks to make sure that the data being entered has the correct number of

characters in it. For example, a six-digit account number will be checked to make sure it contains exactly six digits.
- File/Table lookups – are used to make sure that codes being used are the same as those used in a table or file of codes. For example, a car parts firm has lots of parts, with each part being given its own code. If a person types in a code for a part, it will be checked against the table to ensure it is a valid code.
- Cross field checks – the data in more than one field often need to be checked together to make sure they make sense. For example, when data is entered for a department in an organisation, the extension number is compared to make sure that it is a valid extension for that department.
- Range checks – are performed on numbers. They check that a number being entered is within a certain range. For example, all the students in a college are aged over 14 so a date of birth being entered which would give an age less than this would not be allowed by the range check.
- Format checks – are performed on codes to make sure that they conform to the correct combinations of characters. For example, a code for car parts may consist first of three numbers followed by a single letter. This can be specified for a field to restrict entered data to this format.

Remember

Not only is there a requirement that data is error free, it is essential that data is kept up-to-date. Data that is not kept up-to-date will be accurate at the time it was entered but changes to

details such as name, address, phone number, etc., will mean that errors start to creep in. If personal data is stored, then there is a requirement under the Data Protection Act 1998 to keep such details up-to-date.

Check digits

Check digits are added to important numbers such as account numbers, International Book Numbers (ISBNs), Article numbers (the numbers under the barcode), etc. These numbers are placed at the end of the block of numbers and are used to check that the numbers have been entered correctly into the computer.

ISBN 978-1-85008-280-4

9 781850 082804

The 13-digit number shown underneath the bars is encoded in the bars, which means the bars can be scanned to give the number rather than having to type it in.

When the large number is entered, the computer performs a calculation using all the numbers to work out this extra number. If the calculation reveals that the extra number (called the check digit) is the same as that calculated by the other numbers, it means that all the numbers have been entered correctly.

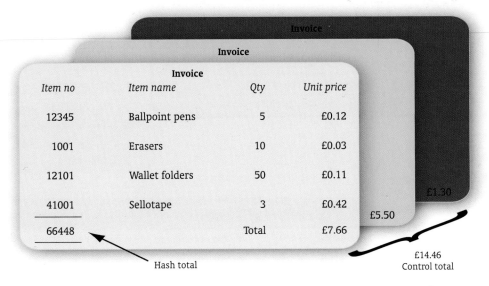

Invoice			
Item no	Item name	Qty	Unit price
12345	Ballpoint pens	5	£0.12
1001	Erasers	10	£0.03
12101	Wallet folders	50	£0.11
41001	Sellotape	3	£0.42
66448		Total	£7.66

Hash total

£5.50

£1.30

£14.46
Control total

How hash and control totals are used to make sure all invoices have been processed.

Error checking during batch processing systems

In batch processing, all the input documents are batched together and inputted in one go. Batch processing uses automatic data capture, so once the input documents have been batched together, the input device (OCR scanner, MICR reader, Mark reader, etc.) can simply read the data into the ICT system. With a batch processing system, there is no human intervention during the processing. Any input forms or other data which cannot be processed will be reported so that they can be dealt with later.

When there are large numbers of input documents used for data entry, it is necessary to check that all the documents have been input and processed properly. There are two checks that can be performed:

- hash totals
- control totals.

Hash totals

Hash totals are meaningless totals used for a check. For example, if each survey form is numbered (e.g. 000001, 000002, 000003, etc.) then the total of all the numbers could be calculated and input to compare with the answer the computer got. If the hash totals were equal, it shows that all the survey forms have been input.

Control totals

Control totals are like hash totals except the totals have meaning. For example, adding up all the totals of a batch of invoices could be used to check that all the invoices had been input. The total would mean the total amount owed for those invoices processed in the batch.

The limitations of error checking

Despite all the checks put in place errors will still occur. It is very easy for someone to think they know how to spell a person's name when they don't. There are many names that sound the same but are spelt differently. All you can do is put in as many checks as possible to reduce the probability of errors occurring.

In order to reduce errors it is best to:

- reduce the amount of typed input to a minimum – to reduce errors it is much better to capture data automatically using optical mark/ character recognition, bar coding, etc., rather than type it in
- allow a user to type in their details – they will be unlikely to make a mistake with their own details
- allow a user to check their details and confirm they are correct
- use as many validation and verification methods as is possible.

Design of data entry: creating validation checks

Introduction

When you create an ICT solution or solutions for your sample work, you will be creating a solution for someone else to use. It is essential that you try to restrict as much as possible the data that a user can enter by using validation checks.

Here you will learn how validation checks can be created using both database and spreadsheet software.

Validation and databases

When databases are created, validation rules are created for some of the fields in the database. Not all database fields can contain validation checks. For example, a person's surname can be almost any combination of characters so it would be hard to distinguish between a correct and incorrect one. You can, of course, specify the type of data that can go into each field and the length (i.e., the number of characters) for each field.

There are many different validation checks for databases depending on the type of field being validated. Many checks are performed by the database software itself. For example, if a field is specified as being numeric, letters cannot be entered.

The actual instructions for the validation check given to the database are called validation expressions. As well as creating the validation expressions, the database designer needs to produce the messages that will appear should the user type in data for the field which breaches the rule. Ideally such text should give them some idea about what is wrong with the data.

Look at the following table. It shows validation expressions for fields using the database software Microsoft Access. The second column contains the validation message which will appear if the user types in data unacceptable for the field.

Validation expression	Message appearing if expression is not valid
>50 And <100	The number entered must be over 50 and under 100. Note this does not include the numbers 50 or 100.
>=10 And <=20	The number entered must be between 10 and 20 including the numbers 10 and 20.
>0	A positive number must be entered.
<>0	A non-zero number must be entered.
>#12/01/07#	A date after the date 12/01/07 must be entered.
>=#01/01/08#	A date on or after the date 01/01/08 must be entered.
Like"????Y"	The data entered must be five characters long ending in the letter Y.
= 3 Or 4	The data being entered must be 3 or 4.
>=#01/01/07# And <#31/12/07#	The data being entered must be in the year 07.
"Male" Or "Female"	Only the words Male or Female can be entered.
<=Date()	The date entered must be today's date or sooner.

Validating entry into spreadsheet software

Many ICT solutions created using spreadsheet software need the user to supply their own data. Validation checks can be created on a cell or a cell range in order to restrict the data a user can enter. In this section you will learn about the various methods used to validate data entry into spreadsheets.

Input message – the message a user will see when they select a cell for the input of data. Usually it gives the user an indication of the sort of data they should be inputting

Validation expression/rule – the command that a developer must type in order to set up the validation for a particular field/cell

Validation message – the message the user will see if they type in data that does not meet the validation rules for the field

▶ Activity 1: Validating cells and creating validation messages

In this activity you are going to find out how validation checks can be applied to cells in the spreadsheet package Microsoft Excel.

1   Load Excel and create a new worksheet.
2   Suppose data is being entered into cells from A3 to A5. We need to put validation checks in all these cells. To choose a range for the validation check, highlight all the cells from cell A3 to cell A5.
3   Click on Data and select Validation… from the pull-down menu like this

4   The following Data Validation screen appears:

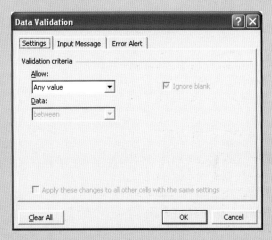

Click on the pull-down menu under <u>A</u>llow

5   Here you can select the type of data that you want to go into the cell. In this worksheet whole numbers need to be entered in the selected cells so click on **Whole number**.
Notice from this list, all the different ways you can specify for data being entered into a cell. Once you have specified a particular type of data it can prevent other different types of data from being entered.

6   Now click on the Data: pull-down menu.

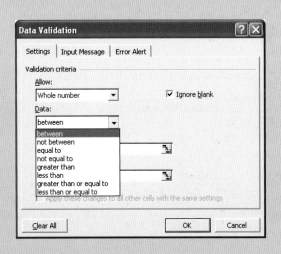

Select **between** from the list.

Design of data entry: creating validation checks
continued

7 In the <u>M</u>inimum box enter **1** and in the Ma<u>x</u>imum box enter **100** like this:

8 You have now added a validation check that will only allow whole numbers between and including 1 to 100 to be entered.

9 **Adding an input message**
An input message appears when the user selects the cell. It lets the user know what values it is acceptable to enter.
Click on the Input Message tab and the following window appears.
Enter the text as shown into the <u>T</u>itle: and **I**nput message: boxes

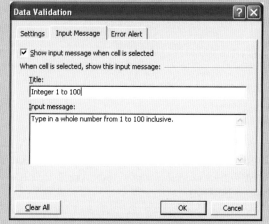

10 **Adding a validation message**
When a user tries to enter invalid data into a cell containing a validation check, the following message appears:

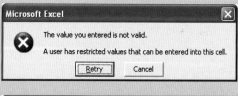

This message is not very helpful because it does not explain to the user what they can and cannot enter.
Click on the Error Alert tab and enter the text as shown:

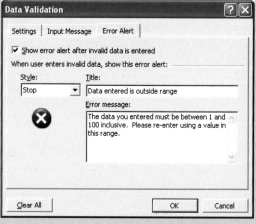

11 **Click on OK to make all the changes.**

12 You now have to test this validation check.
   You need to check that:
   - It only allows whole numbers to be entered.
   - It only allows numbers between 12 and 14 to be entered.

   It is best to create a table and then enter in the values into cell A4 of the spreadsheet and record what happens. You should never assume that a validation check will work as expected without checking it.

13 Type each of the numbers into cell A3 in turn and then copy and complete the validation table shown below.

Validation check for cell: A3			
Value entered	**What should happen**	**What actually happens**	**Action needed**
0	Not accepted	Not accepted	None
1			
2			
20			
99			
100			
101			
7.5			
-2			
A			

Remember – always ensure that your validation checks work as expected. Do not simply assume they will work.

14 To complete the validation you need to check that all the cells in the range from A3 to A5 have the validation check. You can do this by entering valid and invalid values into the cells.

Restricting the user to a list

One way of helping a user enter correct data is to supply them with a list of items to choose from. Using a list prevents the user from entering data that is not on a list. The only problem with lists is that they are only appropriate when there are only a small number of choices, for a field such as M or F, ranking of 1 to 5, etc.

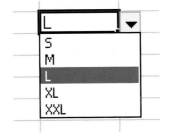

Here the sizes of a shirt are shown as a list from which the user can select.

EXAM TIP

Some of the questions on the examination paper will refer to material created by you as your sample work. Preventing errors is an important aspect of the development of any ICT solution. Make sure that you have included a range of methods of verification and validation appropriate to your solution.

You may be asked to write down the page number where you have done some error checking.

Design of processes

Introduction

In this section you need to design all the processes that need to be implemented. Remember that it is the processes on the input data that turn the data into output information.

Types of processes used in ICT solutions

It is important to note that processing of data is not just performing calculations. Here is a list of types of processes which could need describing:

- calculations (i.e., performing arithmetic on the input data)
- logical operations (i.e., making decisions based on the input data)
- searching
- sorting
- selecting
- re-arranging
- structuring
- classifying
- merging
- recording
- retrieving
- transmitting
- controlling
- producing a graph or chart.

Basically a process is any operation that transfers data into information.

What you have to produce for your sample work

For your sample work, you will need to list all the processes in detail for your ICT solution. You need to specifically itemise each process performed on the input data.

In the case of a spreadsheet you could:

- produce a list of all the calculations that will be used (NB do not supply the formulae printed out from the spreadsheet for this, as this is the design stage)
- produce a list of all the logical operations performed on the data
- produce details of any macros planned.

In the case of a database you could:

- produce details of the planned structure (note putting data into a structure is processing)
- details of sorts and searches
- details of reports produced
- lists of calculations.

What data will be processed?

Your ICT solution will involve the processing of data and this data can be in the following forms:

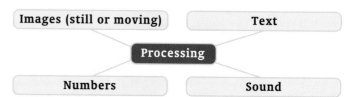

Documenting the processes

In the analysis stage, you should have identified the processes that need to be applied to the input data in order to change it to output information.

In order to document the processes that need to take place, you need to write a list of all the processes needed to produce the ICT solution. The processes need to be in detail so that it is easy to implement to produce the solution.

For example, if your ICT solution involved creating a spreadsheet, then you would need to produce a list of all the processes including:

- every calculation used in the spreadsheet
- any logic expressions used
- any sorts
- any macros used
- any processes where data is turned into graphical information.

Processing images

Raw images, not in the form you require them, can be processed to produce final images that can be included in multimedia products such as presentations and websites.

Processing of images can include:

- Resizing – enlargement and reduction.
- Rotation – rotating the image by an angle.
- Colour corrections – altering brightness or contrast.
- Combining images – creating an image using two or more images.
- Cropping an image – so that only part of the original image is used.
- Digitally retouching an image – using techniques such as airbrushing.
- Conversion of images to different colour schemes – so that they are displayed correctly on websites.
- Changing the file format of images – this can be done to reduce file size which is important when transferring them using networks.
- Conversion of colour images to black and white images.
- Removal of unwanted items in an image (e.g., spots on a model's face, wrinkles on an actor, etc.).
- Adding layers to images.
- Altering the resolution of an image.

Design of output of information and designs that need to be used by other people

▼ You will find out

▶ About choosing the output method

▶ About choosing the output format

▶ About the need for sequencing the output

▶ About how designs can be used by others

Introduction

Finding out what information a client wants output from a system you are designing is the first stage in the design of an ICT solution. This is because the output will determine what processing needs to be done and what input data is needed into the system.

Working backwards from the output

Make sure that you understand what information the client wants output from the ICT solution. In some cases this will involve sketching screen designs or plans of paper documents. Make sure that you involve the client in this process. Keep showing them your designs and modify them based on the comments you receive. Remember that you are developing the solution that they need, not the solution that you think they need or the one you would like to produce.

Once you have worked out the output (i.e., the answers or final product) you can produce a list of the processes you would need to produce the output. Remember that processes are not limited to calculations – there are many different processes that can be performed on data.

Once you have a list of the processes you can then work out what the processes need in terms of the input of data and how this data might be input (i.e., the type of input method).

You can then produce a table which summarises the inputs, processes and outputs for the system.

Designing the output method

Think about answers to the following:

- What hardware or other devices have been chosen for the ICT solutions?
- Why were these devices chosen?

Designing the output format

The output format depends on the type of problem, but output can be:

- displayed on a screen
- printed as a hard copy on paper
- output as sound
- output as transmitted information.

Designing the sequencing of the output

In many ICT solutions the sequencing of the output information is important. For example, websites, multimedia presentations, invoices, spreadsheet models, etc., require that important information is on the top left of the screen.

If information needs to be output on paper, then you need to have several goes at the design of the information on the page and choose the best one. Design of information on screens is also important, as is the sequencing of each screen in a complete product such as a multimedia presentation.

Designs that need to be used by other people

Sometimes you do not have the necessary skills or experience to be able to implement a design. For example, you may have a requirement for a website and software tools may not be able to do what you want to do. You may have to make use of the services of a programmer. You would need to produce enough information about what you want them to do for them to go away and turn your design into a working solution.

Questions, Activity and Case study

▶ Questions 1 | pp. 22–23

1 A website is to be developed for a client. You have been asked to produce this website by using ICT tools and techniques.
   (a) Explain what is meant by ICT tools. (2 marks)
   (b) Explain what is meant by ICT techniques. (2 marks)
2 Explain the methods by which the following data could be captured (2 marks each).
   (a) A piece of text on a piece of paper.
   (b) The results of a paper-based questionnaire.
   (c) An image loaded onto the card of a digital camera.
   (d) An old paper map.
   (e) A photograph in a book.
   (f) A conversation conducted between a group of people.
   (g) A wedding video stored on a digital video camera.
   (h) The details on a paper order form which has been sent through the post.
   (i) A piece of live music.
   (j) A large product number that needs to be input.

▶ Questions 2 | pp. 24–25

1 Think about the types of mistake you make when typing information into a computer. Write a list of **three** different mistakes you can make. (3 marks)

2 A computer manager says 'data can be valid yet be incorrect'. By giving **one** suitable example, explain what this statement means. (3 marks)

▶ Questions 3 | pp. 26–27

1 A college keeps all of its staff details in a file held on their administration ICT system. Shown below is a section of the file showing the data entered into some of the fields.

Surname	Forename	Dept Number	Dept Name	Ext Number
Peter	Hughes	112	Accounts	318
Suzanne	Roberts	121	Accounts	671
Charles	Jones	361	Personnel	432
Jenny	712		Student services	543
James	Wong	361	Accounts	543
Suzanne	Roberts	121	Accounts	671

   (a) During the entry of this data, the validation checks were turned off. By referring to the data held in the above table, state **four** problems that have occurred. (4 marks)
   (b) For each **one** of the problems identified in (a), state the name of the validation check that could have been used to prevent the problems. (4 marks)

2 A Schools Information Management System contains details of all current pupils in the school. On entry to the school the following information must be entered for each pupil:
   • Surname
   • Forename
   • Date of birth
   • Postcode
   (a) Describe **one** different validation check for each of the fields which could be used to validate the data being entered. (4 marks)
   (b) Once the data has been entered for each field the whole record will need to be verified.
      (i) Give **one** reason why this is necessary. (1 mark)
      (ii) Name and describe a method of verification for each record. (2 marks)

1 Using the validation expressions in the table on page 28 to help you, write down a sentence explaining how each validation expression works.
   (a) "Junior" Or "Senior"
   (b) = 1 Or 2
   (c) >=Date()
   (d) Like"A????"
   (e) Like"???????"
   (f) <20
   (g) >=1 And <=50
   (h) >=#01/02/08#
   (i) >=#01/01/08# And <=#31/12/08#
   (j) "M" Or "F"

2 Explain the difference between a validation rule and a validation message. (2 marks)

1 Here is a list of processes that can be performed on data:
   • calculations (i.e., performing arithmetic on the input data)
   • logical operations (i.e., making decisions based on the input data)
   • searching
   • sorting
   • selecting
   • re-arranging
   • structuring
   • classifying
   • merging
   • recording
   • retrieving
   • transmitting
   • controlling.

For each of the following, state which processes in the above list would apply to each of these ICT solutions. (1 mark each)
   (a) Producing a blog on the Internet.
   (b) Producing a multimedia presentation on a popular tourist attraction.
   (c) Storing a collection of MP3 music files on a computer so that they can be found easily.
   (d) The production of an electronic photograph album to produce a set of images with an accompanying commentary.
   (e) The production of a website which will be useful to the local community.

2 Give five examples of types of processes which can be performed by software. (5 marks)

1 Distinguish, by giving examples, the difference between the terms output method and output format. (4 marks)

2 When designing screen output, sequencing of items on the screen is important. Give two factors you would need to consider when deciding the sequencing of items on the screen. (2 marks)

▶ **Activity 1 Producing a mind map for the output from different types of ICT system**

For this mind map you will need to have a good knowledge of a number of different types of popular ICT software and systems. You have to produce a mind map showing the output device, the output method and the output format for the following ICT systems:
   • A multiple choice quiz to be completed using presentation software.
   • A blog on your favourite sport.
   • A podcast on the latest fashion.
   • A spreadsheet which can be used to help analyse the results from a questionnaire.
   • A website that promotes a private tutoring service.
It is up to you to research each of the systems if you need further information and also to present your information in a suitable way.

Questions, Activity and Case study continued

▶ **Case study 1** pp. 24–32

British Gas sends out £2.3 trillion bill

Utility British Gas has admitted sending one of its customers a bill for £2,320,333,681,613. Brian Law of Fartown, Huddersfield, received the bill last month as a final demand after failing to pay an earlier bill of £59. The sum of £2.3 trillion was apparently due for electricity supplied to Mr Law's new home in Fartown. And the letter from British Gas threatened to take him to court unless he paid the amount in full. Mr Law, who runs an exhibition company called Prodis Play in Leeds, had delayed paying the original bill last year because he was away on business.

A penny a day

According to the local newspaper, the Yorkshire Post, Mr Law attempted to call British Gas to resolve the matter but with little result. 'After two hours, I did get through to somebody, and said I had received this bill,' Mr Law told the newspaper. 'I started reading the figure out and the girl I was speaking to said there must have been a mistake. Eventually, I talked to a chap who promised to sort things out and he asked me to fax the bill through. I did that and rang again on the Wednesday, but this gent wasn't in and neither was his manager. I kept leaving all my phone numbers but nobody rang back.' Eventually, Mr Law decided that he would only be able to resolve the matter by going to court and offering to pay a penny a week.

'Simple mistake'

However, after enquiries by the press, British Gas responded, saying it was a 'simple, clerical mistake'. The figure on the final demand was in fact the meter reference for Mr Law's property. 'The clerical error meant that the reference ended up in the bill's total box', said a spokesman for the company in Leeds. The company said it had 'a very amiable conversation' with Mr Law about the mix-up, adding, 'he seemed to see the funny side'. Mr Law will now be setting up a direct debit arrangement to pay his future bills. 'There is certainly no question of us taking him to court or cutting off his supply', the company added.

(Article which appeared on BBC website March 2003 http://news.bbc.co.uk/1/hi/business/2818611.stm)

1 Processing accurate data is a requirement for any ICT system. In this case study inaccurate data was processed to produce ridiculous results.
   Explain **two** different consequences to an organisation of processing inaccurate data. (4 marks)

2 The diagram on page 37 shows a gas bill.
   (a) Explain clearly how the customer in the case study above came to get his extremely large bill. (1 mark)
   (b) (i) Give the name of a suitable validation check that could have been used for the amount of the bill. (1 mark)
       (ii) Describe how the check you have described in part (i) can prevent the error described in the case study from occurring. (1 mark)

3 The customer reference number is a unique number given to each customer and contains 9 digits.
   (a) The first customer entered onto the system has customer reference number 000000001
       (i) Write down the maximum number of unique customer reference numbers it would be possible to have with this ICT system. (1 mark)
       (ii) Name and describe a validation check that could ensure that only numbers are entered into this field. (2 marks)
       (iii) Name and describe a validation check that could be used that would ensure that only 9 digits could be entered for the customer reference number. (2 marks)
   (b) A payment slip similar to that on page 37 is used when a customer pays a bill. Each payment a customer makes is given a unique number. This payment number is a 23-digit number. A bar code is used so that this large number can be entered automatically into the ICT system.
       (i) Give one reason why bar coding is used here for data input. (1 mark)
       (ii) Bar coding often makes use of a check digit. Briefly explain the purpose of a check digit. (2 marks)

Home Energy power

Mr A Nother
123 Park Avenue
Northbridge Wells
Countyshire
NW55 2PL

Your gas bill

Customer account
912345678

Telephone
01912 345678

Website
www.home-energypower.com

	Previous	Present	Units/kWh	Total
Reading	11942 E	12150 E	208 = 2311.47 kWh	

Charges	Standard	Meter number 99999	
965 kWh at 4.266p per kWh (1 May 07 to 12 Jun 07)			£41.17
1346.47 kWh at 2.173p per kWh (1 May 07 to 12 Jun 07)			£29.26
Subtotal (excluding VAT)			£70.43
VAT at 5.0% on £70.43			£3.52
Charges for this period			£73.95
Previous bill 1-May-2007 12345666			£77.42
Payment received – Thank you 8-Jun-2007 01234567			£77.42

Amount to Pay £73.95

Transfer
Cash Company

bank credit

Reference (Customer number)
`123` `912345678`

Credit account number
`1234 56`

Amount due
£ `73.95`

Cheque acceptable

Cashier's
stamp and number

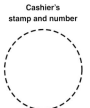

Signature

`9123 4567 8912 3456 789`

Date

Any Bank

Sort code
`11-22-33`

CASH		
CHEQUE		

£

Exam support

Worked example 1

1 **Read the following sentence:**

   Validation checks can ensure that data is reasonable or sensible, but they cannot ensure that data are correct. By giving a suitable example, explain carefully what this sentence means. (4 marks)

Student answer 1

1 Data might be wrong but it still passes the validation check. An example is where a person makes a spelling mistake when typing in a name. The name will still be accepted even though it is wrong.

Examiner's comment

1 The first sentence is true but it needs to mention that the validation checks will check for data that is obviously incorrect or ridiculous data.

   The spelling mistake is a bad example to choose as it is hard to validate a person's name. You can only really use a data type check. The answer does not fully answer the question asked. **(2 marks out of 4)**

Student answer 2

1 The user types in a quantity of laser printer toner cartridges they want to order. They want to order 2 but instead they incorrectly type 20. There is a validation check called a range check which will only query or not accept the quantity if less than 0 or greater than 150. Since 20 is in range it will be accepted even though the number 20 is incorrect. Hence the quantity 20 is incorrect yet still valid and will be accepted for processing.

Examiner's comment

1 Here a clear example has been given for a field that has a stated validation check (i.e., a range check) and there is a clear explanation of how data can be valid yet incorrect. **(4 marks out of 4)**

Examiner's answers

1 Two marks for explanation and two marks for the example.

   Any example here which picks up the fact that validation can only restrict the data but it cannot ensure the correctness of data.

   The user enters a date such as 09/11/75. The validation check on the date field will check that the date is not impossible or a date into the future and perhaps a check to make sure that the date does not make the person ridiculously old. However, if the user makes a mistake whilst typing in and transposes two digits and enters 09/11/57, then as this is a valid date it will not be picked up by the validation check. Hence the validation check can only check that the data is sensible or reasonable.

Worked example 2

2 A tool hire company uses database software to record the details of all its customers. Before a customer can hire tools, the company must record the following details: title, forename, surname, address, postcode and date of birth. Name and describe a validation check that can be used when data is entered into each of the following fields. The validation check must be different in each case.

(a) Surname
(b) Postcode

(c) Date of birth
(d) Title

Student answer 1

2 (a) Format check
  (b) Format check
  (c) Range check
  (d) Format check

Examiner's comment

2 The student should have looked at the mark scheme and noticed that there are a total of 8 marks which means two marks for each part.

As stated clearly in the question they needed to name the type of check and also to describe the check. This student has only named the check. Always look at the mark related to the parts of the questions to prevent this kind of mistake which is so common. This student has reduced the marks they can now get by half.

Answer (a) is incorrect – a format check is used for codes where there is a combination of letters and numbers.

Answer (b) is correct for the postcode.

Answer (c) is correct for the date of birth.

A format check is inappropriate for a name. It is hard to validate a name so a data type check is the only simple check besides checking against a list or a file of names. **(2 marks out of 8)**

Student answer 2

2 (a) A presence check which means that the field cannot be left blank. The name would be needed to contact the customer.
  (b) Postcode could be cross-checked against a database obtained by the Royal Mail of all the postcodes to check that it is a valid postcode.
  (c) A range check so that the age as calculated from the date of birth does not make the person ridiculously too young or too old.
  (d) Title can be validated using a check to make sure that there are no numbers in the person's title.

Examiner's comment

2 Answers (a) to (c) give both a correct name for a suitable check and a suitable description of the check. In part (d) the person has not given a name to the check, so only one mark for this last part. The check they have described is a data type check. **(7 marks out of 8)**

Examiner's answers

2 One mark each for the name of a validation check and one mark for a correct description for each field.
  (a) Data type check – to make sure there are no numbers in the name.
      Presence check – to check that data has been entered into the field.
  (b) Format check – so that the postcode contains the correct combinations of letters and numbers for it to be a valid postcode.
      Table lookup – could be cross-checked against the database obtained from Royal Mail to make sure that the postcode actually exists.
      Length check – to make sure that the correct number of characters for a postcode have been entered (e.g., 7, 8 or 9 characters).
      Cross field check – could check that the postcode matches the address field.
  (c) Format check – check that the data entered is in the correct format for a date, e.g. DD/MM/YY.
      Range check – to make sure that the date is not in the future or does not make the customer too old or young.
  (d) Length check – to make sure the title does not contain too many characters.
      Presence check – to ensure data has been entered for the field.
      Table lookup – to check that a valid title has been entered by comparing the title with a list of titles in a table.
      Data type check – to make sure that the title does not contain any numbers.

Summary mind maps

Select design tools and techniques and apply them to identified problems

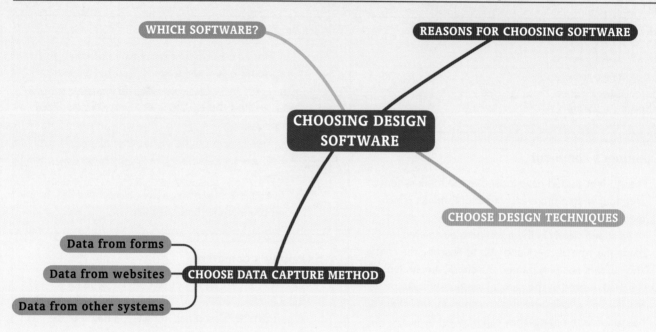

WHICH SOFTWARE?

REASONS FOR CHOOSING SOFTWARE

CHOOSING DESIGN SOFTWARE

CHOOSE DESIGN TECHNIQUES

Data from forms

Data from websites

Data from other systems

CHOOSE DATA CAPTURE METHOD

Design of data entry: problems with errors

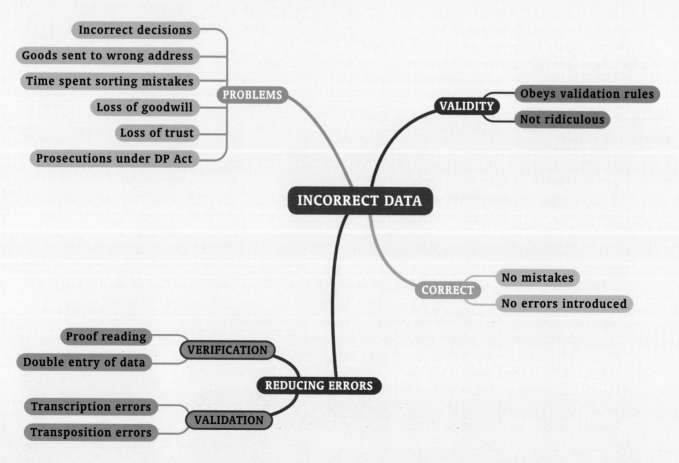

Incorrect decisions

Goods sent to wrong address

Time spent sorting mistakes

Loss of goodwill

Loss of trust

Prosecutions under DP Act

PROBLEMS

VALIDITY

Obeys validation rules

Not ridiculous

INCORRECT DATA

CORRECT

No mistakes

No errors introduced

Proof reading

Double entry of data

VERIFICATION

REDUCING ERRORS

Transcription errors

Transposition errors

VALIDATION

Design of data entry: validation

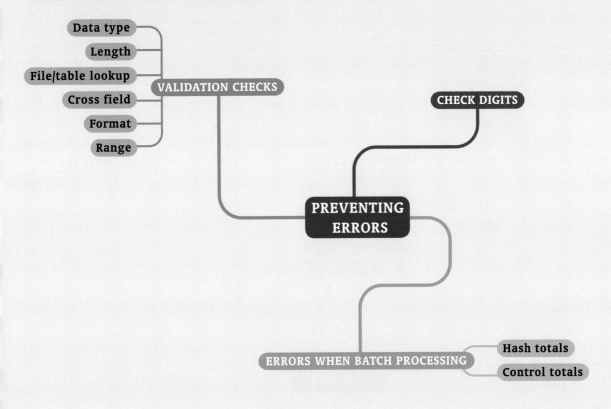

VALIDATION CHECKS
- Data type
- Length
- File/table lookup
- Cross field
- Format
- Range

CHECK DIGITS

PREVENTING ERRORS

ERRORS WHEN BATCH PROCESSING
- Hash totals
- Control totals

Design of data entry: creating validation checks

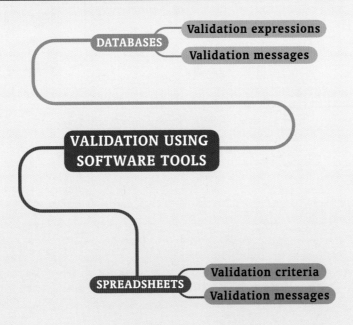

VALIDATION USING SOFTWARE TOOLS

DATABASES
- Validation expressions
- Validation messages

SPREADSHEETS
- Validation criteria
- Validation messages

Summary mind maps continued

Design of output of information and designs that need to be used by other people

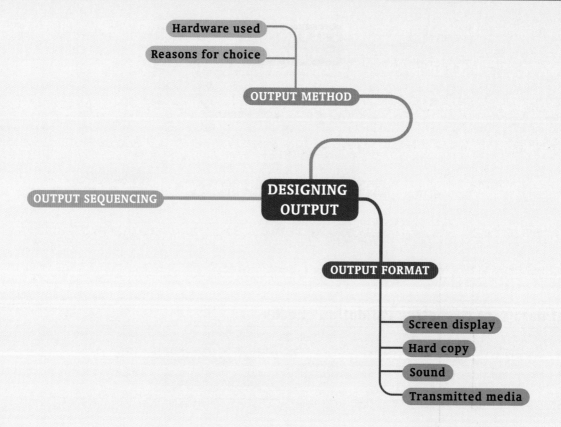

TOPIC 4: Selection and use of input devices and input media

In this topic you will need to know about the range of input devices and input media so that you can choose an input device and media that is best for a particular application.

When you solve your ICT problem, your choice will be limited by the input devices that your school or college has. In the examination you could be asked about the theory of input devices or you could be asked a question about the reasons for your choice of input device to solve the user-identified problem.

▼ The key concepts covered in this topic are:

▷ Select suitable input devices and input media from those available

▷ Justify why the items selected were suitable to solve each particular problem

CONTENTS

Selection and use of input devices and input media: simple devices

Introduction

To get the output from an ICT system it is necessary first to input the data into the system and then process it. Data capture is the term for getting the data into the computer in a form that enables it to be processed.

In many situations this will involve typing in the information but this will be inappropriate if you want to input sound or an image into the computer. In this section you will be looking at the range of input devices so that you can make an informed choice of input device for a particular ICT system you are designing and implementing.

Selecting a suitable input method

The ideal way of entering data into an ICT system would be:

- automatic
- fast
- cheap
- accurate.

Unfortunately it is hard to find a way which satisfies all of these criteria, so a compromise has to be reached. Keyboard entry is the commonest way of entering

KEY WORDS

Data capture – the way the computer obtains its data for processing

Input – the act of entering data into an ICT system

Input device – the hardware device such as a keyboard or a scanner used to feed the input data into an ICT system

data and it is ideal for low volumes of data but it is not cheap because you have to pay someone to key it in. Typing mistakes are common, so it is not very accurate. It does have the advantage that the input device (i.e. the keyboard) is included with all computer systems, so there is no cost for additional hardware.

In the following section you will be looking at different input methods using different input devices from the point of view of the criteria outlined above. Input methods are of two types:

- manual methods of data entry
- automatic methods of data entry.

Manual methods involve a human being present to enter the data. Entering data via a keyboard is a manual method. If a human needs to be involved for most of the time, then it is considered a manual method of data entry.

Automatic methods are methods where a human would batch the work to be done together and then leave the computer to automatically read the data. It can also involve the capture of data from sensors. Automatic methods of data entry are ideally suited to high volume work.

Manual methods of data entry

Manual methods of data entry involve a human user continually interacting with the computer in some way such as by typing or talking to it.

Keyboard entry

The keyboard as a data input device has the following disadvantages:

- Slow – the fastest typists can type a maximum of 100 words a minute so they are not suitable for high volume and fast data entry.

- Costly – someone has to be paid to enter the data.
- Prone to errors – it is so easy to make typing mistakes and they are not always spotted.
- Health problems – typing at high speed can cause certain health problems such as repetitive strain injury (RSI).

Keyboard entry does have some advantages, such as:

- Cheap from a purchase point of view – all computers come with keyboards, so there are no additional hardware costs.
- Universal use – most people know how to use a keyboard.

Using a mouse

A mouse is an input device because it allows you to make selections as well as draw lines and size graphic objects.

Voice/speech recognition

Voice/speech recognition systems allow you to enter data via a microphone directly into a computer. Basically you dictate the data into the computer. The only additional resources needed in addition to a computer are a microphone and the voice recognition software.

Voice recognition is ideal for entry of data into word-processing software or into a structure such as a database by people such as lawyers, doctors, etc., who only use ICT systems as part of their job. Voice recognition can also be used to dictate and send e-mails as well as enter commands into the operating system.

Voice recognition software turns voice into text.

Advantages of voice recognition include:

- Faster than typing – (up to 160 words per minute, which is three times the average typing speed).
- 99% accuracy – provided time has been spent teaching the computer about your voice.
- Cheap – many computers come with a microphone, so the only cost is the cost of the software.

Disadvantages of voice recognition include:

- Takes a while to get used to – can be frustrating for beginners to use.
- Not accurate at first – you may need to train the system about your voice. This is done by entering data and then correcting the mistakes the system has made.
- Errors due to background noise – few people have their own offices. Usually there is lots of background noise (people talking, telephones ringing, etc.). These can cause errors as the system tries to interpret these sounds.
- Does not work with all database software.

Scanning

Scanners are input devices that can be used to capture an image and are useful for digitising old non-digital photographs, paper documents or pictures in books. Scanners can also be used in large organisations to digitise

EXAM TIP

When describing the process of inputting the images from a camera, make sure that you describe the full process, which will involve creating a new folder or finding an existing folder on the hard drive in which to save them. You could also mention that a suitable file format could be chosen depending on the use to which the images will be put.

paper documents so that the original documents can be destroyed. The main purpose for this is to save space by not having to store paper documents.

Scanners are often used with OCR software, so that the actual characters on a page can be recognised and input into other software such as word-processing or desktop publishing software.

Producing images using digital cameras

Digital cameras have almost replaced the older cameras which used film and are ideal for capturing images for use in documents, presentations and websites. They have the advantage that the image is already in digital form so it may be input directly into the computer. Image editing software can then be used to alter the size of the image, use only part of it (called cropping) and so on. To input a digital image from a camera into a computer you can:

- attach a lead from the camera to the computer and load the images into a suitable folder on your hard drive
- take the card used to store the images out of the camera and insert it into a slot which is provided on many computers and then copy the image files onto your hard drive.

Webcams

A webcam is a small video camera used as an input device to send a moving image over an intranet or the Internet. Webcams are used for:

- seeing people you are chatting to using instant messaging services
- seeing the views of different places and parts of the world
- security purposes; for example, in nurseries they have them so that people can see their children whilst they are at work.

Input from a digital video camera (camcorder)

Digital video cameras are able to transmit digital signals, which means they can be connected directly to a computer and used to input video directly into a computer for editing and storing.

Some still digital cameras are also capable of producing short video clips.

Using input from a website

It is possible to take the values from a website (a bit like copy and paste) but instead of the values being static, they will change in your ICT solution when the values change on the website.

This would be useful if you need to use data that is constantly changing but do not want to have to copy the data in again each time there is a change.

It works by there being a link back to the original data so that when you want the data updated it will populate your solution with the latest data.

Suitable applications for this would be:

- Obtaining stocks and share prices from a website to input and keep up-to-date the value of a collection of shares.
- Investigation of the fluctuations of foreign currency prices.

Other input devices

There are many other input devices including:

- joystick – used primarily for playing games
- touch pad – used as an alternative to a mouse with a laptop computer
- tracker ball – like an upside-down mouse
- digitiser – a pen-like device which allows you to draw or write on a flat tablet – usually used by graphic designers or for computer aided design (CAD) work
- light pen – used for selecting items on a screen by touching them with a pen.

Selection and use of input devices and input media: capturing transaction data

▼ **You will find out**

▶ About the use of magnetic strip recognition

▶ About the use of touch screens

▶ About the use of bar codes for input

▶ About the use of point of sale (POS) terminals

▶ About the use of hand-held devices for input

▶ About the different types of input media

Introduction

In this section you will look at the more specialist input devices such as those used in stores and other types of businesses.

Magnetic strip recognition

Magnetic strips can be seen on credit cards, debit cards, reward cards and membership cards. They can also be found on plane and train tickets. Data is encoded in the magnetic strip and when the card is swiped, the data from the card is used to record the transaction.

The data encoded in the magnetic strip of a credit or debit card includes:

- the account number
- the expiry date of the card
- other security information.

This keypad has a strip reader.

Advantages of magnetic strip input include:

- Fewer errors – there are fewer errors made because there is no keying in of data.
- Added security – because there are security details encoded in the card which do not appear on

the card, making it harder but not impossible to commit fraud.
- Very quick – the card is read quickly, which is particularly important in a shop.
- Data cannot be read without a properly programmed machine – decreases the likelihood of fraud.

Touch screens

Touch screens allow a person to make selections by simply touching the screen. They are used as input devices for purchasing train tickets or used as information points in tourist information offices, art galleries and museums. They can also be used to provide information on services provided by banks and building societies.

The main advantage of the touch screen as an input device is that it is so simple and capable of being used by almost anyone

Bar code recognition

Bar code recognition involves using a series of light and dark bars of differing widths to enter a code which is usually printed underneath the bar code.

Using the code, the system can determine from a product database the country of origin, the manufacturer, the name of the product, the price and other information about the product. Suitable applications for bar code recognition include:

- recording of goods in supermarkets
- warehouse stock control systems
- parcel tracking systems
- linking books to borrowers in libraries
- luggage labelling at airports.

Advantages of bar code input

- Faster – scanners are sophisticated and can read bar codes at different angles.
- More accurate – compared to typing in long codes manually.
- Low printing costs – can be printed on labels. You can buy special software which allows an ordinary printer to print bar codes.

Disadvantages of bar code input

- Can only be used for the input of numbers.
- Expensive – the laser scanners in supermarkets are expensive, although hand-held scanners are relatively cheap.

ISBN 978-1-85008-280-4

9 781850 082804

A bar code.

POS terminals

Point of sale terminals are placed in stores where customers pay for goods. There are a variety of input devices used with a POS terminal and these include:

- touch screen displays
- keyboards
- magnetic strip readers (for reading credit/debit card and loyalty card details)
- bar code readers.

This POS terminal is used by the Spar convenience stores and makes use of touch screens.

Hand-held input devices

Portable hand-held input devices are used by meter readers to take readings of gas, electricity and water meters used in the home. The meter reader takes the reading and then inputs it into a hand-held device which uses wireless communication to send the data to the main computer system.

Hand-held devices are also used for:

- tracking parcels
- recording customer signatures for receipt of goods
- stock taking in stores
- taking orders for food in restaurants.

Input media

Input media is the material on which the data is encoded so that it can be read by an input device and digitised so that it can be input, processed and turned into information by the ICT system.

It is important to note that sometimes the output from one ICT system can be used as the input media for a different ICT system. Take the lottery, for example, you shade in the boxes on a card which is used as the input media for the system. You are then given a printed receipt which contains a bar code and also has your numbers printed on it. This receipt can be put into the system when you go back to the till for your winnings for the small amounts.

Examples of input media include:

- forms with marks on them capable of being read by an optical mark reader
- forms containing text capable of being read by an optical mark reader
- a bar code
- a magnetic strip on a credit/debit, loyalty or membership card
- a picture card used by a digital camera
- a CD-ROM used to supply the printer driver for a new printer
- bar code on a bin so the council knows how much rubbish you throw away.

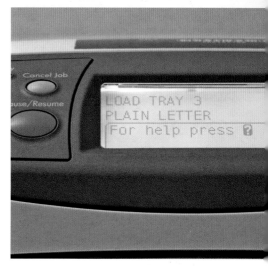

EXAM TIP

In some questions you may be asked about the input method. This is the method used for data capture, so, for example, keyboard entry is an input method. If you just write keyboard then you are describing an input device. Also make sure that you do not confuse the input media with either the input method or input device.

Selection and use of input devices and input media: high volume devices

Introduction

High volume repetitive input demands high speed input devices that can work without human intervention. The main requirements for such input devices are speed and accuracy. Such input devices need input media that can be read directly by the input device attached to the computer.

Automatic methods of data entry involve the ICT system being able to read the input data automatically.

Optical mark recognition (OMR)

Here paper-based forms or cards with marks on them are read automatically by a device called an optical mark reader.

OMR readers can read marked sheets at typical speeds of 3000 sheets per hour. OMR is an ideal method for marking multiple choice question answer sheets for examinations and tests. The students mark the correct bubbles or square by shading them in and the reader can read and process the results at high speed.

Advantages of optical mark recognition include:

- Ease of use – only need one computer and optical mark reader to read the marked sheets.
- Cheap – optical mark readers work in a similar way to scanners and are cheap compared to other input devices. System is automatic so no need to pay people to enter the details.
- Fairly accurate – if the forms have been filled in correctly, then almost 100% accuracy can be achieved.
- Fast – this is particularly important if a large volume of data needs to be input and processed in a short space of time (e.g., tests and assessments).

Disadvantages of optical mark recognition include:

- Only suitable for capturing certain data – data needs to be in a form where there are tick style answers.
- Reject rate can be high – if you have not given precise instructions, users may fill in the forms incorrectly, which will lead to high rejection rates.

- If the form used is creased or folded it may be rejected or jam the machine.

Suitable applications for optical mark recognition include:

- voting forms
- lottery tickets
- market research forms
- tests/assessments
- product evaluation sheets
- time sheets (used to record the time you started and finished each day to work out wages)
- school/college attendance registers.

Optical character recognition (OCR)

Optical character recognition (OCR) uses a scanner as the input device along with special software which looks at the shape of each character so that it can be recognised separately. The software can then convert the image of each letter to text, which can be passed to another software package such as a word-processor or database for processing.

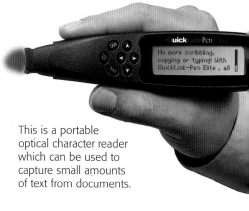

This is a portable optical character reader which can be used to capture small amounts of text from documents.

OCR can recognise:

- typed characters
- hand-written characters (provided they are neat).

Filling in a survey form using OMR.

Here is how optical recognition works:

1 **Scan the text**
A printed page is scanned using a scanner.

2 **Perform the recognition**

The OCR software now converts the image into text which can be edited separately. This process looks at the image of each individual letter in turn and then turns it into text which can be put into a software package.

3 **Save the file**
The file is saved for editing in one of the many different formats such as:

A cheque reader.

Any Bank PLC

15 January 20 07

Some Town Banch
45 Anywhere Parade, Some Town

Pay Somebody   or order
One hundred pounds — £100—00

⑈0000894 ⑈ 65⑈0134⑈ 0254990 5⑈02

cheque number   bank sort code   account number

MICR

Magnetic ink characters are the strange looking characters which you see at the bottom of cheques.

Magnetic ink character recognition (MICR)

The magnetic ink characters can be seen here.

⑆⑉⑈⑇ 0123456789

With MICR, the numbers are printed onto the cheque in a special magnetic ink, which can be read at very high speed by the magnetic ink character reader. Most of the data (cheque number, bank sort code and account number) are pre-printed onto the cheque but the amount is not known until the person writes the cheque. When the cheque is presented for payment, the amount the cheque is for is then printed onto the cheque, again in magnetic ink.

Uses for magnetic ink character recognition are limited mainly because of the cost, and its use is almost entirely for the processing of cheques.

Small magnetic ink character readers can be used to input cheque details into accounts systems. Advantages of magnetic ink character recognition include:

- Accuracy – the documents (usually cheques) are read with 100% accuracy.
- Difficult to forge – because of the sophisticated magnetic ink technology used, it would be difficult to forge cheques.
- Can be read easily – cheques are often folded, crumpled up, etc. Methods such as OCR or OMR would not work with these. MICR uses a magnetic pattern, so this is unaffected by crumpling.
- Speed of reading – documents can be read at very high speed and this is particularly important for the clearing of cheques.

Disadvantages of magnetic ink character recognition include:

- Expense – the high speed MICR character readers are very expensive.

Unit 1 Practical Problem Solving in the Digital World

Questions

▶ Questions 1 | pp. 44–45

1 Speech recognition systems are more accurate and easier to use than in the past.
   (a) Give **two** advantages to a user in using a speech recognition system. (2 marks)
   (b) Describe **two** different ways in which a speech recognition system could be used. (2 marks)
   (c) Speech recognition systems are sometimes not 100% accurate. Give **two** possible reasons for this. (2 marks)

2 A person who worked as a website designer for a company has decided to work freelance designing websites for companies. They have a basic but up-to-date computer system.
   State with reasons **two** input devices other than the mouse and keyboard, they should buy to help them design websites. (4 marks)

▶ Questions 2 | pp. 46–47

1 Magnetic strip is a popular input media for storing credit card details.
   (a) Name **two** other applications where magnetic strip is used as the input media. (2 marks)
   (b) Give **two** advantages in using magnetic strip as the input media on a credit or debit card. (2 marks)
   (c) In addition to the magnetic strip, most credit and debit cards contain a small chip on the card. Explain why this chip is included. (2 marks)

2 Touch screens can often be seen at tourist information offices. Give **one** advantage of using a touch screen as an input device for use by the general public. (1 mark)

3 Bar coding is used for data capture in many different applications.
   Give the names of **two** applications where bar coding is used as an input method, and for each give a reason why it is suitable. (4 marks)

▶ Questions 3 | pp. 46–47

1 (a) Explain the difference between input devices and input media. (2 marks)
   (b) In the following questions, you have to decide whether the image is an input device or input media. (1 mark each)
       (i) A credit card with magnetic strip. (1 mark)

   (ii) A magnetic strip reader. (1 mark)

   (iii) A camera picture card. (1 mark)

(iv) A flash/pen drive. (1 mark)

(v) A CD-ROM. (1 mark)

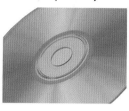

(vi) A bar code. (1 mark)

ISBN 978-1-85008-280-4

9 781850 082804

(vii) A lottery ticket. (1 mark)

(viii) A microphone. (1 mark)

(ix) A digital video camera. (1 mark)

(x) A webcam. (1 mark)

(xi) An optical mouse. (1 mark)

2 MICR rather than OCR is chosen for cheque processing.
   (a) Give **one** reason why this is so. (1 mark)
   (b) Give **two** pieces of data encoded in magnetic ink characters that are present on the cheque when it is printed. (2 marks)
   (c) What piece of information is printed onto the cheque by the bank in magnetic ink characters before the cheque is cleared. (1 mark)

3 (a) Explain the meaning of the term data capture. (2 marks)
   (b) Automatic data capture is preferable when large volumes of data need to be input into an ICT system in a short space of time.
       Give the names of **three** automatic methods of data capture. (3 marks)
   (c) For the three automatic methods of data capture named in part (b), give an application for which the method is appropriate. (3 marks)

4 Which input device would you use?
   For each of the following situations, write down the name of the input device most suited to input the data. For each device you have named, give one reason for your choice.
   (a) For dictating a story direct into a word-processor. (2 marks)
   (b) For recording the numbers on a lottery ticket. (2 marks)
   (c) For inputting loyalty card details when customers are paying for goods in a supermarket. (2 marks)
   (d) For reading account numbers and bank sort code numbers on a cheque. (2 marks)
   (e) For inputting a discussion between three people for incorporation into a presentation. (2 marks)
   (f) For inputting a drawing of a cartoon produced on paper into a desktop published magazine. (2 marks)
   (g) For inputting the printer driver software for a new scanner which you have just bought. (2 marks)
   (h) For inputting a video of a person over the Internet while they are having a conversation using the Internet. (2 marks)
   (i) For helping a blind person input text into a computer. (2 marks)
   (j) For inputting the account number on an electricity bill without having to use a keyboard to type it in. (2 marks)

Case studies

▶ Case study 1   pp. 44–49

Comtech a company keeping an eye on vending machines

Comtech are a company involved in equipment for the remote monitoring and control of vending machines. For the people who own vending machines, there are a number of problems:

- Vending machines running out of certain items, resulting in the loss of sales.
- Vending machines breaking down and the vending machine company not being told they are broken – again this results in lost sales.
- Vending machines being attacked by thieves.

Vending machine companies would also like:

- To know more information that will help them with stock control and supply chain management.
- Better control of the money taken by the machine (remember that some machines do not give change,

so there can be more money in the machine than for the value of goods sold).

The solution was supplied by Comtech, who set up a system where vending machine companies can address all the problems outlined above. Basically, the system collects the data from the machine and then transmits it over a network to the Comtech computer which the vending machine company can access from their computers using the Internet.

As well as monitoring the vending machine remotely, the system can also control the vending machine. For example, if it malfunctions, the vending machine can be turned off remotely. The vending machine company can also alter the prices for the different goods remotely without having to visit the site.

The Comtech system monitors and controls vending machines remotely and captures the signals directly from sensors and sends the data to a remote computer.

You may have to do some research to answer the following questions:

1 What is meant by the term 'supply chain management'? (2 marks)

2 One of the advantages in this system is that it can retain customers.
   Explain how this system retains customers. (2 marks)

3 A vending machine company said one of their problems is that they have no 'real-time data' from their vending machines.
   (a) Explain what is meant by 'real-time data'. (1 mark)
   (b) Briefly explain why data from the Comtech system is real time. (1 mark)

4 With the old system, the vending machines sometimes had to be refilled on a daily basis. Give one way this new system will help with this. (2 marks)

5 M2M means machine to machine. Explain why this system is called machine to machine (M2M). (2 marks)

▶ Case study 2   pp. 48–49

e-counting in elections

Read the following case study carefully and then answer the questions.

Optical mark recognition was used to count the votes for the City of Westminster local elections. The votes in elections in the past were processed manually with huge teams counting the votes by hand. Nine high-speed optical mark readers were used to input the data from the ballot forms into the system.

With OMR, the returning officer was able to announce the result of the vote two-and-a-half hours after the

voting closed. The almost 44,000 voting papers with each person making three votes on each paper, would have taken 140 people around five hours to process them.

Security of the count was very important and the counting software carries out multiple security checks on every ballot paper, which makes it impossible to enter fraudulent papers into the system. If a ballot paper had been confusing (e.g., a person had voted for everyone) then an image of the paper was sent to an election official at a workstation for adjudication.

1 State **one** reason why optical mark recognition was a suitable input method for the voting system. (1 mark)

2 Give **one** disadvantage in using optical mark recognition (OMR) as opposed to counting the votes by hand. (1 mark)

3 OMR is a popular fast automatic input method. Give the names of two different applications for which optical mark recognition would be suited. (2 marks)

Exam support

Worked example 1

1 The results of a survey are input into a computer for further processing using spreadsheet software.

(a) Here are some input methods that were considered:
- keyboard entry
- optical mark recognition
- optical character recognition

(i) Give **two** pieces of information that you would need in order to determine which method of input would be best. Give reasons for why you need each piece of information.   (2 marks)

(ii) For each of the **three** input methods mentioned, give the full name of the input device needed. (3 marks)

(b) The keyboard is the most popular input device but it is not necessarily the best. Give **two** reasons why keyboard entry is not always the best input method. (2 marks)

Student answer 1

1 (a) (i) Whether the input device is available.
The number of forms

(ii) Keyboard
Optical mark reader
Scanner

(b) It is too slow
It is too expensive

Examiner's comment

1 Answer (a) (i) the input device could be obtained even if it was not available so no marks for this part.

The number of forms is relevant but there is no reason given, so only one mark here.

Part (a) (ii) gains two marks. The scanner is the input device but on its own it will not recognise characters, so the answer needs to say with OCR capability or software to get the mark.

Answer part (b) needs further elaboration for the mark. Do not write too slow, faster, cheaper, more expensive, etc., without further qualification. **(3 marks out of 7)**

Student answer 2

1 (a) (i) The amount of data that needs to be input on each questionnaire.
The time it would take for a typist to input all this data.

(ii) Keyboard
Optical mark reader
Optical character reader

(b) Keyboard entry is inaccurate because it is so easy to misread data on the form or introduce typing mistakes. Keyboard entry takes a long time if there are lots of questionnaires to process.

Examiner's comment

1 Parts (a) (i) and (ii) are well answered.

The last part of the answer to (b) only gains one mark since the student has not specifically stated the disadvantage of taking a long time to key in (e.g., the results are not obtained quickly or the cost implications of paying the wages). **(6 marks out of 7)**

Examiner's answers

1 (a) (i) One mark each for two pieces of information needed to make the decision and one mark each for the reasons.

The number of questionnaires that need processing – if there are lots then an automatic method of data capture should be used.

Whether the questions can be structured or changed so that they are multiple choice or graded in some way so that they could be read automatically using a mark reader.

The time it would take to manually type the information in, so it could be worked out how much it would cost to process all the questionnaires and also work out the time it would take.

(ii) One mark each for three of the following:
Keyboard
Optical mark reader
Optical character reader/scanner with OCR software

(b) One mark each for two of the following:
- Inaccurate – it is easy to make a transcription or transposition error when typing.
- Slow – if there are a large number of questionnaires to process, they will take a long time to get the results.

Expensive – paying someone to type the information in is expensive.

Health problems – typist could get RSI.

Exam support continued

Worked example 2

2 All ICT tasks involve the three steps of input, process and output. Using an example of an ICT problem and solution you are familiar with:
   (a) State what the ICT problem was. **(1 mark)**
   (b) Give **two** examples of data that was input and give the method of input used. **(2 marks)**
   (c) State **one** process that was performed on the input data. **(1 mark)**
   (d) State **one** example of information that was output from the ICT solution explaining the method of output. **(2 marks)**

Student answer 1

2 (a) Set up a website for the tourist information office on local attractions.
   (b) Images entered using a digital camera or copied from websites.
       Text which was entered into word-processing software using a keyboard and saved and imported into the website design software.
   (c) Organising the items on each webpage and creating the links between the webpages on the site.
   (d) The complete webpages containing text, images about attractions and links are output on a screen.

Student answer 2

2 (a) Set up a financial model to show the cash flow for a person who is thinking of buying a villa abroad and renting it out to holiday makers.
   (b) The number of weeks rented and the prices charged per week for the different rental periods.
   (c) Multiplying each week by the cost per week (which varies depending on high season, mid season, etc.) to work out the money coming in each week before deductions.
   (d) A worksheet on screen but which can also be printed out showing the money coming in each week and the total income for the year based on the expected number of weeks rented.

Examiner's comment

2 It is harder to identify inputs, processes and outputs for a web-based ICT problem than, for example, a spreadsheet, database, etc., and this student has made a very good attempt.

   The student has correctly answered parts (a) and (b).

   Organising information as well as creating links are both processes so full marks for section (c).

   The student has correctly identified what the information is that is output and also the method of output. **(6 marks out of 6)**

Examiner's comment

2 This is another excellent answer and the student has understood the concepts of input, process and output and has managed to present a clear answer containing all the essential components. **(6 marks out of 6)**

Examiner's answers

2 (a) One mark for a clear explanation of the problem such as:
       The client wanted a worksheet to show the income and expenditure for a holiday cottage they are renting out.
   (b) One mark for each input and method of input x 2.
       The number of weeks the cottage could be rented for entered using a keyboard.
       The prices charged for each period entered using a keyboard.
   (c) One mark for a process such as a calculation.
       The amount of rental for each week was obtained by multiplying the rental by the number of weeks rented.
   (d) One mark for a statement of the output and the method of output.
       The total projected income after costs and expenses taken out was displayed on the screen.

Summary mind maps

Selection and use of input devices and input media: simple devices

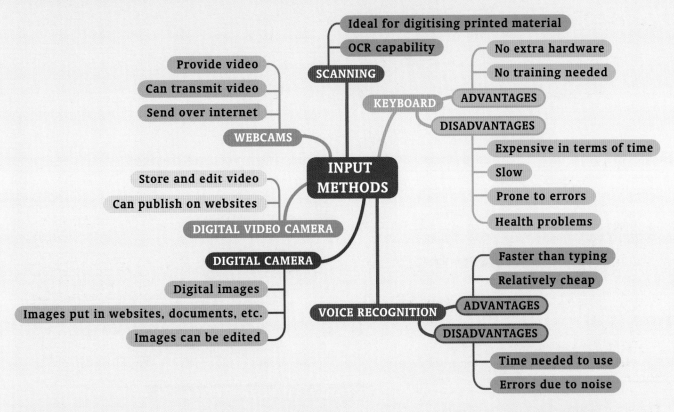

Selection and use of input devices and input media: capturing transaction data

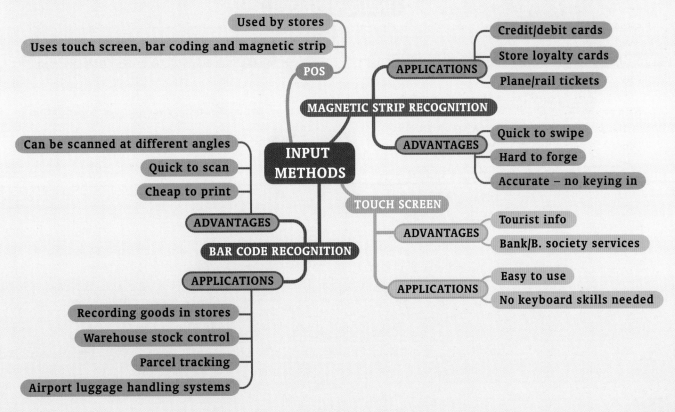

Summary mind maps continued

Selection and use of input devices and input media: high volume devices

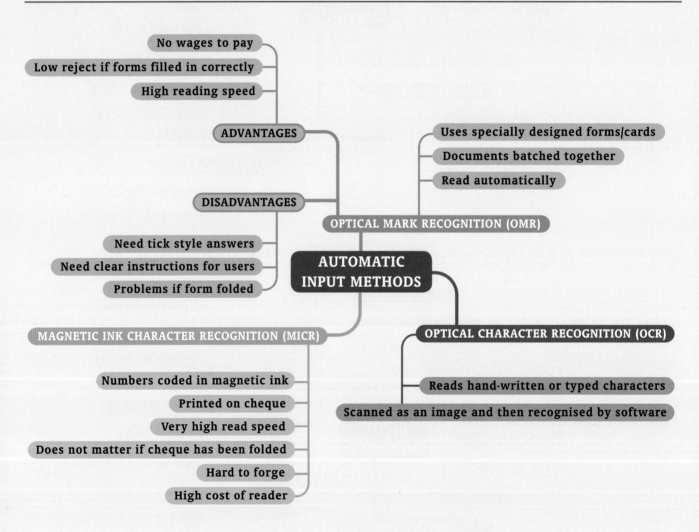

No wages to pay

Low reject if forms filled in correctly

High reading speed

ADVANTAGES

Uses specially designed forms/cards

Documents batched together

Read automatically

DISADVANTAGES

OPTICAL MARK RECOGNITION (OMR)

Need tick style answers

Need clear instructions for users

Problems if form folded

AUTOMATIC INPUT METHODS

MAGNETIC INK CHARACTER RECOGNITION (MICR)

OPTICAL CHARACTER RECOGNITION (OCR)

Numbers coded in magnetic ink

Printed on cheque

Very high read speed

Does not matter if cheque has been folded

Hard to forge

High cost of reader

Reads hand-written or typed characters

Scanned as an image and then recognised by software

TOPIC 5: Selection and use of storage requirements, media and devices

As part of your sample work you will need to decide on the storage requirements for your ICT solution and you must be able to justify your choice. Because of this you need to have a good knowledge of all the storage devices and media available.

▼ The key concepts covered in this topic are:

▶ Select from input devices input media available

▶ Justify why items selected were suitable to solve each particular problem

CONTENTS

Selection and use of storage requirements, media and devices: storage and storage capacity

▼ You will find out

▶ About the difference between primary and secondary storage

▶ About the need for temporary and permanent storage

Introduction

In this section you will be looking at aspects of main memory and backing storage and why there is a need for temporary and permanent storage.

Primary and secondary storage

ICT systems need to store programs and data and this storage can be either in:

- Primary storage – in chips inside the computer.
- Secondary (or backup storage) outside the computer.

Primary storage is of two types:

- ROM (Read Only Memory)
- RAM (Random Access Memory).

With both types of primary storage the programs and data are stored on chips and are available immediately by the central processing unit.

Secondary storage is outside the computer (assuming the computer is defined as being the control unit, the arithmetic and logic unit), although it can be within the casing of the

computer. Unlike with primary storage, there is a short delay while the data is obtained from the secondary storage.

Secondary or backup storage can include:

- Magnetic disk
- Magnetic tape
- CD-ROM
- CD-RW
- DVD.

The need for temporary and permanent storage

The computer needs a working area and a place to hold the data while it is working on it. RAM (Random Access Memory) is used to hold the data temporarily whilst the computer is working on it. If the computer is switched off without saving this data, then the data will be lost.

The RAM is like a whiteboard that is constantly being overwritten with new data. If you are working on a spreadsheet, the spreadsheet is kept in RAM until it is saved on disk. If you want to use it again, you simply load the file into the RAM where you can work on the spreadsheet again.

▶ KEY WORDS

Volatile memory – memory which loses data when the power is turned off

Non-volatile memory – memory stored on a chip which does not lose data when the power is turned off

RAM – random access memory. Fast temporary memory which loses its contents when the power is turned off

ROM – read only memory – memory stored on a chip which does not lose data when the power is turned off

RAM (Random Access Memory)

RAM is a fast temporary memory where programs and data are stored only when the power is supplied.

RAM is:

- held on a computer chip
- called volatile memory because the contents disappear when the power is turned off
- read/write, so can be altered by the user.

ROM (Read Only Memory)

ROM is fast permanent memory used for holding instructions needed to start the computer up.

ROM is:

- held on a computer chip
- called non-volatile memory because it does not lose its contents when the power is turned off
- used to hold instructions to start the computer
- contents cannot be altered by the user.

The importance of memory size

Having a large amount of memory is important. Having more memory means:

- applications run faster on their own
- more applications able to run at the same time
- able to quickly move between applications.

Measuring storage capacity and performance

In order to compare different storage methods it is necessary to look at those things that affect the use of the storage device. The following can be used to measure storage capacity and performance:

Storage capacity – how much data can the storage device/media hold? Usually measured in Mb or Gb.

Storage density – how compact is the storage medium? Ideally you want as much storage as possible in the least possible space.

Access time – this is the time the storage device takes to access a particular piece of data. This has to be an average time. There will also be a corresponding time for the storing of the data.

Transfer rate – once the data has been located, it will need to be read and transferred to the computer. This measures the throughput of the data.

Physical size – storage devices need to be as small and as light as possible. This is particularly important in laptop computers.

Portability – Some storage devices used for backup should be removable. The ease with which they are removed is important.

Units of memory and storage

The amount of data and instructions the computer can store in its memory is measured in bytes. One byte contains 8 bits (a bit is a binary digit 0 or 1).

A single character (letter, number or symbol on the keyboard) can be stored in one byte. This means that one byte is an extremely small unit of storage. We normally measure storage/memory in

terms of kilobytes (Kb), megabytes (Mb) or gigabytes (Gb).

Why you need to know about file sizes

It is always important to know about the size of certain files because it is essential if you want to know how many of them could be stored on a particular storage device. File sizes can be a little confusing but here they are from the smallest to the largest:

> Bit
> Byte
> Kilobyte (Kb)
> Megabyte (Mb)
> Gigabyte (Gb)
> Terabyte (Tb)

The exact file size conversions are shown here:

> Bit (0 or 1) the smallest unit of measurement
> Byte 8 bits
> Kilobyte (Kb) 1024 bytes
> Megabyte (Mb) 1024 kilobytes (Kb)
> Gigabyte (Gb) 1024 megabytes (Mb)
> Terabyte (Tb) 1024 gigabytes (Gb)

These are quite difficult to work out without a calculator so it is easier to estimate file sizes using the following:

> Byte 8 bits
> Kilobyte (Kb) 1000 bytes
> Megabyte (Mb) 1000 kilobytes (Kb)
> Gigabyte (Gb) 1000 megabytes (Mb)
> Terabyte (Tb) 1000 gigabytes (Gb)

Memory card – typical storage capacity 2Gb

File compression

Files are often compressed before saving on the storage medium and this enables more files to be stored in the same space. For example, if an image file stored as a bitmap is compressed and stored as a JPEG file, the resulting file is typically about 8% of the bitmap file size. Music files are compressed into MP3 format.

Storage device capacities

CD – typical storage capacity 700Mb.

Flash drive – typical storage capacity 4Gb.

Magnetic hard drive – typical storage capacity 320Gb

Selection and use of storage requirements, media and devices: devices and media

▼ You will find out

▶ About the storage devices and media available

▶ About how data is stored at a different physical location from where it may be used

▶ About measuring storage capacity and performance

▶ About limitations of storage devices and media

Introduction

It is usually necessary to store data for future use and there is a large range of drives and devices that can be used for this. Each device/media has its own set of advantages and disadvantages and the choice is usually dictated by the requirements of the application. As part of your ICT solution you will need to choose a storage device/media to hold your solution and the data it uses. You will need to justify your choice and also show that you have considered other options.

Storing data for future use: backing storage

Backing storage is storage outside the processor (i.e. CPU) and in many cases uses removable media so that files can be transferred from one computer to another. Backing storage allows data to be stored for future use.

There is a large selection of storage devices and media to choose from and the main ones are outlined here.

Magnetic disk drives

Magnetic disk drives can be classified according to whether the media containing the data is hard or soft.

Floppy disks and drives

Floppy disks are flexible plastic disks which are coated with a material which can store data as a magnetic pattern. The disks are removable and can be transferred from one computer to another.

Floppy disk drives are not popular any more mainly because of how long it takes to transfer the data from them (called the data transfer speed) and the very low storage capacity (1.44 Mb) compared to other backing storage.

Nowadays computers do not have them already built in and many shops are not selling the disks or the drives any more.

Hard drives

Hard drives consist of a series of disks with a magnetic coating and a series of read/write heads which put the data onto or record it off each surface.

Magnetic hard drives have the advantages of:

- a very high transfer rate
- a very high storage capacity.

It is possible to buy additional hard drives for backup purposes and it is also possible to buy hard drives which fit into bays in the computer which may be removed each night and stored safely.

Inside a magnetic hard disk drive. Notice the plinth of disks and the read-write heads which transfer the data on or off the disks.

> **EXAM TIP**
>
> Magnetic hard drives are normally connected to Internet servers and file servers so that files are available to anyone authorised to access them. So try not to think that a hard drive is just a single user storage device in a personal computer.

Additional hard drives can be used for backup purposes. This hard drive connects to the USB port and it is light and transportable.

Optical drives

Optical disks are flat circular disks on which data is stored as a series of bumps. The way the bumps reflect laser beam light is used to read the data off the disk.

CD-ROM (Compact Disk-Read Only Memory)

CD-ROMs are used mainly for the distribution of software. Although most home computers are equipped with DVD drives, a lot more computers, especially those used in businesses, still only have CD drives. You can read a CD using a DVD drive but you cannot read a DVD with a CD drive. This is why software is still being sold on CD rather than DVD.

With CD-ROM:

- data is read only
- data is stored as an optical pattern
- there is a large storage capacity (600 Mb)
- they are used for the distribution of software.

CD-R (CD-recordable)

CD-R allows data to be stored on a CD, but only once. It is ideal for the backing up of data or for storing digital music.

CD-RW (CD-rewriteable)

A CD-RW disk allows data to be stored on the disk over and over again – just like a hard disk. You can treat a CD-RW like a hard drive but the transfer rate is less and the time taken to locate a file is greater. The media is not as robust as a hard drive.

DVD (Digital Versatile Disk)

DVDs have a much higher storage capacity than CDs and are ideal for the storage of multimedia files such as MP3, digital images and video clips.

DVD-ROM (Digital Versatile Disk-Read Only Memory)

DVD-ROM is used for the distribution of movies where you can only read the data off the disk. A DVD-ROM drive can also be used for the reading of data off a CD.

DVD+RW (Digital Versatile Disk+Read/Write)

A DVD+RW drive can be used to write to as well as read data from a DVD.

DVD-RW are sometimes called DVD burners because they are able to be written to and not just read from. Typical storage capacities are:

- 4.7 Gb for the older DVD drives
- 8.5 Gb for the latest DVD drives.

Magnetic tape

Magnetic tape stores the data on a plastic magnetic coated tape which is stored on a reel. Sometimes the tape is in a plastic case a bit like the old-fashioned music cassette tapes. Magnetic tape:

- has a huge storage capacity (around 800 Gb)
- is used for the backup of data and programs in large systems
- is not used for storage needed quickly because of the large access time (it takes time for the data to be found on the tape).

This magnetic tape drive can store 800 Gb of data and is used to back up data from an e-commerce business. The tape cartridges can be removed from the drive and stored off-site for security purposes.

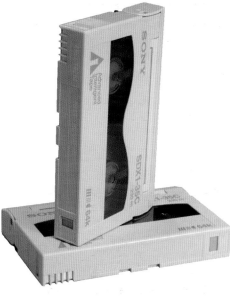

Flash/pen drives

Flash/pen drives are very popular storage media which offer cheap and large storage capacities and are an

Unit 1 Practical Problem Solving in the Digital World

Selection and use of storage requirements, media and devices: devices and media *continued*

Many computers and printers have drives that will read the data on different sized memory cards. There are also portable memory card drives which attach to the USB socket of the computer.

Data stored at different physical locations from where it is used

Data is often stored at different physical locations from where it is used. Take, for example, a website that you create using your computer at home. Unless you have your own web-server/Internet server, which is unlikely, you will have to store your website on your Internet service provider's website. Your website along with other similar websites will be stored on a fast storage device (usually magnetic hard disk) which is permanently connected to an Internet server. This will allow others to gain quick access to your website.

Examples where data is stored at different physical locations to where it is used include:

Flash/pen drives are the most popular portable storage media. Their portability is their main advantage and you simply plug them into the USB port where they are recognised automatically.

ideal media for photographs, music and other data files. They consist of printed circuit boards enclosed in a plastic case.

The main advantages are:

- small and lightweight – easy to put on your key ring or in your pocket
- can be used with any computer
- large storage capacity (up to 30 Gb)
- no moving parts so they are very reliable
- not subject to scratches like optical media.

The main disadvantages are:

- their small size means they are easily stolen
- they are often left in the computer by mistake and lost
- they do not have as high a transfer rate as magnetic hard disk drives.

Memory card drives and memory cards

Memory cards are the thin cards you see in digital cameras. They are ideal storage media for photographs but can also be used for storing other types of data.

- Networked computers – networked computers can store work at a remote location. Centrally storing user data makes it easier to ensure the security of the data and also to back it up.
- A blog – although you can create a blog using your computer, the actual blog is stored on a storage device that is permanently connected to an Internet server that will service the requests from users to view it and add content to it.
- On-line backup companies which for a fee will allow you to store your backup data on their computers. The Internet is used to transfer the files to and from their storage devices.

Memory cards are sometimes called picture cards.

This card reader connects to the USB socket and is capable of reading 15 different sized and types of memory card.

- Websites – those people who do not have their own Internet servers will need to store their webpages and website on the server of an Internet service provider (ISP).
- E-mails – if you are a home user of the Internet, then your e-mails are stored on the storage devices of your Internet service provider. When you log on you can view them and if you need to, store them on your own computer.

Selecting storage devices and media for your ICT solution

When creating your ICT solutions you will have to choose storage devices and media to hold the data.

As there are a whole range of devices and media available, you will need to explain the reasons for your choice. Always explain why you did not choose certain storage devices and media as well as explaining why you chose the one you did.

Limitations of storage devices and media

The ideal storage device would be:

- cheap
- offer a very large storage capacity
- have extremely fast access times
- have an extremely high transfer rate
- be very robust and not be affected by scratches, heat, magnetic fields, etc.
- be of a very small size so that they can be transported easily
- offer the ability to be attached to lots of different devices, e.g. digital cameras, portable media devices, computers, etc.

Unfortunately the ideal storage device and media does not exist for all applications. Instead, one has to be chosen which has as many of the desirable qualities as possible.

If a device or media does not offer some of the above, then it will be a limitation.

Backup storage

Backup storage is used to hold copies of the original files in case they are lost. As most of the time these backups

Zip disks look like a fatter version of the older floppy disks.

Portable hard drives are relatively cheap and are ideal for backing up music, photographs and other data files.

are not needed they do not have to be immediately accessible by the computer unless they are to be used by a network where any downtime is unacceptable. Instead most types of backup storage make use of removable media which can be kept away from the computer and preferably stored off-site.

The main requirement for backup storage is that it should be portable and have a high storage capacity.

Other backup media/devices include:

- Pen/flash drives are ideal for backup of small amounts of data and are popular for transferring data between computers.
- CD-RW and DVD-RW can be used as backup but they are slow compared to other methods.

Magnetic tape is ideal removable media when lots of data needs backing up.

Questions and Activities

▶ Questions 1   p. 58

1 Memory can be classed as volatile and non-volatile. Explain the difference between these two types of memory. **(4 marks)**

2 Explain why it is necessary to have a large amount of memory when running the latest application software. **(2 marks)**

▶ Questions 2   pp. 60–63

1 Data needs to be stored for future use. Here are a number of storage devices/media. For each of these, explain a suitable use and explain clearly why the storage device/media is suited to the application.
  (a) Memory card **(3 marks)**
  (b) CD-ROM **(3 marks)**
  (c) Magnetic hard drive **(3 marks)**
  (d) Flash drive **(3 marks)**

2 Data is often stored at different physical locations. Give **two** applications where data is stored remotely and explain clearly why this is necessary. **(4 marks)**

3 You want to distribute your digital photographs to your friends and family. There are several methods you could choose to do this, namely:
  • distribution on DVD
  • distribution on CD-ROM
  • uploading the digital photographs to a website
Explain with justified reasons which method or methods you consider to be most suitable. **(6 marks)**

▶ Activity 1 Researching storage devices and media

Everyone who uses a computer needs to store their data and programs somewhere. As the number of people who store photographs, music and video on their ICT systems increases and the number of huge databases increase, storage needs to be available to store all the files.

There is a huge range of storage devices and storage media available and which one you choose depends on factors such as the amount of data you need to store, the amount of data you might need to store in the future, whether the data needs to be transferred and so on.

Storage devices are being developed all the time and always get smaller and cheaper, with a higher storage capacity.

For this activity you are going to research the latest storage devices.

You are going to investigate the storage devices available for a home user or a self-employed user, as well as a business user who has fifteen computers all connected to a network where all the data and programs are held centrally.

The research you will do will feature in one of the main computer magazines.

The editor will write the article but has asked you to produce a list of the latest storage devices with their main features. The editor has mentioned that this might be best presented in a table but has left you to work out the best way to present the information. The editor has explained that the idea is that a user should be able to pick out a suitable storage device based on their needs.

The editor has suggested that you might use the following websites for your research:
    http://www.dabs.com/
    http://www.pcworld.co.uk/
    http://www.amazon.co.uk/
    http://www.ebuyer.com/
The editor has asked that you try to condense your material so that it occupies no more than one single page of A4. Your teacher/lecturer may decide you are better working in a small group to complete this task.

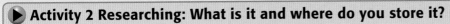

▶ Activity 2 Researching: What is it and where do you store it?

Here is a list of some of the things users might want to do. You have to look at the relevant section in the topic and also do some research for yourself. All storage devices will store data but the way they do it is different and some are more appropriate than others in different situations. You have to choose what you consider to be the best solution and explain your reasoning.

Storing a multimedia presentation

You have produced a multimedia presentation for a salesperson consisting of thirty slides which make full use of the multimedia features of the presentation software. In the presentation you have included sound, slide transition effects, still images, animations and video. The salesperson needs to show customers on the salesperson's laptop computer but they may also present the material to groups of customers using the customer's computer connected to a data projector.

Storing a podcast

You develop a series of podcasts covering various topics for AS-level ICT. You would like to distribute them to all the members of your class.

Storing backup files

You have a huge amount of data stored on your computer, mainly in the form of video files, music files in MP3 format, digital photographs, program files and files containing work you have produced as part of your AS ICT work. You need to back all this data up, but which storage device or media would you choose?

Providing portable storage

You need to do some work in class at school or college and also work in the library or at home on either a laptop or desktop computer. You need a small portable storage device that can be used to store and transfer data but which one is best and why?

Storing end of year accounts for archive purposes

A self-employed painter and decorator needs to keep end-of-year accounts for income tax purposes. He prepares these accounts himself using spreadsheet software. He is required to keep copies of his accounts for six years. He intends to keep one copy on the computer and one on removable media. This media is kept along with all his receipts and paperwork in a box file. Once the accounts have been produced they will not be altered, so he needs to ensure that the files can be read only. Which storage media do you suggest and why?

Keeping a backup of all your family photographs

Most people have a collection of family photographs stored on their computer and Amy is no exception. Because these photographs are stored on the computer she is worried about the computer being stolen or damaged and losing the photographs. She needs to back the files up and preferably on media or a device that she could use with other people's computers. Which storage device or media do you suggest and why?

Distributing a collection of family photographs

You have a large number of family photographs as digital files taken at a family party and you would like to distribute them to all the family members. Which storage media would you choose for this distribution and why?

Exam support

Worked example 1

1   **CD-RW**
    CD-ROM
    DVD-ROM
    Flash memory
    Portable media player
    500 Gb external hard drive
    Choose a suitable storage medium from the list above and

give a reason for:
(a) **Storing your work** .... **(2 marks)**
     Reason...
(b) **Storing a podcast** .... **(2 marks)**
     Reason...
(c) **Keeping a blog** .... **(2 marks)**
     Reason...

Student answer 1

1 (a) Storing your work – CD-RW
        Reason – you can store and alter the contents easily
   (b) Storing a podcast – flash memory
        Reason – flash memory is easily transported from one
        computer to another
   (c) Keeping a blog – portable media player
        Reason – holds a lot of information

Examiner's comment

1   To answer this question successfully a student needs to
    understand what a 'podcast' and a 'blog' are.
        Part (a) CD-RW is quite a cumbersome way for
    storing work which needs to be transferred. There
    are better media in the table. The reason stated is
    superficial and includes little detail. No marks here.
        Part (b) has both parts correct. Any storage media
    can be used for a podcast as the idea is that podcasts
    can be listened to/viewed anywhere and anytime.
        Part (c) shows that the student does not know what
    a blog is. If they knew that a blog is an on-line service
    and that blogs need to be stored on storage attached
    to a server, they would not have given this answer.
    (2 marks out of 6)

Student answer 2

1 (a) Storing your work – portable media player
        Reason – you can treat is just like an additional portable
        hard drive and you can transfer files between the school's
        computer and your home computer.
   (b) Storing a podcast – flash memory – you can load the
        podcast off the Internet automatically and then use the
        flash memory to play it back on any computer you like.
   (c) Keeping a blog – 500 Gb external hard drive
        Reason – a blog is an Internet service so a server is used
        and you need a big and fast storage device to enable users to
        access it and add to it.

Examiner's comment

1   This student has clearly understood the purpose of a
    podcast and a blog and has chosen the correct storage
    devices. The reasons given show a good understanding
    of appropriate storage devices/media for different
    situations. Full marks for the answer to this question.
    (6 marks out of 6)

Examiner's answers

1 (a) One mark for the storage device and one mark for a
        reason.
        Storing your work – flash/pen drive, portable media
        player.
        Reason – small size so easily transported, robust so
        no problem with scratches, inexpensive compared
        to a portable hard drive, can be attached quickly to
        any computer.
   (b) One mark for the storage device and one mark for a
        reason.
        Storing a podcast – any in the table would be
        suitable.

        Reason – depends on media chosen. (Flash drive
        – can be easily be transferred from one computer
        to another. Portable media player – podcast can be
        viewed whilst on the move, etc.).
   (c) One mark for the storage device and one mark for a
        reason.
        Keeping a blog – 500 Gb external hard drive.
        Reason – the blog needs to be connected to an
        Internet server. High storage is needed because the
        server will need to store other people's blogs.

Worked example 2

2 A multimedia presentation is to be transferred between computers.
  (a) Give the names of **two** storages devices that can be used to store the files and explain why they are suitable for this application. **(4 marks)**
  (b) All storage devices and media have limitations. For each storage device/media you have named state **two** limitations. **(2 marks)**

Student answer 1

2 (a) CD because lots of different files can be stored and all computers come with a CD drive.
    DVD – because the storage capacity is high and they work with all computers.
  (b) CD – you cannot store data on both sides of the disk
    DVD – the surface of this disk can easily be damaged which causes them not to work.

Examiner's comment

2 Just stating either CD or DVD will not gain marks. As the presentation has been created on one computer and needs to be transferred to a different computer, there needs to be a write facility so it is necessary to give the names DVD+RW or CD-RW.
In other questions where the write facility is not needed the proper terms DVD-ROM or CD-ROM should be used rather than CD or DVD.
No marks for part (a)
Part (b) the lack of storage on both sides could (loosely) be considered as a limitation. The problem here is that the top surface tends to get scratched and also where would you put the label!
Optical media is easily damaged so part (b) is an acceptable answer. **(2 marks out of 6)**

Student answer 2

2 (a) CD-RW because the data can be recorded onto a CD-RW disk, which has a high storage capacity that is ideal for all the multimedia files. Also all computers have a drive that is capable of reading the data off the disk.
    Flash drive – the drive can be used just like another drive and has a high enough capacity to hold all the files needed and it is easy to transport, being small in size and light.
  (b) CD-RW you have to take care when handling them as it is very easy to scratch the disk surface and prevent the CD-RW from being able to transfer data.
    Flash drive – the access time is lower than that for an internal magnetic hard drive which means the data takes longer to load.

Examiner's comment

2 Part (a) the student has identified suitable storage devices/media and has clearly related their reasons to the transfer of multimedia files for a presentation. This part gains full marks.
  Part (b) two limitations to each storage media/device have been identified so full marks for this.
(6 marks out of 6)

Examiner's answers

2 (a) One mark for each device and one mark for the reason x2.
     Pen drive – small size means easily transferred from one computer to another.
     Pen drive – can be used by all computers as it simply plugs into the USB port/socket.
     Pen drive – can get cheap storage capacity up to 4 Gb which is enough for large music, animation, image files needed for a multimedia presentation.
     CD-RW – has a large storage capacity which is needed because multimedia files are usually large.
     CD-RW – small in size which means they are easily transferred between computers.
     CD-RW – can be read by any computer with a CD drive or a DVD drive.

  (b) One mark for each limitation. Note the limitations must refer to the named storage devices in part (a).
     CD-RW – easily scratched which causes read problems (1).
     CD-RW – limited amount of storage capacity (1).
     Pen drive – low transfer rate compared to a magnetic hard drive (1).
     Pen drive – easily bent and broken when in the socket (1).
     Pen drive – often left in the machine by mistake and lost (1).

Summary mind maps

Selection and use of storage requirements, media and devices: storage and storage capacity

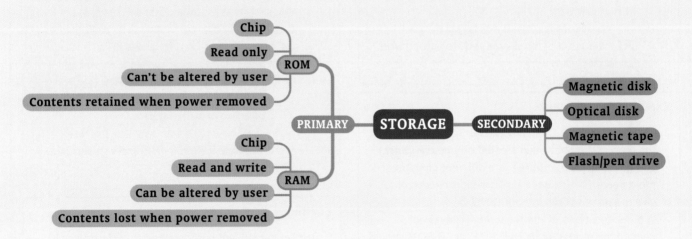

Selection and use of storage requirements, media and devices: devices and media

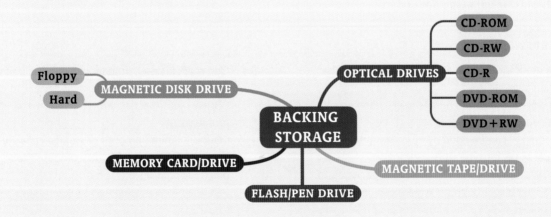

TOPIC 6: Selection and use of output methods, media and devices

In this topic you will need to know about the methods used to get output from ICT systems, and the output devices and media needed to do this. You will have to choose output methods, media and devices for the output from your sample work. You may be asked about the theory or about your sample work and where you have indicated output details in the documentation.

▼ The key concepts covered in this topic are:

▷ Selection and use of output methods, media and devices

CONTENTS

Selection and use of output methods, media and devices: printers

Introduction

The output from an ICT system are the results and there are a number of output methods which make use of output devices and output media.

Output methods

The most popular output devices are the screen and the printer, but there are other output methods. Multimedia webpages and presentations can be displayed on screen and the sound can be output from loudspeakers.

Output in digital form – the output from one system can be transmitted or saved and used as the input to a different ICT system.

Here are the main output methods:

- hard copy – printed on paper or card
- screen display – sometimes referred to as soft copy
- output in digital format – to be used as input to another system
- sound – speech, music, sound effects
- output to portable devices such as iPods, MP3 players, etc.
- output as control signals used to control devices such as electric motors, switches, valves and so on.

In many situations you will not want a hard copy all the time – for example, you could output the availability of a holiday or an item on the screen and then be given the opportunity to print the information out.

Output devices

Once data has been entered and stored and processed by an ICT system it is necessary to output the results of processing. The results of processing are output using one of the many output devices. There are many different types of output device but the commonest ones are:

- printers
- screens
- plotters
- speakers.

Printers

Printers are an essential part of any ICT system and are used to provide hard copy. There are several different types of printer available, each one more suited for a particular purpose. You need to be able to name the printers and be able to match a printer to an application.

The main types of printer are:

- ink-jet printers
- laser printers
- dot matrix printers
- thermal printers.

Ink-jet printers

Ink-jet printers are popular with home users but less popular with businesses because of the high cost of the ink cartridges. Ink-jet printers work by spraying ink onto the paper and can produce high quality printouts that almost look as though they have been printed professionally.

Advantages of ink-jet printers:

- High quality print – ideal for most business uses where appearance is important.
- The ability to produce photographic quality print – makes it ideal for printing photographs, brochures, etc.
- Quietness of operation – this is important as you can make telephone calls whilst jobs are printing.
- Cheap to buy – initial costs are low.

Disadvantages of ink-jet printers:

- High cost of ink cartridges – cost of the actual printer is low but the ink refills are very expensive.

▶ KEY WORDS

Continuous stationery – long sheets of paper with perforations between the pages and down each side. There are sprocket holes down the side which enable the paper to be pulled through the printer

Impact printer – the shape of the letters is formed by hitting an inked ribbon against the page

- Ink smudges – there is a tendency for the ink to smudge on the paper unless you are very careful.
- Need special paper – for the best quality printouts (e.g., for photographs) glossy paper is needed, which is expensive.

Laser printers

Laser printers are very popular with businesses because of their high speed when printing in colour or black and white. They make use of photocopier technology and different colour inks.

Advantages of laser printers:

- Supplies (e.g., toner cartridges) last longer – means the on-going printing costs are less than for an ink-jet printer.
- High printing speed – this makes it an ideal printer for an office where most of the printouts are in black and white.
- Very reliable – you have very few problems compared with ink-jet printers.
- No wet pages to deal with – the pages from ink-jet printers can get very wet and start to smudge when other paper slides across it. There is no problem like this with a laser printer.

- Uses ordinary and cheap photocopier paper – no special expensive paper needed.

Disadvantages of laser printers:

- Higher initial cost – compared to other printers the initial cost of the printer is higher.
- Colour printing is expensive – you have to use a colour laser printer.
- Higher power consumption – means running costs are higher.

Dot matrix printers

Dot matrix printers are not often seen at home but they are very common in businesses. They are called impact printers because they work by hitting little pins (usually 9 or 24) against an inked ribbon to mark out the characters.

Advantages of dot matrix printers:

- Can be used to print multi-part stationery – this is important in organisations, as different parts of the printouts can be sent to different people/departments.
- Can be used with continuous stationery – the sprocket feed enables continuous (and also multi-part) stationery to be printed. This is ideal for product lists, stock lists, customer invoices, etc.
- Reliable – the technology is simple and has a very high mean time between failures.
- Easy to use with different paper sources – you can have different paper sources set up ready to be chosen by the software being run.

Disadvantages of dot matrix printers:

- Very noisy – because they are impact printers.
- Characters are not as clear – shape of the characters is made up from a series of dots.
- Unsuited for printing graphics – no good for desktop publishing or word-processing work where high quality text is usually needed.
- Limited colour printing – need to use a ribbon which consists of bands of different colours so restricted to certain colours.

Dot matrix printers are able to switch between many different paper sources.

Thermal printers

Thermal printers are printers which use heat in order to produce an impression on paper. Typical applications for thermal printers include:

- printing receipts in cash registers or point of sale terminals
- printing tickets in car parks
- printing lottery tickets.

Thermal printers are becoming quite popular owing to their silent printing, high speed and the quality of the printing.

Multifunction printers

These are very popular printers because they combine the following in one machine:

- printer (usually laser)
- scanner
- photocopier
- fax.

Advantages of multifunctional printers:

- Small footprint – takes up little more than the space of an ordinary printer. If you had separate devices they would take up a lot more space.

Hardware drivers

Hardware such as printers, scanners, cameras, etc., often comes with software. In most cases this software will come on a CD-ROM for the following reasons:

- many computers no longer have floppy disk drives
- the storage capacity on floppy disks is small which means several disks are needed – installation involves the hassle of inserting and removing disks
- most computers can read CD-ROMs but not all can read DVDs. DVD drives can read CD-ROMs but not vice versa.

Printer drivers

Printer drivers are programs that control the operation of a printer. When a document is printed, the printer driver takes over the operation of the printer and feeds it commands which it understands.

Where do you get drivers from?

Drivers are an important part of any hardware that is linked to a computer.

This top of the range multifunctional laser printer can print, copy, fax and scan in colour

Sometimes a computer will need to have software re-installed because of damage to the original software or loss. As well as the re-installation of systems software and applications software any drivers for the hardware attached will also need to be re-installed.

Here are ways of providing the drivers:

- Install them from the system software – drivers are often provided as part of the system software/operating system.
- Installation CD/DVD – drivers are provided on the installation CD/DVD that comes with the hardware.
- From a website – drivers can be downloaded from the hardware manufacturer's website and can also be downloaded from other sites which specialise in supplying drivers.
- By e-mail – drivers can be e-mailed from a help desk.

⮕ KEY WORDS

Printer driver – software that converts commands from the systems or applications software into a form that a particular printer can understand

Selection and use of output methods, media and devices: output devices

Introduction

As with input methods, input devices and input media covered earlier, it is important to be able to distinguish between output methods, devices and media.

In this section you will look at all the other possible output methods and devices besides the printer. You will also look at the range of output media.

Screens

Screens (sometimes called VDUs (Visual Display Units) and monitors) allow users to view processed information. Most screens are now flat screens which offer the advantages that they take up less space on the desk and are much lighter, which means cleaning around them is easier. These screens make use of LCD (Liquid Crystal Display) which produces less heat than cathode ray tube screens.

Flat screens have become the norm.

Copyright 2002 by Randy Glasbergen.
www.glasbergen.com

'See? If you get close enough to the screen, a 15-inch monitor looks just as big as a 20-inch monitor!'

A large screen is needed when there is lots of detail on the screen such as in CAD (computer aided design) or desktop publishing work.

Plotters

Plotters are used for the printing of graphs, plans, maps and designs from a computer system. Plotters produce very accurate and precise drawings to scale, which look much more professional compared to the same produced using a printer.

There are two types of plotter: the flat-bed plotter for small drawings and the drum plotter for large drawings. They work by drawing lines, curves, etc., using a pen.

Sound output

Speakers

Speakers are a very important output device and many users make use of them more than a printer. Using speakers, you can:

- listen to voicemail
- listen to radio stations anywhere in the world using the Internet
- listen to music you have stored on your computer
- listen and watch video
- make use of multimedia presentations, websites, interactive quizzes, etc.
- make and receive phone calls over the Internet.

Computer speakers are an important output device for multimedia systems.

Limitations of current output devices

The following shows some limitations of an ink-jet printer:

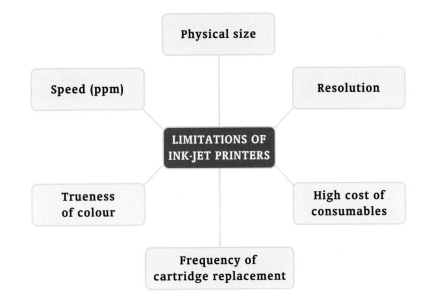

Headphones

Sound may also be output to headphones in order not to disturb others.

Output to portable devices

Music needs to be portable – people want to be able to store or download it onto their computer and then transfer it to other devices such as iPods or MP3 players or transfer it to players located in different rooms in their homes.

Output media

The output media is the material or something on which information can be stored or conveyed. Using this definition you can see that the following are classed as output media:

- hard copy (i.e., output printed on paper, card, acetate, etc.)
- magnetic media such as flash drives, picture cards, removable hard drives
- optical media such as CD-ROM, CD-RW, DVD, etc.

> **EXAM TIP**
>
> In the examination for Unit 1 you could be asked to identify where you have specified the output methods, the output devices and output media (if applicable) for your ICT solutions. Make sure you clearly identify this section or these sections as you may need to refer to them by page number.

Questions and Activities

▶ Questions 1 | pp. 70–71

1 A brochure prepared using desktop publishing software needs to be printed. The brochure contains both text and graphics.
Name **two** types of printer that can be used. (One word answers are acceptable for this question) (2 marks)

2 A kitchen company needs some high quality photographs of kitchens they have supplied to show potential customers.
They have supplied these as image files on a DVD.
(a) Give the name of the type of printer that would be most suitable for printing these photographs out. (1 mark)
(b) Give two reasons why the printer you have named in part (a) is suited for this. (2 marks)
(c) Give two limitations of the printer you have named. (2 marks)

3 A small business is being set up and it is planning a small local area network containing five printers. The business needs to produce invoices, stock lists, price lists, brochures and so on.
(a) Give the name of one type of printer it should purchase. (1 mark)
(b) Give one reason why the printer you selected in (a) would be a suitable choice. (1 mark)
(c) Give one limitation of the type of printer you have suggested in part (a). (1 mark)
(d) The business owner has asked if he should purchase all the same type of printer or whether two different types of printer would be better. Explain, by giving reasons, why two different types of printer would be better. (2 marks)

▶ Questions 2 | pp. 70–71

1 A laser printer is purchased which offers normal printing functions.
A CD-ROM is supplied with the printer containing drivers.
(a) State **three** functions of a printer driver. (3 marks)
(b) State **one** reason why the printer drivers are not provided on a floppy disk. (1 mark)
(c) State **one** reason why the printer drivers are not provided on a DVD. (1 mark)

2 You have a very large collection of family photographs stored on your computer. You would like to make the digital files available to other members of your family who live in different parts of the country. You think about outputting the contents of your collection and consider the following methods:
 • outputting to a DVD
 • outputting to a CD-ROM
 • uploading the photographs to a website which your family can access.

Explain with reasons which of the methods of getting the photographs to your family would be best. (6 marks)

3 Ink-jet printer
Laser printer
Dot matrix printer
Plotter
Choose the best output device from the list above for:
(a) Printing a plan of a kitchen drawn to scale. (1 mark)
 Reason (1 mark)
(b) Printing a high quality colour photograph. (1 mark)
 Reason (1 mark)
(c) Printing invoices using continuous stationery. (1 mark)
 Reason (1 mark)

▶ Activity 1 Mind maps for the different types of printer

For this activity you are required to produce a mind map or a series of mind maps which outline the functions and features of the different types of printer and also identify the tasks to which each is particularly suited.

Using your mind map, it should be possible to determine the most suitable type of printer for use for a certain task.

You can produce your mind map by hand or use specialist mind mapping software.

▶ Activity 2 Output devices that are also input devices

In order to make portable devices small, it is necessary to develop output devices that can also be used as input devices. Touch screens can be used to output information in the same way any screen can output information but they can also be used to make selections by touching the screen, so they also act as input devices.

You have been asked to write a short illustrated article about the use of touch screens for the input and output of information and about the applications for which they are particularly suited. Don't just think about computers – think about the whole range of ICT devices.

Here are two pictures of touch screens being used to help you with your ideas.

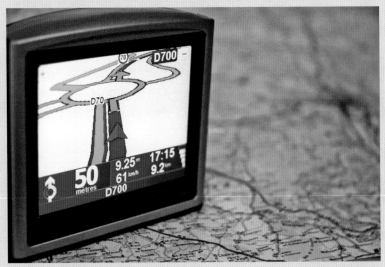

Satellite navigation systems.

Information kiosk.

▶ Activity 3 Screen resolution – what's it all about?

Screen resolution, measured in pixels, refers to the resolution of the computer screen. A particular screen has a maximum screen resolution determined by the manufacturer, but you can lower the screen resolution using the operating system.

You have been asked about screen resolution by someone who knows very little about ICT. You will need to do some research on screen resolution and then write a short piece about why it is important and its relevance to using ICT.

You need to address the following in your article:

- Why the same website can appear differently on a laptop and desktop computer.
- Why you need to consider screen resolution when designing websites.
- How screen resolution is important when displaying digital photographs on the screen.
- How screen resolution affects the quality of the picture displayed.
- About typical maximum resolutions for computer screens.

Remember that this piece of text is aimed at a novice user, so you must either avoid the use of technical language or explain any words carefully as you go along.

Exam support

Worked example 1

1 (a) A webpage is being designed for a client using website development software.
        The client has been asked to see some initial designs of a few pages.
   (i)   Give **one** reason why it might be better to show them the webpage on a screen rather than printed out on paper. **(1 mark)**
   (ii) If the client wants to see a printed version. Give the name of **one** type of printer that could produce a suitable printout. **(1 mark)**
   (iii) Describe **one** limitation of the printer you have named in part (ii). **(1 mark)**
   (b) Name and describe **one** output device other than a screen and a printer that a user would need in order to use the multimedia features of a website. **(1 mark)**

Student answer 1

1 (a) (i) It is quicker to show a screen than print it out.
        (ii) Laser printer.
        (iii) Speed.
   (b) Loudspeaker so that the user can hear a commentary about the content of a webpage.

Examiner's comment

1 Part (a) (i) is a typical faster, better, cheaper kind of answer and the time to print a page is not a real factor here, so no marks.

Part (a) (ii) is not acceptable as the majority of laser printers are black and white printers – need to say colour laser printer to get the mark.

Part (a) (iii) Speed on its own is not enough and the student needs to explain why it is a limitation.

Part (b) is an adequate description for one mark.

(1 mark out of 4)

Student answer 2

1 (a) (i) You are seeing the output in the way the user will view it so it is better because it is more realistic.
        (ii) Ink-jet printer.
        (iii) Colour reproduction – it is hard to mix inks in such a way that the colour is exactly the same as that produced on the screen.
   (b) Loudspeaker so a user can hear sound effects and music which adds interest to the output of a website.

Examiner's comment

1 (a) (i) is a good answer and gets a mark.

Answers to 1(a) parts (ii) and (iii) get both marks.

Part (b) is ok and the student has clearly stated the output device and given an advantage that the form of output brings. **(4 marks out of 4)**

Examiner's answers

1 (a) (i) One mark for an answer such as one of the following:
             The colours will be more true to life on a screen than on a printout.
             You are seeing the website in the same way a user will see it.
             They will need to see how clear the elements (e.g., text, images, etc.) are on the screen.
   (ii) One mark for either an ink-jet printer or colour laser printer.
         Laser printer will not get a mark on its own – need the word 'colour'.
   (iii) It should be clearly indicated what the limitation is and why it is a limitation.

One mark for one of the following:
Not able to reproduce actual colours exactly.
Speed of the printer when lots of printouts need to be produced in a short period.
High cost of consumables such as toner or ink-jet cartridges and special paper.
Not easily portable – especially with laptop computers.

   (b) One mark for a name and how the device is used.
        Loudspeaker – so that sound can be output.
        Speakers – so that music accompanying the website can be played.
        Headphones – so that sound can be heard without others having to listen to it.

Worked example 2

2 Name and explain the facilities offered by output device or devices that you would use to carry out the following tasks efficiently:

(a) Output an accurate and detailed scale drawing of a plan of a kitchen using specialist kitchen design software. **(3 marks)**

(b) Output a printout of an order where there are three copies produced at the same time: one for the customer, one for the accounts department and one for the warehouse staff. **(3 marks)**

(c) Output a presentation to be shown to a small number of staff in a room. **(3 marks)**

(d) Output an interactive multimedia display for a tourist information centre. **(3 marks)**

Student answer 1

2 (a) Printer because it could produce the plan in colour and show all the dimensions on the plan.

(b) An impact printer so that stationery that contains several sheets can be put through the printer at the same time and printed because the impact marks all the sheets. The sheets can then be separated and sent to the different departments.

(c) An electronic whiteboard can be used to output the presentation onto a screen and the presenter can control the presentation and can even draw on the screen to point things out.

(d) A large LCD and speakers so that the user can see the attractions as well as hear a running commentary or music.

Examiner's comment

2 (a) The word printer is not enough at AS level, as there are several types of printer, some of which would be ok but a dot matrix or thermal printer would be unsuitable. A good plan is drawn to scale so does not need dimensions on it.
No marks for this answer.

(b) Impact printer is ok here – but better to use the name dot matrix printer. The student clearly explains two additional points: 'impact marks all the sheets' and 'sheets put through at the same time'. Full marks for this part.

(c) Student has named the device, and made two points about the facilities so full marks for this part.

(d) Two output devices are mentioned here and the student has identified facilities offered, so full marks here. **(9 marks out of 12)**

Examiner's answers

2 (a) One mark for the name of the device and two marks for the facilities it offers.
Name of device:
Ink-jet printer (1)
Laser printer (1)
Graph plotter/drum plotter/flat-bed plotter/plotter (1)
Facilities offered:
Can print in colour (1)
Can produce accurate scale drawing (more accurate for plotter) (1)
Can print large plans (for plotter) (1)
Can produce very neatly drawn plans (1)

(b) One mark for the name of the device and two marks

Student answer 2

2 (a) Graph plotter as it is able to offer an accurate and neatly drawn diagram and can also print in colour. Also if a drum plotter is used, then very large plans can be produced.

(b) A dot matrix printer because the dots are created by lots of small pins which hit the inked ribbon against the paper and cause the characters to be formed. The paper has a chemical on it which means that the impact is transferred though the sheets.

(c) A large plasma display as the output can be fed to it from the computer. The high quality of the display will mean that high quality still and video images can be seen by the audience. Loudspeakers can relay hi-fi sound to accompany the images.

(d) A screen is used to output the information.

Examiner's comment

2 (a) and (b) gain all three marks for a correct name and a description of two of the facilities.

(c) Gives two names and a description so three marks for this.

(d) Only gives the name of the device, so only one mark here. **(10 marks out of 12)**

for the facilities it offers.
Is an impact printer so can print multi-part stationery (1)
Can print several sheets simultaneously (1)
Is a very fast printer so useful if lots of orders need printing quickly (1)

(c) One mark for the name of the device and two marks for the facilities it offers.
Ink-jet printer (1) for the printing of acetates in colour (1) which may be placed on an overhead projector and projected onto a screen (1)
Laser printer (1) for the printing of acetates in colour (1) which may be placed on an overhead projector and projected onto a screen (1)
Data projector (1) and speakers (1) to project the presentation from the screen of the computer (1) onto a large screen (1) and to output music/commentary (1)
Plasma screen (1) projector (1) and speakers (1) to use the screen as the display of the computer (1) and to output music/commentary (1)

(d) LCD screen (1) and two suitable facilities (2)

Summary mind maps

Selection and use of output methods, media and devices: printers

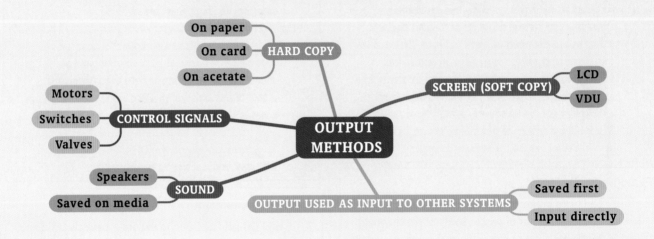

Selection and use of output methods, media and devices: output devices

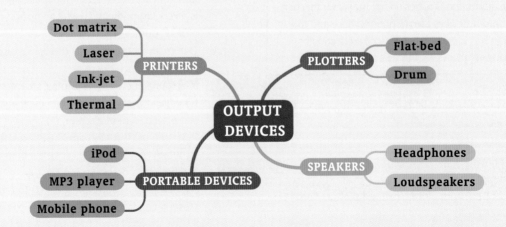

In this topic you will need to know about the different types of software and what they do. When you solve your ICT problem you will have to choose the most appropriate software for the job. Sometimes your choice will be limited by the availability of the software (i.e., software that your school/college has). You may be asked about the theory or be asked about your sample work and where you have described your justification for the software you used.

▼ The key concepts covered in this topic are:

▷ Identify the software available

▷ Justify why the selected software was suitable to solve each particular problem

▷ Systems and applications software

CONTENTS

Systems software and applications software: operating systems

Introduction

In order for ICT hardware to do a useful job it needs two types of software:

- systems software
- applications software.

Applications software

Applications software is software that allows the computer to be applied to a particular problem. Applications software would not normally be applied to the management of the resources of the computer such as memory, time spent processing jobs, and dealing with input or output.

Applications software is software used for a particular purpose or application such as order processing, payroll, stock control, games, creating websites, image editing, word-processing and so on.

Systems software

Systems software is any computer software that manages and controls the hardware thus allowing the applications software to do a useful job. Systems software is a set of programs which instructs the hardware what to do. Systems software consists of the following programs:

- Operating system
- GUI (graphical user interface)
- File management
- Utilities.

Remember – systems software is not just one program, it is several.

Systems software can be broken down into the operating system, GUI (graphical user interface), file management and utility software

The operating system

The main purpose of the operating system is to allow the applications software (databases, browsers, word-processors, games, etc.) to interact with the computer hardware. It allows the computer hardware to behave in a predictable way so that the applications software can use it.

Tasks the operating system would perform include:

- diagnostic checks – performs some diagnostic checks when the computer is switched on (i.e., booted up)
- controls the receipt of input from the input devices such as the keyboard and mouse
- controls output – sends information to the screen or other output devices

- memory management – controls the memory allocation needed by programs – this is important because several programs could be held in memory simultaneously
- controls the flow of data to and from the main processor
- works out where to store the data on the hard disk drive
- deals with security issues such as usernames and passwords
- handles the interrupts which occur when applications software contains bugs or there is a hardware fault.

Brands of systems software include:

- Windows
- Macintosh OS-X
- UNIX
- Linux.

Windows

Microsoft Windows is by far the most popular make of systems software and it owes its success to the way it was developed to work on lots of different types of computers from different manufacturers.

There are many different versions of Windows such as Windows 2000, Windows NT, Windows XP and now Windows Vista. Each new version needs to run more demanding applications and also cope with the increased security issues.

UNIX

UNIX is systems software that has evolved from the early years of computing. It can be used by different types of computer such as mainframes as well as PCs. It uses a

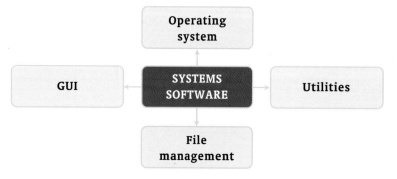

graphical user interface like Windows but it also makes use of a command line interface. UNIX is an example of systems software.

Here are some of the main features of UNIX:

- it is written in the programming language C
- it is a multi-programming operating system
- it is a multi-tasking operating system
- it can be used to run hundreds of terminals.

UNIX is quite difficult for first time users to use and tends to be used more by computer professionals than ordinary users. Universities are likely to use UNIX as are Internet service providers (ISPs).

Linux

Linux is a free (called open source) operating system which has gained popularity. Many users of this operating system prefer it (not just because it is free) but because of its security and stability. It also has the cutest logo!

Linux is mainly used as server software but its popularity with home and small business users is on the increase.

Macintosh OS

Macintosh is systems software developed by Apple who developed the first operating system to make use of a graphical user interface which is now so popular.

The Mac operating system is used with Mac computers which are popular in the area of graphic design.

The latest Mac operating system called Mac OS-X Leopard makes use of a GUI.

Systems software and applications software: interfaces

▼ **You will find out**

▶ About the need to provide the user with a method of communicating with the computer

▶ About the different types of interface

▶ About the relative advantages and disadvantages of each type of interface

▶ About the main features of a graphical user interface

Introduction

Systems software has to perform many different tasks and needs to be used by anyone who uses a computer. It is important that the interface makes it as easy as possible for the user to be able to complete a task using the software.

There are three main types of interface:

- Command line/driven interface – here you have to type in a series of commands. This type of interface is very hard to use.
- Menu-driven interface – here you are presented with a list of things to do and you have to choose one of them by typing in either a number or a letter. These are easy to use but are limited in the sorts of things you can do with them.
- Graphical user interface (GUI) – these are very easy to use and have all the features such as windows, icons, menus, pointers, etc.

There are also other interfaces such as natural language interfaces and form-driven interfaces.

Windows is a graphical user interface.

Command line/driven interface

Command line interfaces are interfaces where you have to type in commands in a certain language (a bit like a programming language) in order to get the computer to do something.

A menu-driven interface.

The commands had to be precise and correctly worded in order that the computer understood them. This was their problem. It made it difficult for an inexperienced user to use them.

> **List Employee No, Surname For Job = "Production"**

When commands are entered like this a common interface is used

Advantages of a command line interface:

- Quicker – in some instances you can do a task quicker by typing a command line rather than using the mouse and all the features of Windows.

Disadvantages of a command line interface:

- Very difficult for beginners to use – you have to learn the structure (called the syntax) of commands.
- Have to remember instructions – hard to remember the instructions/commands you need to do a particular task.

Graphical user interfaces (GUIs)

Graphical user interfaces (GUIs) are very popular because they are easy to use. Instead of typing in commands, you enter them by pointing and clicking at objects on the screen. Microsoft Windows and Macintosh OS are examples of graphical user interfaces.

The main features of a GUI include:

- Windows – the screen is divided into areas called windows. Windows are useful if you need to work on several tasks.
- Icons – these are small pictures used to represent commands, files or windows. By moving the pointer and clicking, you can carry out a command or open a window. You can also position any icon anywhere on your desktop.
- Menus – menus allow a user to make selections from a list. Menus can be pop-up or pull-down and this means they do not clutter the desktop whilst they are not being used.

- Pointers – this is the little arrow that appears when using Windows. The pointer changes shape in different applications. It changes to an 'I' shape when using word-processing software. A mouse can be used to move the pointer around the screen. Other input devices can be used to move the pointer such as light pens, touch pads and joysticks.
- Desktop – this is the working area of the GUI and where all the icons are situated.
- Drag and drop – this allows you to select objects (icons, folders, files, etc.) and drag them so that you can perform certain operations on them such as drag to the recycle bin to discard, add a file to a folder, copy files to a folder and so on.
- Taskbars – show the programs that are open. This facility is handy when working on several programs together.

Important note – although most systems software makes use of a GUI, this can be used with any software. For example, most applications software uses a GUI. Other examples of devices making use of a GUI include mobile phones, satellite navigation systems, etc.

Advantages of GUIs:

- No language needed – in the past you had to type in certain instructions to communicate with the computer.
- Use of icons – novice users can simply select programs or things they want to do by pointing and double clicking.
- Easier to use a mouse – most users would prefer to use a mouse to point and click rather than use the keyboard.

Disadvantages of GUIs:

- More memory is needed – sophisticated GUIs have large memory requirements so older computers may need upgrading or new computers bought.
- Increased processing requirements – faster and more

powerful processors are needed to run the latest GUIs. This could involve upgrading the processor or buying new computers.

Menu-driven interfaces

Here a user is presented with a list of options and they type in the letter or number of their selection.

Advantages:

- A simple interface which is very easy to use.

Disadvantages:

- Only suitable where there are a few items to select from on the menu.

Form-driven interfaces

Form-driven interfaces are used to collect information from a user in a step-by-step manner. The user supplies this information by typing it into a form. Validation checks ensure that the customer only enters valid data into the form and that all the important fields are completed.

The form below is an on-line booking form for a holiday. Notice the red asterisks next to some of the fields. These fields contain presence checks, which means the user always has to enter data for these fields for the booking to be continued to the next stage.

Natural language interface

An interface that allows the user to interact using natural written or spoken language (e.g., English) as opposed to computer language and commands. It has the advantage that learning how to use it is easy because it uses words we are all familiar with and can remember.

The main problem with a natural language interface is that natural language is so ambiguous at times so it is necessary to restrict the language to certain words.

Passenger Details

Please enter passenger names to match those shown on your passports.

Example of form-driven interface

Systems software and applications software: utilities and file management

▼ You will find out

▷ About the utilities that are provided as part of systems software

▷ About the file management facilities offered by systems software

▷ About peripheral drivers and the function they perform

Introduction

Besides the operating system and the user interface, system software also provides utilities and file management software.

Utilities

A utility is a program that performs a very specific task and a series of utilities comes as part of the systems software. Utilities are not regarded as applications because they are fairly simple and will only perform one very specific task, which is always related in some way to managing the computer's resources.

Examples of utilities include:

- File converters – used to save files in different formats. For example, a file created using word-processing software could be saved as a text file (.txt) or as web page.

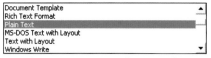

- Virus scanners – used to scan the memory and hard drives for viruses.
- Security and accounting – used to check user IDs and passwords and to keep a record of network activity.

File management software

File management software is provided as part of the systems software. Typically, file management software would perform the following:

- File/folder organisation – used to create folders, copy folders/files, rename folders/files, delete folders/ files, move files/folders, etc.
- Backup copy creation – used for the taking of backup copies for security purposes.
- File compression – used to compress files before storing or before being sent over a network. WinZip is an example of a file compressor.

> ### EXAM TIP
>
> Remember to always relate your answer to the context of the question. Usually there is a situation or brief scenario given and you need to refer to it in your answer.

File compression utilities such as WinZip reduce the size of files, which reduces disk space and the time needed to send an e-mail with the files attached.

- Defragmentation – each time a file is saved using Windows it puts the data anywhere it can find on the hard drive. After a while the data and programs become scattered over the surface. This reduces the access time and also wastes hard drive space. Defragmentation software is used to tidy up the surface of a magnetic hard drive so that files can be accessed and read more quickly by the operating system.

The windows defragmentation program shows the fragmented files as red lines.

KEY WORDS

Driver – a short specially written program that understands the operation of the device it controls/operates. It is needed to allow the systems or applications software to use the connected device properly

Peripheral – a device connected to and under the control of the central processing unit (CPU)

They reorganise the surface of the magnetic hard drive more efficiently.

- File recovery – used to recover deleted or damaged files.

If you accidentally delete the wrong group of files, help is at hand. A file recovery program may be able to get them back again.

- Uninstallers – software used to remove all the files put onto the computer when a piece of software was installed.

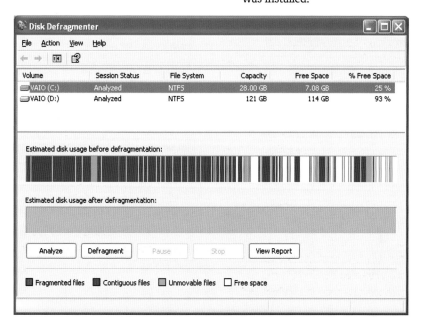

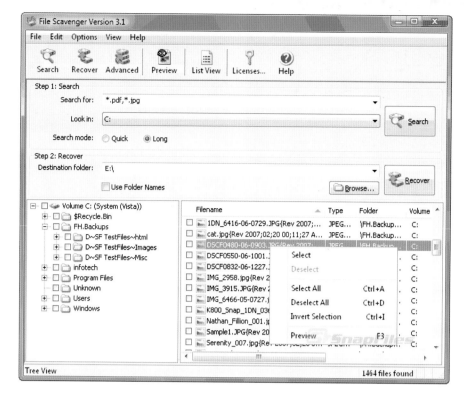

Peripheral drivers

Each peripheral device (e.g., printer, scanner, digital camera, webcam, etc.) needs some software to work with the hardware. This software is generally called peripheral drivers.

Many drivers come with the operating system. For example, the keyboard and hard disk drive already have their drivers included in the operating system.

The problem arises when a new peripheral is attached and because the operating system did not know about the device when the operating system was developed, it needs driver software installed.

What does peripheral driver software do?

All peripheral devices attached to computers need software to make them work properly. For example, a printer may not be able to print envelopes if the printer driver has not been installed. Here are some of the things peripheral drivers do:

- Provide communication between the operating system/applications software and the peripheral device.
- Convert instructions from the software into a form that the peripheral device can understand.

- Enable the peripheral device to work with other applications and operating systems software.
- Produce error messages such as printer or scanner not ready, etc.
- Tell the computer what the printer is and what it is capable of doing.

Where do you get peripheral driver software?

Here are the main ways of obtaining printer driver software:

- If the device you are attaching uses plug-and-play, as soon as the device is connected the operating system will look to see if it has the appropriate driver software and will install it automatically.
- You may find that you have them as part of your operating system, so you just need to install them.
- You can reinstall them from the disks which originally came with the device.
- You can install them from your backups of the hard drive.
- You can download drivers from the manufacturer's website.
- You can download driver software off driver sites on the Internet.

Printer drivers

There are many different types of printer. Different makes and models of printer communicate with the operating system and application software slightly differently.

This means printer drivers are needed to convert the instructions from the applications or systems software into a form that the printer can understand.

There are many drivers included as part of the operating system and if you attach, say, a new printer to the computer, the operating system will search for the driver needed to run it. It does this automatically without you having to do anything except plug in a cable to the device. This is called plug-and-play.

Notice the huge range of devices here that require driver software.

Systems software and applications software: types of application software

Introduction

Applications software is software that is capable of performing a certain job or application. This is distinct from the other type of software, the systems software, which shields the user from the intricacies of having to communicate with the hardware. The position of applications software in relation to the systems software and the hardware is shown in the following diagram:

Package software

A bundle of files necessary for a particular program to run along with some form of documentation to help a user get the program started.

Generic software

This is an applications package that is appropriate for a wide range of tasks and can be used in lots of areas of work. It can be appropriate for home users, businesses and organisations. For example, word-processing software is generic software because it can be used in virtually any job and for lots of different tasks that are completed on a day-to-day basis.

Examples of generic software include word-processing, database, presentation, browser, DTP (desktop publishing), etc.

Integrated software

This is an application package consisting of software for several distinct applications. There will always be two or more applications packages in integrated software.

Office software is integrated software consisting of word-processing, database, presentation, spreadsheet and desktop publishing software.

Microsoft Office is an integrated package as well as each of its components being a generic package. Office-type suites bundle popular application packages together.

There are other Office-type packages apart from Microsoft Office. One such package is called Star Office by a company called Sun Microsystems.

Advantages of integrated packages over separate application packages:

- Cheaper than buying individual packages.
- Easier to transfer data from one of the modules to another. For example, it is easy to process data in a spreadsheet, draw a graph and then incorporate the graph in a document produced using word-processing software.
- Consistency of the user interface between the modules making it easier to learn.
- Easier to install as you only have to install one package as opposed to several.

Disadvantages of integrated packages over separate application packages:

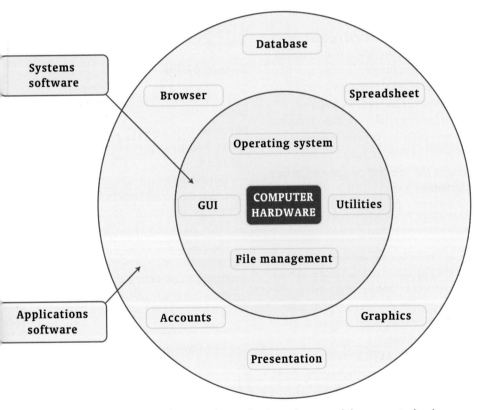

The systems software sits between the application software and the computer hardware.

Applications software

Applications software can be divided into:

- package software
- generic software
- integrated software
- specific software
- bespoke software.

EXAM TIP

Some exam questions will ask about advantages and disadvantages. You need to refer to either an advantage or disadvantage by comparing it with another method.

```
                    ┌──────────────┐
                    │   Database   │
                    └──────────────┘
┌──────────────────┐        ┌──────────────┐
│ Word-processing  │        │ Presentation │
└──────────────────┘        └──────────────┘
              ┌─────────────────┐
              │   INTEGRATED    │
              │    PACKAGE      │
              └─────────────────┘
┌──────────────┐          ┌─────────────────────┐
│ Spreadsheet  │          │ Desktop publisning  │
└──────────────┘          └─────────────────────┘
```

- The integrated package may be weaker in one or more of the separate applications. By choosing separate applications you can choose the best one of each.
- Have to pay for modules you may never use so it could waste money.

Specific software

This is software that performs one particular task. Examples of specific software include payroll (for working out wages), stock control, programs for working out income tax, garden design software, etc.

Bespoke software

Sometimes called tailor-made software, as it is specifically created and written for a particular business or organisation. It is produced when there is no suitable

software package available and is a very expensive option.

It has the advantage that it gives exact functionality and it can give a greater competitive advantage because it always gives exactly the right information. With bespoke software:

- An organisation does not have to change how it works in order to fit around the way the software works.
- You can specify exactly what the software must do.
- The software can be designed to work with the existing hardware and software.
- There may not be a suitable software package on the market.

Disadvantages of bespoke software:

- More expensive than buying an off-the-shelf package.
- May contain more errors that were not discovered during testing.

Advantages of buying off-the-shelf software:

- Much cheaper than developing software from scratch.
- No delay between buying the software and using it.
- Other users to contact for help if it is needed.
- Likely to be more rigorously tested because it is being used by so many users.
- Ready availability of training courses.
- Books are usually available on the software to help users to learn how to use it.

Purposes of applications software

Applications software is software that has been produced to allow the user to carry out a specific task. Applications software is not concerned with the control and management of system resources (e.g., memory, allocation of processing time and storage) of the computer, as that is the job of the systems software.

Generic packages

Generic packages are software that is not restricted to any particular job or application and can be used by any business on a day-to-day basis for completing lots of different tasks. Generic software would include:

- word-processor
- database management software
- spreadsheet
- presentation software
- desktop publishing
- web browser
- website creation software.

Copyright 2001 by Randy Glasbergen.
www.glasbergen.com

'Our new office suite software will automatically save your work if it feels you've created any work worth saving.'

Systems software and applications software: word-processing and spreadsheets

▼ **You will find out**

▶ About the range of facilities provided by word-processing software

▶ About the range of facilities provided by spreadsheet software

▶ About the range of facilities provided by database software

Introduction

You will already have a good knowledge of features of word-processing, spreadsheet and database software. You will need to develop a solution to an ICT problem using appropriate software. It is important to be able to choose the most appropriate software for the task, and to be able to do this you have to have a good understanding of the capabilities of a range of software. Often you have a choice between several pieces of software to solve a particular problem. For example, if you were designing a website, then you could use word-processing, desktop publishing software or specialist website design software. You would need to justify your reasons for your choice of software.

Word-processing

Word-processing packages are used to produce documents containing text such as letters, reports, etc., and for preparing text for other applications. For example, text could be typed in using word-processing software and then the file could be imported into desktop publishing software.

Before starting any document you need to consider the page layout/format which consists of the following:

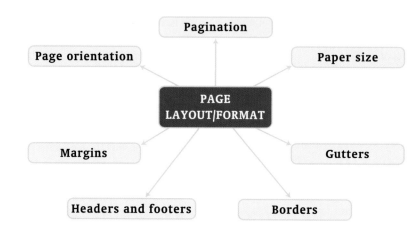

Things to consider when creating the page layout/format for a document.

Once text has been entered it can be formatted to add structure and emphasis. Text can be formatted by altering the characteristics of the font. The formatting text features are shown here:

EXAM TIP

You could be asked about formatting text, formatting cells, etc. Make sure that you know the different types of format. Cut and paste is not a method of formatting.

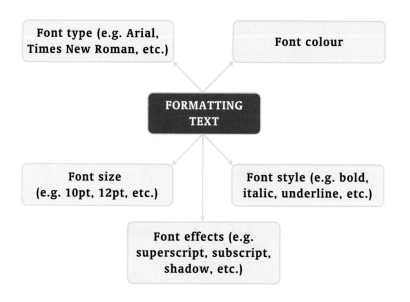

KEY WORDS

Header – text placed at the top of a document

Footer – text placed at the bottom of a document

Bullet point – a block or paragraph of text that has a symbol placed in front to make the section of text stand out

> **KEY WORDS**

Templates – files which hold standardised document layouts. Templates hold the design of the document so that only the variable information needs to be added

> **KEY WORDS**

Relational database management system (RDMS) – database system where the data is held in tables with relationships established between them. The software is used to set up and hold the data as well as to extract and manipulate the stored data

Relationship – the way tables are related to each other. Relationships can be one-to-one, one-to-many or many-to-many

- Grammar checker – used to check the grammar in a sentence and to highlight problems and suggest alternatives.

Spreadsheet software

Spreadsheet software is used to manipulate numbers and text arranged in cells. Formulae are used to relate one cell with other cells. Once a formula has been entered, then if one value of a cell on which the formula is based changes, the formula will automatically perform the calculation with the new value.

Spreadsheets are ideal for:

- budgets
- cash flow forecasts
- accounts (e.g., profit and loss, end of year accounts, etc.)
- creating and using models
- performing statistical analysis on data
- producing graphs and charts from sets of data.

Formatting paragraphs/blocks of text

Blocks of text or paragraphs can be formatted in a number of ways which are shown below:

FORMATTING BLOCKS OF TEXT
- Justification (e.g. left centre and right)
- Bullet points/numbering
- Line spacing (single 1.5 and double)
- Tabs and indents
- Hyphenation

> **EXAM TIP**

When asked about macros, remember that it is not just a set of stored instructions but also that these instructions can be executed automatically.

Additional features of word-processing software

There are a number of more advanced features of word-processing software that can be used:

- Templates – used to specify the structure of a document, such as fonts, page layout, formatting and styles.
- Mail merge – combining a list of names and addresses with a standard letter so that a series of letters is produced with each letter being addressed to a different person. The list of data used for the mail merge can be created using the word-processing software or it can be imported from a database or spreadsheet.
- Indexing – allows words to be highlighted so that they can be used to form an index. The word-

processing software keeps a record of the words along with their page number and when instructed to, it will create the index.
- Macros – these are used to record a series of keystrokes so that, for example, your name and address can be added to the top of the page simply by pressing a single key or clicking on the mouse.
- Thesaurus – allows a word to be chosen and the word-processor will list synonyms (i.e., words with similar meanings). This is useful in creative writing where you do not want to repeat a word.
- Spellchecker – word-processing software has a dictionary against which all words typed in are checked. There is usually the facility to add words, which is important if you use specialist terms.

> **KEY WORDS**

Macro – a series of commands and instructions that you can group together as a single command in order to complete a task automatically. Macros save time when you wish to perform tasks on a regular basis

> **EXAM TIP**

Many of the questions you will be asked about software will relate to your sample work. Make sure that your write up of this sample work includes a section relating to your selection and choice of software. Reasons for selecting software as well as rejecting other software should be given.

Systems software and applications software: word-processing and spreadsheets *continued*

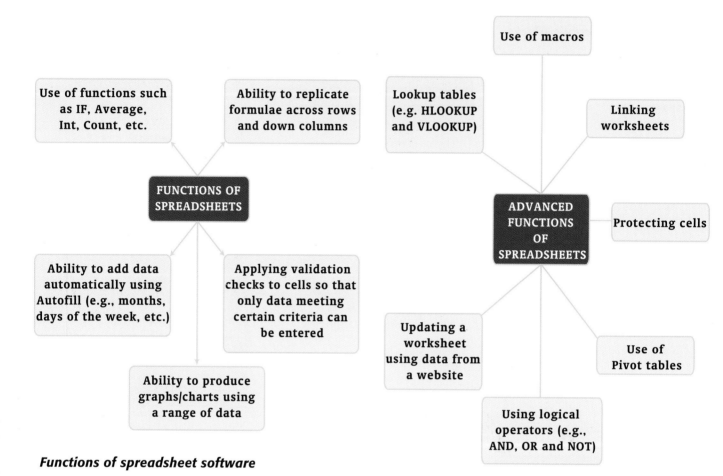

FUNCTIONS OF SPREADSHEETS

- Use of functions such as IF, Average, Int, Count, etc.
- Ability to replicate formulae across rows and down columns
- Ability to add data automatically using Autofill (e.g., months, days of the week, etc.)
- Applying validation checks to cells so that only data meeting certain criteria can be entered
- Ability to produce graphs/charts using a range of data

ADVANCED FUNCTIONS OF SPREADSHEETS

- Use of macros
- Lookup tables (e.g. HLOOKUP and VLOOKUP)
- Linking worksheets
- Protecting cells
- Updating a worksheet using data from a website
- Using logical operators (e.g., AND, OR and NOT)
- Use of Pivot tables

Functions of spreadsheet software

Macros

A macro consists of a series of keystrokes and menu choices which are recorded by the user as a small program. Instead of issuing the same series of instructions and commands, you can simply run the macro. Macros are used to save time.

Macros can be set up so that a complex task can be reduced to simply pressing a button. In this way, more experienced users can help less experienced users to complete complex time-consuming repetitive routines simply.

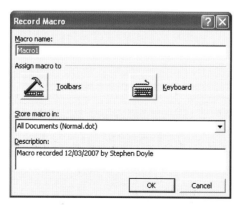

The Record Macro window for the word-processing package Word. Notice that to run the macro you can either type in a command using the keyboard or click on an icon in the toolbar.

Database software

Database software allows data to be entered and stored in a structured way which aids its retrieval.

Database management systems keep the data separate from the programs themselves, so once the data has been created it can be accessed using different software. This is important as when a business or organisation expands, it may decide to use different database management software and will not want to have to input all the data again.

Databases used by businesses and organisations are called relational databases, with the data being held in lots of different tables with links called relationships between the tables.

Presentation software

Presentation software is not just restricted to viewing a series of slides containing content. You can actually build a multimedia application such as a multiple choice or other type of computer-marked test using presentation software. In this type of problem you would use the feature of presentation software of being able to hyperlink one slide to another. This means that the slides do not have to be displayed in only one particular order. There are many other features of presentation software and these are shown in the following diagrams:

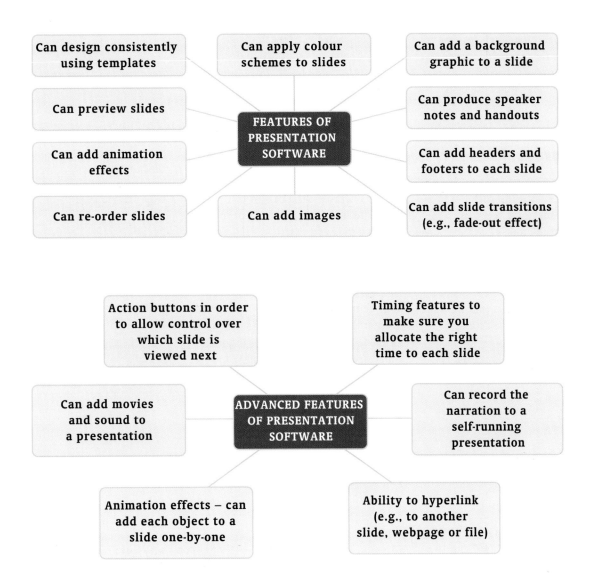

Activity 1: Using advanced features of generic applications software

Generic applications software can be used for a huge variety of different tasks no matter what line of work you are in. Examples of generic software include:
- word-processing
- spreadsheet
- presentation.

By loading the above software in turn and looking through the various menus, find out about the more advanced features that you may never have used before.

For each piece of software, write down a list of the advanced features and give an example of the type of task they are suited to.

Systems software and applications software: web browsers

Introduction

Other generic software includes web browser software and web design software. Most people use web browser software and many others use web design software to help promote their business or just to create a home page.

Web browser software

Web browser software is the software you use to access the Internet. Microsoft Internet Explorer is an example of a web browser.

Favourites or Bookmarks

This is a storage area where the URL (i.e., the web address) of a website can be stored so that it can be accessed later using a link.

Using Favourites/Bookmarks it is easy to access a website that you want to return to.

E-mail facilities

An e-mail is an electronic message sent from one communication device (computer, telephone, mobile phone or portable digital assistant) to another. All web browser software has e-mail facilities.

Search

Search allows you to find an e-mail using keywords in the title or you can search for all the e-mails from or to a certain e-mail address.

Reply

This allows you to read an e-mail and then write the reply without having to enter the e-mail address. As the recipient can be sent both the original e-mail and your reply they can save time because they know what your e-mail is about.

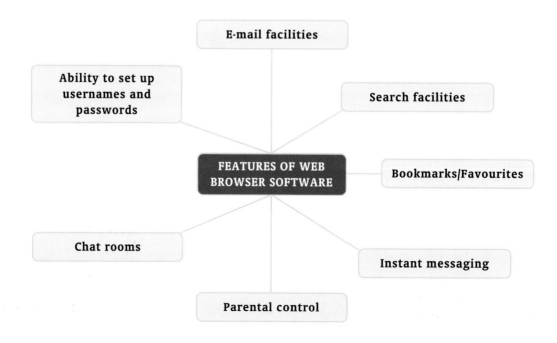

There are many e-mail facilities but the ones show here are the main time-saving ones.

Forward

If you are sent an e-mail that you think others should see, you can forward it to them. An e-mail, for example, sent to you by your boss, could be forwarded to everyone who works with you in a team.

Address book

In the address book are the names and e-mail addresses of all the people to whom you are likely to send e-mail. Instead of having to type in the address when writing an e-mail, you have just to click on the e-mail address or addresses in the address book.

You can get the e-mail software to automatically add people to your address book if they have sent you or you have sent them e-mail.

The screenshot shows an address book. Rather than type in the e-mail address of the recipients and maybe make mistakes, you can simply click on their address. Notice the facility to create groups.

Groups

Groups are lists of people and their e-mail addresses. They are used when a copy of e-mail needs to be distributed to people in a particular group. For example, if you were working as part of a team and needed to send each member the same e-mail, then you would set up a group. Every time you needed to send the members of the group e-mail, then you could just send the one e-mail to the group thus saving time.

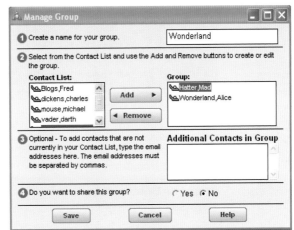

> ## ▶ Activity 2: Creating and sending an e-mail to a group

For this activity, you are required to produce a distribution list so that the same e-mail can be sent to a group of people. You will need to find out how to do this yourself.

Send the same e-mail to four of your friends and check that they all received it.

Systems software and applications software: web browsers *continued*

EXAM TIP

Many questions on e-mail will refer to the facilities that are provided that will make team working easier. Make sure that you can give three such facilities.

File attachments

You can attach files to e-mails. For example, you could attach a file containing a photograph of yourself obtained from a digital camera, a piece of clip art, a picture that you have scanned in, a long document, etc. Basically, if you can store it as a file, then you can attach it to e-mail.

You can attach more than one file to e-mail, so if you had six photographs to send, then you could attach and send them all at the same time.

Before you attach a file you must first prepare an e-mail message to send explaining the purpose of your e-mail and also giving some information about the files that you are sending (what their purpose is, what file format they are in, etc.).

Once the e-mail message has been completed, you click on the file attachment button and select the file you want to send. A box will appear to allow you to select the drive, folder and eventually the file that you want to send.

If you want to send more than one file, repeat the file attachment process. Usually, if there is more than one file to send, then the files will be compressed to reduce the time taken to send them.

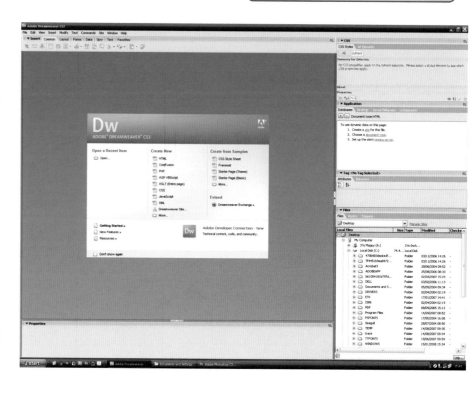

Website design software

In order to develop a website, website development software is needed. This need not be specialist software, as there are many common packages that could be used provided the site is not too complicated.

Generic software which could be used to develop websites includes:

- Word-processing software (e.g., Microsoft Word)
- Desktop publishing software (e.g., Microsoft Publisher).

Specialist web design software has many more functions but is more difficult to use but the end result will be more professional. Specialist web design software includes packages such as:

- Microsoft FrontPage
- Adobe Dreamweaver.

In order to develop websites many more pieces of software will be needed:

- Word-processing software – it is easier to word-process pieces of text using word-processing software.
- Scanning software – old photographs may need to be digitised so that they can be added to a webpage. Large amounts of text could be scanned in and then recognised using optical character recognition (OCR) software.

- Photo/image editing software – images sourced may not be the right shape or size for the space on the webpage so they will need to be edited. Contrast or brightness can also be altered.
- Browser software – needed to check how the webpage/website will look on the screen. Usually more than one browser is used to make sure the webpage looks as good in each browser.

Features of websites

Simple websites can be developed in packages such as Word or Publisher but for a better website it is advisable to use specialist website design software.

You will probably have created your own website using a suitable package at either Key Stage 3 or 4.

Simple features of website design software

- Ability to add and format text.
- Just like in word-processing software text can be added and formatted with different sized headings and sub-headings, etc.
- Adding tables to help layout text and images.
- Ability to import data from other packages.
- Ability to add hyperlinks to other webpages.
- Ability to use anchors to link to different sections in the same webpage.
- Ability to add a mailto link. This allows a viewer of a website to send an e-mail by opening the user's e-mail application.
- Ability to preview the website in different browsers for testing purposes.

Advanced features of website design software

Cascading style sheets (CSS)

It is hard to keep consistency from one web-page to the next but the use of cascading style sheets helps with this. Instead of applying certain formatting to each block of text, you can apply an existing cascading style sheet to it. This means that this block of text will have the same font, font size and colour as defined in the CSS. The use of these sheets can save a huge amount of time when building websites.

The cascading style sheets are a way of separating the content from the presentation (e.g. font size, positioning, colours, etc.).

Ability to create a webpage using frames

Creating a webpage using frames means that you can have multiple webpages in a single browser window. By doing this the user can select a link in one frame that loads content into another existing frame, thus enabling the user to stay in the same browser window.

Ability to create a form and use it to collect data

Forms can be created which enable you to collect data from a user. For example, you could collect name and address details for a person asking for further information about a product. You could also ask the user to sign a guestbook and add their comments to a feedback page.

Ability to look at the HTML code

When a website is being developed using website development software, behind the scenes the program is generating a series of HTML codes that are the instructions that explain how you want the website set out.

Some website developers prefer to alter the HTML codes because it offers them more flexibility than using the website design package on its own.

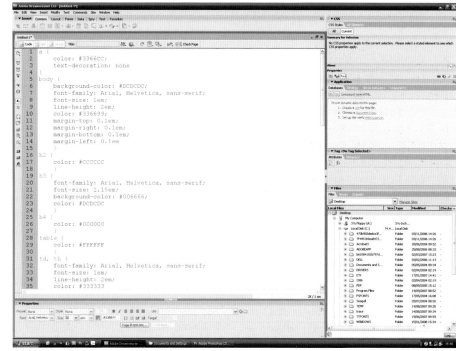

▶ Task
pp. 92–95

1 Explain the facilities of an e-mail software package that you would use to carry out the following tasks efficiently.
   (a) Pass on an e-mail message that you have received.
   (b) Send a copy of a scanned picture.
   (c) Send regular e-mails to a group of friends.

2 Give **three** functions of a spreadsheet package that you have found useful and explain how you have used each function.

Unit 1 Practical Problem Solving in the Digital World

Questions and Activities

▶ Questions 1   pp. 80–81

1 Explain, giving an example for each, the difference between applications software and systems software. (Note do not give brand names in your answer) (4 marks)

2 Systems software is not just a single program. Give the names of three of the **four** main types of program that would normally be found as part of systems software. (3 marks)

3 An operating system is part of the systems software. Briefly describe **three** of the tasks performed by an operating system. (6 marks)

▶ Questions 2   pp. 82–83

1 UNIX is a make of operating system and it uses both a GUI and a command line interface.
  (a) Explain the meaning of the term operating system. (2 marks)
  (b) What does the abbreviation GUI stand for? (1 mark)
  (c) Briefly explain **one** difference between a GUI and a command line interface. (1 mark)
  (d) New users tend to prefer a GUI, whilst an experienced user may prefer to use a command line interface. Give **one** reason for this. (1 mark)

2 E-commerce sites often make use of a form-driven interface.
  (a) Explain the meaning of the term form-driven interface. (2 marks)
  (b) Give **one** reason why such an interface is appropriate for an e-commerce site. (1 mark)

3 (a) Give the names of **three** different types of human/computer interface (HCI). (3 marks)
  (b) For each of the human/computer interfaces you have named in part (a) describe a situation where each of them could be used. (6 marks)

▶ Questions 3   pp. 84–85

1 You buy a new computer and sell your old one through the free ads but decide to keep your old printer to use with the new computer. When you connect the old printer to the new computer, it does not print properly. You ring the computer supplier's help-desk who say that you need to install the printer drivers.
  (a) Explain what a printer driver is and describe **one** thing that a printer driver does. (2 marks)
  (b) The original printer drivers have been lost. Describe **three** possible ways of getting the printer drivers for the printer. (3 marks)

2 Older printer drivers were often provided on floppy disks but now they are provided on CD-ROMs.
  (a) Give **one** reason why printer drivers are no longer provided on floppy disks. (1 mark)
  (b) Installation software including drivers is supplied on CD-ROM rather than DVD, despite DVDs being able to store much more data. Give **one** reason for this. (1 mark)

3 For users to interact with computers there needs to be an interface. An interface can be hard or easy to use and the most popular interface is the graphical user interface (GUI).
  State **three** factors of a GUI and for each one describe briefly how it aids the communication between the user and the computer. (6 marks)

1 The terms 'integrated package' and 'generic package' are often confused.
   (a) Describe, giving an example, the meaning of the term integrated package. (2 marks)
   (b) Describe, giving an example, the meaning of the term generic package. (2 marks)
2 Many ICT solutions to problems can be solved using generic software.
   (a) Explain what is meant by the term generic software. (1 mark)
   (b) Give **three** examples of generic software (note not trade names). (3 marks)

3 Staff in a small office use an integrated package which contains word-processing, spreadsheet, presentation and database software. All these items of software have a common user interface.
   (a) Explain the meaning of the term integrated package. (2 marks)
   (b) Give **two** advantages of purchasing an integrated package over buying separate packages. (2 marks)
   (c) Give **four** advantages of having a common user interface. (4 marks)
   (d) State **four** specific features of a user interface which would benefit from being common between each of the components of the integrated package. (4 marks)

1 A new company is to be formed. The directors have decided that everyone in the organisation who uses a word-processing package should use a series of templates. By doing this, the company can help promote its corporate image.
   (a) Explain what is meant by a template. (2 marks)
   (b) Give **one** reason why companies are keen on their employees all using a series of templates for the different types of document. (2 marks)
2 Which type of software would be best used for the following tasks?
   (a) viewing websites
   (b) writing a novel
   (c) creating a financial model such as a cash flow prediction

   (d) querying a large set of records
   (e) creating folders for the storing of different types of file on a computer
   (f) a business preparing end of year accounts
   (g) producing a high quality glossy brochure
   (h) keeping financial records. (8 marks)
3 A small company is being set up and the owner of the company wants to purchase new hardware and software.
   (a) Give the names of **three** items of software that they should buy. (3 marks)
   (b) For each of the items of software you have given for (a) state why it would be required. (6 marks)

1 A website developer is developing a website for a company. The developer is using specialist website development software. In addition to this piece of software, state, giving reasons, **two** other pieces of software that they may need to use. The reasons must be different in each case. (4 marks)

2 Three website developers live in different parts of the country and are working together on a large website for a company.
   The website developers make constant use of e-mail facilities to keep in touch with each other.
   Give **three** different features of e-mail software that will enable them to work together on this project and for each feature describe briefly why it is useful. (6 marks)

▶ **Activity 3: Researching memory and processor requirements for Windows Vista**

Use the Internet to find out the minimum memory and processor requirements needed to run the systems software Windows Vista.
   Also find the same information for the older systems software Windows XP.
   Is it true that more sophistication of the systems software means increased resource requirements?

Exam support

Worked example 1

1 (a) Explain what is meant by a generic software package. (2 marks)
  (b) Give three examples of generic software packages.
    (Please note: do not use brand names). (3 marks)

Student answer 1

1 (a) Software that can be used for any purpose and anyone can use it
  (b) Word
    Spreadsheet
    Database

Examiner's comment

1 (a) Software is also used for a purpose so what the student probably meant to say is that the software can be used for lots of different purposes and can therefore be used in lots of different businesses. This is not clear. **(0 marks out of 2)**

  (b) Despite the question saying not to use brand name the brand name Word appears in the answer. Never give brand names. Spreadsheet and database software are correctly named as types of generic software. **(2 marks out of 3)**

Examiner's answers

1 (a) Two marks for an answer similar to this:
    A software package that is not specific to a particular job/application. It can be used in many different areas of a business and can be used on a day-to-day basis.
  (b) Any three from the following list – one mark each:
    Word-processor
    Database management software/database software
    Spreadsheet
    Presentation software
    Desktop publishing
    Web browser
    Website creation software

Student answer 2

1 (a) Software that almost anyone has a use for, as it can be used for so many different tasks. For example, word-processing software can be used to produce letters, memos, posters, newsletters and it can even be used to produce websites.
  (b) Desktop publishing
    Presentation
    Spreadsheet

Examiner's comment

1 (a) The main point that generic software is not used for the one task is mentioned and the example (which is not asked for) adds to the explanation. **(2 marks out of 2)**

  (b) All of these are correct names of generic software. **(3 marks out of 3)**

EXAM TIP

Don't use brand names when talking about software.

Say spreadsheet instead of Excel or Microsoft Excel.

Say word-processing software and not Word or Microsoft Word.

Don't answer questions as if you have been asked to write everything you know about a certain topic. Examination questions are carefully worded and you must make sure that you read and understand each word. Tailor your answer to the context.

Make sure that you have fully justified your choice of software in your sample work.

Remember that many problems need to be solved using a range of software.

In any case you will need at least two pieces of software: the systems software used and the type or types of applications software.

Use the correct terminology in your answers.

Be precise and do not waffle.

Do not write part of the question out in your answer – this simply wastes time and gains no marks.

Worked example 2

2 A software developer is working as part of a team of ten developers who are developing new software for an on-line loans company. The team members work in different parts of the country. The developers need to keep in touch with each other and need to pass work (mainly programs, screen designs, etc.) to each other.

(a) Explain **three** advantages of the developers contacting each other by e-mail rather than by post. **(6 marks)**

(b) Describe **two** facilities provided by e-mail software that will make it a lot easier to work as a team. **(4 marks)**

Student answer 1

2 (a) Cheaper
       Faster
       Better

(b) Being able to send the e-mail to more than one person
     Being able to attach a file to an e-mail

Examiner's comment

2 (a) The word 'explain' means that a one word answer is not enough. There are 6 marks allocated here. One mark will be allocated to the clear explanation of the advantage, with the other mark for the brief explanation of how it relates to working in teams. Avoid general words like 'better'. You need to be specific.
       General words such as faster, cheaper, better gain no marks. **(0 marks out of 6)**

(b) 'Being able to send the e-mail to more than one person' is a facility of e-mail software but there needs to be a fuller explanation as to how this facility will make things easier when working as a team.
     It is important to tailor answers to the information given in the question.
     Again 'Being able to attach a file to an e-mail' is a facility provided by e-mail software. There needs to be further elaboration on why this is an advantage. **(2 marks out of 4)**

Student answer 2

2 (a) Sending e-mails speeds things up. An e-mail can be sent and replied to in seconds, whereas a letter sent and replied to takes several days.
       It is cheaper as there is no cost for paper, printing, envelopes and stamps.
       It is faster to send an e-mail and get a reply.

(b) It is possible to create groups and send the same e-mail to all the members of the group rather than send each e-mail separately.
     They can attach other files to the e-mail such as programs and screen design and this avoids them having to save them onto removable media such as CD.

Examiner's comment

2 (a) The first two answers are good answers and would get full marks.
       The third answer is almost a repeat of the first answer. It is always important to check your answer is not similar to an answer already given. **(4 marks out of 6)**

(b) Both answers are good and gain full marks. **(4 marks out of 4)**

Examiner's answers

2 (a) Any three advantages (two marks each) such as:
- E-mail is cheaper than a letter. No stamp, envelope or paper is needed. There is also a time saving so this makes e-mail cheaper. Even if the e-mail is sent across the world it will not cost any more than a local e-mail.
- Quick to write. They are informal, meaning that people do not spend time on the layout and the odd spelling mistake is acceptable.
- Ideal if there is a time difference. The reader can check e-mail when they are ready.
- Inexpensive and easy to send the same e-mail message to lots of different people.
- You can attach a copy of the sender's e-mail with your reply so this saves them having to search for the original message.
- You do not have to go out to a post box, so it saves time.
- You do not have to waste time shopping for stamps, envelopes and paper.
- Fast. It takes seconds to send and receive e-mail. If the person at the other end checks their e-mail regularly, then a reply can be sent very quickly.

(b) Two facilities (two marks each) such as:
- Groups/distribution lists – allowing you to send the same e-mail to a group of people without having to select individual e-mail addresses.
- File attachments – being able to attach files to an e-mail so others can download the work onto their own computers and can comment on it.

Summary mind maps

Systems software and applications software: operating systems

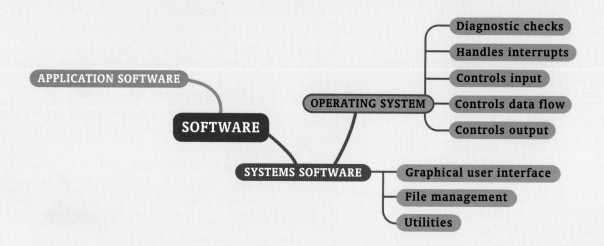

Systems software and applications software: interfaces

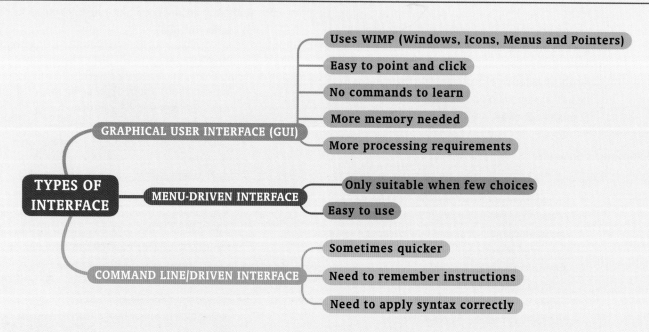

Systems software and applications software: applications software

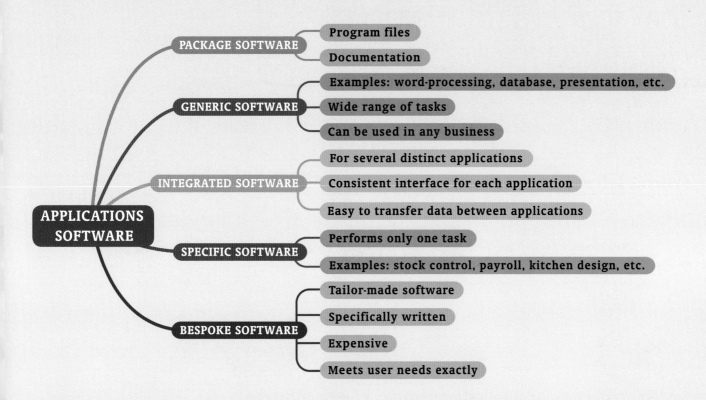

APPLICATIONS SOFTWARE

- **PACKAGE SOFTWARE**
  - Program files
  - Documentation
- **GENERIC SOFTWARE**
  - Examples: word-processing, database, presentation, etc.
  - Wide range of tasks
  - Can be used in any business
- **INTEGRATED SOFTWARE**
  - For several distinct applications
  - Consistent interface for each application
  - Easy to transfer data between applications
- **SPECIFIC SOFTWARE**
  - Performs only one task
  - Examples: stock control, payroll, kitchen design, etc.
- **BESPOKE SOFTWARE**
  - Tailor-made software
  - Specifically written
  - Expensive
  - Meets user needs exactly

Systems software and applications software: systems software

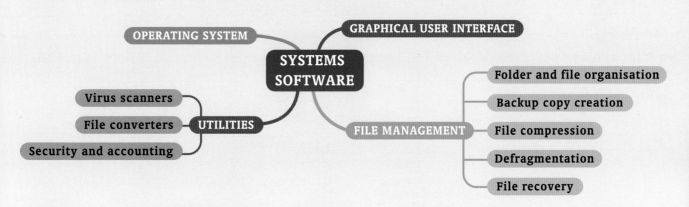

SYSTEMS SOFTWARE

- **OPERATING SYSTEM**
- **GRAPHICAL USER INTERFACE**
- **UTILITIES**
  - Virus scanners
  - File converters
  - Security and accounting
- **FILE MANAGEMENT**
  - Folder and file organisation
  - Backup copy creation
  - File compression
  - Defragmentation
  - File recovery

Systems software and applications software: generic software

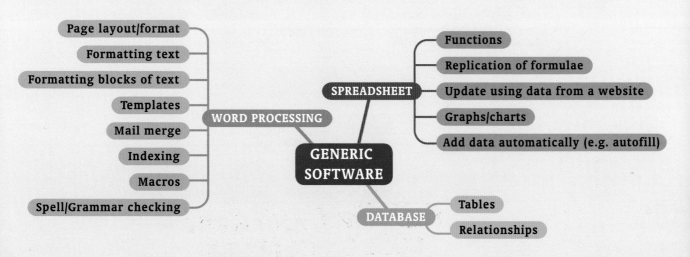

GENERIC SOFTWARE

- **WORD PROCESSING**
  - Page layout/format
  - Formatting text
  - Formatting blocks of text
  - Templates
  - Mail merge
  - Indexing
  - Macros
  - Spell/Grammar checking
- **SPREADSHEET**
  - Functions
  - Replication of formulae
  - Update using data from a website
  - Graphs/charts
  - Add data automatically (e.g. autofill)
- **DATABASE**
  - Tables
  - Relationships

Summary mind maps continued

Systems software and applications software: applications software

Performs a certain job — **APPLICATIONS SOFTWARE** — Needs systems software to function

Systems software and applications software: web software

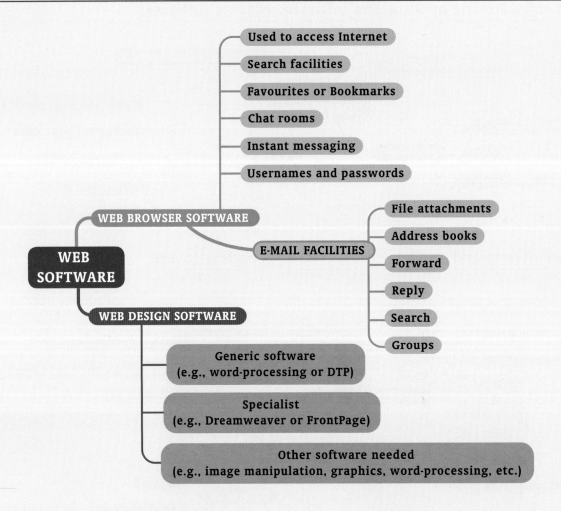

Used to access Internet

Search facilities

Favourites or Bookmarks

Chat rooms

Instant messaging

Usernames and passwords

WEB BROWSER SOFTWARE

WEB SOFTWARE

E-MAIL FACILITIES

File attachments

Address books

Forward

Reply

Search

Groups

WEB DESIGN SOFTWARE

Generic software (e.g., word-processing or DTP)

Specialist (e.g., Dreamweaver or FrontPage)

Other software needed (e.g., image manipulation, graphics, word-processing, etc.)

TOPIC 8: Implementation of ICT-related solutions

In this topic you will be creating the solution or solutions to the ICT problem or problems you have previously analysed and designed. Creating the solution from the designs is called implementation.

▼ The key concept covered in this topic is:

▷ Production of working solutions

CONTENTS

Implementation of ICT-related solutions

Introduction

This is the stage where you get to actually use the software tools to build the solution to the client-identified problem or problems.

During this stage you will need to spend most of your time getting your solution to work properly but you will also need to spend some time producing some documentation explaining how the problem or problems were solved.

The assessment for the sample work

Remember that the assessment for the sample work is by examination, so it is not like completing a project that is marked. You will have to explain your understanding of the processes you have completed by repeating either what you did in the examination or by referring to your sample work.

What documentation needs to be produced for the implementation stage?

The examination board stipulates that the sample work should address at least one problem and provide evidence as follows:

1 A problem identification with a list of requirements for that problem. Interpretation of those requirements as input, processing and output.
2 A test plan and clearly annotated samples of testing evidence that is cross-referenced to the test plan. This evidence needs to be provided as documentation.

You will notice that implementation is not listed here. You are not required to document the implementation but you can still be asked about it. There are some questions on the paper for Unit 1

that concern aspects of the solution that you do not have to specifically document. You can still be asked about them though.

The last two topics in this unit are:

9 Testing of ICT-related solutions.
10 Evaluation of ICT-related solutions.

You need to produce documentation for the testing but not the evaluation. Testing is not something you leave to the end of the solution, so you will need to test the solution and make corrections as you go along.

Important limitation

The main limitation in producing your sample work is the number of pages you are allowed to bring into the examination.

If you are working on two ICT problems then you will have to be very careful that you do not go over the 10 to 20 pages that you are allowed for the whole of the documentation.

Your work will need to be succinct – remember that you are marked on an examination that refers to parts of your project and not directly the project itself. One of the main criteria for the project of documentation is that the sections should be clearly marked and easy to find. You will need to find relevant parts quickly during the examination and refer to them on your exam script, so having a clear structure to your work is essential.

Implementation

Implementation is the stage where you start to build the ICT solution by making use of the design tools. The implementation stage will make use of:

- Hardware: input, storage and output devices.
- Software: software tools used to create the solution to the problem

and don't forget the systems software needed to run them.
- Communications technologies: your solution may make use of a network or the Internet.

As you go along, it is useful to produce evidence such as:

- screenshots
- printouts
- annotated printouts (i.e., printouts with your comments handwritten on them)
- sound recordings in a suitable file format
- photographs or images
- text.

You should collect any material that you consider shows how you went about solving the ICT problem. If you collect this material as you go along, it is much easier and you may like to use it for the next stages of the project which are testing and then evaluation.

During the implementation you need to keep records of any changes that you needed to make to your design in order to simplify things or get your solution to work. Keep records of things that did not work and how you corrected them to get them to work.

Implementation advice

Here are some tips that should help you with the implementation of your ICT solution:

- Whatever you produce you should always keep looking at the client requirements to check that they are being met. You are producing what the client wants not what you want to produce.

EXAM TIP

Always make sure that what you implement is what was set out in the design stage.

If you need to make any changes then this is ok but you need to explain why the change to the design was needed.

- You should make sure that you use the previous stages (i.e., the analysis and design stages). The whole sample work should flow from one stage to the next.
- Do not be too ambitious with your solution. It is better to produce a simple version that works, rather than an all bells and whistles version which looks good but does not produce the correct output.
- Ensure that validation checks are built into your solution or other ways of making sure that only accurate data is processed.
- Test your solutions as you go along. You made need to change things and it is easier to do this sooner.
- Do not get bogged down in the solution. If you cannot produce what you intended, then you may need to simplify your problem (with the client's consent).

General rules to follow when implementing spreadsheets

Here are some rules to help you when implementing spreadsheets. You will find it easier to implement spreadsheet solutions to ICT problems if you follow these general rules:

- type labels in cells first
- type raw data in cells
- use formulas wherever possible
- in formulas, reference the cell locations rather than the numbers themselves
- use functions where possible instead of formulas
- use the copy commands or fill commands to copy formulas
- do not type anything that the spreadsheet will type for you
- check for correct formulas with test values

- format the spreadsheet to make it readable and attractive (e.g., present material graphically if it helps the user understand the output)
- use comments to help users know what data is to be put into certain cells
- create validation checks.

Organising folders and files

In order to successfully implement your solution, you will need to be organised. You will need to create and name suitable folders for your work and give the files they contain suitable and logical names. You will be creating lots of different files for your ICT solution and they need to be found quickly.

Remember the importance of backing up your work. Organising your files means this can be done quickly.

Health and safety aspects of the implementation

You need to bear in mind the following when implementing your solution:

- You will be spending long periods working at the computer – remember how to work safely by sitting up straight in your seat, taking breaks, etc.
- Make your sure your solution does not cause health problems for others (e.g., user interface should be stress free to use, minimal use of the keyboard to avoid the likelihood of RSI, etc.).

EXAM TIP

Get into the habit of writing clear explanations as to what you are doing. You will have to produce explanations as part of the exam. Show your explanations to others and see if they can understand them.

Questions

▶ Questions 1 | pp. 104–105

1 You are creating a multimedia presentation for a client. The client has agreed the design with you and you have completed the analysis stage.

   Write down **three** things you must now do as a part of the implementation stage, in order to complete the presentation. **(3 marks)**

2 Describe **three** enhanced features of presentation software and explain how each of them can be used. **(3 marks)**

3 Images are sourced for inclusion in ICT solutions.
   (a) State three sources for images. **(3 marks)**
   (b) Describe three things you would have to do with the images before you can use them in your own work. **(3 marks)**

4 During the implementation of the ICT solution you will need to spend long periods working at the computer.
   (a) Give **two** health problems that can be caused when working at the computer for long periods. **(2 marks)**
   (b) For each health problem identified in part (a), explain one way that the health risk can be minimised. **(2 marks)**

If I am stuck can I get help?

No, you are not allowed any help from your teacher/lecturer when producing your sample work. The work has to be your own. You can of course do research for sites that explain how to use certain software tools, use books and use your notes, etc., if you get stuck with the implementation.

   Do not get help from outside school with your ICT solution – the work must be your own and you must sign a form confirming that the work is your own. If you submit work that is clearly beyond your talents, then your teacher/lecturer will spot this and you may be disqualified from the assessment/examination.

Tips on implementation

During the implementation you will be turning your designs into working ICT solutions using a variety of software tools.

   Here are a few tips on implementing your solution:
   • Involve your client throughout the implementation stage.
   • Keep showing them what you have done so far and make sure they are happy.
   • The client may be able to spot things you are doing wrong or have not considered.
   • Listen to any comments your client makes and act on them.
Remember that the most important thing is that the ICT solution should work, so do not spend too much time on the appearance of the solution at the expense of producing a solution that works.

   Read as much as you can about the software tools you are going to use to solve the ICT problem before starting the implementation. You need to understand the capabilities of each piece of software.

   Although the whole solution is performed after the implementation stage, you also need to test that various components of your solution are working before starting on the next component.

   Remember that you can be asked about the implementation stage in the examination so it is a good idea to write a few notes explaining what you did and any problems you had and this can be included in the evaluation part of the sample work later.

Exam support

Worked example 1

1 When implementing an ICT solution it is necessary to back up your files.
   State a suitable storage medium for backing up each of the following files, explaining why it is suitable.
   (a) A multimedia presentation. (2 marks)
   (b) A short financial model created using spreadsheet software. (2 marks)

Student answer 1

1 (a) CD because it there is a lot of data to store and CD is able to store a lot.
   (b) Floppy disk because it can be re-used again and again.

Examiner's comment

1 (a) CD or CD-ROM or DVD is not an acceptable answer. It needs to be a media that can be writeable by a user/developer. More detail is needed such as CD-R, CD-RW, etc. Statements such as 'store a lot' are vague and not worth a mark at AS. A better answer would be 'CD-RW has a high storage capacity which is necessary to store large image and sound animation files needed for the presentation'. **No marks for this part.**
   (b) This answer is ok and gains two marks.
   (2 marks out of 4)

Student answer 2

1 (a) A CD-RW which has a high storage capacity of 700 Mb which will be enough for the files such as images, video, sound that will be needed for the presentation.
   (b) A flash/pen drive because it is a removable medium and very portable, which means that the data is easily loaded into different computers.

Examiner's comment

1(a) and (b) Both of these answers have used suitable media and have justified their choice.
   (4 marks out of 4)

Examiner's answer

1 (a) One mark for a suitable media with a large storage capacity such as:
   • CD-RW
   • CD-R
   • DVD-(+/-)
   • Zip disk
   • Portable hard drive
   • Memory card
   • Flash/pen drive
   • Removable hard drive
   One mark for a reason such as:
   • High storage capacity needed for storing multimedia files
   • Small size so easily transferred from one computer to another
   • Re-useable medium so more presentations may be added or the existing presentation edited

   (b) One mark for a suitable media such as:
   • Zip disk
   • Portable hard drive
   • Memory card
   • Flash/pen drive
   • Removable hard drive
   One mark for a reason such as:
   • Re-usable so that models containing different data can be saved
   • Need a removable medium because the data may be private/sensitive
   • Small size so easily transferred from one computer to another

Summary mind map

Implementation of ICT-related solutions

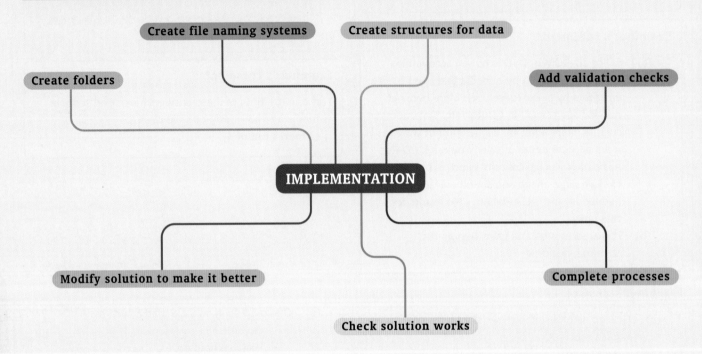

TOPIC 9: Testing of ICT-related solutions

ICT solutions need to be thoroughly tested before use. In this topic you will learn how to test ICT solutions and how to test that the solution does not fail when certain data is entered. You will also learn about how to check that the ICT solution you develop matches the client's requirements.

▼ The key concepts covered in this topic are:

▶ Construct test plans that include a range of suitable test data, identify expected outcomes and test that the client's requirements have been met

▶ Follow a test plan in a systematic way

CONTENTS

Testing of ICT-related solutions

Introduction

Testing of any solution to an ICT problem must be thorough. In order to make testing thorough it is necessary to draw up a document called a test plan. This document outlines what testing will be done and also includes the results of the testing and an evaluation of the testing.

Reasons for thorough testing:

- A client will not be happy with a solution that does not do what it is supposed to do.
- A user will get frustrated with solutions that do not work properly.
- There are health and safety issues which say that solutions should not frustrate/stress the user.
- Faulty software could cost the client money.

Detecting errors while the ICT solution is being developed is much better than the client or user discovering them whilst they are using the solution.

What needs to be tested?

Where a user is able to enter data into a system, testing is needed to check that:

- allowable/normal data is accepted into the system
- data just outside the acceptable range is rejected
- erroneous (i.e. ridiculous) data is rejected by the system.

Additionally you would also test to ensure that:

- the solution meets all of the user requirements
- the solution is capable of being used by a typical user
- error messages are clear
- any paper forms used to input data to fields are in the same order as on the screen

- the correct output is produced
- all output is complete and clearly arranged
- any reports are clear, dated and numbered.

There are some tests that are specific to the development of multimedia solutions, such as websites, and these are outlined later.

Testing using normal data

Testing using normal data involves entering data that should be acceptable to the solution to check that it is allowed to be entered and that it produces the correct output.

Boundary test data

Many ICT solutions fail at input boundaries. For example, suppose a user is allowed to enter a value from 50 to 100 inclusive. The boundaries of the numbers are therefore 50 and 100. The numbers you would test would be one either side of 50 and the number itself (i.e., 50).

You would then test the following values for the lower boundary and the upper boundary.

| 49 50 51 | 99 100 101 |
| lower boundary | upper boundary |

Example

The age of a student in a secondary school needs to be input into a system as a number from 11 to 19 inclusive.

Test values for the lower boundary would be 10 11 12

Test values for the upper boundary would be 18 19 20

Testing using erroneous data

There is also the chance that a user will enter data which is ridiculous for a field and this is called **erroneous data**.

In the previous example, the value input for the age (i.e., 11 to 19) could be tested using erroneous data. Test values for erroneous data could be:

121
-9
D
%
25
eighteen

A thorough test plan will ensure that all the inputs are tested for boundary values of data as well as for a range of erroneous data.

Requirements-based testing

At the start of the ICT solution, the client will have identified a list of the requirements of the solution.

Requirements-based testing involves checking that each of the requirements have been met by the solution you have developed.

Testing ICT solutions that do not involve numbers

The previous section refers to ICT solutions that use numbers as some of the data input. But what if your solution does not use numbers for input?

You can still have normal data or erroneous data and you need to think about the form this data is likely to take in the context of your solution.

Remember that data is not just about letters and numbers, it can also be:

- images
- video
- sound.

So what form would erroneous sound data take? It could be:

- distorted – the sound file could be corrupted
- too loud or too low – the sound might not have been recorded at the correct sound level

- the wrong sound used – files may have become mixed up
- the wrong length – for example, a podcast which should be 10 minutes ends up being 30 minutes long.

Testing a podcast

Podcast websites frequently have a section where people who subscribe and then listen to the podcast can leave their comments. Here are a few typical comments taken from such sites. The podcast in question was a podcast about building websites and was part of a series of podcasts with each of them lasting 10 minutes.

Here are some of the comments made:

- ummmmmm… It's only 12 seconds long!
- It won't let me subscribe.
- I love the podcasts you have produced, but this one, number 5 in the series, is so low I cannot hear it properly.
- The latest one is very poor in quality – think you need a better mike?

You can see from the above comments that testing the podcast should have revealed the problems, rather than the users discovering them when downloading them.

To test a podcast you can:

- Check the length of the podcast by timing it with a watch to ensure it meets the client's requirements.
- Check that the subscription to your podcast works properly by subscribing to it yourself.
- Check that the podcast can be downloaded from the site onto an MP3 player such as an iPod or iPhone.
- Check, by listening to the podcast, that the sound levels are correct, the content is accurate, the content is all there, the content conforms to what the client wanted and that the sound is not distorted.

For more information on podcasts and the problems you can have with them refer to the Apple iTunes site at: http://www.apple.com/itunes/store/podcasts.html

Creating and following a test plan

▼ **You will find out**

▶ About what a test plan is and what it should include

▶ About how to structure a test plan

▶ About how to follow a test plan

▶ About how to test multimedia solutions

Introduction

Testing should be done throughout the development of the solution. The reason for this is that you would not want to move onto the next part of a solution unless you were sure that the first part worked properly.

It is important, therefore, to keep records of all the tests you have performed. This is put together in a document called a test plan. A test plan provides evidence to the client that the solution has been properly tested.

A test plan should show the design of representative examples of tests to ensure:

- validity of data input
- accuracy of output
- presentation of output
- that the solution meets the requirements of the client
- that the solution is usable by the end user and/or intended audience.

Validity of data input

Validation checks should have been set up to restrict the user to entering only certain allowable data. Please note that it is impossible to restrict data so that only correct data can be entered.

The steps involved in testing the validity of data input are:

- devise the test
- carry out the test
- match the results of the test with those required by the client
- take corrective action if the results do not match.

Checking the validity of data input involves checking that any validation checks are working properly.

Accuracy of output

Checking the accuracy of output involves:

- Putting data into the solution and checking that the results are accurate (e.g., for a spreadsheet, all the calculations could be worked out with pen, paper and calculator to check they match).

Presentation of output

The way the output is presented is important. This would involve:

- checking that the output is in the correct format
- checking that the output is in the correct order
- checking that the output is clearly presented
- checking that any colour schemes used are appropriate.

That the solution meets the requirements of the client

During the analysis and design stage a list of client requirements will have been produced. This list can be compared to check that all the requirements have been met by the solution. Meeting the client requirements could involve:

- checking all the client's requirements against the solution to check they have all been met
- showing the solution to the client
- obtaining client feedback
- acting on the feedback from the client if necessary.

That the solution is usable by the end user and/or the intended audience

The best way to test whether the ICT solution is easy to use is to ask a range of users to use it and give you feedback. In order to focus them on what you want to know about, it is a good idea to produce a questionnaire containing questions such as:

If there is an audience as well as a user for the solution, then you will need to evaluate the ease of use with both sets of people.

How should a test plan be structured?

Here are some tips for producing test plans. Because ICT solutions to problems can be very different, you may need to modify a test plan to suit your own solution. The main function of any test plan is to supply evidence that the solution has undergone rigorous testing.

Here are some tips:

- number each test plan
- explain briefly what you are testing for
- explain briefly how that test is constructed
- give the test data that is to be used – note that sometimes it is better to provide a reference here to a table of test data situated elsewhere (e.g., see table on page #)
- have a column for expected results – this is what should happen
- have a column for actual results – what actually happens.

	Totally agree				Totally disagree
I had no problem loading the product	5	4	3	2	1
Once loaded, it was clear what I had to do next	5	4	3	2	1

Following the test plan in a systematic way

The test plan you produce to test your ICT solution should be followed in a systematic way. You may need to refer to it when asked questions as part of the exam for Unit 1.

Test Number	Reason for testing	How test is constructed	Test data used	Expected results	Actual results	Action taken
1						

As ICT solutions are so very different it is difficult to explain a test plan that would cover all types of solutions. If you feel that your solution is different from those covered in this section, all you need to consider is how you can ensure that the solution works properly. You can then set about designing a structure for tests that will be suitable.

Testing multimedia solutions

The testing of multimedia solutions such as interactive presentations or websites is different to testing solutions such as spreadsheets and databases.

With a multimedia solution you would need to test that:

- The content is correct, engaging and conveys the right meaning – there should be no spelling or grammatical errors. Ask typical users to comment on this.
- Every link works and goes to the correct page – there is nothing more annoying than links to non-existent pages.
- All the interactive features work as intended – here you would need to check that buttons, hot spots, image maps, menu selections, etc., all work properly.

- The solution is robust and cannot be made to fail – make sure that there is nothing in the solution that will cause a computer to freeze.
- The product works properly with different browsers – remember with websites that users will use many different browsers to access your website. You need to check your site with a few different browsers.
- People are able to use the solution without help – make sure that you have developed a solution that is capable of being used by the majority of your users.
- The solution meets all client requirements – as always check that you have met all the client's requirements with your solution.

What to do if you discover any problems

During the testing process you will find things that do not work or need altering. You should:

- Note any potential problems as they occur.
- Decide how you are going to put them right.
- Check that any changes you make do not affect other parts of the product.

You must always provide evidence of testing and any remedial action you take to get your multimedia product working properly.

Important note

As this is a chapter near the end of the unit, you may think that testing is a process that comes at the end of the development. This is not the case. Testing should be a process that should be done at all the stages of the development. If you create, for example,

a link to another page, then before you move on to do something else, it makes sense to test that the link works.

It is always worthwhile having a group of potential users to bounce ideas off. It is much easier to get agreement on an idea before doing too much work on it.

Supplying testing evidence

The evidence for testing will depend on the type of solution you have produced. Here are some examples of evidence you could supply:

- You could supply tables of data showing data entered and the results.
- You could supply a list of the user requirements (as determined in the analysis and design stages) and then work through the solution and tick them off to check they have all been met.
- Any printouts or screenshots you produce as part of the testing evidence should be annotated, which means that you can write on them to explain the testing that has taken place.

Using the results of testing evidence in the evaluation

The final stage is to produce an evaluation and this is covered in the next topic.

You will be using the results of testing evidence to evaluate your solution. Not all solutions work perfectly and often compromises have to be made, so the solution may not satisfy all the user requirements. Maybe the user's expectations of the solution were unrealistic or they could not be completely realised because the software was not up to the task. In all these cases you will need to use the evidence from testing and refer to it in your evaluation.

Questions

▶ Questions 1   pp. 110–113

1 A client has an ICT problem and has asked you to develop a solution to it. A list of client requirements has been provided.
   (a) Explain briefly what is meant by a client requirement. (2 marks)
   (b) Once you have developed the solution, describe how you would evaluate that all client requirements have been met. (2 marks)
2 A quantity between 100 and 500 is to be entered into a database.
   (a) The developer decides first to test the solution using normal data.
   Explain, by giving an example, what this means. (2 marks)
   (b) Explain, by referring to this example, what is meant by boundary test data. (2 marks)
   (c) Testing is also performed using erroneous data. Explain, by referring to this example, what this means. (2 marks)
3 Give **two** reasons why solutions to ICT problems should be thoroughly tested. (2 marks)

▶ Questions 2   pp. 112–113

1 You have just developed a website for a client. Describe **three** tests you would perform on the website to check that it works properly. (3 marks)
2 (a) Explain the meaning of the term test plan. (1 mark)
   (b) Give **two** things that would be included as part of a test plan. (2 marks)
3 It is important to involve the client in your solution as much as possible throughout the development of the solution.
   Give **two** reasons why this is important. (2 marks)

Worked example 1

1 Testing
   (i) Explain how your solution is tested with **normal** data (2 marks)
   (ii) Give a page reference of a test using **normal** data. (1 mark)
       (Write Q1 (ii) in the margin, in the correct place, on that page)
   (iii) Give a page reference showing an item of **erroneous** test data. (1 mark)
       (Write Q1 (iii) in the margin, in the correct place, on that page)
   (iv) Explain what is meant by **erroneous** test data. (2 marks)
   (v) Give a page reference showing an item of **extreme/boundary** test data. (1 mark)
       (Write Q1 (v) in the margin, in the correct place, on that page)
   (vi) Explain what is meant by **extreme/boundary** test data. (2 marks)

Exam support

Student answer 1

Note the type of answer to this question depends on the type of ICT solution the student has produced.

1 (i) A range of share prices were obtained and entered manually using the keyboard. All the share prices used were actual and valid prices. The output is compared with that produced manually using paper and calculator.

(ii) Page 12

(iii) Page 12

(iv) This is data that is wrong. It will not be accepted and a message will appear why it is wrong.

(v) Page 12

(vi) This is data that is on the boundary and is put into the computer to see if it is rejected or accepted for processing.

Student answer 2

1 (i) Test data which will pass the validation rules is entered into a field and it should be accepted by the ICT solution and duly processed.

(ii) Page 10

(iii) Page 10

(iv) Erroneous test data is data that is wildly incorrect and it is entered to make sure that it is rejected by the validation rules. It could be data not accepted by a range check or data that is of the wrong type (e.g., putting a number into a name).

(v) Page 10

(vi) Data just outside the boundary of the range check which should be rejected, or data that is just inside the range check which should be accepted. This is to check that a range check is working correctly.

Examiner's comment

1 (i) Here the student has not explained that test data is being entered. They have not grasped that the purpose of the test data is to check that the validation checks are working properly to prevent wrong data from being processed. No marks for this part.

(ii) and (iii) have the correct page references.

(iv) The student has not made it clear in what way the data is wrong. They needed to mention that the data is ridiculous and should therefore be rejected by the validation checks.

(v) This is the correct page reference.

(vi) It is hard to talk about a boundary test without giving an example. If you find it hard to explain something, then always try giving an example to help.

The student needed to explain that the data needed to be slightly inside or slightly outside or on the boundary and they have not made it clear.

They have made a comment that the data will be accepted or rejected but there is no reference to which data. No marks here. **(3 marks out of 9)**

Examiner's comment

1 (i) Student has specified that allowable data is entered and that this will be accepted and processed so two marks here.

(ii) and (iii) are correct – two marks.

All the other answers are correct and have been clearly communicated showing that the student fully understands testing. **(9 marks out of 9)**

Examiner's answers

1 (i) One mark for specifying test data to be used.
One mark for explaining that the test data should be accepted by the solution.

(ii) One mark for correct page no. showing that the normal data has been accepted by the solution.

(iii) One mark for correct page no. showing an item of erroneous data that is outside the boundary or of the wrong type so that it would be rejected by the solution.

(iv) One mark for explanation that it is wildly wrong data (ridiculous numbers or wrong data type) and one mark for the fact that it should be rejected by the validation check.

(v) One mark for correct page showing an item of extreme/boundary test data.

(vi) One mark for the definition and one mark for example or fact that data should not be accepted for processing.

Data that is either side of the boundary or on the boundary of acceptable data (1). For example, if the maximum number that can be entered is 20, then 19, 20 and 21 are examples of boundary test data (1). The solution should reject data that is outside the boundary (1).

Summary mind maps

Testing of ICT-related solutions

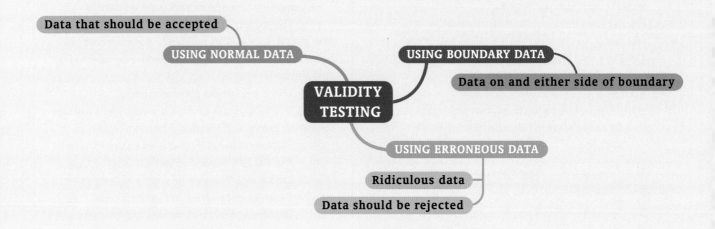

Data that should be accepted

USING NORMAL DATA

VALIDITY TESTING

USING BOUNDARY DATA

Data on and either side of boundary

USING ERRONEOUS DATA

Ridiculous data

Data should be rejected

Creating and following a test plan

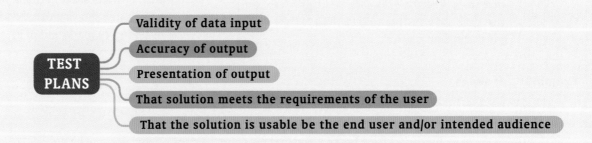

TEST PLANS

Validity of data input

Accuracy of output

Presentation of output

That solution meets the requirements of the user

That the solution is usable be the end user and/or intended audience

TOPIC 10: Evaluation of ICT-related solutions

This topic is the final topic of Unit 1 and it completes the practical work for the AS examination. On completing the ICT solution you will need to reflect on the sample work you produce and assess how well it met the user requirements. From this topic you will learn how to produce an evaluation.

CONTENTS

Unit 1 Practical Problem Solving in the Digital World

Evaluation of ICT-related solutions

Introduction

After you have completed some work, it is always useful to look back and reflect on the solution and how well you feel it met the client's needs. You may also like to reflect on the way you went about completing the work and the problems you had and how they were overcome.

This topic will explain to you the various processes involved in evaluation.

Does the solution do what it is supposed to do?

In the previous topic you will have tested the solution and as part of this you should have produced documentation showing how closely your solution matched the user requirements. You can refer to this document in your evaluation or maybe actually include a copy of the table here for reference.

Here are some questions you could answer as part of this section of the evaluation:

- How closely did the solution match the user requirements?
- If the solution did not match user requirements perfectly was there a reason for this and what was it?
- What modifications needed to be made in developing the solution?
- Did you make any compromises and if so what were they?
- Does the solution have any limitations and what are they?

> **KEY WORDS**
>
> **Evaluation** – the act of reviewing what has been achieved, how it was achieved and how well the solution works

Does the solution do it how it was supposed to do it?

When you first start developing a solution to a problem it is sometimes hard to envisage the problems that might arise. You may have to change things slightly or go back to the client and ask if it is possible to solve the problem in a different way.

You need to include in your evaluation details of any changes that were made to the solution and the reasons why they were necessary.

What makes an ICT solution effective?

It is hard to generalise about the effectiveness of ICT solutions as ICT problems are so different. For an ICT solution to be effective it must:

- meet all the client's requirements
- ensure as far as is possible that inaccurate data is not processed
- use the most appropriate method of input
- use the correct output method
- produce the correct output
- produce the output in a logical order
- produce clear messages if the wrong data is entered
- ensure that any health and safety issues are addressed for the user
- have a user interface that is easy to use
- be easy to use by a user and/or any intended audience
- not contain any spelling or grammatical mistakes in any text used
- contain material that is accurate and up-to-date
- use design elements (fonts, font sizes, colour schemes, etc.) that are appropriate
- meet the capabilities of the user/audience

If the solution is not effective, what would make it effective?

Once you have decided on all the factors that would make the solution effective, you can produce a list of any shortfalls in your solution. With any problem, if you were given more time or had the chance to start again, then the second attempt would almost certainly be better.

In this section you need to identify anything that is wrong with your solution and what you might do to correct it.

Here is a comment made by a student about a model they created using spreadsheet software:

'I produced the output data in a table but on reflection I should have also produced graphs of the data. Graphs could be discussed at meetings since trends are much easier to spot using graphs rather than numbers in tables.'

Asking the client, user and/or audience for their comments

As part of the testing, you should have asked the user for their comments or got them to fill in a questionnaire about the usability of the solution. You can refer to this in your evaluation and it is also useful to include any comments they made.

> **EXAM TIP**
>
> Avoid making comments similar to the following as part of your evaluation:
>
> 'I thought it worked well and I really enjoyed doing it and the client thought it was good, too!'

How to produce a well written evaluation

Here are some pointers that will help make your evaluation of your ICT solution the best it can be.

- Evaluations of ICT projects can end up being an afterthought and not enough thought is given to them. Evaluations should identify where your solution has worked well and where there is the opportunity for improvement.
- It is important to remember that you are not evaluating your own performance in the project in the sample work. All this evaluation should cover is how good a solution has been produced. So don't include comments like 'I was ill for two weeks and left things to the last minute so I did not complete the whole solution as I would have liked to'.
- You should not refer to difficulties/problems you had with the software because you were unfamiliar with it.

- It is useful to add the client's, user's and audience's views to your evaluation. It is best to add quotes. Remember that these comments could be obtained by giving the client, user and audience a questionnaire to complete.
- Remember to refer to any testing in your evaluation. Referring to the section which checks that the client's requirements have been met is essential.
- The evaluation should be honest. No ICT solution is ever perfect, so you need to include both criticism and praise.
- When you are matching to see if the client's requirements have been met by the solution, you need to make a small comment on each about the extent to which the requirement has been met.

- For example, you developed a website as your ICT solution and one of the client requirements was that the website should be easy to use by all staff. To evaluate this you could ask the staff who need to use the website how easy it was on a scale from 1 to 5 with 5 being the easiest. You could then say in your evaluation what score it had been given and also refer to comments they had made.
- Obtain feedback on your solution from client, user and audience. Use a questionnaire and remember to add a part where they can write in comments.

EVALUATION SHEET

Superb

Excellent

Great

Good

Questions

▶ **Questions 1** pp. 118–119

1 Give **two** reasons why after developing an ICT solution to a problem the solution should be evaluated. **(2 marks)**

2 Describe **three** factors that would make a solution an effective solution. **(3 marks)**

Worked example 1

1 (a) (i) Give a page reference showing where you have assessed the effectiveness of the solution in meeting the client's requirements. **(1 mark)**

   (ii) Explain **one** way it is possible to assess the effectiveness of the solution in meeting the client's requirements. **(2 marks)**

(b) Describe two criteria by which a solution could be assessed as being effective. **(4 marks)**

Student answer 1

1 (a) (i) Page 14

(ii) You can ask the client if the solution did the job properly.

(b) The solution was easy to use – I sent a usability questionnaire to the user and they used the solution and marked the solution out of 20 and gave it 16 which was good.

I used the list of user requirements and then went through the solution carefully to check off that the each requirement was met. It met all but one of the requirements, which I thought was good.

Student answer 2

1 (a) (i) Page 14

(ii) Use the list of client requirements and work through each item checking that the requirement is met by the solution. Flag up any requirements that have not been met.

(b) The solution satisfied all of the user requirements as identified during the design stage. This means that the solution sets out to do what the user intended it to do.

The ICT solution should have an easy to use interface. It is possible to test this by giving the user a questionnaire to fill in.

Examiner's comment

1 The answer to (a) (i) is correct but part (ii) is too general an answer. Also there are two marks allocated here and the student has only made one insufficient point so no marks for this part.

Part (b) was well answered although the student has answered it as if it were a question about their own work rather than a general question.

They have, however, shown a good understanding and the examples given, meaning that they gain the four marks for both criteria. **(5 marks out of 7)**

Examiner's comment

1 (a) (i) is correct so one mark.

(ii) The student has confused the user and client. As the client is the person who has asked for the ICT solution, they are the person who will supply the user requirements.

It is very easy to confuse the user, client and audience for an ICT solution and the terms are not interchangeable and should be used with care. Only one mark for part (ii).

Part (b) has both parts correct and is worth two marks each. **(6 marks out of 7)**

Examiner's answers

1 (a) (i) The correct page number where the reference to assessing the effectiveness of the solution in meeting the client's requirements is shown.

   (ii) Two marks for an answer similar to the following:
   - Use the list of requirements as agreed by the client (1) produced at the analysis and design stage and check each requirement is met by the solution (1).

(b) Two criteria (two marks each) from the following list:
   - The solution satisfies all the client requirements.
   - The solution works in the way the client intended it to work.
   - The solution provides the correct output.
   - The solution has an easy to use interface.
   - The solution restricts ridiculous data from being processed.

Exam support

Worked example 2

2 (a) After an ICT solution has been produced and completed, the solution should be evaluated. Give **one reason** why the ICT solution should be evaluated. **(2 marks)**

  (b) (i) Give the page number where you begin to write your evaluation in your sample work.
      (In your sample work write 2(b)(i) page next to the beginning of your evaluation in the margin of that page)

     (ii) Give the page number where you have evaluated how well **one of the client's requirements** has been satisfied by the ICT solution.
      (In your sample work write 2(b)(ii) page next to the beginning of your evaluation in the margin of that page) **(2 marks)**

  (c) Describe **two ways** in which it is possible to assess the client's satisfaction with your ICT solution. **(4 marks)**

Student answer 1

2 (a) So that the solution can be checked to make sure that it works properly.

  (b) (i) Page 12
     (ii) Page 13

  (c) You can ask them what they think of the solution. You can see if they complain about it.

Student answer 2

2 (a) To assess whether it met the needs.

  (b) (i) Page 10
     (ii) Page 13

  (c) Give the client a questionnaire to answer which asks them to rate certain aspects of the solution such as user friendliness, design of screens, etc.
  Interview the client and ask them to identify good and bad points of the solution you have produced. Get them to give you truthful comments.

Examiner's comment

2 (a) Checking that the solution works properly is not the purpose of evaluation because that is the purpose of testing. Evaluation is a reflective look at how well the solution produced meets the client's requirements. No marks for this part.

  (b) (i) Here the student has just put a page number in and there is no section on the page that refers to the start of the evaluation. In fact the student has missed the evaluation section out completely. No marks here.

     (ii) Again as there is no evaluation section present in the sample work and the student has simply put a page number in and hoped it won't be noticed, there are no marks for this.

  (c) Asking the client for their comments is a valid answer but waiting for them to complain is not, so only two marks out of the four here.
  (2 marks out of 8)

Examiner's comment

2 (a) Notice that there are two marks for this answer. There needs to be two separate points or one point with a detailed answer. The answer given here is only worth one mark.

  (b) (i) and (ii) The sample work has been clearly referenced and both references refer to correct evidence.

  (c) Both of these answers are correct and worth two marks each, so full marks for this answer.
  (7 marks out of 8)

Examiner's answers

2 (a) One mark for the reason and one mark for further explanation or an example.
  In order to see how near the solution is (1) in meeting all the client's requirements (1).
  To review what has been achieved (1), how it was achieved (1) and how well the solution works (1).
  To reflect on the problems which were overcome (1), to make the solution an effective solution (1).

  (b) (i) and (ii) The sample work has been clearly referenced and both references refer to correct evidence.

  (c) Two distinctly different ways (two marks each) such as:
  Conduct an interview with the client and ask them what they thought the strengths and weaknesses of the solution were (1).
  Ask the client (1) how close or otherwise the solution met their needs/requirements (1).
  Ask the client to complete a questionnaire (1) which can be used to assess their satisfaction with the solution (1).

Summary mind maps

Evaluation of ICT-related solutions

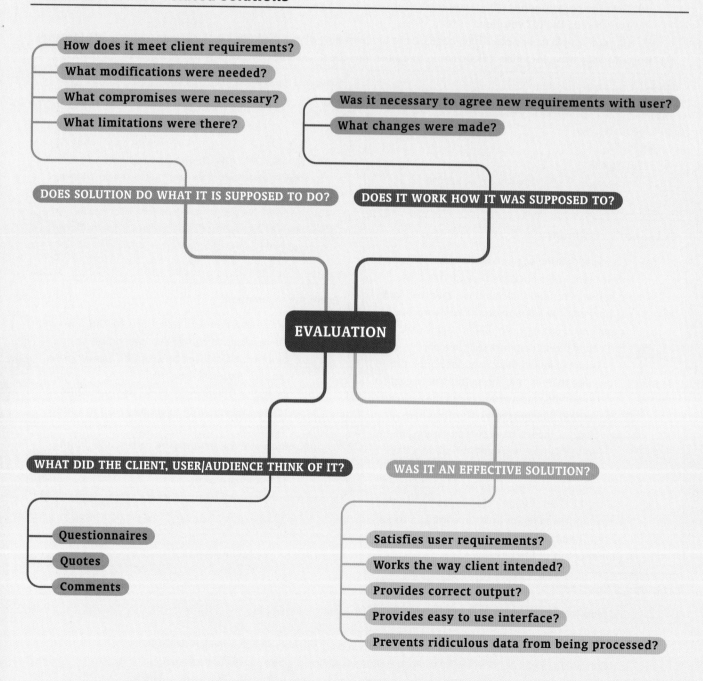

This topic is the first topic in the second AS module: Unit 2 Living in the Digital World. In this module you will be learning about how ICT is used in the world we live in and how its use affects individuals, society and organisations.

This first topic looks at the concept of the ICT system and its components.

▼ The key concepts covered in this topic are:

▶ What is ICT?

▶ What is a system?

▶ What is an ICT system?

▶ The components of an ICT system

CONTENTS

An ICT system and its components

You will find out

▶ About what ICT is

▶ About what a system is

▶ About what an ICT system is

▶ About the components of ICT systems

Introduction

In this topic you will learn about what ICT is and how it is used to create ICT systems for individuals, businesses and organisations. ICT is part of everyday life and it is almost taken for granted and it is growing all the time. In this topic you will be looking at the components of ICT systems and their purposes.

What is ICT?

ICT stands for Information Communications Technology. It is a hard term to define because the subject changes so rapidly. ICT concerns any device or system that allows the storage, retrieval, manipulation, transmission and receipt of digital information.

ICT covers hardware such as:

- computers
- scanners
- digital cameras.

ICT covers software such as:

- systems software
- word-processors
- databases
- spreadsheets.

It is not just about computers (this is simply called Information Technology (IT)). The 'C' in ICT stands for communications and covers all the communications technologies we use such as:

- digital TV
- digital radio
- e-mail
- Internet
- broadband
- networks (wired and wireless)
- mobile phones
- GPS (global positioning systems)
- videoconferencing
- instant messaging
- fax.

What is a system?

A system in everyday life is a way of doing things. For example, we all have a system for getting ready in the morning to go to school or college.

All systems involve input, process and output. Can you think of getting ready in the morning as inputs, processes and outputs?

What is an ICT system?

A system is a way of doing something, so an ICT system is a way of doing something using ICT.

Businesses need many different ICT systems including:

- systems for paying staff (payroll systems)
- stock control systems
- order processing systems
- purchasing systems
- accountancy systems
- personnel (human resources) systems
- e-commerce systems
- banking systems.

What do all systems have in common?

All systems have one thing in common. They all involve the three steps of input, processing and output.

ICT systems are those where the output from the system goes directly to a human being or into another ICT system.

Input – this involves capturing or entering the data. In many cases this will involve entering data via the keyboard but there are many other faster and more accurate methods such as bar coding, scanning, etc. The input involves turning the data into a form that can be processed by the computer. In other words the data needs to be encoded.

Processing – means performing actions on the input data. Typically this would involve performing calculations, searching, sorting, arranging, presenting, converting, transferring, classifying, etc.

Output – these are the results or the information produced when the data has been processed. All information systems produce output.

The six components of an ICT system

There are six components of any ICT system:

People – are needed to supply the data to the ICT system and also to make judgements and decisions from the output supplied from the system.

Data – is the raw material of any ICT system and this is processed by the system to provide the information which is the output produced by the system.

Procedures – determine what needs to be done and when. It also covers the passing of data or information between different people. Administrative procedures are needed to deal with problems such as customers not paying bills, problems with deliveries, etc.

Hardware – these are the physical components that make up the ICT system. If you can touch it, then it is hardware. Hardware includes input devices (keyboards, mouse, scanner, etc.), storage (memory, hard drive, etc.), the processor and the output devices (screen, printer, plotter, etc.). Also included in hardware are the communication devices needed to send data across networks.

Software – these are the computer programs which provided the step-by-step instructions to get the job done.

Information –the results from processing data. Information is the output from an ICT system.

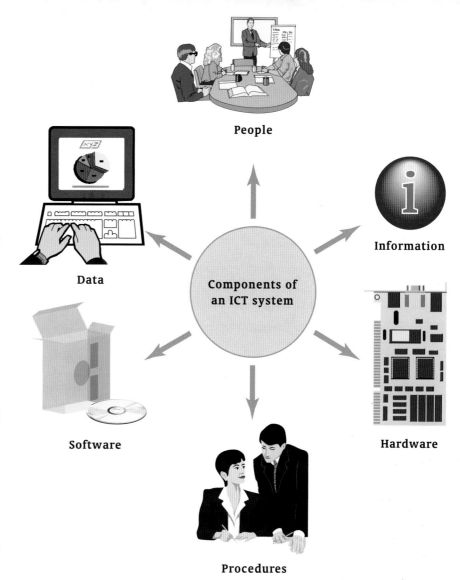

People

Data

Information

Software

Components of an ICT system

Hardware

Procedures

EXAM TIP

Do not get the steps or stages of computing (input, process and output) mixed up with the components of an ICT system. They do not have any common components.

Remembering the above

Use the following to help you remember the above:

Pe DISH Pro

Pe **Pe**ople
D **D**ata
I **I**nformation
S **S**oftware
H **H**ardware
Pro **Pro**cedures

KEY WORDS

Data – raw facts and figures for processing

Hardware – the physical components of a computer system

Information – output from an ICT system

Software – the programs which supply the instructions to the hardware

Unit 2 Living in the Digital World

Questions and Activities

▶ Questions 1 | pp. 124–125

1 ICT and IT are not the same thing. Give a careful definition of the term ICT. (2 marks)

2 A company uses a system where hourly paid employees clock in and out each day. The system records the times and uses these to work out an employee's wages each week.

(a) Describe **three** inputs to the payroll system. (3 marks)

(b) Describe **two** processes performed on the input data you have described in part (a). (2 marks)

(c) Describe **one** output from the payroll system. (1 mark)

▶ Activity 1 The components of ICT systems

The six components of an ICT system are:
- hardware
- software
- data
- people
- procedures
- information.

Look carefully at the following system where you will see that all six of the above components have been identified and described.

Type of system: School/college attendance system

Hardware – Local area network in the school office connected to two laser printers and two optical mark readers.

Software – Systems software and SIMS (Schools Information Management System) software.

Data – The attendance data for each pupil in a class is shaded in on a mark form by the class teacher.

People – Teachers and school administration officers.

Procedures – Teachers fill in a form at the start of each class, marking who is present by shading boxes on a form. At the end of the day the forms are passed to the school office for processing. The forms for all the classes for the day are batched and put into the optical mark reader, which reads the data off the form and inputs it into the SIMS software where it updates all the attendance details.

Information – Any unauthorised absences are identified by the system and this information is merged into letters which are printed and then sent to parents telling them of the absence.

For this activity you need to identify three different ICT systems which you are familiar with and then describe them in a similar way to the above system by identifying and explaining the six components.

It will be easier to do this if you choose fairly simple examples. Try to choose single systems. Remember to set out your three examples using the following headings:
- Hardware
- Software
- Data
- People
- Procedures
- Information

Exam support

Worked example 1

1 Give the names of **six** components of an ICT system. **(1 mark each)**

1

2

3

4

5

6

Student answer 1

1 Hardware
  Internet
  Storage
  Processing
  Output
  Input

Examiner's comment

1 This student has not remembered the six components and has given a mixture of terms associated with ICT.
   Students need to actually learn this type of material as it is impossible to simply guess it.
   Only hardware was correctly listed.
   (1 mark out of 6)

Student answer 2

1 Data
  Hardware
  Software
  People
  Information
  Ways of working

Examiner's comment

1 This student has remembered 5 out of 6 of the components. Ways of working could be taken to mean procedures but the actual word procedures is needed for the mark. **(5 marks out of 6)**

Examiner's answers

1 One mark for each of the following:
   • People
   • Data
   • Information
   • Software
   • Hardware
   • Procedures

Summary mind maps

An ICT system and its components

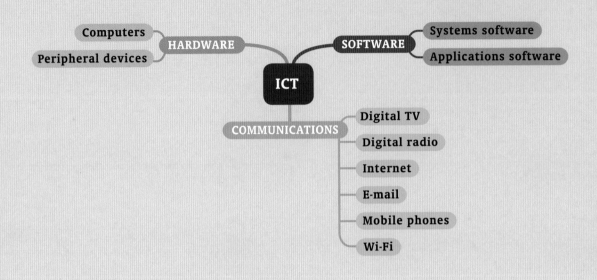

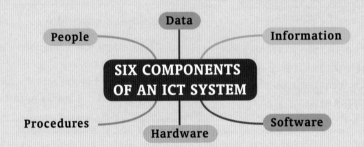

In this topic you will learn about what constitutes data and information and the difference between these two terms. You will learn that there are different forms of data and that it is sometimes necessary to code data during collection to enable effective processing. Data is also always encoded on input to an ICT system because ICT systems are only able to process digitised data. You will learn about how a variety of processes turn data into useful information.

▼ The key concepts covered in this topic are:

▶ Data

▶ Data is processed to produce information

▶ Information

CONTENTS

Unit 2 Living in the Digital World

Data and information: aspects of data

Introduction

In this section you will learn about data and how it is sometimes coded during collection and how it is encoded on entry to an ICT system.

What exactly is data?

There are a number of forms that data can take. Data can be:

- numbers
- words
- images
- sound.

Data are details that are meaningless because they lack relevance. If you look at data, it is either no use to you or not in a form that you can use.

Ways in which data can arise

There are lots of ways data can arise and these are summarised in the following diagram:

Coding data

Data is often coded during collection or when input into an ICT system. The reasons for this are:

- coded data takes less effort to type in
- more data can appear on the screen
- takes up less storage space (less important as storage media is cheap)
- it is easier to check that a code is accurate using validation checks.

Encoding data

Encoding is the process of putting information/data (e.g., text, numbers, symbols, images, sound and video) into a specified format that allows effective transmission or storage by an ICT system.

ICT systems are only able to process data in binary code, so any data has to be converted to this format before processing. Luckily we do not have to get involved in this process – the ICT system does it for us.

The opposite of encoding is decoding where the coded information is changed back into its original form.

Examples of encoding

ASCII encoding – here characters on the keyboard (i.e. letters, numbers, symbols and punctuation marks) are changed into a series of binary digits. For example, the letter A is stored as 01000001.

There are a number of reasons for encoding:

- To compress data – this makes it occupy less space on a storage device and makes it faster to send to another computer over a network.
- To enable a file produced in one software package to be read by someone who does not have that software package available on their computer. For example, a user could save a file as a text file in ASCII, so that it can be read and used by other users.

WAYS IN WHICH DATA CAN ARISE

- From automatic measurement of environmental quantities
- From the results of an experiment
- From a survey
- From a transaction
- From the ouput of a management information system

Encoding image files

Image files are encoded which means the image is represented in a certain way when it is stored. There are many different ways in which an image can be encoded and it depends on how the image is produced (e.g., by digital camera, scanned in, produced using paint/drawing software, etc.).

Data representation

When a character (letter, number or symbol) is typed from the keyboard it is converted to a binary code which consists of a series of 1's and 0's. This is then processed by the computer.

On a network these binary coded characters are transmitted along a wire until the character is received at the other end where it is decoded and converted back to the character again. Most computers represent characters using ASCII code (American Standard Code for Information Interchange) and below is the 8-bit code for the 26 letters of the alphabet (representing letters in ASCII).

A	0100 0001
B	0100 0010
C	0100 0011
D	0100 0100
E	0100 0101
F	0100 0110
G	0100 0111
H	0100 1000
I	0100 1001
J	0100 1010
K	0100 1011
L	0100 1100
M	0100 1101
N	0100 1110
O	0100 1111
P	0101 0000
Q	0101 0001
R	0101 0010
S	0101 0011
T	0101 0100
U	0101 0101
V	0101 0110
W	0101 0111
X	0101 1000
Y	0101 1001
Z	0101 1010

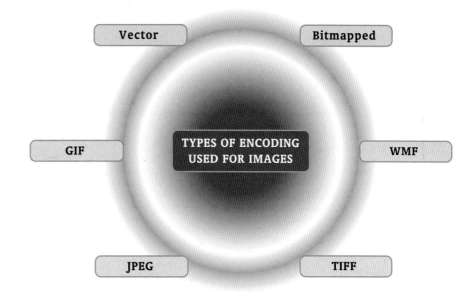

Vector — Bitmapped — GIF — **TYPES OF ENCODING USED FOR IMAGES** — WMF — JPEG — TIFF

Types of encoding for sound files

Sounds are not digital, so to save sounds on a computer requires the data to be encoded. Sound (i.e., speech and music) is quite complex and requires a lot of storage space, so to reduce the storage needed for sound files, a technique called compression is used during encoding.

There are many formats for sound files but here are the most popular ones:

- WAV – used with Windows for storing sounds. Files in this format are not highly compressed.
- MIDI (Musical Instrument Digital Interface) – used mainly to communicate between electronic keyboards, synthesisers and computers. MIDI files are compressed and the files are quite small.
- MP3 – this format uses compression to reduce the file size considerably and this is why the MP3 file format is so popular with portable music playing devices such as iPods.
- Shockwave Audio – used for very high quality sound with very small file size.

KEY WORDS

ASCII – a code for representing characters in binary

American Standard Code for Information Interchange (ASCII) – a code for representing characters in binary

Binary code – code made up from a series of binary digits – 0 or 1

Encoding – putting information/ data (e.g., text, numbers, symbols, images, sound and video) into a specified format that allows effective transmission or storage by an ICT system. This normally involves digitising the information

Unit 2 Living in the Digital World

Data and information: differences and details

Introduction

In this section you will learn about the difference between data and information and how data is processed to produce information. Information is a valuable commodity and its worth is determined by its quality. This section will also explain how the quality of information can be assessed.

The differences between data and information

Data are the raw values put into, stored and processed by a data processing system and that information is produced together with a context that adds meaning.

Raw data is relative because data processing often occurs in stages so the 'processed data' from one stage can be the raw data for the next stage of processing.

| £23,712 | £28,932 | £35,067 |

The above set of numbers is data. It tells us nothing because there is no context. We do not know if they are a premiership player's weekly wage, the price of a car or the value of sales of own brand baked beans in a week. No new knowledge is gained by looking at these figures and on their own, they are impossible to understand.

If we are told that the data refers to the first three months' sales of baked beans in a store, then 'the first three months' sales have steadily increased' is information. 'Sales for the second month have increased by 22% and for the third month by 17.5%' is information.

Information informs you of something you did not already know or it is presented in a way that has meaning and is useful. Converting data (sometimes called raw data) is what ICT systems do.

Information

Information comes from the processing of data. People or computers can find patterns in data which gives them information and the information enhances their knowledge about the subject.

Information is data which has been:

* processed
* converted to give it meaning
* organised in some way.

A word of warning about the terms information and data

In general usage, the words information and data are often used interchangeably. However, in ICT there is a very clear and distinct difference between the terms and you must be very precise in using and explaining them.

It is extremely important that you can distinguish between data and information.

Examples of processing are shown below:

Producing useful information

To be useful, information has to be meaningful to the person using it. Many information communications systems fail to give users the information they need and this is frustrating to users.

> **EXAM TIP**
>
> When asked to describe the difference between data and information you need to be very precise in your answer. In many ways it is better to remember a definition word for word, rather than try to put your own definition together.
>
> You may be asked to give an example to show that you understand the difference between the two terms. Remember, when giving your answer, that data is not a single value.

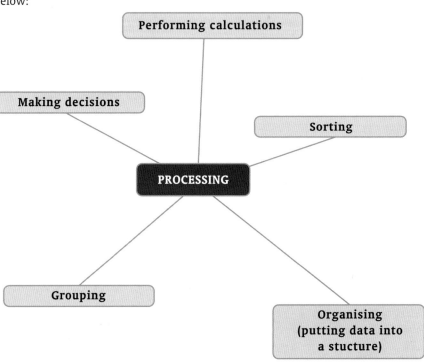

Performing calculations

Making decisions

Sorting

PROCESSING

Grouping

Organising (putting data into a stucture)

Quality of information

Some information is better than other information. For example, you need to decide how reliable the information is. This is particularly important, as decisions are usually made on the basis of the information. The quality of the information is a measure of:

- the accuracy of the information
- how easy the information is to understand
- the relevance for a particular use
- how up-to-date the information is.

Here are some examples of the above:

Accuracy – credit card statements must have the correct rate of interest applied to the balance, otherwise customers will complain and the card company could be prosecuted.

How easy the information is to understand – a copy of personal information has been sent to a customer and this contains coded information which they do not understand. The company would waste time explaining the codes.

The relevance for a particular use – a group has asked their record company for a breakdown of their royalties for all months over the last three years and the record company only gave them the total royalties for each year. The group wanted to look at the seasonal variations in their royalties but the information given would not show this.

How up-to-date the information is – food is usually date stamped so that after a certain date it would be best not to eat it.

Information should be date stamped as using out-of-date information could result in problems such as bills being sent to the wrong address, decisions being based on incorrect information and so on.

All reports and printouts from a computer should be date stamped so that the user knows how recent the information is.

A report showing out of stock items in a store printed out on Monday should not be used to place orders for more stock on a Friday, as many more items would have gone out of stock by then and there is the possibility that more stock may have replaced previously out of stock items.

Timeliness of information – if a business can identify from its ICT systems, users that are about to make a purchase or change something in their lives, then they will be at a huge competitive advantage. For example, if a marketing questionnaire was sent out containing the question: 'Are you thinking about switching your credit card to one with an introductory rate of 0% interest?', then if some promotional material about a new credit card were to drop through the letterbox the day after, the response rate would be high.

The importance of keeping data up-to-date

There is a requirement under the Data Protection Act 1998 for anyone who processes personal data to keep that information accurate and up-to-date.

It is very difficult for a business to do this alone. For example, if you move house, you are likely to tell your bank, credit card companies, utility companies (gas, electricity, telephone, etc.) but unlikely to tell the company you booked a holiday with last year so they can stop sending you brochures.

There are companies that keep details of people who:

- have moved house (including their new address)
- have deceased
- have asked not to be sent unsolicited mail (i.e., mail that they have not asked for)
- have never responded to a mail-shot.

The companies provide a service where you can update your data with all the changes.

You are probably wondering where these organisations get this data. Here is where it comes from:

- The moving details come from the utility companies who are contacted with the new address details when people move.
- The deceased data comes from the Registers of Births, Marriages and Deaths.

- The people who do not want to be sent mail-shots comes from a database set up by the Mailing Preference Service (MPS).
- Data concerning people who have never responded to a mail-shot comes from all the companies who send mail-shots who pool this information together.

Processing huge amounts of data

Sometimes the main problem with data is that there is too much rather than too little. Within hours of the terrorist attack on the London Underground on 7 July, police were gathering huge amounts of data which included:

- CCTV footage
- mobile phone records
- witness statements.

They managed to process all of the available data and managed to arrest the people involved.

Processing huge amounts of data requires a powerful computer coupled with sophisticated software.

Questions and Activities

▶ Questions 1 | pp. 130–131

1 Explain, by giving a relevant example in each case, the difference between coding data and encoding data. (4 marks)

2 Data is often coded so that less data needs to be entered into the computer which saves time typing and also reduces the likelihood of the user contracting RSI.
Give **one** different reason why data is sometimes coded. (2 marks)

3 Look at the following:
12, 23, 3, 42, 76, 16, 29
(a) Can you understand what these numbers mean? (1 mark)
(b) Explain, giving a reason, whether the numbers are data or information. (2 marks)

4 Data can take different forms.
Give the names of **three** different forms that data can take. (3 marks)

▶ Questions 2 | pp. 132–133

1 By giving a suitable example, explain the difference between data and information. (3 marks)

2 An IT manager explains that 'data is processed to produce information'.
Give **three** distinctly different examples of processing. (3 marks)

▶ Activity 1 Is it data or information?

For this exercise you need to decide whether each of these examples is data or information.
1 A bar code on a tin of baked beans.
2 A graph showing the way sales have varied over a twelve-month period.
3 Your bank balance has jumped 102%.
4 12.78.
5 A graph showing how the annual mean temperature varies with latitude.

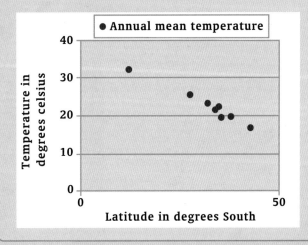

▶ Activity 2 What codes are these?

Codes are all around us. Here are some popular codes. Can you work out what the codes are used for and where you have seen examples of each code being used?
1   10/12/76
2   M or F
3   L23 5TA
4   01519307766
5   90-12-45
6   LPL, MAN, LGW, LHR
7   GB, F, CH, D

Exam support

Worked example 1

1 Data is encoded before being processed by an ICT system.
Describe what data encoding means. (2 marks)

Student answer 1

1 Encoding means turning the data into a code. You could have a code for each course in a college, like this ASICT01 means AS level ICT Group 1. It saves typing in the whole thing.

Examiner's comment

1 This student has mixed up coding data before input and encoding during input.
Encoding and coding are frequently mixed up and this has cost this student the two marks. **(0 marks out of 2)**

Student answer 2

1 Encoding means putting the data into a code during input into the ICT system. For example, when a bar code is read by the computer, a binary code is input into the computer which the computer can understand and process.

Examiner's comment

1 The student needed to make it clear that the 'putting' the data into a code is actually done by the input device although later on the example is clearly explained. As the student has mentioned that the code is produced during input (rather than before or during the collection) this is enough for two marks.
(2 marks out of 2)

Examiner's answers

1 One mark each for two of the following:
The data is converted to binary (or a code) during input (1) which can be understood by the computer (1) and can be saved for subsequent use in a file format understood by the computer such as ASCII or bitmap (1).

Worked example 2

2 A old photograph is scanned in using a scanner so that it can be used on a website. The software used by the scanner encodes the image and then stores it so that it can be added to a webpage.
Give the names of two types of encoding that can be used. (2 marks)

Student answer 1

2 MP3
Bitmapped

Examiner's comment

2 MP3 is a compressed file format for music and not a type of encoding used for images. Bitmapped is a type of encoding used with images. **(1 mark out of 2)**

Student answer 2

2 JPEG
BMP

Examiner's comment

2 Both file formats are acceptable for images.
(2 marks out of 2)

Examiner's answers

2 Any two types of encoding for images (one mark each) such as:

Bitmapped	JPEG (Joint Photographic Experts Group)
Vector	TIFF
Compressed bitmapped	GIF
WMF	

Data and information: aspects of data

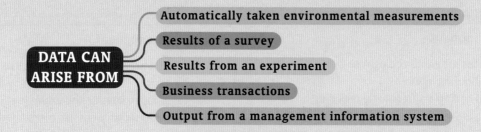

Data and information: quality of information

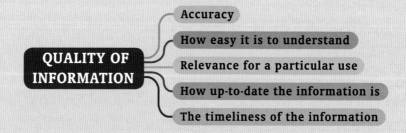

ICT systems are designed for people and are used by people for a particular purpose. In this topic you will be looking at the characteristics of users and how ICT systems need to take these characteristics into account. You will also be looking at how users interact with ICT systems and why this is important when providing systems that should communicate effectively with users. You will look at different types of user interface and their relative advantages and disadvantages.

▼ The key concepts covered in this topic are:

▶ ICT systems are designed for and used by people

▶ ICT systems are commissioned for a purpose

▶ Characteristics of users

▶ How users interact with ICT systems

▶ Working in ICT

CONTENTS

Unit 2 Living in the Digital World

People and ICT systems and characteristics of users

Introduction

Users are all different. They are usually different ages with different educational backgrounds, interests and ICT experience. Because of this, producing systems that everyone can use is challenging. If you make things too simple, you may annoy or frustrate experienced users. The challenge is to produce systems capable of being used by your average user.

Characteristics of users

Users are the people who use the systems designed by others on a day-to-day basis. In many cases they will spend long periods using these systems, which could be a major part of their work. There is therefore an obligation on people who design and develop these systems to make them as easy and user friendly as possible.

Users have differing requirements dependent upon:

- experience
- physical characteristics
- environment of use
- task to be undertaken
- age.

Experience

When a new system is introduced most users will need to be trained to use it. In small organisations this may not be feasible and users will be expected

to learn the new software themselves using manuals, on-line tutorials and books. Users will all have different experience in using ICT and any ICT solution needs to take this into account.

Physical characteristics

People with special or particular needs need to use computers as do disabled people. ICT systems can present these people with many new opportunities and make their lives more fulfilling.

Users with a sensory impairment – the user may not be able to read the letters on the screen properly – use a font that is easy to read and make sure that the size of the font is large enough for these users to read.

If a person is blind, then ICT can help them by the use of a 'talking' computer where the words are spoken when typed in by the user, or output on the computer. Blind users can also use special Braille keyboards to enter data and they can use Braille printers to produce output in Braille with raised dots.

Users with a physical disability – this usually affects the user's mobility. For example, they may not be able to use their arms or hands or may be unable to walk. In some cases the

disability is so severe that the person is almost paralysed.

People who are unable to write because of their disability can use voice-activated systems to put data into the computer.

Environment of use

ICT systems may be used:

- at home
- on the move (on trains, planes, etc.)
- at work.

The requirements of any ICT system must take this into account. For example, the screen on a laptop is generally smaller than with a desktop computer, so systems may need to have a less cluttered screen design, if the system is to be used mainly on laptop computers.

Task to be undertaken

The task to be undertaken will determine the user requirements. For example, if there is a lot of text to be entered, then you would need to look at the possibility of entering the text without the user having to type it in. Automatic methods of data entry could be used, making use of MICR, OCR and OMR. If none of these techniques are suitable, then a system making use of voice recognition could be considered.

The user requirements for a website could be:

- easy to navigate – to quickly find the information they require
- regular updates – so they do not rely on wrong information
- use of the correct font, font colour, font size, background, etc., to make text easy to read
- fast load times – so they do not waste time waiting for webpages to load.

Age

Age is a big factor when designing systems. You would not design the interface for a piece of multimedia software aimed at primary school children in the same way as for an adult user.

As people are living longer there are more older people who want to use ICT systems. They may want to keep in touch with children and grandchildren who may be located all over the world. They may want to use chat rooms to make new friends. As they have more time on their hands, older people are making full use of the benefits that ICT brings.

Ways in which the accessibility of a website or other ICT system can be improved

Websites and other ICT systems are often designed to be used by the general public. This would include people of all ages, all nationalities, in different situations (at work, for leisure, etc.), with a range of disabilities, with different educational backgrounds and different ICT skills. This covers just about everyone.

Look at the following showing what can be done to make a website more accessible to users:

Use plain, simple language.

Explain difficult words or phrases.

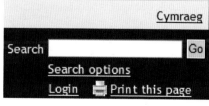

Offer different languages. This site can be translated into Welsh.

Read Text

Allow a user to have the webpage read out aloud to them – ideal for people with sight impairment.

Text smaller

Text larger

Allow a user to change the size of the text.

Allow a user to change the colour of the text and background.

Provide users with on-line help.

How users interact with ICT systems

Introduction

Humans need to interact with ICT systems and this needs to be done in the most effective way, taking into account the characteristics of the users. There needs to be an effective dialogue between humans and machines. The commonest interface involves using a graphical user interface (GUI), with the user issuing instructions and making selections using the mouse. In this section you will be looking at the different types of user interface and how user interfaces can be designed to provide effective communication between the ICT systems and users.

You should already know quite a lot about interfaces as you came across them when looking at systems software in Unit 1 Topic 7: Selection and use of appropriate software.

The need for effective dialogue between humans and machines

When using any ICT device, there needs to be a dialogue between the machine and the human user. The user needs to be able to issue instructions to the device to tell it what to do and the device needs to tell the user what to do or if there is a problem, what that problem is.

Human/computer interfaces provide the means by which the user can tell the computer what to do and at the same time the computer can interact with the human user by giving them a response. These interfaces are important because they determine how easy it is to use the ICT system to do a certain task.

The standard interface for the human inputting data into the computer is via the keyboard with the computer giving its response on the screen. This is not the only type of human/computer interface, although it is fair to say that it is the most common. There are many other systems that make use of ICT and need another type of interface. Process control screens, digital TVs, mobile phones, computer games, cockpit controls on fly-by-wire aircraft, information systems that can be used by members of the public, all make use of innovative user interfaces.

Appropriate interface design to provide effective communication for users

If you are playing a game such as simulating driving a Formula One racing car around the track, then you would

▼ **You will find out**

▶ About the need for effective dialogue between humans and machines

▶ About how interfaces can be designed to provide effective communications for users

▶ About the need for the provision of appropriate help and support for users of ICT systems

▶ About the benefits and limitations of different types of user interface

want the game to be as realistic as possible. You can easily show the view of the cockpit on a computer and it is easy to show the indicators and the instruments on the screen. All this adds to the realism. The part that would let the game down might be the human/computer interface. The worst interface would be using the cursor keys and other keys to steer the car, change gear, accelerate and so on. A better interface would be to use a joystick, although this will not be ideal as cars are normally fitted with steering wheels, gear sticks and foot pedals. You can actually buy these to make the interface as near to the real thing as possible.

The interface must be designed to enable the user to communicate effectively with the device and to also enable the device to communicate with the user.

A graphical user interface (GUI) is the most popular human/computer interface used by software manufacturers for systems and applications software. With a GUI the mouse is used as the main input device. You will remember that a GUI consists of some or all of the following features:

- windows
- icons
- menus
- pointers
- desktop
- drag and drop
- taskbars.

Command-driven interfaces

With command-driven interfaces the user has to remember and issue commands to the ICT system to get it to do something. Sometimes the commands are entered using the keyboard and sometimes they are entered using lists of commands.

Natural language interfaces

It would be easy if we could issue instructions to the ICT system in the same way that we can issue instructions to another human. This would be the ideal interface for us, as it is the way humans communicate with each other. There are interfaces that are able to do this and they are called natural language interfaces.

> **KEY WORDS**
>
> **Interface** – the point where two objects meet. In ICT this is usually between a device such as a computer, printer, scanner, etc., and a human

The need for the provision of appropriate help and support for the users of ICT systems

Everyone has been a beginner at using ICT systems at some time. It can be frustrating to know what you want to do but not be sure how to do it. This is where help screens come in.

On-line help

All software packages should have an on-line help facility where users can get help supplied by the package, rather than have to look through manuals or user guides.

On-line help for novice users

Some help screens can be very off-putting and frequently use unfamiliar terms in their explanations. Help screens should explain things simply and giving the user examples best does this.

Most users perform a variety of tasks using the software and are expert at some tasks whilst novice at others. Besides providing help should the user need it, the software should recognise and anticipate the users' goals and offer assistance to make the task easier. Microsoft Office uses Wizards that help you through some of the more complex tasks. This form of assistance allows the users to accomplish their tasks in as short a period as possible.

Appropriate training

Users should not be left to figure out new ICT systems for themselves. It is much more productive to train them properly on any new systems they have to use. There are a number of ways this can be done:

- on-line tutorials which guide them through the essential features of the system
- interactive multimedia training resources provided on CD-ROM or DVD
- classroom face-to-face teaching/training
- paper-based instructional guides
- individual tuition on a one-to-one basis.

Existing user base

If you are working in an office with other more experienced users and you encounter a problem with a particular piece of software, then it may be prudent to ask someone you work with for their help before approaching anyone else. It is reckoned that about 80% of IT problems are solved by

non-IT staff. If the problem cannot be solved in this way, then you can make a telephone call to a help-desk that may be in-house (i.e., within the company) or provided externally by the company who supplied the hardware or software.

Help-desks

Problems will always occur when people use ICT systems and these problems can often leave the user unable to use the facility. This can be frustrating to users.

In most large organisations user support is provided by the use of help-desks. Help-desks are usually manned by someone from the IT department, although with the growth of outsourcing, the help-desk could be outside the organisation. Their purpose is to give expert advice to users regarding any software and hardware problems they might have.

As most organisations use networks, it is possible for staff on the help-desk to look at the user's screen and offer them advice over the phone without actually leaving their desk.

The benefits and limitations of different types of user interface

These were covered in Unit 1 Topic 7: Selection and use of appropriate software. You should look over this.

Working in ICT

▼ You will find out

▶ About the many different jobs available to ICT professionals

▶ About the personal qualities and general characteristics necessary for an ICT professional to work effectively within the industry

▶ About the characteristics of an effective ICT team

Introduction

The area of ICT is dynamic and fast moving and ICT professionals are constantly needed, to keep abreast of the technology and provide managers and users with the best possible systems. This section will introduce you to the types of jobs in ICT and what personal qualities and characteristics you need to take up such as job.

You will also look at what makes an effective ICT team.

The many different jobs available to ICT professionals

There are many different roles in ICT and many of the roles tend to overlap in small organisations. The main roles held by ICT professionals are:

- business analyst/systems analyst/ project manager
- software developer/programmer
- web designer
- IT trainer
- technician/engineer/network administrator
- help-desk operator.

All the above roles also have management positions, where the person would be responsible for the management of a team of people.

The difference between technical skills and personal skills

Technical skills are those skills that are necessary in order to complete a specific job in ICT. For example, a software developer would need programming skills in a particular computer language in which the program is being written. Programming is a technical skill and not a personal skill.

Personal skills are those skills a person possesses and which are transferable to any job or task. Examples of personal skills are shown on the right:

Business analyst/systems analyst

Typical roles of a business/systems analyst/project manager include:

- Interview business users to determine their requirements for the system.
- Apply the techniques of systems analysis to business problems.
- Be knowledgeable about the technical options for a particular business problem.
- Work with developers and other computer professionals in teams.
- Work within a budget to produce the best system to solve a business problem.

Technical skills needed:

- Knowledge of formal techniques – to be able to apply all the techniques of systems analysis to solve business problems.
- Knowledge of the application of hardware/software – to be able to understand what is technically possible.
- A good understanding of both business and ICT – so that they understand the business problem being solved and can use the best ICT solution.
- Project management skills – to coordinate the activities of everyone involved in a project.

Personal skills needed:

- Communication skills – to be able to talk to users about what they want from the system and to present ideas to management.
- Written skills – to be able to produce clear reports to managers, software developers, etc.
- Ability to work in teams – to be able to brief ICT staff such as software developers, web designers, etc.
- Problem solving skills – to be logical in going about solving a business problem.
- Attention to detail – need to be meticulous about attention to detail.

Software developer/programmer

Typical roles of a software developer/ programmer include:

- Writing new programs to solve business problems as per the brief given by the business/systems analyst.

- Altering existing programming code to get the programs to work differently.
- Debugging and testing programs to remove errors.
- Producing program documentation.

Technical skills needed include:

- Programming skills – need to be proficient in a programming language such as Visual Basic.
- Testing skills – need to be able to thoroughly test programs to ensure they are 'bug' free.

Personal skills needed include:

- Problem solving skills – need to be able to solve problems by the writing of programming code.
- Ability to work in teams – need to work with other programmers, business analysts working on the same project.
- Meticulous in attention to detail – small errors can cause programs to crash, so detail is extremely important.
- Ability to work under pressure – programs are written to deadlines, so pressure is always on to complete tasks on time.

Web designer/administrator

Typical roles of a web designer/ administrator include:

- Creating websites that are functional and look good.
- Liaising with other staff who supply content for the website.
- Using programming skills and graphic design skills to create webpages.
- Liaising with other business and technical staff.
- Make changes to an existing website to cope with the changing demands of the website.
- Ensure that the website works with the back-office software such as order processing, payment and accounts packages.
- Evaluating the effectiveness of the website using user comments.

Technical skills include:

- Proficiency in web design packages – need to be able create websites and webpages using web design packages such as Dreamweaver.
- Design skills – need to understand elements of design to produce webpages that are attractive, eye-catching and functional.
- Understanding of networks – to be able to link the website to other systems such as stock control and accounts.
- Knowledge of psychology – to understand how users interact with websites.

Personal skills needed:

- Creative skills – to produce eye-catching designs.
- Communication skills – to be able to liaise with other staff.
- Willingness to keep up-to-date – as the designs and expectations of websites change over time.

- Listening skills – so that they understand fully the purpose of the website and how it will be used.

Help-desk operator

Typical roles of a help-desk operator include:

- Helping users with their ICT problems.
- Answering user problems by telephone.
- Finding out whether a problem needs a visit by an engineer.

Technical skills needed include:

- Good knowledge of software/ systems being used or willingness to learn about them – to answer user/customer problems.
- Networking skills – so that network problems can be solved remotely.
- Hardware skills – need to be able to detect hardware problems.

▶ Activity 1 Investigating careers in ICT

There are huge opportunities in ICT for interesting and well-paid employment. Here is a website which is used by many ICT professionals to find jobs:

> http://www.computingcareers.co.uk
> Use the above site to research each of the following ICT jobs:
> - **business analyst**
> - **software developer**
> - **web designer.**

Produce a written summary for each job outlining the personal and technical skills needed.

Copyright 2005 by Randy Glasbergen.
www.glasbergen.com

'When he walked into my office, I knew he was the perfect geek to join our IT team. His shoelaces were USB cables.'

Personal skills needed include:

- Listening skills – to make sure the user's problem is correctly understood.
- Communication skills – to be able to explain clearly to users what they need to do to solve the problem.
- Ability to work under pressure – user may become frustrated with events such as a queue of customers being unable to pay for their goods at a point of sale terminal.
- Willingness to learn new skills – in order to keep up-to-date with the latest software.
- Ability to work as part of a team – sometimes collective skills and experience are needed to solve a tricky problem.
- Approachable – so that users do not feel stupid when they ask for help.

ICT trainer

Typical roles of an ICT trainer include:

- Designing courses to help users.
- Delivering courses to users on software packages, procedures, new programs, etc.
- Keeping up-to-date with the latest developments in ICT.

Technical skills include:

- Skills in the software being used.
- Trouble-shooting skills – to sort problems out.
- Business skills – in order to understand how the users are likely to use the ICT systems.

Personal skills needed include:

- Teaching skills – being able to explain systems/software to users so they understand how to use them.
- Technical knowledge – a good understanding of the material being taught is essential.
- Communication skills – needed to impart knowledge and skills during training sessions.

© Randy Glasbergen, 1996.

'I want everyone at the meeting to dress up like Lego blocks. Then we can see exactly how each team member interlocks with the other team members in the project.'

- Willingness to keep skills up-to-date – need to ensure that they understand and can explain to others all the latest developments in ICT.

Technician/network administrator

Typical roles of a technician/network administrator include:

- Installing hardware and software.
- Maintaining all the equipment including networks.
- Ensuring that all programs and data on the server are safely backed up.
- Upgrading hardware and software.
- Archiving files.
- Repairing hardware and correcting software faults.
- Setting up user accounts with user-IDs and passwords.
- Setting up permitted levels of access for different users.

- Checking that all security hardware/software is working properly and is up-to-date.

Personal skills needed include:

- Good technical knowledge – need to fully understand the workings of hardware, software and networks.
- Problem solving skills – need a systematic way to solve user problems with equipment and software.

Effective ICT teams

ICT projects are usually too large and complex to be completed by a single person and are normally completed by an ICT team. A project which would take one person five years to complete should only take ten people six months to complete.

Each person in the team brings different types of expertise and experience to the project.

Advantages of working in teams

- The project manager can assign tasks to the team member with the most appropriate experience and skills to carry them out.
- Team members are able to bounce ideas off each other.

- The project can be completed in a reasonable time frame.
- If a member of the project team leaves, then there is always someone else with project knowledge to take over.
- Teams are able to help and motivate each other.
- Teams can produce work which is far superior to that produced individually.
- Team members can work collaboratively on a project.

Disadvantages of working in teams

- Project teams are harder to manage.
- Team members may fall out, causing friction.
- Some people are better working on their own and do not like to be dependent on others.
- If one team member does not complete their task on time, then it can affect other team members and cause their tasks to run late.
- Lots of meetings are needed to coordinate all the activities.
- Team members are dependent on each other.

Leading an ICT team

Team leaders are usually chosen for a particular project, as they will need specialist knowledge and skills in the area of the business which the project covers. This means that a team leader for one project might be a member of the project team for a different project.

The success or failure of a project rests with the team leader, so it is essential to choose a team leader with these skills:

- Leadership skills to ensure all team members have faith in the decisions being made and to make sure everyone in the team works well together.
- Technical skills and knowledge about the area of business being developed.
- Management skills to be able to assign tasks to team members who are the most capable of carrying them out.
- Skills in using project management software – team leaders need to use software to manage the project to produce critical path analysis charts and Gantt charts.

'I'm pleased to report that our project is ahead of schedule and under budget... not bad for the first hour!'

- Previous team leader experience to understand all the likely pitfalls and problems.
- Skills in budget control to make sure that the project does not go over budget.
- Being able to work under pressure, especially being able to deal with the unexpected (technical problems, staff illness, etc.).
- Presentation skills – being able to present proposals to ICT and non-ICT staff.
- Motivational skills – to be able to bring out the best work in their team members.

Good project managers are judged by how well their solution works and whether it is completed on time and under budget.

Skills of team members

The main skills for any ICT professional are as follows:

- problem solving skills
- strong communication skills
- ability to work in teams – team working skills
- be able to adhere to deadlines – time management skills.

EXAM TIP

As always, read the question carefully.

Check the meaning of every word in the question.

Do not read anything into the question that is not there.

Questions and Activities

Questions 1 pp. 138–139

1 Users of ICT systems can be identified as having certain characteristics. Give **one** reason why each of the following characteristics needs to be taken into account for these users.
   (a) Age (1 mark)
   (b) Physical characteristics (1 mark)
2 You have been asked to develop a website for retired people. State, giving reasons, **three** things you would need to consider in your design for these users. (3 marks)

Questions 2 pp. 140–141

1 Give the names of **three** different types of user interface. (3 marks)
2 A user is having problems using a new ICT system. Describes **two** ways in which help can be given to this user. (4 marks)

Questions 3 pp. 144–145

1 ICT projects are usually completed by ICT teams. Give **three** reasons why projects are completed by teams rather than by an individual. (6 marks)
2 An e-commerce site is to be set up for a completely new business. An ICT project team is to be set up and suitably qualified people need to be appointed to various roles.
   (a) Give **three** skills each of the following people should possess in order to carry out their role effectively.
      (i) Software developer (3 marks)
      (ii) Business analyst (3 marks)
      (iii) Web designer (3 marks)
   (b) There needs to be someone in overall charge of the project team. Give **three** skills the team leader/project manager must have. (3 marks)
3 You are employed as a manager responsible for the help-desk team. One of your team members leaves and you write a job advertisement for the local paper.
   Describe **two** personal qualities that a person employed in the help-desk team would need to have. (4 marks)

▶ Activity Personal qualities needed for a person employed as a member of a help-desk team

In the following table there is a list of the qualities needed by a member of a help-desk team. The reasons for the quality are jumbled up. You have to match the reason to the correct quality.

Personal quality	Reason
Good oral communication skills	Problems often prevent users from completing a task so they will want you to help no matter how busy you are
Willingness to learn new skills	So that users are not put off asking them for help
Approachable	Ability to work out a series of questions to analyse the problem
Ability to work under pressure	To talk to users to explain clearly what they need to do to solve their problem
Prepared to work flexible hours	To enable them to understand all the organisation's systems and software
Good team worker	Able to exchange information with other members to build up a body of knowledge
Good written communication skills	So that user problems can be documented and analysed to see if software could be improved
Logical approach to problem solving	Users will expect a speedy reply to their problems sometimes at any time in the day or night they are working

Exam support

Worked example 1

1 An organisation is creating a new system and needs a large ICT team to plan, design and implement it.
   Describe **four** characteristics of a good ICT project team. (8 marks)

Student answer 1

1 Problem solving skills to help solve ICT problems.
   A willingness to learn new skills to help the organisation.
   People who work well together and will help each other.
   People who will develop ideas with others and produce good
   collective work.

Examiner's comment

1 The first two characteristics do not specifically apply
   to an ICT project team and are personal skills, so no
   marks for these two answers. The student needed to
   tailor their answer to team work.

   It is important for the student to look at the marks
   allocated here. Two marks for each characteristic
   means that the characteristic will need to be clear and
   then there is some further explanation or amplification
   which explains why the characteristic improves the
   performance of the team.

   The third answer gives two characteristics but does
   not give a reason how this helps. Only worth one of
   the two marks.

   The fourth answer has given an appropriate
   characteristic and a mention of how it applies to
   working in teams so this is worth two marks. **(3 marks
   out of 8)**

Student answer 2

1 Team made up of people with different expertise and strengths so
   that there are no weaknesses in the solution in certain parts.
   Team made up with members who can produce much better work
   as a team than they ever could on their own.
   Team has got members who are willing to agree with what needs
   to be done and how to do it, so that they can concentrate on their
   contribution.
   Good team leadership by a project manager who will motivate
   and help solve any problems team members may have.

Examiner's comment

1 All of the answers have identified a characteristic
   and have clearly explained why this characteristic is
   important in members of an ICT team, so full marks for
   this question. **(8 marks out of 8)**

Examiner's answers

1 Any four characteristics (one mark for the characteristic and one mark for further
   explanation) similar to the following:
   A team consisting of people who bring complementary skills to a problem, so
   they are able to bring strengths and skills in different areas.
   A team consisting of people who work well together and bring support to each
   other, so that they do not waste time arguing with each other.
   Able to share and bounce ideas off each other so that different solutions to
   problems can be explored and developed.
   Can produce a much better solution to a problem than any team member could
   produce individually.
   Contains individuals who respect other team members' opinions so every
   solution is explored and the best chosen.

Unit 2 Living in the Digital World

Exam support continued

Worked example 2

2 Projects being developed inevitably have problems. A good project team leader will be able to deal with and solve such problems.

(a) Describe **four** types of problem the project leader could face when dealing with an ICT team. (8 marks)

(b) Describe **two** skills a project manager should possess in order to be able to deal with the problems you have outlined. (2 marks)

Student answer 1

2 (a) A member of the team being ill for a long time.
Team members refusing to work with each other.
Only some of the team working hard while the others sit back.
The project going over budget.

(b) Diplomacy skills.
Budgeting skills.

Examiner's comment

2 In part (a) the student has not noticed that two marks have been allocated for each problem identified. They needed to identify the problem and then add some further explanation for the two marks.

All the answers to part (a) are correct but they needed to say a bit more – particularly what effect the problem might have on the project.

This student only gained half the marks for this part.

Part (b) has identified two skills relevant to part (a), so full marks for this part. **(6 marks out of 10)**

Examiner's answers

(a) One mark for the statement/name of the problem and one mark for a brief explanation of the problem.
A member going off sick or leaving – this would remove a person with a good knowledge of the problem being solved.
Members not agreeing with each other – this could waste time and cause friction in the team.
Keeping track of the parts of the project – more people involved means more time is spent keeping track of how the project is progressing.
Certain individuals working harder than others – having to manage people not pulling their weight and letting the team down.
Using too many resources – not sticking to the budget allocated.
Individuals not meeting deadlines – individual tasks running late can cause the whole project completion date to be delayed.

Student answer 2

2 (a) Staff arguing about and not reaching agreement on how to solve a particular ICT problem and thus causing friction with some team members.
A project running behind schedule and likely causing a delay in completion of the whole project due to team members not working hard enough at the start.
Staff not working well as a team and not sharing ideas and work which leads to the ICT solution not being the best they could produce.
Some people always taking time off sick, causing other staff to have to work harder to complete the project.

(b) Leadership skills to ensure all team members have faith in the decisions being made and to make sure everyone in the team works well together.
Management skills – to be able to bring out the best work in their team members and to make them feel as though they let the side down by being off.

Examiner's comment

2 (a) All four types of problem have been correctly identified and further explanation clearly shows understanding of the problem. Full marks for part (a).

(b) The main point here is that the skills that the manager must possess should be the skills to sort out the problems identified in part (a). Leadership skills and management skills are too like each other. Only one mark here.
(9 marks out of 10)

(b) One mark for a statement of each skill to a maximum of two marks.
Diplomacy
Enthusiasm
Project management skills
Budgeting skills
Motivational skills

Summary mind maps

People and ICT systems and characteristics of users

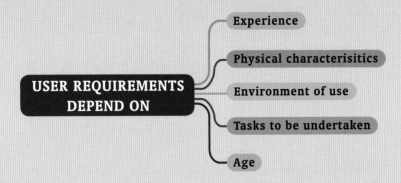

USER REQUIREMENTS DEPEND ON
- Experience
- Physical characterisitics
- Environment of use
- Tasks to be undertaken
- Age

Working in ICT

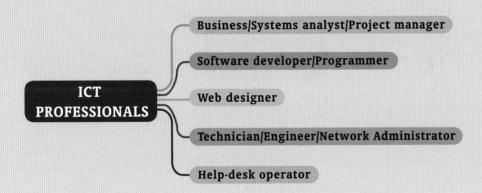

ICT PROFESSIONALS
- Business/Systems analyst/Project manager
- Software developer/Programmer
- Web designer
- Technician/Engineer/Network Administrator
- Help-desk operator

Working in teams

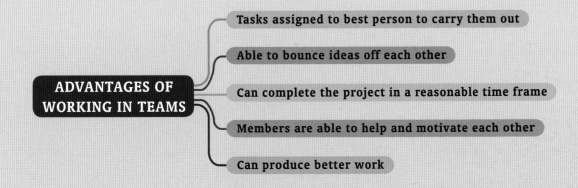

ADVANTAGES OF WORKING IN TEAMS
- Tasks assigned to best person to carry them out
- Able to bounce ideas off each other
- Can complete the project in a reasonable time frame
- Members are able to help and motivate each other
- Can produce better work

Summary mind maps
continued

How users interact with ICT systems

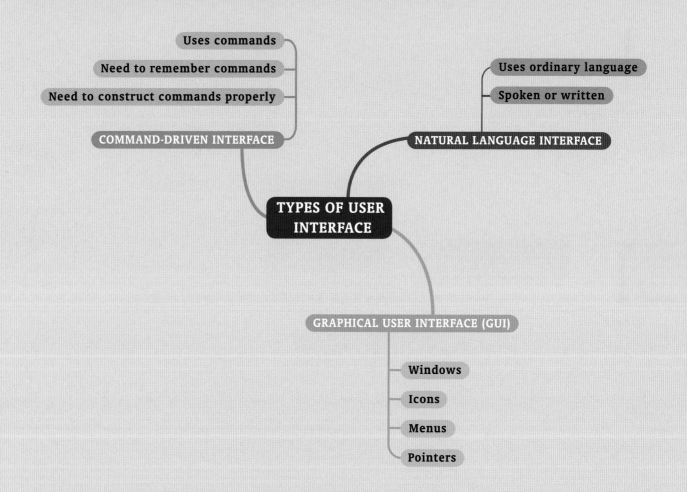

Nowadays most computers are connected to a network. If you connect your personal computer at home to the Internet then your computer becomes part of the network.

If a computer is used on its own without any connection (wireless or wire) to a network (including the Internet), then it is said to be a stand-alone computer.

The importance of being able to transfer data is the most important advantage in using a network and it is why networks are used in organisations of all sizes such as banks, schools, hospitals and shops as well as homes.

In this topic you will learn about how data is transferred in ICT systems.

▼ The key concepts covered in this topic are:

▶ Basic elements of an ICT network

▶ Characteristics of networks

▶ Use of communications technologies

▶ Standards

CONTENTS

Unit 2 Living in the Digital World

Basic elements of an ICT network: network components

▼ You will find out

▶ About communication devices

▶ About networking software

▶ About data transfer media

▶ About standards and procedures

▶ About ICT networks for different geographical scales and uses

Introduction

A basic network consists of a collection of computers and other hardware devices such as printers and scanners that are linked together so that they can communicate with each other.

Basic elements of an ICT network

There are four basic elements of an ICT network in addition to the computers themselves:

- communication devices
- networking software
- data transfer media
- standards and procedures.

Communication devices

Communication devices are those pieces of hardware that are needed to turn stand-alone computers into networked computers.

Network interface card (NIC)

Before a computer can be connected to a network it will need to have a network interface card. Most modern computers have these when you buy them. A network interface card is simply a card containing circuitry along with a socket. The socket allows the connection between the computer and the cabling. The card is simply slotted into the motherboard (the main circuit board) of the computer. The purpose of the network interface card is to convert the data from the form in which it is stored into a form that can be transmitted through the network media (e.g., metal cable, fibre optic cable or air).

Basically, a network interface card:

- prepares data for sending over the network
- sends the data
- controls the flow of data from the computer terminal to the transmission medium.

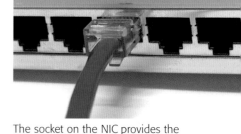

The socket on the NIC provides the connection to the transmission medium.

A network interface card (NIC).

Hub

A hub is a simple device which is used to join computers in a network so that they are able to share files and an Internet connection.

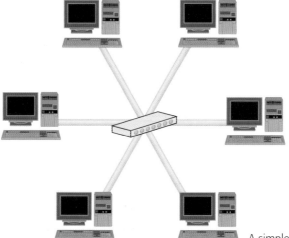

A simple network makes use of a hub.

KEY WORDS

Transmission medium – the material which forms the connection between the computers in a network (e.g., air in the case of wireless, metal wire, optical fibre)

Network – a group of computers that are able to communicate with each other

Networking software – this is systems software which allows computers connected together to function as a network

Switches (network switches)

Switches are similar to hubs in that they are used to join multiple computers together in a network. Switches, however, contain more intelligence because they are able to inspect packets of data so that they are forwarded appropriately. Because a switch only sends a packet of data to the computer it is intended for, it reduces the amount of data on the network, hence speeding the network up.

Routers

Routers are hardware devices that join several wired or wireless networks together.

Routers are usually a combination of hardware and software which often act as gateways so that small home computer networks can be connected to the Internet using a single connection.

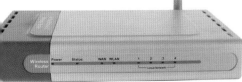

A wireless router.

Networking software

Networks need software to tell the connected devices how to communicate with each other.

Network operating systems software

Small networks can be run using existing Windows software, but for larger client-server networks, specialist network operating systems software is needed.

Network operating systems have more complexity because they need to coordinate the activities of all the computers and other devices connected to the network.

Examples of network operating system software include:

- UNIX
- Linux
- Novell Netware – this is a very popular client-server network operating system.

Network management software

If you were the network manager responsible for a network consisting of several hundred computers, you would need help in looking after them all to keep the network running.

Luckily there is software called network management software that will help you do this.

Some tasks the network management software would help with include:

- Making sure that all the computers have up-to-date software with the latest security patches, so that hackers cannot get into the network.
- Keeping track of the software being run on each computer and checking that there are licences for all the software being used.
- Keeping all application software up-to-date.
- Providing remote control facilities so that help-desk staff can sort a user's computer problem out by seeing exactly what is on the user's screen.
- Check that bandwidth is being used correctly.
- Finding out if a user has installed non-licensed software without permission on a networked computer.
- Checking the speed of the processor and the memory used for a particular computer on the network. This can be useful to identify computers that need upgrades.

Data transfer media

Data transfer media is the material through which data travels from one computer to another in a network. For small, simple networks, this is usually wire, but many networks are now implemented wirelessly. Wires add considerably to the cost of a network, especially the cost of installing them.

The main forms of data transfer media are:

- metal wires
- fibre optic cable
- wireless.

Metal wires

Metal wires offer a high transmission speed but they do need to be installed

Fibre optic cable.

and this can be expensive. There are three different types of wire.

Unshielded twisted pair

The main features are:

- thin wires are twisted to help cancel out interference
- thin wires mean easier installation
- only suitable for small networks.

Shielded twisted pair

The main features are:

- wires are twisted
- wires have a copper braiding which protects the data signals from outside interference/corruption
- more expensive than unshielded twisted pair
- greater transmission speeds than unshielded twisted pair.

Non-metal cables

Light travels faster than electricity, so this is why in many networks pulses of light are used to carry data.

Fibre optic cable

In fibre optic cable, the data being passed is encoded as pulses of light through a very thin glass fibre. Bundles of fibres are used to carry the data to and from the network.

The main advantages of fibre optic cable are:

- speed – the data travels much faster
- small size – a huge amount of data can travel through a very small cable
- lack of electrical interference – they do not suffer from interference like metal wires.

The main disadvantage is:

- cost – the devices needed to connect up the cable and the cable itself are more expensive.

Basic elements of an ICT network:
network components *continued*

No cables at all

Many computers are now able to connect to the Internet or communicate with other computers in a local area network wirelessly. With wireless communication, the data transfer medium is the air through which the radio waves travel.

Wireless

Wireless networks enable people to connect to the Internet or to a LAN wirelessly. This means they can work anywhere they can get a radio signal for their network.

Many people, especially people who travel a lot, need to access the Internet regularly. There are many public places where the Internet can be accessed wirelessly using a person's laptop computer or other portable devices such as mobile phone or PDA.

These places where you can access the Internet using Wi-Fi are called hot spots.

To set up a small Wi-Fi network you would need:

- a broadband connection to the Internet
- a router
- Wi-Fi enabled computers (most computers have a wireless adapter installed in them). You can buy wireless adapters for older computers.

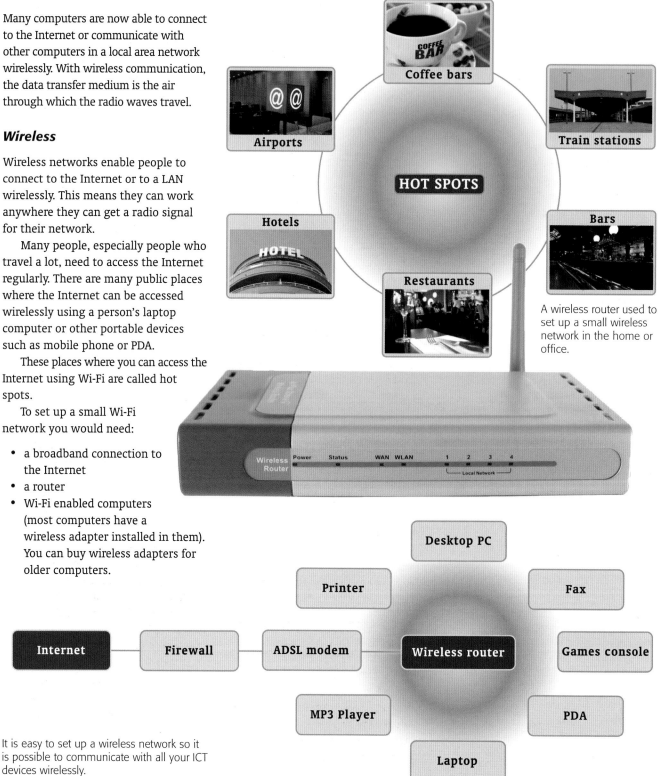

Coffee bars

Airports

Train stations

HOT SPOTS

Hotels

Bars

Restaurants

A wireless router used to set up a small wireless network in the home or office.

Wireless Router   Power   Status   WAN   WLAN   1   2   3   4   Local Network

Desktop PC

Printer

Fax

Internet — Firewall — ADSL modem — Wireless router — Games console

MP3 Player

PDA

Laptop

It is easy to set up a wireless network so it is possible to communicate with all your ICT devices wirelessly.

> **KEY WORDS**

Hot spot – a region where the Internet can be accessed wirelessly

Wi-Fi – a trademark for the certification of products that meet certain standards for transmitting data over wireless networks

How Wi-Fi works

1. The router is connected to the Internet by a high-speed broadband connection.
2. The router receives data from the Internet.
3. It transmits the data as a radio signal using an antenna.
4. The computer's wireless adapter picks up the signal and turns the radio signal into data that the computer can understand.

When sending data, the above processes work in reverse.

Wi-Fi zone sign.

Wi-Fi user.

Advantages of Wi-Fi:

- allows inexpensive LANS to be set up without cables
- allows people the freedom of working anywhere a signal can be received
- ideal for networks in old listed buildings where cables would not be allowed to be installed
- global set of standards – you can use Wi-Fi all over the world.

Disadvantages of Wi-Fi:

- power consumption is high – which means laptops soon exhaust their rechargeable batteries
- there may be health problems in using Wi-Fi
- there may be security problems even when encryption is used
- home networks have a very limited range (e.g., 150 ft)
- can get interference if wireless network signals start to overlap.

Network standards and procedures

For devices to communicate with each other in a network certain standards need to be used. Standards are important because without them, one device could be sending data to another device in a form that the other device does not understand.

Manufacturers of devices that are connected to networks agree these standards so that the devices can work together. Standards will be looked at in a later section in this topic.

In order for a network to run properly it is necessary to adopt certain procedures and make sure that all users are aware of them. Without proper procedures:

- the security of the network may be compromised
- the network may run slowly
- users may fall foul of legislation (e.g., Data Protection Act, Computer Misuse Act, etc.)
- work may be lost
- actions may inconvenience or annoy other users

- actions may cost the organisation time in terms of employee time needed to sort out problems.

ICT networks for different geographical scales and uses

ICT networks can be divided into two types:

- Local Area Networks (LANs)
- Wide Area Networks (WANs)

The geographical area covered by each of these networks is different with LANs being confined to a single building or site and WANs being distributed over multiple sites, even in other countries.

LANs

The main features of LANs are:

- Confined to single building or site – the hardware and communications equipment is contained in one building or site.
- Ownership of the communications equipment – the organisation actually own all the communications equipment (such as wiring, etc.) that links the terminals.

WANs

The main features of WANs are:

- Hardware is spread over a wide geographical area – devices (computers, point-of-sale terminals, storage, etc.) are spread over a wide geographical area. The devices are spread over multiple buildings and sites.
- Third party telecommunications equipment is used – hardware in a WAN is situated in many sites, which can be in different countries. Telephone, radio and satellite communications are needed, which are supplied by a third party (e.g., BT). The organisation with the WAN has to rent these services from a telecommunications supplier.

Basic elements of an ICT network: network topologies and types

Introduction

In this section you will look at the way the terminals in a network are linked. We use the word linked rather than connected, as many networks are wireless.

This section will also cover the two main types of network: peer-to-peer and client-server.

Network topologies

The devices in a network can be set up in many different ways and the way this is done is called the topology.

A network topology shows how the computers are connected when wires are used and if wireless (radio, infra-red and microwaves) is used, it shows how the devices in the network communicate with each other.

The ring topology

This is a ring network which is also a peer-to-peer network because there is no server.

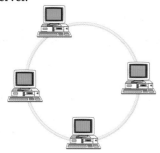

With the ring topology:

- all the computers are arranged in circle
- data sent by one computer passes around the ring until it reaches the correct computer.

Advantages of ring networks:

- easy to add extra devices
- each computer has the same access as the others so no one computer can 'hog' the network.

Disadvantages of ring networks:

- if there is a break in the connection (wire or wireless), then the whole network fails
- faults are difficult to locate
- it is impossible to keep the network running whilst equipment is added or removed because there is only one path for the data to follow.

The bus topology

With a bus topology, all the devices connected to the network are connected to a common shared cable called the backbone. Signals are passed in either direction along the backbone.

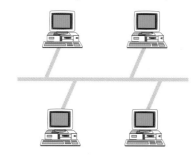

Advantages of bus topology networks:

- cost effective because of the small amount of cable needed
- simple cable runs makes it easy to install
- easy to add extra devices to the network.

Disadvantages of bus topology networks:

- if more than about 12 devices are connected to the network, then the performance of the network is degraded
- if there is a break in the backbone cable, then the network cannot be used.

The star topology

The star topology uses a central connection point to connect all the devices on the network together. The central connection point can be a hub, a switch or a router.

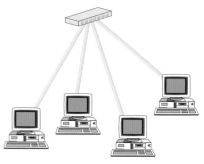

Advantages of star topology networks:

- fault tolerant – if one of the cables fails, then the other computers can still be used
- load tolerant – extra computers can be added without much loss in performance because all computers have their own path to the hub
- easy to add extra computers – extra computers can be added without disturbing the network.

Disadvantages of star topology networks:

- higher cost – the large amount of cabling needed makes it a more expensive topology
- dependence on the central hub/ switch or router – if the device at the centre of the network fails, then the whole network will fail.

The mesh topology

Unlike the other topologies, data sent using a mesh topology can take several different paths to its destination.

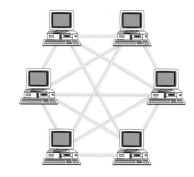

Advantages of mesh topology networks:

- fault tolerant – as there are many paths data can take to get to its destination, if one of the paths fails, there is always another path that can be taken
- easy to locate faults.

Disadvantages of mesh topology networks:

- higher cost – there are lots of cable runs needed to create a mesh network
- harder to maintain – the greater length of cable means that the network is harder to set up and maintain.

Peer-to-peer or client-server

Networks can be divided into two main types:

- peer-to-peer
- client-server.

Peer-to-peer (P2P) networks

Peer-to-peer networks are networks where each computer has the same status and they are able to communicate with each other on an equal footing. This means that every computer on this type of network can access all the resources of any of the other computers on the network.

Peer-to-peer networks are used for home networks. If you simply want to share files and printers using several computers in your home, then a peer-to-peer network will be fine.

P2P has become very popular with Internet users for the sharing of files between users. Each user is able to

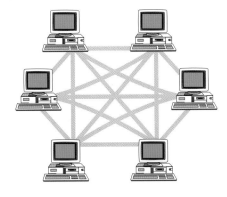

Kazaa is a free peer-to-peer file sharing system.

connect to another user's computer over the network so there is no central management. There have been many problems with this over the legality of sharing copyrighted music, video, images, etc.

P2P software systems such as Kazaa and Napster are one of the most popular software applications with users.

With peer-to-peer networks all the computers are of equal status and can access each other's resources.

Advantages of peer-to-peer networking:

- cost saving – no server is needed, so all the computers can be the same
- no network manager is needed – all users take responsibility for the network
- easy to set up – they are the simplest of computer networks, so they can be set up by anyone
- there is no reliance on a server – so no worry about the server breaking down
- lower operating costs – less setup and maintenance costs
- peer responsibility – users decide what resources other users can use on their computer.

Disadvantages of peer-to-peer networking:

- backups cannot be made centrally – this places responsibility on all the users to backup their own data; you cannot be sure that all users will do this
- users need more IT knowledge – as they will be responsible for the files on their own computers
- poorer security – resources are shared, so users have to decide what resources of theirs other users on the network can use
- some computers may run slowly – those computers that have resources on them that all users use will run very slowly.

Client-server networks

Client-server networks are the preferred choice for large networks. In a client-server network all the computers are not the same status. Usually a more powerful computer is used as the central computer, where all the files and programs are stored, and this computer is called a server. The other computers on the network are called clients.

As the server is such an important part of a client-server network, a person, called the network manager, is usually appointed to be in charge of it.

Advantages of client-server networks:

- security is better – because it is centralised and a person is given responsibility for it
- centralised data – data is all held on the file server which means that all users have access to the same set of data
- backups are taken centrally – regular backups are taken by the network manager which means data and programs are unlikely to be lost
- faster access to programs and files – servers are used which are powerful computers, so the whole network runs faster
- centralised administration – all the administration of the network (e.g., allocation of usernames and passwords, help, etc.) is performed centrally so users do not have to worry about it.

Disadvantages of client-server networks:

- more expensive – servers are expensive
- need specialist knowledge – need to have a person who understands the technicalities of a network in charge of the network
- software is sophisticated and expensive – network operating systems are expensive. For larger client-server networks it may be necessary to buy network management software.

Characteristics of networks

Introduction

In this section you will be looking at types of network that use Internet technology and the Internet itself. You will also be looking at the difference between the commonly used words the Internet and the World Wide Web.

The differences between the Internet and the World Wide Web

The Internet and the World Wide Web are not the same thing. Look carefully at the differences between the following definitions:

Internet – the Internet is a huge group of networks joined together. Each of these networks consists of lots of smaller networks. This means that the Internet consists of hardware.

World Wide Web (WWW) – the World Wide Web, simply called the Web is a means of accessing information contained on the Internet. It is an information-sharing model that is built on top of the Internet. The World Wide Web uses HTTP, which is one of the languages used over the Internet, to transmit information. The World Wide Web makes use of browser software to access documents called webpages.

The Internet provides more services than accessing webpages.

Using the Internet you have:

- e-mail facilities
- instant messaging
- Usenet news groups
- FTP (file transfer protocol), which is a way of exchanging files between different computers connected to the Internet
- P2P (peer-to-peer) networking, which allows you to exchange files (usually MP3 files) with other users.

All of the above services require different protocols to that required by the World Wide Web.

The Internet is therefore the actual network whereas the World Wide Web is the accessing of webpages using the Internet. It is important to realise that the World Wide Web is only one of the facilities based on the Internet.

Intranets

An intranet is a private network that uses the same technology as that used by the Internet for the sending of messages around the network. The main use of an intranet is to share organisational information and share resources.

The concepts of client and server are used for the computers in an intranet along with the same protocols (HTTP, FTP and e-mail) as used by the Internet.

The main feature of an intranet is that only employees of the organisation are able to use it.

Please note that an intranet need not be confined to a single site and it is still possible for people on an intranet to access the Internet.

Extranets

The use of an intranet is restricted to employees of the organisation, whereas with an extranet, customers, suppliers and other partners, as well as the employees of the organisation, can access the information. Extranets are not accessible by the general public and this is ensured by the use of usernames and passwords. Because the people who need access to the information are not on the same site, data needs to be sent using third parties for the communication lines. Data can be sent via the Internet or it can be sent using the more expensive private communication lines which offer more security and performance.

If the Internet is used for the sending of the data in an extranet, the following security measures have to be put in place:

- gateways
- firewalls
- encryption
- user authentication.

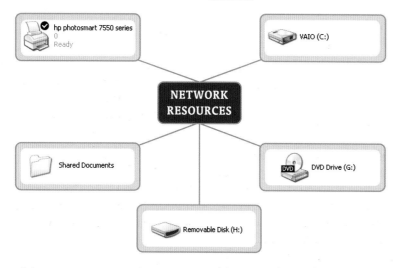

Some of the resources you can share on a network.

Uses of communication technologies and standards

Introduction

In this section you will be looking at the advantages and disadvantages of networks and the appropriate and inappropriate use of networks.

Different manufacturers make different network devices and to get them to communicate with each other it is necessary for the manufacturers to agree on certain standards. In this section you will also look at communication standards.

Relative advantages and disadvantages of networks

There are many advantages of networking computers and they far outweigh the disadvantages. Advantages include:

Ability to share files – no need to make copies of files as all the files can be accessed by all the computers on the network if needed.

Ability to share hardware resources – no need to have a printer for each computer as any hardware device (e.g., printer, scanner, plotter, etc.) can be shared.

Ability to share software – software can be shared, meaning that everyone will be using the same version. Maintaining software by keeping it up-to-date is made much easier.

Lower software costs – it is cheaper to buy one network version with a licence for so many users compared to buying individual copies for each computer. It also saves time as only one copy needs to be installed on the server.

Improved security – it is easier for network managers to control access from computers to the Internet. It is much easier to make sure that any material from the Internet is checked with the latest virus checking software.

Easier to implement acceptable use policies – centralising applications software simplifies the process of implementing software policies in an organisation. Software policies refer to what software may be installed on computers and how it may be used.

Easier to back up files – backing up is performed by the network manager rather than the individual users. This means backing up is taken seriously and users are less likely to lose data.

Improved communication – networks have e-mail facilities which will improve communication between workers.

Central maintenance and support – new upgrades to software need only to be added to the server. Network managers and support staff can see what the users are looking at on their screen, so they can be given help if they are having problems with a task.

Disadvantages include:

Technical knowledge needed – more IT knowledge is needed to run a network so specialist staff are usually needed.

Lack of access when file server fails – if a file server fails (i.e., goes down) the entire network may fail, which means that users might not be able to access files and data.

Cost – although a network will save money over time, there is the initial high cost of all the network equipment and training needed.

Standards for communication

There are many different hardware devices that can be attached to a network. In order for these devices to communicate with each other, it is necessary for them to have certain characteristics in common. They must be able to present electronic signals in a certain way, so that they are able to understand each other.

For this to happen, the manufacturers need a common standard for electronic communication. The most popular standard used for electronic communication is defined by an organisation called the CCITT (the International Committee for Data Communication).

The need for standards when transferring data

Communications software makes it possible for computers to send and receive data over a network.

When data is sent over a network the communications software manages the flow of data across the medium (metal wire, fibre optic cable, air (in the case of wireless), etc.) and also establishes certain rules, called the protocol, by which computers can communicate.

Typical tasks performed by the communications software are:

- collecting the bits of data and putting them into packets before sending
- adding information to each packet regarding which computer the data came from (i.e., the source of the data) and which computer it needs to go to (the destination computer)
- performing some error checking to make sure that the packets sent out by the source are exactly the same as those received at the destination
- establishing connection with remote computers
- changing the packets back into ordinary data which can be understood by the receiving computer.

In order to do all the above, both the network hardware and software need standards for communication.

Questions, Case studies and Activities

▶ Questions 1 pp. 154–155

1 Most schools use networked computers to form a LAN rather than using stand-alone computers.
   (a) Explain the difference between computers in a LAN and stand-alone computers. (2 marks)
   (b) Describe **two** advantages to the students in using a LAN rather than using stand-alone computers. (2 marks)
   (c) Describe **two** disadvantages to the students in using a LAN rather than using stand-alone computers. (2 marks)

2 Describe **two** differences between a local area network (LAN) and a wide area network (WAN). (2 marks)

3 Briefly explain the purpose of a network interface card. (2 marks)

▶ Questions 2 pp. 156–157

1 There are two main types of local area network (LAN): peer-to-peer and client-server.
   (a) Describe **four** features of a peer-to-peer network. (4 marks)
   (b) Describe **four** features of a client-server network. (4 marks)

2 In computer networking the word topology means the layout of the connected devices on the network. A local area network is to be set up. Give the names of **two** topologies which could be used for this LAN and draw a diagram to illustrate each one. (4 marks)

▶ Questions 3 p. 158

1 Explain the main difference between the Internet and the World Wide Web. (2 marks)

2 Intranets and extranets are now very popular networks for large and small organisations.
   (a) Give **two** features of an intranet. (2 marks)
   (b) Give **two** features of an extranet. (2 marks)

▶ Questions 4 p. 159

1 Explain why standards are needed when transferring data using a network. (2 marks)

2 Give the names of **three** devices whose resources may be shared using a network. (3 marks)

Network procedures at a university

In this case study you will look at network procedures for a university. All universities, colleges and schools use networks and having a set of procedures for staff and students helps prevent problems.

This document sets out the network procedures. Read these procedures carefully and then answer the questions that follow.

1 Usernames and passwords
  (a) All staff and students need a username and password to log on to the network.
  (b) Usernames are the member of staff's employee number and for students it is their student number.
  (c) Passwords should be at least 7 characters and contain at least 3 numbers.
  (d) Passwords should be changed every three months.

2 Unauthorised use
  (a) Do not share your password with anyone.
  (b) Any unauthorised use of the network must be reported to the network manager so that they are able to assess the network for damage.

3 Confidentiality
  (a) Staff should not allow students to enter or view other students' electronic grades or records.
  (b) Periodic directory maintenance is performed by network administration staff to help ensure the network performance and integrity. They will only view information related to file size, number of files, etc.
  (c) When network administration staff need to troubleshoot a user problem, or need to access or view a user's files, they will obtain the user's permission first.

4 Student use
  (a) Students must be monitored/supervised when using the network.
  (b) Students should only log in to the network with their own username and password.
  (c) All data must be saved on the student's area on the network. Data must not be stored on the local hard drive.
  (d) Students are not allowed to install software on the hard drives or the network.

5 Logging out
  (a) When staff leave their work area they should log out of the network.
  (b) All computers should be turned off at the end of the day.
  (c) Always log out before turning off computers.

6 Viruses
  (a) If you bring media from home or another place, scan it for viruses.
  (b) All internal hard drives will be scanned for viruses by support staff before they are connected to the network.
  (c) When using laptops on the network, make sure that there is a current copy of a virus scanner installed on them and ensure that this is updated regularly.
  (d) If files are downloaded from the Internet, make sure that they are downloaded as a temporary file which you should then scan before opening the file.

7 Backups
  (a) The network is backed up every day. It is also best if you take you own backup copies of your personal work on removable media.

8 Software
  (a) Your amount of storage on the network is limited. You should therefore maintain your files by copying them to removable media and deleting them off the network.
  (b) Staff but not students are able to install legal and original software on the hard drive of their computer.
  (c) Software can only be added to the network by the network manager.

9 Copyright
  (a) All staff and students must comply with current copyright laws.
  (b) Software on the network should not be copied.
  (c) Non-copy-protected audio (e.g., MP3) and video files for personal use should not be stored on the network.

10 Hardware
  (a) All networked hardware must remain on-site and must be kept connected to the network.
  (b) Computer and other equipment must not be borrowed and taken home.
  (c) Hardware must only be modified or repaired by the network technicians.

11 Removable media
  (a) Care must be taken when pen drives are inserted into or removed from computers.
  (b) Keep magnetic media away from magnetic fields (top of screen, metal cabinets, electric pencil sharpeners, etc.).

12 Problem solving
  (a) All help requests should be referred to the help-desk on ext. 3232.
  (b) Help is available 7 days per week from 8.00 am to 6.00 pm.

See over for questions.

Questions, Case studies and Activities continued

▶ Case study 1 (continued) | p. 159

Questions: Network procedures at a university

All the following questions refer to the case study.

1 This question concerns usernames and passwords which are needed to log on to this network.

(a) Explain why usernames are displayed whilst passwords are never displayed on the screen. (1 mark)

(b) Explain the purpose of:
   (i) a username (1 mark)
   (ii) a password (1 mark)

(c) The network manager has said that users of the network need more guidance about choice of passwords. Describe **four** different things users should bear in mind when choosing passwords. (4 marks)

(d) To be effective, passwords need to be changed regularly. For this network, the passwords should be changed every three months. Give **one** reason why the network manager might be opposed to a proposal to make users change their password every week. (1 mark)

2 (a) Give **one** reason why the network manager will only allow students to store data on the network and not the local hard drive of the computer they are working on. (2 marks)

(b) Explain why the procedures make it a requirement for students to maintain their own storage area on the network. (2 marks)

3 Some networks in businesses do not allow removable media to be inserted into networked computers.

(a) Give **one** reason why this is done. (1 mark)

(b) Explain why this is not a real option for a network for a college or university. (1 mark)

4 Explain why software should only be added to the network by the network manager. (2 marks)

5 Students are able to use removable media to store their work for backup purposes.

(a) Give the names of **three** examples of removable media which the students could use. (3 marks)

(b) Students are able to bring in pen-drives and other media from home. Give **one** danger that this presents to the network and state what can be done to minimise the risk. (2 marks)

▶ Activity Peer-to-peer file sharing

In this activity you are going to research peer-to-peer networks and peer-to-peer file sharing.

Use the Internet and access the following website: http://www.kazaa.com/us/help/glossary/p2p.htm

Look through the glossary until you have a good grasp as to what peer-to-peer is, how it works and why it is useful, and then answer the following questions:

1 Explain how a peer-to-peer network differs from a client-server network.

2 Peer-to-peer networking using the Internet is very popular. Give **two** things you can do using a peer-to-peer network.

3 People often have on their computers personal files that they would not want to share with others. How does the Kazaa P2P file sharing system deal with this?

4 File sharing systems are not popular with music publishers.

(a) Give the name of the Act which protects musicians and music publishers from having their work copied.

(b) Give **one** reason why musicians may not like systems such as Kazaa.

(c) Some groups trying to get on the ladder might like systems such as Kazaa. Give **one** reason why.

5 Give **two** reasons why a user might be worried about the security implications of the Kazaa system.

6 Kazaa can be downloaded free from the website: http://www.kazaa.com/us/index.htm

Explain how Kazaa can be provided free, yet Kazaa can still make money from the venture.

Exam support

Worked example 1

1 (a) Explain what is meant by the term intranet. **(2 marks)**
  (b) Explain what is meant by the term extranet. **(2 marks)**

Student answer 1

1 (a) An intranet is an internal network and can be used for sending internal data.
  (b) An extranet is an external network and can be used for sending external data.

Examiner's comment

1 Part (a) is correct about the internal network but the second part needs to be more specific to gain the second mark. They needed to say, for example, that '... for sending internal data such as e-mails'.
Part (b) the main point that needs to be made here is that data needs to be shared by people who are external to the organisation yet still need shared data. This is not specific enough to gain any marks.
(1 mark out of 4)

Student answer 2

1 (a) An intranet uses the same technology as the Internet but is used internally within an organisation for the sharing of data such as e-mails.
  (b) An extranet again uses Internet technology and is used to allow trading partners such as customers and suppliers, who are outside the organisation, to access certain data.

Examiner's comment

1 Part (a) is a good answer. They should have said it is a network – it is always best to assume that you are explaining it to someone with only a basic knowledge. This part is still worth the two marks.
Part (b) is a good answer but needed to mention that it is network and that it is a private network and only authorised persons are able to access it.
Still worth two marks though. **(4 marks out of 4)**

Examiner's answers

1 (a) One mark for what it is and one mark for how it can be used.
    An intranet is an internal network that can be used by all the employees of an organisation for the sending of internal e-mail, sharing diaries, sharing data, etc.
  (b) One mark for what it is and one mark for how it can be used.
    An extranet is an external private network which is made available to an organisation and their trading partners so they can share information about orders and payments.

Summary mind maps

Basic elements of an ICT network: network components

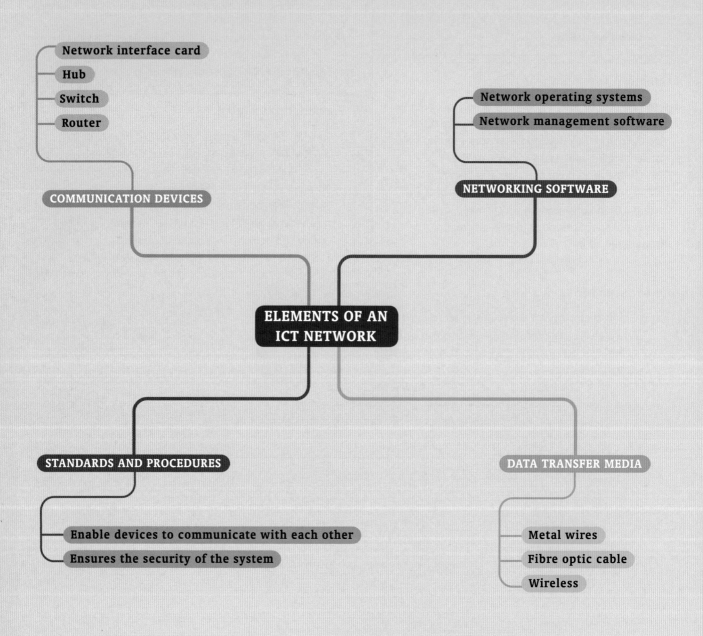

Network interface card
Hub
Switch
Router

Network operating systems
Network management software

COMMUNICATION DEVICES

NETWORKING SOFTWARE

ELEMENTS OF AN
ICT NETWORK

STANDARDS AND PROCEDURES

DATA TRANSFER MEDIA

Enable devices to communicate with each other
Ensures the security of the system

Metal wires
Fibre optic cable
Wireless

Basic elements of an ICT network: network topologies and types

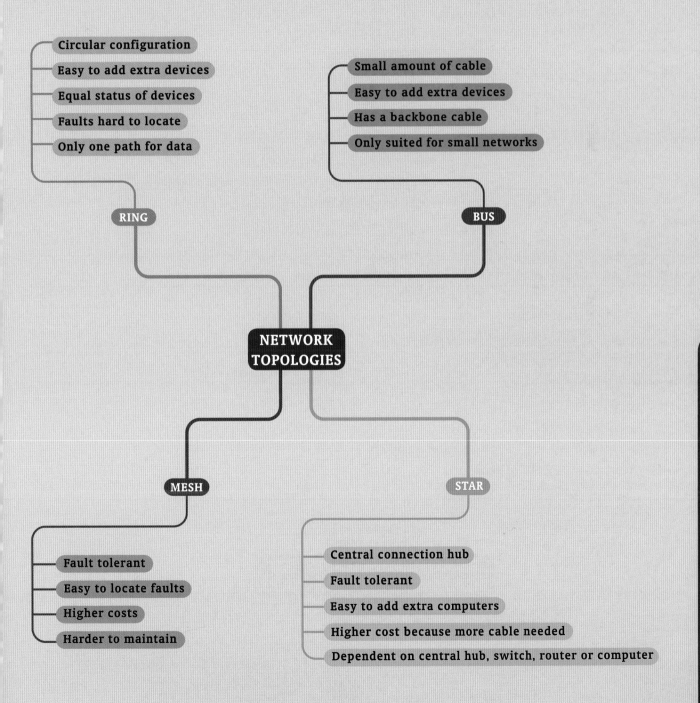

- Circular configuration
- Easy to add extra devices
- Equal status of devices
- Faults hard to locate
- Only one path for data

RING

- Small amount of cable
- Easy to add extra devices
- Has a backbone cable
- Only suited for small networks

BUS

NETWORK TOPOLOGIES

MESH

- Fault tolerant
- Easy to locate faults
- Higher costs
- Harder to maintain

STAR

- Central connection hub
- Fault tolerant
- Easy to add extra computers
- Higher cost because more cable needed
- Dependent on central hub, switch, router or computer

Summary mind maps continued

Characteristics of networks

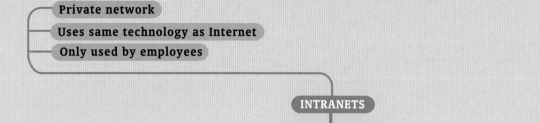

- Private network
- Uses same technology as Internet
- Only used by employees

INTRANETS

NETWORKS

EXTRANETS

- Not restricted to just employees
- Suppliers, customers and other trading partners can access it
- Can use public or private communications
- Uses same technology as Internet

Uses of communication technologies and standards

- Ability to share files
- Ability to share hardware resources
- Ability to share software
- Lower software costs
- Improved security
- Easier to back up files
- Easier to implement acceptable use policies
- Improved communications
- Central maintenance and support

ADVANTAGES

RELATIVE ADVANTAGES AND DISADVANTAGES OF NETWORKS

DISADVANTAGES

- Technical knowledge needed
- Lack of access when file server fails
- Cost

In this topic you will need to know about the threats to ICT systems and what can be done to minimise them.

You will also learn about the legislation (laws) relating to the safety and security of data in ICT systems.

▼ The key concepts covered in this topic are:

▶ Privacy of data in ICT systems

▶ The need to protect data in ICT systems

▶ The threats to ICT systems

▶ Protecting ICT systems

▶ The Data Protection Act 1998

▶ The Freedom of Information Act 2000

▶ The Computer Misuse Act 1990

▶ The Copyright, Designs and Patents Act 1988

CONTENTS

Unit 2 Living in the Digital World

The need to protect data in ICT systems: privacy and passwords

Introduction

The word privacy means freedom from intrusion by the public and others. Privacy is normally regarded as a right that we all have, but with the introduction of ICT systems and monitoring systems, it is very hard for an individual to keep aspects of their personal life private. It is also hard for an individual to control the flow of personal information about themselves.

Keeping your private life private is very difficult now, as there are so many ICT systems that are designed to collect as much information about you as they can. Much of this information is used for marketing purposes but other information can be collected and used by government departments such as councils, HM Revenue and Customs, the Police and the security services. The constant threat of terrorism has meant that the amount of monitoring and surveillance has greatly increased.

Some of the personal details held about you on ICT systems:

ICT systems that erode privacy

Many ICT systems are set up to collect, process and store personal information. By linking the information from all the systems, it would be possible to build up a complete picture about a person's life. The erosion of privacy comes from a number of areas, which are summarised here:

KEY WORDS

Privacy – being able to choose to keep certain aspects of your life private

Credit-checking agencies (cards you have, loans, mortgages, payment history, etc.)

Surveillance cameras (number plate and face recognition systems, etc.)

Internet service provider records (websites visited, e-mail sent)

Phishing (an illgal activity which tries to find out bank details)

Records of purchases you have made

ERODING PRIVACY

Spyware (used to snoop into your Internet use)

Mobile phone records (details of all your calls including your conversations)

Cookies (record details of visits to websites, what pages you looked at, etc.)

Marketing database (builds up a profile of your lifestyle)

PERSONAL INFORMATION HELD ON ICT SYSTEMS

- Earnings
- Credit history
- Likes and dislikes
- Purchases made
- Insurance details (home, car, life, etc.)
- Vehicle details
- Exams and qualifications
- Medical details
- Phone call details
- Marketing information (gained from replies to questionnaires)
- Criminal records
- Bank account details (statements, loans, direct debits, etc.)

The use of user-IDs or usernames

The same computer is often used by different people so the computer needs a way of identifying who is using the computer.

Here are some facts about user-IDs:

- A user-ID is unique to a particular user and will normally be an abbreviation for the person's full name.
- Using the user-ID, the computer can allow users to have their own personal settings and files.
- When the user-ID is entered, the computer will know who is using the computer. It then has to know that it is the genuine person using the computer and this is where the password comes in.

Part of a login screen for Internet Banking.

The use of passwords

Passwords are the first step in protecting an ICT system against illegal access. Passwords are known only by the person who set up the password and therefore are used to ensure only this person has access to the ICT resources. Passwords are a series of characters that need to be typed in before access to the ICT system is allowed.

Passwords are not displayed on the screen. Instead they appear as a series of asterisks so that they cannot be observed by anyone standing behind you.

Choosing a password

Choosing a password should be easy but it isn't, as most passwords that people choose are easily determined (or cracked as it is called) by hackers. It has been estimated that 80% of all passwords can be cracked by an experienced hacker in less than 18 minutes.

Many people think hackers enter passwords manually and hope to hit on the right one. If this was the case, hacking would not be the problem it is. Hackers are extremely determined and use ICT themselves to determine passwords. For example, there are programs that have been created to crack passwords.

The trouble with passwords is:

- people choose simple words because they are easy to remember – these make it very easy for hackers to crack
- or they choose pet names, names of football teams or even their own names – all of these are easily guessed by friends or colleagues
- people often have to remember so many passwords, so they write them down, thus increasing the security risk
- they are not changed regularly enough – this increases the risk of hackers cracking the password and using the personal information obtained.

© 2003 Randy Glasbergen. www.glasbergen.com

'Yesterday I changed everyone's password to "password". I sent it to everyone in a memo, put it on a big sign on the wall and printed it on all of the coffee cups. Guess how many people called me this morning because they forgot the password.'

Changing passwords can cause problems with users ringing up the help-desk because they have forgotten them.

Rules for passwords

When selecting and using passwords:

- Do not use a word that can be found in a dictionary.
- Do not use your own or any other name or surname even if you put numbers after it.
- Always use the maximum number of characters the system allows. So, if the password can be up to 10 characters, use all 10 and not just, say, 4 of them.
- Include numerals as well as letters.
- Include a mixture of upper and lower case letters but try not to make the first letter a capital letter.
- If the password system allows, put other characters in your password like £, &, %, $, @, etc.
- Do not write your password down.
- Change your password regularly (usually the system will prompt you to do this automatically).
- Do not tell anyone else your password.
- Do not use your user-ID as your password.
- Never respond to an e-mail that asks you for your password.

EXAM TIP

There is often confusion between the terms privacy and security. Exam questions often ask you to determine between the terms. Here are definitions you can use.

- Ensuring the privacy of data means making sure that personal data is not disclosed to anyone not entitled to see it.
- Security means making sure that the hardware, software and data of an ICT system does not come to any harm.

Unit 2 Living in the Digital World

The need to protect data in ICT systems: monitoring

▼ You will find out

▶ About how ICT is used to monitor you at work, at home and when just performing everyday tasks

▶ About spyware and cookies and their threats to privacy

▶ About how loyalty card systems erode privacy

Introduction

The UK is the most closely monitored country in the world. We are continually monitored as we go about our lives, and a huge picture of all our activities could be built up. Much of this information is stored and never used but many people are worried about the erosion of the basic right to privacy.

Monitoring

Monitoring at work

Many organisations monitor their employees' use of the Internet. Using a person's user-ID to identify them, a network manager can find out the amount of time spent on the Internet, the websites visited and even look at the e-mails they have sent. This monitoring could be used to collect evidence about an employee's use of ICT resources so they could be disciplined.

Network managers can also look at what programs and data are stored on a user's hard drive. They can do this so that they can look to see what versions of software a user is using but they can look for unauthorised software, music files, video files, etc., as well as look at all other data stored.

Monitoring at home

Even when sitting in the privacy of your own home, you are not safe from prying eyes. Your connection to the Internet provides others with lots of ways of finding out about you and what you do whilst on-line.

Internet service provider records

Internet service providers (the organisation that provides your Internet connection, e.g. AOL, Tiscali, BT, etc.) are required to keep records of your Internet use. Such records include:

* pages visited
* how long was spent on each page
* downloads made.

ISPs also record the following about your e-mail activity:

* e-mail addresses of the recipients
* contents of each e-mail
* dates and times each e-mail was sent.

You can buy anti-spyware software as a separate package.

As you can see, your Internet use is tracked but most of the time there is so much information stored that it would only be accessed in special situations by the Police or the security services (MI5, FBI, etc.).

Spyware

Spyware is software which collects information without their consent about the user of a computer connected to the Internet.

Spyware records details such as:

* keystrokes used
* web browsing history.

It can even scan your hard drive for any information it has been instructed to find. Typical uses of spyware include:

* to investigate your searching history on the Internet, so you can be targeted for an advertising campaign
* intercepting passwords and credit card details for fraud/theft.

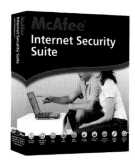

McAfee Internet Security Suite is a software package which provides anti-spyware, anti-virus, firewall, anti-spam, anti-phishing and backup software all in the same package.

> ### KEY WORDS
>
> **Cookie** – a small text file downloaded to your computer, used by websites to collect information about how you use the website
>
> **Internet service provider (ISP)** – the organisation that provides a connection service to the Internet (e.g., AOL, BT, etc.)
>
> **Spyware** – software which collects information without their consent about the user of a computer connected to the Internet

---

AOL Spyware Protection	Download Now

Some Internet service providers provide free anti-spyware software.

There are many different problems spyware causes such as:

- identity theft/fraud – spyware can search for passwords and credit card details
- computer crashes – software may have bugs which cause your computer to crash
- poor performance – spyware runs in the background, so it slows your computer down
- lots of pop-ups and banner advertisements – targeting you for advertising, means lots of annoying pop-ups/banner ads appear, which wastes your time having to close them down
- software problems – spyware can interfere with existing software
- security software is disabled – spyware can disable firewall and anti-virus software.

To remove spyware:

- install anti-spyware software
- install a security suite of software or anti-virus software – anti-spyware software is often included in security packages or as part of anti-virus software
- install software provided by your Internet service provider (ISP).

Anti-spyware software will:

- scan the memory for any spyware running
- scan any new programs that have been downloaded
- scan any programs that try to reinstall themselves
- scan the entire hard drive periodically.

A receipt from a supermarket

Cookies

Cookies are used by websites to collect information about how you use the website.

A cookie is a small text file downloaded to your computer. They can be used to find out whether the computer (and usually the user) has visited the site before. They can also be used to investigate the pages on the site the user has visited and this can be used to tailor the content of the site to a particular user.

To the owner of a website, cookies provide a way of investigating how users use their site. In many cases a website will try to promote products that a user has shown a previous interest in.

The main problem with cookies is that they erode our privacy by effectively following our paths through certain websites. In most cases this is done without the user's consent and in some cases without their knowledge.

Monitoring by others

Monitoring occurs when you are walking along a road or driving a car or using your mobile phone. When you enter a shop and buy goods, then your purchasing habits may be investigated by ICT systems.

What your shopping can tell about you

Look at the receipt from a supermarket on the left:

If you paid by cash and you did not use a loyalty card, the supermarket would not be able to link you to the purchases you made. The data about your purchases would be private.

If, however, you use a credit card and a loyalty card, they will know a lot more about you and be able to link you to the purchases made.

The need to protect data in ICT systems: identity theft

▼ You will find out

▶ About the problems with on-line banking

▶ About the meanings of the terms phishing and Trojans

▶ About what identity theft is and how it can be prevented

Introduction

The huge increase in people performing financial transactions on-line has led to a number of problems. Paying for goods or services on-line using credit or debit cards raises a number of security problems. Similar problems occur when viewing on-line bank accounts. You have to be very aware and careful when performing on-line transactions.

Problems with on-line banking

What happens if you are one of the many people who bank using the Internet and someone gets unauthorised access to your account and cleans it out?

Well, banks offer some protection if this happens, provided you have taken sensible precautions. These sensible precautions would typically involve you making sure that you have a firewall and anti-virus software installed on your computer and that this software is kept up-to-date.

Most of the banking problems are caused by the following:

Phishing – this is where fraudsters send random e-mails asking people who are using the on-line banking system to update their account details. When the user clicks on the link in

Online Banking Guarantee

We guarantee to refund your money in the unlikely event you experience fraud with our Internet banking service – as long as you've been careful, for example, by taking reasonable steps to keep your security information safe. We protect you with safeguards that meet industry standards. **Visit our security pages.**

The online banking guarantee given by LloydsTSB to its customers.

the e-mail or copies the URL into their browser, they are taken to a fake website which looks similar to the proper bank site. The user is then asked to type in personal information such as name, address, credit or bank details and password. Once this has been done, the fraudster has access to the bank and credit card details.

Trojans – these are lines of computer code that are stored in your PC without you knowing. They are loaded into your computer when you look at an e-mail or visit a fake website. Their aim is to gather details of your username and password which the code transmits back to the fraudster.

Identity theft/fraud

There has been a lot on the news recently about the problems of identity fraud, but what is it?

Everyone knows the dangers of losing or having their credit cards stolen. If someone has your account details, they can start siphoning money out of your account. If they do it gradually and not in one go, many people do not notice it. In fact in many cases of identity theft, the victim takes 14 months to work out what is happening.

How can I prevent this from happening?

Be very suspicious of any e-mails sent to you. The Internet e-mail system is very insecure and you should never divulge personal information in an e-mail or follow a link to a site from an e-mail and divulge personal information.

Always view official looking e-mails with scepticism despite them having the right logos and using official language. Do not be tricked into inputting your

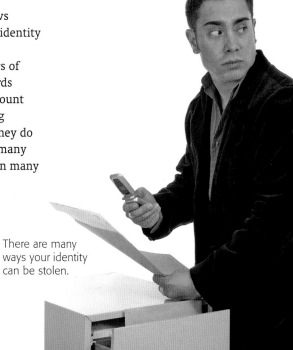

There are many ways your identity can be stolen.

details, even if they say things like 'your account will be suspended unless you enter these details'.

How your identity can be stolen

Identity theft is the fastest growing crime in the UK. Here is how it could happen.

First week

Someone roots through your recycling bin containing papers thrown out. They find old bank statements, bills, credit card slips and so on. A few days later they have re-directed your mail to a new address and with the details they can now start to buy goods on-line.

Second week

With the information from the redirected mail, they start to open new credit card accounts in your name. They may even pay for broadband or mobile phone services using your details.

Third week

The thief is getting a bit greedy. They decide to buy a car using a card in your name. They pay for insurance using a credit card in your name.

Fourth week

They are involved in a car accident and give your name and address to the police. Because you don't appear in court, you are arrested.

Keeping banking details private

Encryption

If information needs to be sent over the Internet or another network and it needs to be kept secure, then encryption needs to be used. This basically codes the data whilst it is being sent and only the true recipient is able to decode it. Should the data be intercepted by a hacker, then the data will be in code and totally meaningless.

The process of coding data, sending it over the Internet and then deciphering it when it reaches the true recipient, is called encryption. Encryption should be used for:

- sending credit card details such as card numbers, expiry dates, etc., over the Internet
- on-line banking
- sending payment details (bank details such as sort code numbers, account numbers, etc.)
- confidential e-mails
- sending data between terminals where confidentiality is essential.

Problems with encryption:

- security forces (the police and MI5) do not like people using codes they cannot crack themselves because they cannot read the e-mails
- encryption can be used for secret conversations between criminals and terrorists.

Unit 2 Living in the Digital World

Threats to ICT systems: what they are

Introduction

A threat to an ICT system such as fire, theft, deliberate damage, power loss, etc., is a source of danger.

The potential threats to ICT systems are many and some are very likely to happen compared to others. The amount of damage done can also vary from a slight inconvenience (e.g., having to remove a virus) to the complete loss of hardware, software and data.

Any user of ICT systems needs to be aware of the threats, because only then can measures be taken to minimise the damage should the threat turn into reality.

Threats to ICT systems can cause the loss of data which causes loss of money in terms of:

- lost business
- lack of confidence by customers or members of the public
- lost computer time
- the need for staff to spend time sorting problems out.

Where do the threats come from?

There are a huge number of threats to computer systems. Here is a list of the main threats but you may be able to think of some more:

- viruses
- Trojans
- worms
- spyware
- adware
- spam
- abuse by staff (accidental or deliberate)
- hacking
- fire
- theft
- natural disasters
- faulty hardware or software.

Earthquakes – loss of power, loss of communication lines, damage to ICT systems caused by building collapse, etc.

Tidal waves – usually these occur after earthquakes, when they are called tsunamis.

Volcanoes – fire and smoke damage, destruction of buildings

Lightning strikes – lightning strikes can cause momentary losses of power which can cause data loss. Lightning can also cause more serious damage with the complete loss of hardware, software and data.

Floods – water damage to hardware, software and data, loss of power or communication lines.

Gales – loss of power lines, destruction of communication equipment, etc.

▼ You will find out

▶ About the threats to ICT systems from natural disasters

▶ About the threats to ICT systems from faulty hardware and software

▶ About the threats from fire

▶ About the threats from loss of power supply

Threats from natural disasters

In Britain we do not generally suffer from natural disasters like a lot of other countries, but with climate change this may change. Some natural disasters and their consequences are shown below to the left:

Threats from faulty hardware or software

Like any electrical device, computers can and do go wrong. The trouble is that although hardware can be repaired or replaced, it is not easy to replace programs and data, especially if no backup copies have been kept.

Faulty hardware – computer hardware is fairly reliable but can and does break down and you have to be prepared for this. The main problem would be caused by the hard drive becoming damaged, rendering the data and the programs unusable.

Faulty software – software especially bespoke software and sometimes packaged software can contain errors (or bugs as they are called) and these can cause damage or loss of data.

Threats from fire

Fire is a serious threat in any workplace and loss of ICT systems can occur, so precautions need to be taken to minimise the threat such as:

- no smoking in all computer rooms
- power sockets should not be overloaded
- wiring should be checked regularly for safety
- bins should be emptied regularly
- do not leave large quantities of paper lying around

- fire alarms/smoke detectors in all rooms
- install a sprinkler system
- use fireproof safes to store media containing programs and data
- remove backup copies off-site.

Computer or hardware theft

Computer theft involves a thief stealing the computer or other hardware. If a computer is stolen then the hardware, software and data will be lost. A firm may be in contravention of the Data Protection Act 1998 if it can be proved that they did not have adequate security to prevent the loss of any personal data stored.

Computer theft is common, particularly with laptops. Laptops are particularly vulnerable to theft because they are:

- small, light and easily concealed
- often used in public places (cafes, on a train, at an airport, etc.)
- put into car boots
- very desirable and easy to sell by thieves.

Hacking

Hacking involves attempting to or actually breaking into a secure computer system. Usually a hacker (i.e., the person who does the hacking) is a proficient programmer and has the technical knowledge to be able to exploit the weaknesses in a security system. Once a hacker has gained access to an ICT system they may:

- do nothing and be content that they have managed to gain access
- gain access to sensitive or personal data
- use personal data to commit blackmail
- cause damage to data
- deliberately alter data to commit fraud.

The spread of viruses

Connection of an organisation's computers to the Internet increases the risk of viruses being spread to the internal network. The latest virus scanning and removal software should be installed on all computers.

Denial of service attacks

A denial of service attack is an attack on a secure system of an organisation so that the organisation is deprived of some of their resources. For example, a denial of service attack on an on-line bookshop could mean that the bookshop's network is so overwhelmed with requests that there is a temporary loss of network connectivity. This means that if you tried to place an order for a book, while the attack was taking place, you would not be able to. As well as inconveniencing customers, there is usually a loss of business, owing to customers not being able to place orders.

Problems with power

Power loss can occur for all sorts of reasons. It can be the result of natural disasters, extreme weather and/or simply from a workman cutting through a cable whilst doing road repairs. Computer equipment needs electricity and problems with the power can include:

- power loss
- changes in the power supply (you see these when your lights flicker) such as power surges.

Power loss

When the mains power goes off, unless you have standby power, you will lose the use of the computer equipment. If a network is affected by the power loss, then the server may not be shut down properly and so it is possible to lose data or it can take time to restore the server when the power is restored.

This UPS contains batteries which will give only around 65 minutes of power.

A standby power system will keep the power supplied and the computers running until the mains power is restored. Standby power will usually consist of either stored power (for short losses of power) or a combination of stored power and a generator. Stored power consists of banks of batteries. Generator power is generated using diesel or petrol.

Because there is a slight delay between losing the power and starting the generator, batteries are also needed to provide power during this interval.

Standby power is sometimes referred to as a UPS (uninterruptible power supply).

Changes in the power supply

Power fluctuations, sometimes called spikes and surges, occur more often than complete power loss. You notice these when your lights start to flicker. Power fluctuations can cause problems with computers and can be a cause of data loss. They can be caused by nearby high power consumption devices being turned on or off, lightning and interference from devices such as light dimmers and mobile phones.

Uninterruptible power supplies also have the facility of being able to protect against power surges.

Surge protectors like these can protect home computers from power surges.

Threats to ICT systems: internal or external, malpractice or crime

▼ You will find out

▶ About how threats can be divided into internal and external threats

▶ About the difference between malpractice and crime

Introduction

In this section you will learn about how it is possible to categorise the threats to ICT systems in a number of ways. For example, they can be categorised into whether they are internal or external or whether they are a result of malpractice or crime.

Internal and external threats

Threats which come from inside the organisation are called internal threats and those coming from outside the organisation are called external threats.

For example, hacking would normally be considered an external threat, because hacking involves obtaining access to a computer system using communication links (usually the Internet). However, if a person employed by the organisation wanted to gain access to part of the ICT system they were not normally allowed to access, then this is also hacking and would be considered an internal threat.

Malpractice and crime

There are lots of different types of activities which human users might or might not do which cause a threat to ICT systems. Malpractice means improper or careless use or misconduct. Crime obviously means all those acts which are against the law. There is a bit of blurring with the word malpractice, as this can also involve illegal acts according to the strict dictionary definition; however, for the exam you need to make the distinction that malpractice is not against the law, whereas crime is.

Examples of malpractice

Examples of malpractice include:

- accidentally deleting data
- not taking backup copies
- not scanning for viruses regularly
- copying an old version of data over the latest version
- allowing your password to be used by others
- not logging off the network after use.

KEY WORDS

Crime – an illegal act

External threat – a threat to an ICT system that comes from outside the organisation

Internal threat – a threat to an ICT system that comes from inside the organisation

Malpractice – improper or careless use or misconduct

Examples of crime include:

- hacking
- deliberately distributing viruses
- illegally copying data or software
- stealing hardware.

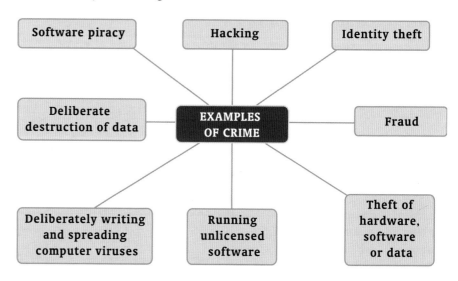

Internal threats would include:

- Employees introducing viruses deliberately or accidentally.
- Staff stealing hardware, software or data.
- Disgruntled staff deliberately damaging hardware, software or data.
- Staff accidentally damaging or losing data.
- Staff compromising the privacy of personal data by leaving computers logged on.
- Staff compromising the security of ICT systems by letting others know their usernames and passwords.
- Staff hacking into ICT systems that they are not allowed access to.

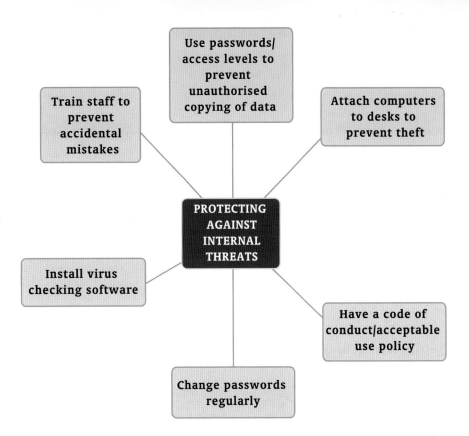

External threats would include:

- People from outside the organisation stealing hardware, software or data.
- People from outside the organisation hacking into the ICT system to view or change information stored.
- Natural disasters such as flood, earthquakes, etc.
- Loss of telecommunications services.
- Viruses introduced from file attachments, etc.

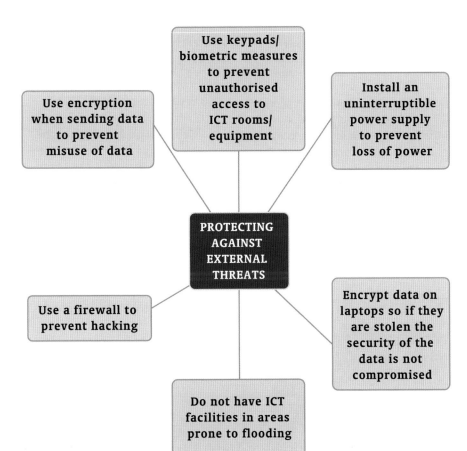

Protecting ICT systems: methods

▼ You will find out

▶ About the hardware measures that can be taken to protect against threats

▶ About the software measures that can be taken to protect against threats

Introduction

There are lots of threats to ICT systems and measures should be taken to reduce or eliminate these threats. The measures that can be taken may be:

- hardware measures
- software measures
- procedures (i.e., ways of working that will minimise threats).

Hardware measures

Hardware measures include computer and other equipment that can be used to reduce the threats.

Protecting data from loss by fire and theft

Data on removable media can be locked away in a fireproof safe.

Access restrictions

To prevent theft and illegal access to ICT systems, access to computer rooms can be restricted by the use of keypads. Access to rooms and computers can also be restricted using hardware which involves biometric testing. Biometric testing involves face recognition, voice recognition or fingerprint recognition. The advantage of this form of access is that there are no passwords or combination codes to remember.

Face recognition systems can restrict access to both rooms and computers. They can even be used to monitor the time that the users are at their workstation.

Locking keyboards

This system uses a card and a card reader to restrict access. When the card is removed, you cannot use the mouse, keyboard and see anything on the screen. When the card is inserted into the reader the system is restored.

EXAM TIP

If you are asked to give two possible methods of managing access to the contents of a file, make sure that your methods are distinctly different. For example, if you said 'iris recognition' and 'fingerprint recognition' then these are both biometric methods and you would only gain one of the marks. Always make sure that two completely different methods are chosen.

Software measures

There are many ways in which software can be used to limit how a user uses a stand-alone computer or networked computer.

Use of passwords and user-IDs/ usernames

A user-ID/username is a name or number used to identify a user of a network. Once the network knows who is using the network, it can allocate resources such as storage area and access to certain files.

Passwords are strings of characters kept secret by the user and are used to access the ICT system. The password makes sure that the person who gives the user-ID/username is the person who they say they are.

It is never a good idea to write your password down.

Access rights

Access rights restrict a user's access to only those files they need in order to perform their job. Their rights are initially allocated to them by the network manager and when they log on by giving their user-ID and password, these rights are allocated by the computer.

A user can have a number of different levels of access to files including:

- Read only – a user can only read the contents of the file. They cannot alter or delete the data.
- Read/write – a user can read the data held in the file and can alter the data.

© Randy Glasbergen, 1997.
www.glasbergen.com

'Sorry about the odour. I have all my passwords tattooed between my toes.'

- Append – they can add new records but they will be unable to alter or delete existing records.
- No access – they cannot open the file so cannot do anything to it.

Firewalls

A firewall is either hardware and/or software that works in a network to prevent communication that is not allowed from one network to another. Suppose an internal network (called an intranet) is connected to the Internet. The intranet will be protected with high security but the Internet is a very low security network. A firewall basically controls the data traffic between the two networks and it looks at each packet of data to see if there is anything about the data that breaches the security policy. If it does then the packet of data will not be allowed into the intranet. Firewalls are used to prevent spread of viruses and also to prevent unauthorised access (i.e., hacking).

Firewalls are also used to control what outside resources users have access to on the intranet.

Norton Personal Firewall can be used to protect your computer from unauthorised access whilst connected to the Internet. This particular firewall is software.

Firewalls can be:

- hardware
- software
- a combination of hardware and software.

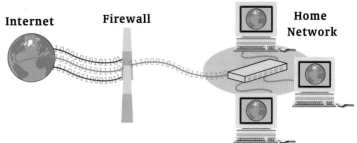

How requests from the Internet are accepted or rejected.

'Somebody broke into your computer, but it looks like the work of an inexperienced hacker.'

Encryption

Encryption scrambles data as it is passed along communication lines or wirelessly so that even if it is intercepted, it makes no sense to the interceptor. Encryption is also a feature of the latest operating systems, where the data stored on the hard drive is automatically encrypted so that if the computer is stolen or the data copied it cannot be understood.

KEY WORDS

Encryption – the process of coding files before they are sent over a network to protect them from hackers. Also the process of coding files stored on a computer so that if the computer is stolen, they cannot be read

Firewall – a piece of software, hardware or both that is able to protect a network from hackers

Password – a series of characters chosen by the user that are used to check the identity of the user when they require access to an ICT system

User-ID – a name or number that is used to identify a certain user of the network or system

'Encryption software is expensive...so we just rearranged all the letters on your keyboard.'

Unit 2 Living in the Digital World

Protecting ICT systems: from staff

Introduction

Procedures means the management controls that are put in place to ensure that users work in a way that reduces or eliminates the threats to ICT systems.

Procedures

Separation of duties

Separation of duties is an important procedure to protect against fraud. This ensures that two or more people should be involved in, for example, dealing with an order. One person would place the order but they would not be the same person who issued the payment for it. This would help prevent the company from paying for bogus orders because collusion between the staff would be needed to commit the fraud.

Non-disclosure

Many staff deal with confidential information that would be of commercial interest to their competitors. They may also view sensitive personal information stored on ICT systems as part of their work. Non-disclosure agreements are sometimes added to prevent employees passing on confidential information to others.

Some public servants may be asked to sign the Official Secrets Act as part of their conditions of employment.

Training

It is possible for users to delete important data by accident. Proper training will make users more confident in using ICT systems so that this type of mistake is less likely to happen.

Careful selection of staff

Choosing staff carefully can prevent problems in the future. ICT staff are in a position of trust and can present a number of threats if they are not chosen carefully.

Taking up references and thoroughly vetting staff working in ICT is essential.

Retention of staff

Turnover of staff in ICT departments can be damaging to ICT systems. It is hard to find suitably qualified and trained ICT staff and it is essential that good staff members are retained. The best way of doing this is to make their jobs interesting and let them know they are valued. Obviously paying them properly helps as well!

Audit trails

Many transactions occur using ICT systems without any paperwork being generated, which may seem to make it quite difficult to trace transactions. Luckily all ICT systems provide audit trails where it is possible to track all the details of a particular transaction.

For example, for a sales processing system it could be checked that a customer made an order, the money for the order was paid and that the goods were dispatched and received by the customer. Any irregularities in the process could be identified by the audit trail and investigated. Audit trails provide records which can be used to track the transactions. Audits are performed at regular intervals and they act as a deterrent, since staff realise that someone is checking things.

'We don't pay much attention to information security.
We're hoping our competitors will steal our ideas
and become as unsuccessful as we are.'

Acceptable use policy

Misusing the ICT facilities in an organisation by their own staff can lead to a number of threats. For example, downloading music onto the firm's computers can introduce viruses.

In order to prevent their own staff from misusing the ICT systems in an organisation, many organisations have an acceptable use policy. This policy makes it clear to all employees or users what is acceptable use and what isn't. The policy will usually make it clear about what disciplinary action will be taken if the ICT systems are abused.

An acceptable use policy protects both the organisation and individuals by providing clear guidelines as to what constitutes use and abuse. There can then be no ambiguity as to how the ICT systems can be used. There are six main areas on a typical IT acceptable use policy:

1 Introduction – this gives general information about the organisation and also outlines the main reasons for having the IT acceptable use policy.
2 General computer use – information here about general use such as health and safety information, advice about keeping workstations clean, eating and drinking near computer equipment, etc.

3 Network and Internet usage – information about network security – passwords and usernames, logging on and off, warnings about visiting undesirable and non-work-related sites. Warnings about downloading files from sites and doing non-work-related tasks.
4 E-mail – ensuring that e-mails sent internally and externally are appropriate. Warnings about opening e-mails from unknown sources which could contain viruses.

5 Security – outline of the Data Protection Act if personal data is being processed. Details about access and unauthorised access. Security measures that must be followed.
6 Training – training must be offered so that all staff understand all aspects of the IT acceptable use policy. They will also need training in all the legislation that applies to ICT use.

The problems and the need for legislation: personal data

Introduction

With the development of ICT systems, new laws had to be passed by parliament in order to protect the individual against misuses of personal data held about them. New laws also needed to be passed to cover other misuses such as writing and spreading viruses, illegally accessing computer resources (i.e., hacking), etc.

The Data Protection Act 1998

The widespread use of ICT has made the processing and transfer of data much easier and to protect the individual against the misuse of data, a law was passed called The Data Protection Act 1998.

Another reason for the Act was the fact that all Member States in the European Economic Area (EEA) had data protection laws, so the UK had to have them as well. This would allow the free passage of personal data from one Member State to another which is essential when conducting business.

The Data Protection Act 1998 covers the misuse of personal data, whether by the use of ICT systems or not. The Act gives rights to the individual to find the information stored about them and to check whether it is correct. If the information is wrong, they can have it altered and may be able to claim damages if they have suffered loss resulting from this wrong information.

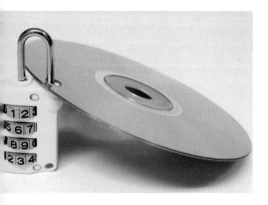

What data is classed as personal data?

The Data Protection Act 1998 refers to personal data. Personal data is:

- data about an identifiable person
- who is alive
- and is specific to that person.

The data subject must be capable of being identified from the information. Usually this would mean that the name and address would be part of the data but it could be that the person could be identified simply by other data given. Data specific to a particular person would include:

- medical history
- credit history
- qualifications
- religious beliefs
- criminal records.

The padlock/signpost symbol is used to alert individuals to the fact that their personal information is being collected. The symbol directs them to sources that will explain how their information is to be used.

Personal data held about you

Personal data is particularly important to people who are trying to sell you something. Generally this marketing data can be put into the following data types, demographic data (where you live) and lifestyle data (what your interests are, what you spend your money on, etc.).

Marketing people need to know more about our personal lives in order to target us for advertising and promotional material.

The eight Data Protection Principles

The Data Protection Act 1998 contains the following eight principles:

1 Personal data shall be processed fairly and lawfully.
2 Personal data shall be obtained only for one or more specified and lawful purposes, and shall not be further processed in any manner incompatible with that purpose or those purposes.
3 Personal data shall be adequate, relevant and not excessive in relation to the purpose or purposes for which they are processed.
4 Personal data shall be accurate and, where necessary, kept up to date.
5 Personal data processed for any purpose or purposes shall not be kept for longer than is necessary for that purpose or those purposes.
6 Personal data shall be processed in accordance with the rights of data subjects under this Act.

7 Appropriate technical and organisational measures shall be taken against unauthorised or unlawful processing of personal data and against accidental loss or destruction of, or damage to, personal data.
8 Personal data shall not be transferred to a country or territory outside the European Economic Area (EEA) unless that country or territory ensures an adequate level of protection for the rights and freedoms of data subjects in relation to the processing of personal data.

Processing personal data

The Data Protection Act refers to the processing of personal data. Processing can mean:

- obtaining data (i.e., collecting data)
- recording data
- carrying out any operation or set of operations on data.

Summary of the eight Data Protection Principles

The eight Data Protection Principles require that data shall be:

1 fairly and lawfully processed
2 processed for limited purposes
3 adequate, relevant and not excessive
4 accurate
5 not kept longer than necessary
6 processed in accordance with the data subjects' rights
7 secure
8 not transferred to countries outside the EU without adequate protection.

The problems and the need for legislation: Data Protection Act 1998

Introduction

The Data Protection Act 1998 is used to protect personal data from misuse. In order to do this it requires certain procedures to take place.

Notification

Notification is the process of letting the Information Commissioner's Office know that an organisation is storing and processing personal data. The person in the organisation who is responsible for the processing of the data (i.e., the data controller) will inform the Information Commissioner of certain details such as:

- Company registration number (a unique number given to each company/organisation).
- The name and address of the data controller.
- The classes of the data that is held (e.g., medical details, financial details, employment details, etc.).
- A general description of the reasons for storing the personal data (debt collection, research, criminal investigation, etc.).
- A description of the data subjects who the data are about (e.g., pupils, patients, customers, etc.).
- Lists of other organisations to which the data is passed (e.g., police, HM Revenue and Customs, universities). These are called recipients.

- Information about whether the information is passed to other countries outside the EEA (European Economic Area).

Notification can be done:

- by post using a special form
- over the Internet
- by phone to the Information Commissioner's Office.

Once these details have been supplied, they will be added to a register that will be made available to the public. This will allow the public to find out about organisations processing their personal data.

It is an offence for an organisation to process personal data without notification.

Exemptions from notification

There are some exemptions from notification under the Data Protection Act. The implication of this is that the data subjects no longer have the right to see the data, have it changed or claim compensation. Data is exempt:

1. Where data is being held in connection with personal, family or household affairs or for recreational use.
2. Where data is used for preparing the text of documents. This is often referred to as the 'word-processing exemption'. This would cover references for jobs, universities, etc., stored on a computer.
3. Where the data is used for the calculation of wages and pensions, or the keeping of accounts or keeping records of purchases and sales for accounting purposes only.
4. Where the data is being held in the interests of national security.

▼ You will find out

▶ How notification that an organisation is processing personal data takes place

▶ About the exemptions from notification

▶ About how data subjects can apply for access to personal data held about them

▶ About how mistakes in personal data can be rectified

▶ About the exemptions from subject access

5. Where data is being used for mailing lists, provided that only names and addresses are stored and the individuals must be asked if they object to personal data being held by the user.

Subject access

Under the Data Protection Act, data subjects (i.e., the people whom the personal information is about) can ask to see the information held about themselves. To do this, they have to write to the organisation they believe is processing the data. There is a fee payable to the organisation of up to £10 but if it is a credit reference agency, then the fee is £2. A reply from the organisation must be within 40 days and if the reply comes from a credit reference agency, then it must come within 7 days.

The purpose of subject access is so that the data subject can see the personal information to check that it is

▶ KEY WORDS

Data subject – the person whom the personal information is about

Information Commissioner – the person responsible for the Information Commissioner's Office and the administration of the Data Protection Act 1998

Notification – the process of letting the Information Commissioner's Office know that personal data is being processed

correct. Many decisions, such as being able to borrow money, whether you are suitable for a job, what medical treatment you are given, etc., are based on this information, so it is very important that the information does not contain errors.

What happens if the personal data is wrong?

The whole point of the Data Protection Act is to allow subject access to allow a person to check the data held about them. If the data subject finds wrong information about them they:

- have the right to compensation for financial loss or injury caused by the incorrect data
- have the right to the data being corrected or even deleted.

Exemptions from subject access

Unless the data falls into one of the categories for exemption from notification, all other personal data must be notified. Notification will allow data subjects to access the personal information about them, but there are exemptions.

Consent to process and pass personal information to others

You can consent to allowing your personal details to be processed and passed to other organisations.

When returning from a holiday you may have been asked to fill in a questionnaire to give the holiday company feedback on the sort of holiday you had. You may at first glance think that this form is entirely about collecting information on your opinions of the holiday but there are some questions about things that are unconnected to the holiday such as the date your house or car insurance is up for renewal. Personal information is valuable, especially if the person has consented to it being passed to others.

The Information Commissioner

The Information Commissioner is the person responsible for the Information Commissioner's Office. The Information Commissioner's Office is the UK's independent authority set up to promote access to official

The Information Commissioner is responsible for another Act called the Freedom of Information Act 2000. This Act gives the right of access to information held by public authorities. Using this Act, an individual can access information such as e-mails, meeting minutes, research reports, etc., held by local authorities. Typically this information would be about:

- how public authorities carry out their duties
- how they make their decisions
- how they spend public money.

Public authorities include:

- central government and government departments
- local authorities
- hospitals, doctor's surgeries, dentist's surgeries, etc.
- schools, colleges and universities
- police and prison service.

Unlike the Data Protection Act, the Freedom of Information Act is not restricted to personal information. It covers all types of information provided that the information is not covered by the following exemptions:

- where the information could jeopardise the prevention or detection of a crime
- where the release of the information would harm the public more than not releasing the information.

These exemptions mean that if the personal data being stored and processed falls into one (or more) of the following categories, then the data subject may be refused access to the personal data. Data where subject access could be refused includes:

- data used for the prevention or detection of crime
- data used for the apprehension or prosecution of offenders
- data used for the assessment or collection of tax or duty.

information and to protect personal information. Duties of the Information Commissioner include:

- responsibility for administering the two acts: The Data Protection Act 1998 and the Freedom of Information Act 2000
- to promote good information handling
- to investigate complaints
- to provide guidelines
- to bring legal proceedings, if necessary.

EXAM TIP

Although the Information Commissioner is responsible for both the Freedom of Information Act and the Data Protection Act, do not get confused between the Acts when answering questions. Basically, the Freedom of Information Act does not concern itself with personal information but instead it concentrates on information about public authorities.

The problems and the need for legislation: Computer Misuse Act 1990

Introduction

Other Acts had to be produced to deal with some of the misuses that started to cause problems after ICT systems became more widespread.

The Computer Misuse Act 1990

The Computer Misuse Act 1990 was passed to deal with a number of misuses as the use of computers became widespread. The Act makes it an offence to:

- deliberately plant or transfer viruses to a computer system to cause damage to programs and data
- use an organisation's computer to carry out unauthorised work
- hack into someone else's computer system with a view to seeing the information or altering it
- use computers to commit various frauds.

Problems with gaining prosecutions under the Computer Misuse Act 1990

In order to prosecute someone under the Computer Misuse Act 1990 the police would need to prove that they did the misuse deliberately. In other words, the person committing the crime knew what they were doing and knew it was wrong to do it.

Proving this intent is very difficult. For example, if you had a virus on your flash drive from home and took it to work and put it into a computer and it transferred a virus, this is an easy thing to do unknowingly. It would be difficult and almost impossible to prove whether or not this had been done deliberately.

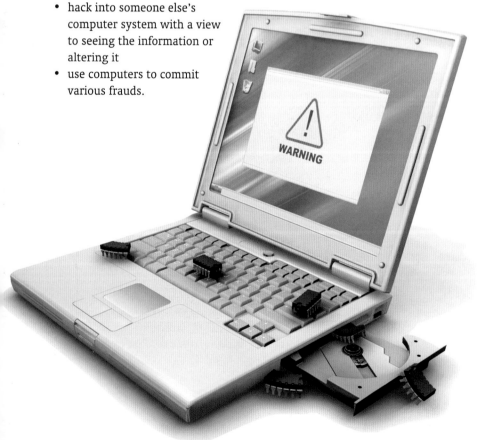

kshdofysw784cnguikng
nsdiyugfuycbrhjnhodr
ub43giumgoisfmcohsu4
yigsfbuy4tg5fiuiyhf
tv7icgirhciacshri7d
zhgd8oiz8s3cyh87fzs7
ngri3wchgikchgkseru7
78csyuihbguzfheyrgic
guea623vab2xuixnuam3
zxifyugiw6739dhcrdsi
kbgk64389b2bikcjmuhi
y7eh7riv74xjf7icjgbc
aigy3dywd2uaayezrs37
jekyhfc3o8wbrclkjmfs
nc798hs0cyo9jvghgnio
jocx7w9465fgisuyfgci
jkshgsyuisglasgfijfe
siubcoac3yhrocnhoiut
n90hvwbaoity7iy475yt
iusauitisyguciyuigti
cgsauigf648cngiog248
bavbwovnityv378nciru
t985y89eygre9iusghye
8397675n1vrqsigyrinc
iso587hsigf46fgtynot

Some organisations would not want others (especially the media) to know that their security has been compromised, so many cases go unreported and unpunished.

Offences under the Computer Misuse Act 1990

There are three sections that define the three offences under the Act.

It is useful to summarise the three sections:

Section 1

A person is guilty of an offence if:

(a) he/she causes a computer to perform any function with intent to secure access to any program or data held in any computer;

(b) the access he/she intends to secure is unauthorised; and

(c) he/she knows at the time that it is unauthorised.

The maximum sentence for an offence under this section of the Act is six months imprisonment.

Section 2

A person will be guilty of an offence under Section 2 of the Act if he/she commits an offence under Section 1 of the Act with the intent of committing a further offence such as blackmail, theft or any other offence which has a penalty of at least 5 years imprisonment. They will also be guilty if they get someone else to do this further offence.

The maximum sentence for an offence under this section of the Act is 5 years imprisonment.

Section 3

A person is guilty of an offence under this section of the Act is he/she does any act which causes an unauthorised modification of the contents of any computer, and at the time that he/she knows that the modification is unauthorised and he/she has the requisite intent. The requisite intent is intent to cause a modification and by so doing:

(a) to impair the operation of any computer;
(b) to prevent or hinder access to any program or data; or
(c) to impair the operation of any program or reliability of any data.

The maximum sentence for an offence under this section of the Act is 5 years imprisonment.

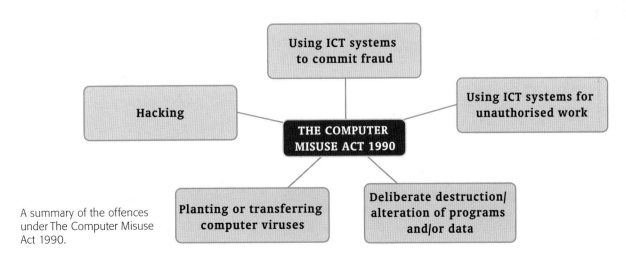

A summary of the offences under The Computer Misuse Act 1990.

The problems and the need for legislation: Copyright, Designs and Patents Act 1988

Introduction

Many people make a living out of writing software and manuals for others to use. These people are protected from having their work copied, in the same way as the writer of a best-selling novel is protected.

Copyright and licensing

There are the following problems with computer software:

- it is very easy to copy
- it is very easy to transfer files over the Internet
- people don't view copying software as like stealing goods from a supermarket.

There are the following problems with copied software:

- not entitled to technical support
- do not qualify for upgrades

- software may be incomplete
- it may contain viruses.

The process of illegally copying software is called software piracy.

The Copyright, Designs and Patents Act 1988

This Act makes it a criminal offence to copy or steal software. In addition if you copy software illegally then you are depriving the owner of the software of some of their income/profits and they will be able to sue you.

The Copyright, Designs and Patents Act 1988 allows the software owner to copy the software and also allows someone else to copy the software provided they have the owner's permission. It is not just programs that are protected by this Act, databases of data, computer files and manuals would also be covered.

Remember that you can legally copy software if you have the permission of the owner. This is necessary in order to take backup copies of software for security purposes.

Under the Act it is a criminal offence to:

- copy or distribute software or manuals without the permission or licence from the copyright owner
- run purchased software covered by copyright on two or more machines at the same time unless there is a software licence which allows it
- compel (i.e., force) employees to make or distribute illegal software for use by the company.

Consequences of breaking this law

Offences under this Act are considered serious and the consequences could include:

- unlimited fines and up to 10 years imprisonment
- you could lose your reputation, promotion prospects and even your job
- you could be sued for damages by the software owner.

Software piracy

Software piracy is the illegal copying of software and data. Just like software, data has a value and many companies would love to get their hands on

The illegal copying of software is called piracy.

their competitors' data. It has been estimated by FAST (Federation Againt Software Theft) that around 27% of the software used in Britain is illegal.

Software piracy means unauthorised copying of software. In many cases this copying will be for personal use but in some cases the people making the copies will sell them at car boot sales, computer fairs, etc. Such copying is illegal since it deprives the software manufacturer of the revenue they would have received had they sold the software.

There are other infringements of the law that are less blatant. For example, a company may have a site licence for 20 computers to use the software when the actual numbers are more than this. Nevertheless, this is still illegal and if caught doing this, the company can face being sued by the manufacturers for loss of sales revenue and fines or even imprisonment for the employees.

EXAM TIP

When software is bought, you do not own it, you only have a licence to use it. Make sure that in exam questions you specify what site licences usually allow you to do.

Never say in an answer that you are not allowed to copy software – this is not true.

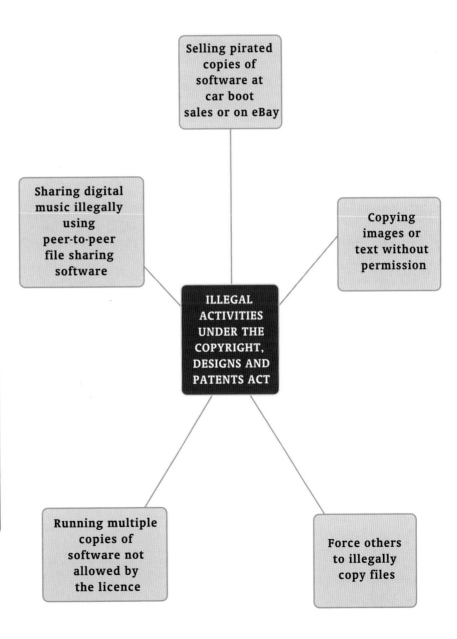

ILLEGAL ACTIVITIES UNDER THE COPYRIGHT, DESIGNS AND PATENTS ACT

- Selling pirated copies of software at car boot sales or on eBay
- Sharing digital music illegally using peer-to-peer file sharing software
- Copying images or text without permission
- Running multiple copies of software not allowed by the licence
- Force others to illegally copy files

Case studies

▶ Case study 1   pp. 172–173

Phishing – tricking people to part with account information

Phishing is where fraudsters set up a fake website which looks the same as a bank website and then send out lots of e-mails to attract people to the site. When they go to the fake site, they are asked to supply personal/financial details, which can be used to steal their identity and money. The name phishing arises because they are 'fishing' for personal information. Shown below is an example of a 'phishing' e-mail.

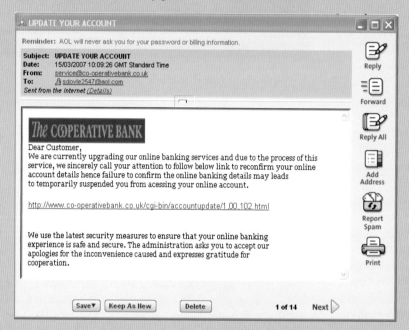

The phishing e-mail looks genuine, but read it and see if there is anything that would make you suspicious.

When you click on the link in the e-mail, you are directed to the following website:

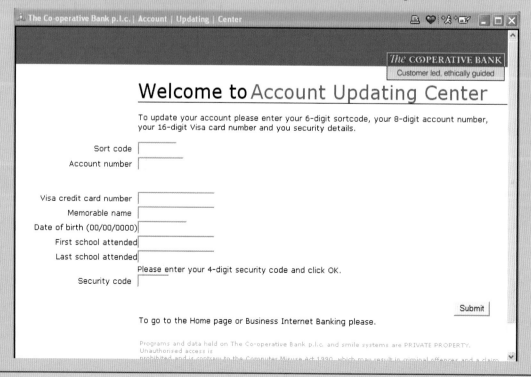

If you were to supply this personal information, the fraudster would have enough detail to be able to steal your identity and buy goods and services using your credit card. Notice that there is no indication that encryption is going to be used to scramble the information entered.

To combat phishing, banks now address you by name when sending you an e-mail and also write down the last few numbers of your account. Anyone sending you these fake e-mails would be unlikely to have these details normally, so you can be sure you are looking at an e-mail from your bank.

Banks would never send you e-mails to confirm or change your security details, account numbers, card numbers, PINs, or expiry dates.

1 As more people use the Internet for banking and buying goods and services on-line, there has been a huge increase in phishing. Describe the meaning of the term phishing and give an example of how it works. (2 marks)

2 When credit card or other personal/financial details are sent over the Internet, they are always encrypted before sending.

(a) Explain what is meant by the term encryption. (2 marks)

(b) Give **one** reason why encryption is necessary. (2 marks)

(c) Many banks ask a security question before a transaction can be completed. Give an example of a security question. (1 mark)

3 Banks and credit card companies are very worried about the increase in phishing. Give **two** pieces of advice you would give to people who buy goods/services or who bank on-line, to help prevent them falling for these fake e-mails and sites. (2 marks)

 Case study 2 pp. 174–175

Pupil hackers

Schools are having problems with school hackers breaching schools' firewalls to access forbidden material. They are using software and special techniques to crack passwords and special websites which can be used to bypass the firewall to access data held on the network.

In one school, a pupil had managed to hack into a teacher's e-mail account and then sent a message to her boyfriend dumping him.

There are a huge number of sites that hackers use to give them information about hacking or can give them access in some other way. Teachers try to block the pupils' access to such sites but it is difficult because there are so many of them and more are being created all the time.

Another way pupils are hacking into ICT systems is by standing behind a teacher and looking at what they are typing in for their username and password. Because of the slowness by which some teachers enter these details, they are able to follow the keystrokes.

Many pupils see Internet misuse as a challenge and almost a game but it does cause all sorts of problems and wastes a lot of time and money.

Security experts have said that there is a real need to educate pupils about their rights and responsibilities when using the Internet and the sanctions for misuse must be spelt out.

1 Briefly explain the purpose of a firewall. (2 marks)

2 Unauthorised access to computer resources is called hacking. There are many different ways a hacker can get access to a network. Briefly describe **two** such ways. (2 marks)

3 A school is likely to hold personal information about its pupils on the network.

Give **five** items of personal information that would be stored about a pupil. (5 marks)

4 Once a pupil has gained access to the school's network, outline **two** things they could do with the information. (2 marks)

5 A school should have an acceptable use policy governing the way the school's computer facilities should be used.

Outline **two** things that should be in the acceptable use policy that would help protect against the abuses outlined in the case study. (2 marks)

6 Hacking is illegal. Give the name of the law which covers hacking. (1 mark)

Unit 2 Living in the Digital World

Case studies continued

▶ Case study 3 — pp. 182–183

Big Brother is watching you!

A Big Brother database is being planned by the government which will hold large amounts of data about each one of us that can be used by government departments as well as some private organisations.

The trouble is that many government departments have data about us which is untrue or out-of-date. The idea is that government departments would be able to share the data that has been collected. This would help individuals such as the family member who needed to contact the different government departments to sort out the affairs of someone who had just died. With the new database only the one set of data about a person is held so it would only be necessary to contact one of the departments to update the details.

One problem that the government would have is that the law would need to be changed regarding the sharing of information.

As the data contained on such a database would be very personal, the use of the database would need to be carefully monitored. Each time someone used the database the details of who accessed it and why the information was needed would be recorded. This in itself would add a huge amount to the data being stored. For example, if a building society needed to check on someone's identity before they decided to give them a mortgage, then the details of the mortgage application would also be recorded.

With this information added, the government have access to huge amounts of information and can build up a picture of a person's life.

1 (a) Give the name of the Act that would have to be changed in order for the transfer of personal data to be allowed. **(1 mark)**

   (b) (i) Which of the eight principles would be contravened if the database went ahead? **(1 mark)**

       (ii) Describe the principle which is being contravened. **(2 marks)**

2 (a) Describe what is meant by the term privacy. **(2 marks)**

   (b) Give **one** way that could be used to make sure that the data in the database is not out-of-date. **(1 mark)**

   (c) Describe, with a reason, why it is more efficient to hold personal details in one huge database compared to lots of separate smaller databases. **(2 marks)**

3 People are worried that their right to privacy is being eroded with the development of this database.

   (a) Give **two** reasons why a person's privacy could be eroded by this database. **(2 marks)**

   (b) Describe **one** benefit to the government in sharing the data in the database between departments. **(1 mark)**

   (c) Give **one** advantage to a private company in being able to use some of the data contained in the database. **(1 mark)**

An ICT system that verifies the information candidates give on application forms for jobs

Around 71% of employers found that people had lied on their CVs or application forms for jobs. They had lied about their qualifications as well as about the jobs they had done and the salary they had earned. This ICT system allows employers to check the information given to them by candidates for jobs, over the Internet.

Here is a report which compares their actual GCSE grades with those they say they have on an application for a job.

John Smith

Secondary Education

Name of school	The School
Town	Nottingham
Attended	Mar 1982 to Nov 1986

Qualifications obtained			
Subject	Type	Grade	Confirmed
Maths	GCSE	B	Yes
English Literature	GCSE	C	No
English	GCSE	C	Yes
Science	GCSE	C	No
History	GCSE	B	No
Geography	GCSE	C	Yes
Religious Studies	GCSE	C	Yes
Physical Education	GCSE	A	Yes
English	A Level	B	Yes

The school have confirmed the following grades achieved:
English Literature – D
Science – E
History - D

candidate verifier

Home | Account Information | Products and Services | About Us | Contact Us | Need Help?

About Candidate Verifier

Selecting the right staff is one of the most time consuming, expensive and complex tasks for any personnel manager. Candidate Verifier from Experian® is the simple, cost effective pre-employment screening solution.

Through its unique, fully automated online system, Candidate Verifier provides fast, accurate and up-to-date information directly to you over the Internet. It allows you to tailor your pre-screening requirements depending on the degree of detail you require and compliments your recruitment process by helping to determine whether candidates not only have the right competencies, but also have integrity, reliability and honesty.

The standard financial report is sent to you instantly via email and confirms residency, as well as identifying any adverse financial details about the candidate. Additional reports can also be requested on a stand-alone basis or to further support your screening process - these include our secondary education check, higher education check, employer reference check, personal reference check and professional membership check. Candidate Verifier gives you the information you need, when you need it and the ability to monitor your enquiry 24 hours a day, 7 days a week.

Subscribe to the service
Report types
Employee Verifier
Data Sources
Demonstration

Copyright © 2004 Experian Ltd (Site Map) and subject to terms of use.

There is a short demonstration of this ICT system which you need to access using the Internet. Type the following URL into your browser: http://www.cvverifier.com/cv/verifier_demo.html

There is also further information about this ICT system on the following website which you should now read: http://www.cvverifier.com/cv/about_cv.html. Please note that this product can only be used by an employer with the written consent of the subject/applicant.

1 Give **one** advantage to the employer in using this system. (1 mark)
2 Give **one** advantage to the employee in using this system. (1 mark)
3 ICT systems are usually judged by the capacity to save organisations money.
   Describe briefly how this candidate verification system can save a school or college money. (2 marks)

4 This ICT system uses several sources of data.
   Give the names of **three** sources of this data. (3 marks)
5 Experian, the company who market this candidate verification system, are data providers and they store and process personal data about data subjects.
   (a) Explain the term data provider. (1 mark)
   (b) Explain the term data subject. (1 mark)

   (c) Give **two** examples of ways in which Experian process data. (2 marks)
6 As a data provider, under the Data Protection Act 1998, Experian must keep the data they use accurate and up-to-date.
   (a) Give **three** different items of data that must be kept up-to-date. (3 marks)
   (b) Give **one** reason why the data they hold must be accurate. (1 mark)

Unit 2 Living in the Digital World

Case studies continued

 Case study 5 p. 185

Freedom of Information Act 2000

The argument the government and others put forward in favour of CCTV and ID cards is that people who have nothing to hide have nothing to worry about. However, the same people are worried about the Freedom of Information Act and how it is used to embarrass them. Although they think the Freedom of Information Act is a good thing, they do not like it being used by the press and broadcasters to gain information about their mistakes, which make good articles or programmes.

There is a threat to the Freedom of Information Act 2000 at present because the government claims that it costs too much money and that this money could be better spent. They would like to see the Freedom of Information Act being used by the general public only and not to fuel stories in the press.

It is interesting to note that MPs voted in 2007 to exempt themselves from the Freedom of Information Act!

1 Give the name of the person who is responsible for the Freedom of Information Act 2000. (1 mark)

2 Describe **one** of the rights that the Freedom of Information Act gives to ordinary people. (1 mark)

3 Give **four** examples of organisations you could ask for details under the Freedom of Information Act 2000. (4 marks)

4 State with reasons whether your request for information to be revealed under the Freedom of Information Act by the following organisations would be successful:

(a) A local authority when they refused you planning permission for an extension to your house. (1 mark)

(b) An NHS doctor's surgery when you wanted to compare their expenditure with other practices in the area. (1 mark)

(c) A school that refused to tell you statistics regarding attendance (both teachers and pupils). (1 mark)

(d) A local authority who refused to supply information regarding the expense claims that their councillors have made. (1 mark)

 Case study 6 pp. 186–187

Cases brought under the Computer Misuse Act 1990

Many successful prosecutions have been brought under the Computer Misuse Act 1990. Here are some of the more interesting ones. Read them carefully and then answer the questions that follow.

1 A teenager bombarded his ex-employer's mail server with 5 million e-mails causing the e-mail server to crash. This caused a denial of service. He pleaded guilty and was sentenced to a two-month curfew.

2 A computer engineer deleted a company's files after a dispute over money he was owed. He was convicted and given an 18-month prison sentence.

3 A man who infected thousands of computers across the world with a fast spreading virus has been jailed for two years. The virus was sent as an e-mail which, when opened, put a virus on the computer hard drive. The e-mail was automatically sent to everyone in the e-mail address book, so the virus soon spread. The virus corrupted data on the computer's hard drive and 'seized-up' 27,000 computers worldwide.

To make a user open the e-mail it had the interesting title 'You have a secret admirer'!

4 A computer student was sentenced to three years psychiatric treatment after he hacked into websites and gained the details of 23,000 Internet shoppers around the world.

The judge said that he had a sense of humour after he sent a consignment of Viagra to Microsoft's founder Bill Gates after hacking his credit card details.

His activities brought FBI agents and Canadian Mounties to the small Welsh village where he lived where he was arrested and had his computer confiscated.

The cost of stopping all the credit card details and reissuing the new credit cards was in the region of £1.5million.

5 A female police officer used the Police National Computer to access the electoral rolls and car registration records to find the address of a woman who was having an affair with her boyfriend. She was sentence to three months imprisonment.

1 Case 1 was an example of a denial of service attack. Explain briefly what this means. (2 marks)

2 (a) Explain what is meant by a computer virus. (2 marks)

(b) Computer viruses can cause annoyance to computer users in a number of ways. Describe two ways in which viruses cause annoyance. (2 marks)

3 Give one reason why users of ICT systems should never open e-mails from people or organisations they do not know. (1 mark)

4 The Computer Misuse Act 1990 has been around for many years, yet there have been relatively few convictions. Give one reason why this is. (1 mark)

5 State three actions by a computer user which are illegal under the terms of the Computer Misuse Act 1990. (3 marks)

▶ Case study 7 | pp. 188–189

The Federation Against Software Theft (FAST)

FAST is the abbreviation for the Federation Against Software Theft.

The Federation Against Software Theft is an anti-piracy organisation who work to protect the work of software publishers. In 2006 FAST announced research findings that 79% of respondents would report someone they saw shoplifting but only 19% would report a colleague for sharing illegal software.

The person in charge of FAST said: 'In my opinion, digital software theft is exactly the same as walking out of PC World with a CD stuffed up your jumper – stealing is stealing, and I'm shocked at the blasé attitude of so many of our survey respondents. There seems to be a huge morality gap.'

Maybe people think they cannot be caught stealing software as there are no CCTV cameras or store detectives. However, FAST has developed ways of finding where illegally downloaded versions of software come from.

It has been estimated by FAST that a reduction in software piracy of 10% could create 40,000 additional jobs and contribute £6bn to the UK economy.

1 Give the meaning of the abbreviation FAST. (1 mark)

2 Explain what is meant by software piracy. (1 mark)

3 Give one way in which software piracy is morally wrong. (1 mark)

4 Give the full name of the organisation that helps protect software producers' rights. (1 mark)

5 Explain what is meant by a software licence. (2 marks)

6 Explain two things an organisation can do to help prevent staff putting illegal copies of software onto the organisation's computers. (2 marks)

7 The copying of software illegally without permission is covered by a law.
Give the full name of this law. (1 mark)

Questions and Activities

▶ Questions 1 | pp. 168–169

1 Many ICT systems are used to process personal information about individuals. Many people say that such systems erode privacy.
   (a) Explain the meaning of the term 'privacy'. (2 marks)
   (b) Give **three** items of personal information which a bank or building society would hold about you. (3 marks)
   (c) Give **three** items of personal information that you would not want to be disclosed to others and for each item give a reason why you would not want this information disclosed. (6 marks)
   (d) Name the Act which governs the way organisations must deal with personal information. (1 mark)
2 Protection of your privacy is essential if you bank or shop on-line.
   (a) Give the names of **three** different pieces of personal information you would need to supply in order to complete an on-line purchase. (3 marks)
   (b) Give **one** item of personal information (that you would not want others to know) that you need to supply in order to complete an on-line purchase. (1 mark)
   (c) Give **one** method by which the item of personal information in your answer to (b) can be kept private. (1 mark)

▶ Questions 2 | pp. 170–171

1 Give **two** reasons why a network manager might need to check the contents of the hard drive of your computer attached to the network. (2 marks)
2 Some organisations monitor their employees' use of the Internet.
   Give **two** reasons why an organisation might do this. (2 marks)

3 Give **one** reason why an employee might object to their network manager monitoring their Internet use. (1 mark)
4 Network resources are protected by a series of passwords and user-IDs.
   Explain clearly the difference between a password and a user-ID. (2 marks)

▶ Questions 3 | pp. 172–173

1 Give **two** ways in which your computer use could be monitored at work. (2 marks)
2 When credit card or banking details are sent over the Internet, they are always encrypted.
   (a) Explain what encrypted means. (2 marks)

   (b) Some government departments are worried about the use of encryption.
      Give **one** reason why they are worried. (1 mark)
3 Internet service providers can erode privacy. Give **one** way they do this. (2 marks)

▶ Questions 4 | pp. 174–175

1 (a) List **six** distinctly different potential threats to an ICT system. (6 marks)
   (b) Threats to ICT systems can be categorised as internal or external threats.
      Explain, by giving a suitable example in each case, the difference between internal and external threats. (2 marks)
2 Fire is a major threat to any ICT system. Give **three** things that can be done to minimise the risk to an ICT system by fire. (3 marks)

▶ Questions 5 | pp. 176–177

1 Threats to hardware, software and data are many.
   (a) Name and briefly describe **two** threats that are not human in origin. (2 marks)
   (b) Name and briefly describe **two** threats that are caused by humans. (2 marks)
2 Explain, by using suitable examples, the difference between malpractice and crime as applied to ICT systems. (4 marks)

Questions 6 pp. 178–179

1 When a customer pays for goods or services using the Internet, the data is always encrypted. Explain, by giving a suitable example, the meaning of the term encrypted. (2 marks)

2 Give **two** methods, besides the use of passwords, for preventing malicious or unauthorised access to data. (2 marks)

Questions 7 pp. 180–181

1 The people who work in an organisation can be responsible for loss or damage to the organisation's data. This can be done maliciously or accidentally. Organisations take regular backups to recover data damaged or lost but they also try to prevent employees from causing loss or damage to data.
   (a) Describe **two** measures that could be incorporated into the hardware which could prevent loss or damage to data. (4 marks)
   (b) Describe **two** software measures that could be used to prevent the loss or damage to data. (4 marks)
   (c) Describe **two** procedures the organisation could adopt to prevent the loss or damage to data. (4 marks)

2 Access to network resources is often managed using passwords and different levels of permitted access for users.
   (a) Explain what is meant by a password. (2 marks)
   (b) Explain the meaning of the term 'levels of permitted access for users'. (2 marks)

Questions 8 pp. 182–183

1 Write down **three** different ways by which personal data could be obtained. (3 marks)
2 Explain simply what recording data would typically mean. (2 marks)
3 Describe **three** different operations that can be carried out on personal data. (3 marks)

4 (a) Give the name of the legislation that protects the privacy of individuals whose personal data is stored and processed by others. (1 mark)
   (b) Give two reasons why this piece of legislation was passed by parliament. (2 marks)

Questions 9 pp. 184–185

1 The Information Commissioner is the person responsible for the Data Protection Act 1998. Give **one** reason why you think the Information Commissioner is independent. (1 mark)
2 Under the terms of the 1998 ata Protection Act, an organistion must notify their use of personal data.
   (a) Give **one** reason why this notification is necessary. (1 mark)
   (b) Give **three** pieces of information the data controller would need to give as part of the notification process. (3 marks)

3 A person applies for subject access under the Data Protection Act 1998.
   (a) Explain what subject access means. (1 mark)
   (b) Subject access is not always granted. Describe, by giving an example, a situation where subject access could be refused. (2 marks)
4 In the context of the Data Protection Act 1998, describe the meaning of the following terms:
   (a) The Information Commissioner (1 mark)
   (b) A data subject (1 mark)
   (c) A data controller (1 mark)
   (d) Notification (1 mark)

Questions 10 pp. 186–187

1 Give the name of the Act which is designed to allow organisations to prosecute anyone accessing their ICT systems illegally. (1 mark)
2 Explain, by giving an example, what is covered by the Computer Misuse Act 1990. (2 marks)

3 Passwords are one method used to protect against unauthorised access to ICT systems. Give **one** other way in which unauthorised access can be prevented. (2 marks)

Questions and Activities continued

▶ Questions 11 pp. 188–189

1 Briefly explain the term software piracy. (2 marks)
2 A network manager is worried that unauthorised and illegally copied software is being used by some employees in the organisation.
   (a) Give **two** consequences to the organisation of using illegally copied software. (2 marks)
   (b) Give the name of the Act that makes it an offence to illegally copy software. (1 mark)

(c) Explain **two** things the network manager could do to prevent employees from copying software illegally onto the organisation's computers. (2 marks)
3 Briefly explain **two** instances in which it might be legal to make a copy of a piece of software. (2 marks)

▶ Activity 1

For this research activity you have to look at the Data Protection Act 1998 carefully to see what the term 'personal data' means. Write a definition for the term personal data.

▶ Activity 2 Creating a mind map on threats

For this activity you have to create a mind map which covers the broad subject of 'threats to an ICT system'.

You can use mind mapping software, such as Inspiration, for this task, or if you do not have the software then you can draw the mind map on paper.

You can use the following list of threats to start you off:
- viruses
- Trojans
- worms
- spyware
- adware
- spam
- abuse by staff (accidental or deliberate)
- hacking
- fire
- theft
- natural disasters
- faulty hardware or software

If you teacher lets you, you can work in small groups which will allow you to work collaboratively and bounce ideas off one another.

▶ Activity 3 Collecting data using surveys

Collecting personal data for processing is big business. For this activity you have to look at the 'Voice in a Crowd website' at www.voiceinacrowd.co.uk. This website allows people to complete lots of different questionnaires with the chance of winning a prize.

This website encourages people to part with their personal information for the chance of winning a prize.

When you are looking at this site, think about the types of questionnaires and which companies each set of answers to the questions would be useful to. Also, look at the privacy statement which tells the user how the information will be used.

Exam support

Worked example 1

1 A health and fitness club would like to offer past members who have let their membership lapse, special deals to rejoin the club. They use data they collected five years ago to decide what special deals and promotions should be offered.
   (a) Explain why the data from five years ago might not be suitable to decide on the offers made to past members today. **(2 marks)**
   (b) Explain the effect on the health club if they used this data from five years ago. **(2 marks)**

Student answer 1

1 (a) Data from five years ago would be out of date. For example, they could have changed address so they would not hear about the offers.
   (b) The health club would lose money and they could be prosecuted.

Student answer 2

1 (a) The data would no longer be accurate. Their circumstances could have changed and they may have a family and not have time to attend a health club.
   (b) The response rate for the offer would be low and not justify the time, effort and cost of letters sent out.

Examiner's comment

1 (a) A fairly simple question if it had been read carefully. This student has answered a completely different question such as 'what are the consequences of using out-of-date data'. This answer does not answer the question – it needs to refer to the data being used to make a decision. **(0 marks out of 2)**

   (b) There are two marks here so at least two points are needed.
   General statements, such as 'lose money' without saying why, gain no marks.
   Again 'could be prosecuted' is too general to be given credit, without giving the reason why. **(0 marks out of 2)**

Examiner's comment

1 (a) There are two marks here. You are safer explaining two separate points rather than give a fuller description of a single point.
   This student should have given two points or made it clearer that the two points made are distinctly different. **(1 mark out of 2)**

   (b) Again there are two marks and one point is given.
   Answer is correct but two separate answers should have been given. **(1 mark out of 2)**

Examiner's answers

1 (a) One mark each for two of the following:
   Market conditions may have changed from five years ago, e.g. there may be more competition.
   People's tastes change so what attracted them five years ago might not attract them today.
   People will be five years older so could have more demands on their time, e.g. families.

   (b) One mark each for two of the following:
   They may waste time and money offering deals no-one wants.
   The price offered may be wrong owing to the competition being cheaper thus losing money.
   They would be in violation of the Data Protection Act 1998 for keeping data for longer than necessary and for processing out-of-date data.

Unit 2 Living in the Digital World

Exam support continued

Worked example 2

2 Under the terms of the Data Protection Act 1998 a data subject may ask to see the personal data held about them.
   (a) Give one reason why the Data Protection Act allows subject access. (2 marks)
   (b) It turns out that some of the data subject's personal information is wrong. Explain two things that the data subject could now do. (2 marks)

Student answer 1

2 (a) To let the Information Commissioner know that personal data is being processed.
  (b) Sue the firm
      Ask them to correct the data.

Examiner's comment

2 (a) They are getting confused here and have supplied a definition of the notification process. Candidates often confuse terms in exam questions. (0 marks out of 2)
   (b) The firm can only be sued if it can be proved that the data subject has suffered loss in some way from the incorrect information. This answer is not in enough detail for a mark. The second point gains a mark. (1 mark out of 2)

Student answer 2

2 (a) Only the data subject would know whether the data is correct or not. For example, if the information said that they owed lots of money when they didn't, they could have it corrected. If they did not do this, it could affect them getting loans, credit cards, etc.
  (b) Apply to have the incorrect data corrected.
      Sue the organisation for damages, if they have suffered as a result of the wrong information. They may not have been able to buy a house if the incorrect information had them as a bad credit risk.

Examiner's comment

2 (a) The two points made in the first two sentences are enough for two marks.
         The example is given to help explain, although it starts to answer the next part of the question (i.e., part (b)). It is good exam technique to always read the entire question before answering it. It stops you wasting time answering the next part of the question. (2 marks out of 2)
   (b) This is a good answer and is worth full marks. (2 marks out of 2)

Examiner's answers

2 (a) Need to mention that the person to whom the data refers is to look at the data and that the personal data is to be checked for accuracy.
         Two points (one mark each):
         To allow a data subject (1) to check the personal data held about them (1).
         So that the person who the data is about can check (1) the accuracy of the personal data held (1)
   (b) One mark each for two answers similar to:
         They can have the data changed if it is incorrect.
         They can have the data deleted if it is incorrect.
         They can sue the organisation if they have suffered loss as a result of decisions being made on the basis of the incorrect information.
         Have the right of compensation caused by incorrect data.

Summary mind maps

The need to protect data in ICT systems: privacy and passwords

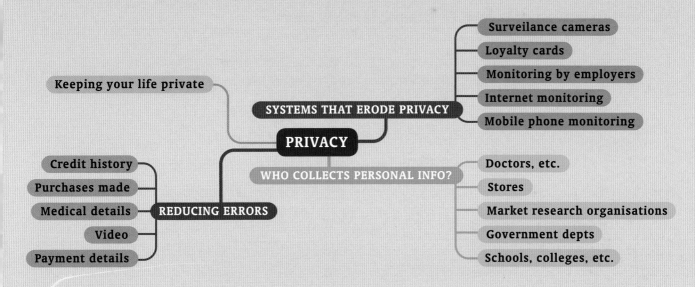

Keeping your life private

SYSTEMS THAT ERODE PRIVACY
- Surveillance cameras
- Loyalty cards
- Monitoring by employers
- Internet monitoring
- Mobile phone monitoring

PRIVACY

WHO COLLECTS PERSONAL INFO?
- Doctors, etc.
- Stores
- Market research organisations
- Government depts
- Schools, colleges, etc.

REDUCING ERRORS
- Credit history
- Purchases made
- Medical details
- Video
- Payment details

The need to protect data in ICT systems: monitoring

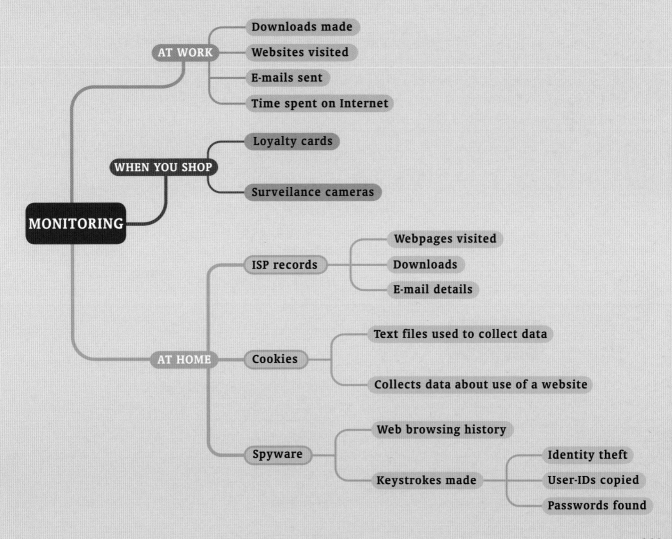

MONITORING

AT WORK
- Downloads made
- Websites visited
- E-mails sent
- Time spent on Internet

WHEN YOU SHOP
- Loyalty cards
- Surveillance cameras

AT HOME
- ISP records
  - Webpages visited
  - Downloads
  - E-mail details
- Cookies
  - Text files used to collect data
  - Collects data about use of a website
- Spyware
  - Web browsing history
  - Keystrokes made
    - Identity theft
    - User-IDs copied
    - Passwords found

Summary mind maps continued

The need to protect data in ICT systems: identity theft

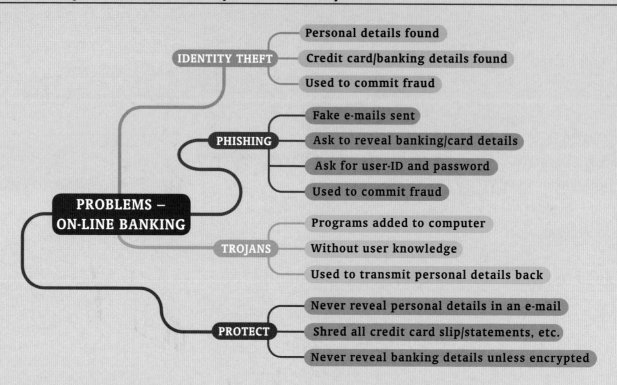

IDENTITY THEFT
- Personal details found
- Credit card/banking details found
- Used to commit fraud

PROBLEMS – ON-LINE BANKING

PHISHING
- Fake e-mails sent
- Ask to reveal banking/card details
- Ask for user-ID and password
- Used to commit fraud

TROJANS
- Programs added to computer
- Without user knowledge
- Used to transmit personal details back

PROTECT
- Never reveal personal details in an e-mail
- Shred all credit card slip/statements, etc.
- Never reveal banking details unless encrypted

Threats to ICT systems: what they are

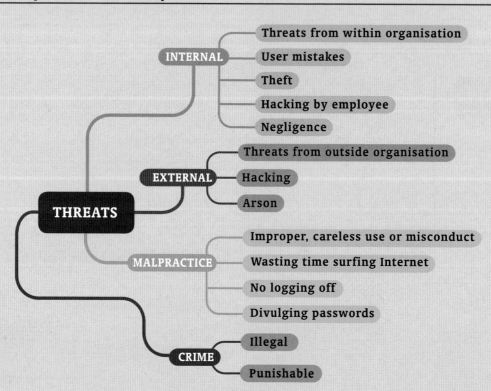

THREATS

INTERNAL
- Threats from within organisation
- User mistakes
- Theft
- Hacking by employee
- Negligence

EXTERNAL
- Threats from outside organisation
- Hacking
- Arson

MALPRACTICE
- Improper, careless use or misconduct
- Wasting time surfing Internet
- No logging off
- Divulging passwords

CRIME
- Illegal
- Punishable

Threats to ICT systems: internal or external malpractice or crime

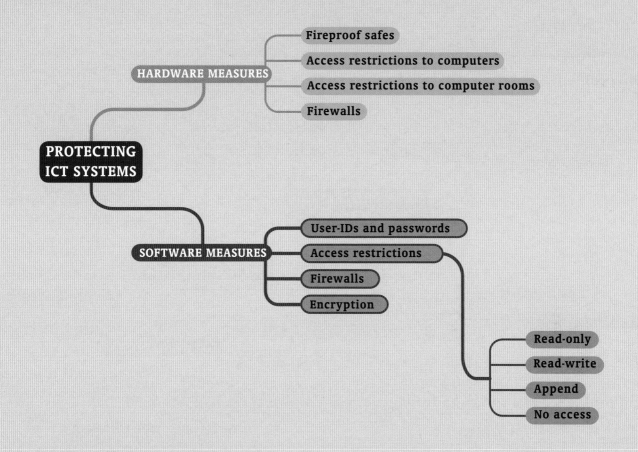

PROTECTING ICT SYSTEMS

- **HARDWARE MEASURES**
  - Fireproof safes
  - Access restrictions to computers
  - Access restrictions to computer rooms
  - Firewalls

- **SOFTWARE MEASURES**
  - User-IDs and passwords
  - Access restrictions
    - Read-only
    - Read-write
    - Append
    - No access
  - Firewalls
  - Encryption

Protecting ICT systems: methods

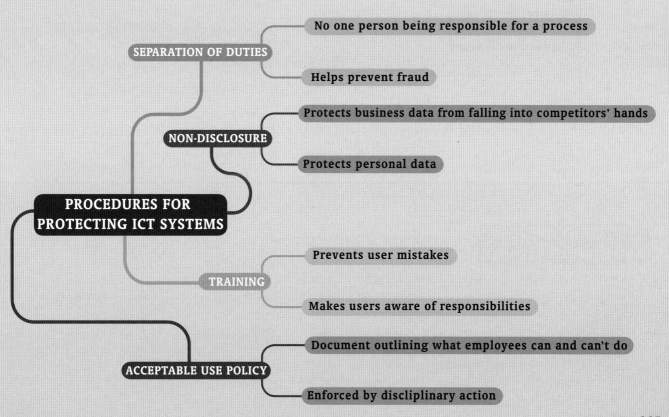

PROCEDURES FOR PROTECTING ICT SYSTEMS

- **SEPARATION OF DUTIES**
  - No one person being responsible for a process
  - Helps prevent fraud

- **NON-DISCLOSURE**
  - Protects business data from falling into competitors' hands
  - Protects personal data

- **TRAINING**
  - Prevents user mistakes
  - Makes users aware of responsibilities

- **ACCEPTABLE USE POLICY**
  - Document outlining what employees can and can't do
  - Enforced by disciplinary action

Summary mind maps continued

The problems and the need for legislation: Data Protection Act 1998

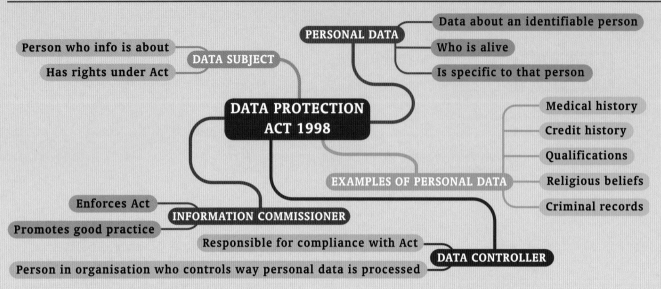

PERSONAL DATA
- Data about an identifiable person
- Who is alive
- Is specific to that person

DATA SUBJECT
- Person who info is about
- Has rights under Act

DATA PROTECTION ACT 1998

EXAMPLES OF PERSONAL DATA
- Medical history
- Credit history
- Qualifications
- Religious beliefs
- Criminal records

INFORMATION COMMISSIONER
- Enforces Act
- Promotes good practice

DATA CONTROLLER
- Responsible for compliance with Act
- Person in organisation who controls way personal data is processed

The problems and the need for legislation: Computer Misuse Act 1990

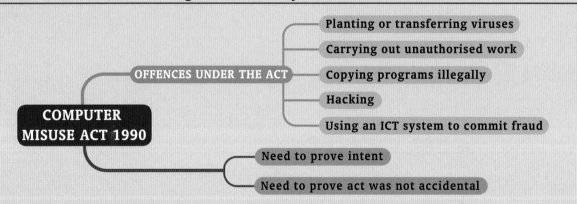

COMPUTER MISUSE ACT 1990

OFFENCES UNDER THE ACT
- Planting or transferring viruses
- Carrying out unauthorised work
- Copying programs illegally
- Hacking
- Using an ICT system to commit fraud

- Need to prove intent
- Need to prove act was not accidental

The problems and the need for legislation: Copyright, Designs and Patents Act 1988

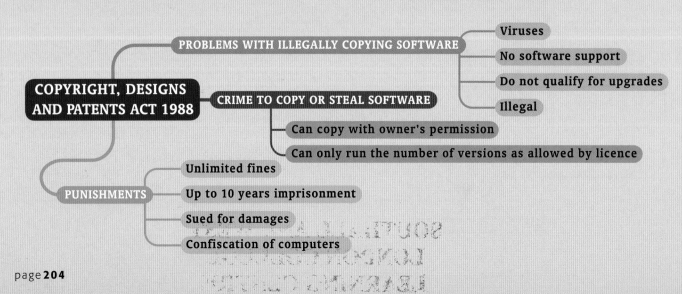

COPYRIGHT, DESIGNS AND PATENTS ACT 1988

PROBLEMS WITH ILLEGALLY COPYING SOFTWARE
- Viruses
- No software support
- Do not qualify for upgrades
- Illegal

CRIME TO COPY OR STEAL SOFTWARE
- Can copy with owner's permission
- Can only run the number of versions as allowed by licence

PUNISHMENTS
- Unlimited fines
- Up to 10 years imprisonment
- Sued for damages
- Confiscation of computers

It is essential that the data and programs in all ICT systems are properly backed up. This topic looks at the subject of backup and in particular why, when and how they are taken and also how the original data is recovered should the worst happen.

Many ICT systems need to keep running 24/7, so this topic will look at how this can be achieved.

▼ The key concepts covered in this topic are:

▶ The need to take regular and systematic backups

▶ Different individuals and organisations have different needs for backup and recovery

▶ Responsibility needs to be allocated for backup and recovery procedures

▶ The need for continuity of service

CONTENTS

Unit 2 Living in the Digital World

The need for regular and systematic backup

Introduction

Most people realise the importance of taking backups but still never take them. Losing personal data on a home computer is annoying, especially when some files such as digital photograph files of people and events can never be recovered. For an organisation or business it is a real disaster.

Threats to ICT systems

You saw in the previous topic that there are a large number of threats to ICT systems and these include:

- computer/hardware failure
- deliberate damage
- accidental damage
- theft
- hacking
- fire
- terrorist attack
- natural disasters (flood, earthquake, tidal wave, lightning strike, etc.)
- viruses
- software bugs
- power cuts.

Malpractice and crime

Those security problems caused by humans can be divided into two types:

- malpractice
- crime.

Malpractice is improper, careless or unprofessional conduct. This means that someone who forgets to log off the network when they go for a break or lunch, allowing others to see and use their computer, would be guilty of malpractice but not of a crime.

A crime is an illegal act. When a crime is committed, the person is punishable by law normally by a fine or imprisonment. In ICT, crime would involve a person doing something that contravened one of the Acts such as:

- passing on sensitive data in contravention of the Data Protection Act 1998
- hacking into a network contrary to the Computer Misuse Act 1990
- illegally copying software contrary to the Copyright, Designs and Patents Act 1988
- sabotaging an ICT system
- spreading computer viruses.

Viruses

Malicious damage can arise from inside or outside the organisation and can vary from a disgruntled employee altering a program so that it does not work properly or printing an insulting message on all the invoices when the employee has left the company, to a person deliberately introducing a virus.

Viruses pose the main threat under the heading malicious damage. A virus is a program that replicates (i.e., copies) itself automatically and usually carries with it some payload which causes damage.

Once a computer or media has a virus copied onto it, it is said to be infected. Most viruses are designed to do something apart from copying themselves. For example, they can:

- display annoying messages on the screen
- delete programs or data
- use up resources, making your computer run more slowly.

One of the main problems is that viruses are being created all the time and that when you get a virus infection it is not always clear what a new virus will do to the ICT system.

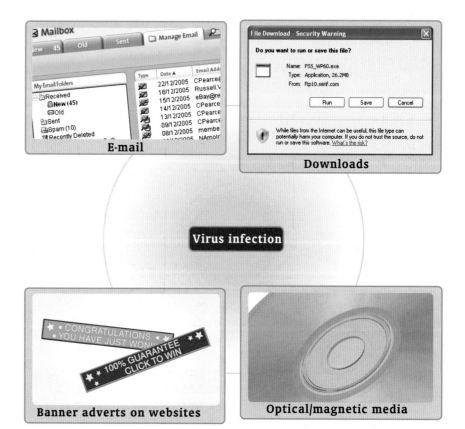

Places where you are likely to get viruses.

Apart from the dangerous payload many viruses carry, one of the problems with viruses is the amount of time that needs to be spent sorting out the problems that they create.

All computers should be equipped with a virus checker, which is a program that is able to detect and delete these viruses. These virus checkers need to be updated regularly, as new viruses are continually being developed and would not always be detected by older versions of virus checkers.

Trojans

A Trojan is a program that performs a legitimate task but also carries with it an undesirable function. You may install this as a downloaded file from the Internet as a useful file, say for teaching you maths. It does this, but each time you load it, it secretly deletes a file from your hard disk.

Worms

A worm is a program that keeps replicating itself automatically, and as it does so it take more and more disk space and also uses a greater proportion of the system's resources for each copy. The net effect of all this is to slow down the system considerably. Worms are able to affect the performance of a network considerably.

Ways by which viruses can be spread

Viruses can be spread by:

- external e-mail
- internal e-mail
- the organisation's intranet (an intranet is an internal network that makes use of Internet technology)
- shared disks
- clicking on banner advertisements on the Internet
- downloads from sites such as games sites.

How to prevent viruses

The best way to avoid viruses altogether is to use virus checking software and adopt procedures that will make virus infection less likely.

Here are some steps that can be taken to prevent viruses entering an ICT system:

- install virus checking software
- do not open e-mails from unknown sources
- keep virus checking software up-to-date – configure the virus checking software so that updates are installed automatically
- have a clear acceptable use policy for all staff who use computers
- train staff to be aware of the problems and what they can do to help
- do not allow programs such as games, video or movies to be downloaded onto the organisation's ICT systems
- do not open file attachments to e-mails unless they are from a trusted source
- if possible, avoid users being able to use their own removable media (floppy disks, removable magnetic drives).

The importance of backup

Backup means keeping copies of software and data so that the data can be recovered should there be a total loss of the ICT system.

The data an organisation holds is a very valuable commodity and is usually worth more than the cost of the hardware and software added together. Think how a business would be able to operate without the following:

- customer database
- supplier database
- product database
- records of all correspondence, price lists, quotes, etc.
- accounts information.

Couple the loss of all this data with the fact that there could be no hardware or software to use and you have a real problem.

It does take effort to back data up, but the latest backup products will do this automatically and without anyone thinking about it.

A recent study has shown that of the companies that lose their data in a disaster:

- 29% are out of business within two years, and
- nearly 43% never open their doors after the disaster.

Backup procedures

Backup involves the creation of data and programs so that if the data or programs are damaged or lost they can be recreated from the backup copies.

Backup procedures are those actions a person or organisation can take to ensure that regular backup copies are taken. Backups should be taken regularly and on a routine basis and the backup copies should be away from the computer system and preferable off-site.

Where to keep backup copies

It is always best to keep backup copies off-site but this is sometimes inconvenient.

Keeping backup copies in a fireproof safe

You could keep backup copies in a fireproof safe. In most cases this will protect them from theft and the damage caused by a small fire. However, they are only fireproof for a certain period of time – usually two hours.

Backups can be kept in fireproof safes. This fireproof safe has a fire rating of 120 min for computer disks and backup tapes.

The need for regular and systematic backup *continued*

KEY WORDS

Backup – copies of software and data kept so that the data can be recovered should there be a total loss of the ICT system.

Keeping backup copies off-site

Backup copies need to be kept off-site if possible. This is because if a building was completely destroyed, then the likelihood is that all the data, software and hardware would be destroyed. Although complete destruction of buildings is rare, it does happen – the terrorist attack on the Twin Towers is an example.

The attack on the Twin Towers caused the complete loss of two entire buildings.

One method of keeping backup copies off-site is to use removable storage media. Removable magnetic hard drives, pen/flash drives, zip drives and memory cards are all quite portable and can be used for backups.

On-line backup services

There are a number of organisations that provide a service where you can backup your essential files on-line using the Internet. This is a good service and you pay for the service according to the amount of data stored using the service.

The advantage with these services is that once you tell the system which data you want backing up, you simply forget about it and your data is backed up in the background while you are not actively using the computer. Additionally, the backup data is stored on the server of the backup provider – so the backup is not kept on the same site as the original data. To prevent security problems, all the data is encrypted before being sent over the Internet and only the person who owns the data can actually access it.

The main disadvantage of on-line storage is trusting your data to another organisation who could possibly go out of business.

For more information on on-line backup look at the following website: http://www.datadepositbox.com

There is also a nice demonstration of the software and its facilities available at: http://www.datadepositbox.com/demo-citytv.asp

Procedures for backup

Backups should be taken seriously. Here are some essential pieces of advice:

- use a different tape or disk each day and have a system for rotating them
- make one person responsible for the taking of backups
- keep backups safe (i.e., in a fireproof safe) and preferably off-site
- rehearse backup recovery procedures – you need to be sure it is possible and you know how to recover data.

Scheduling backups

The main requirement for backups is that they should be easy to take. In many cases backups can be taken automatically and this is achieved by scheduling a time for the backups to start. In most cases, whilst the backups are taken, the ICT system will slow down. Network users will notice this loss of speed, so it is best to take backups when the computer is not being used by users. In a lot of situations this can be achieved at night but there are many ICT systems that are in use 24 hours a day so the taking of backups has to be scheduled to the least busy periods.

Backups can be:

- taken manually
- scheduled to be taken automatically.

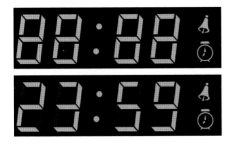

The grandfather, father and son system (the ancestral file system)

In some large ICT systems, which have large storage needs, two types of files are kept: master files and transaction files. The master file is the most complete version of a file and if it were

lost or damaged then the whole system would be rendered useless. Transaction files are used to hold details of all the transactions (i.e., bits of business) since the master file was last updated. The transaction file is used to update the master file with the changes periodically (e.g., each night, every week, etc.).

There is always the chance that data held on either a disk or tape master file may be destroyed, for example by an inexperienced user, a power failure, fire or even theft. For most companies, the loss of vital data could prove disastrous. However, using the grandfather-father-son principle it is possible to recreate the master file if it is lost.

The principle works like this. Basically three generations of files are kept. The oldest master file is called the grandfather file and is kept with its transaction file. These two files are used to produce a new master file called the father file that, with its transaction file, is used to create the most up-to-date file, called the son file. The process is repeated and the son becomes the father and the father becomes the grandfather and so on. Only three generations are needed and the other files may be re-used. Usually this system, called the ancestral file system, is used for tapes, although it may also be used for disks.

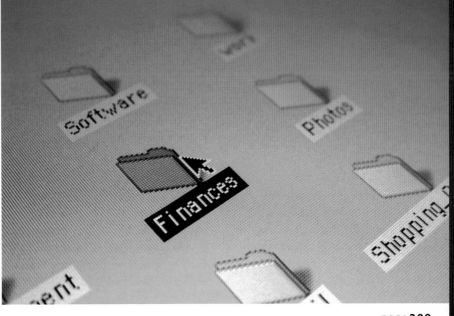

The needs of individuals and organisations for backup and recovery

▼ **You will find out**

▶ About what needs to be backed up

▶ About when backups should be taken

▶ About how the backups are taken

▶ About the storage devices and media used for backup

Introduction

Individuals and organisations have different needs for backup and recovery. Usually the amount of data stored by individuals would be small compared to the databases of large companies such as utility (gas, electricity, water and telephone) companies.

No-one, however, likes to lose data, and to an individual, the loss of irreplaceable digital camera images can be a disaster. To a company, the complete loss of data could mean the company goes out of business.

The amount of data that needs to be backed up varies considerably, so the needs for backup and recovery need to be tailored to the requirements.

Backup strategy

Everyone who stores data on a computer should have a backup strategy. This is a plan for taking backups and also covers the recovery of data should the worst happen and data is lost. This strategy needs careful thinking about.

The strategy used for backup and recovery depends on:

- what
- when
- how
- storage.

What

- You need to decide what needs to be backed up.
- For a home user this may be data and some programs.
- You may already have backup disks when the programs were first installed. Even if you downloaded them from an on-line site, then you can usually download them again without paying.

The different types of backup

There are three different types of backup called:

- full backup
- incremental backup
- differential backup.

Remember – a backup will usually involve taking copies of both the programs and the data.

Full backup

As the name suggests, full backup involves making a copy of all the files on the system.

Incremental backup

This type of backup backs up the files which have changed since the last full backup. This type of backup is useful because it is possible to have an audit trail of the file changes.

Suppose the files are corrupted four days after a full backup was made. There would be four data sets with all the changes on them – one for each day. To restore the files it would be necessary to update the full backup with each of these data sets of the changes in turn.

Differential backup

A differential backup is a cumulative backup of changes made since the last full backup. Every day the differential backup is made, the system adds further data that has changed since the last full backup. Eventually the next full backup is made and the process starts all over again.

When

How often backups are taken depends on how much data changes and how often it changes. For organisations, large amounts of data are continually changing.

Individuals

- Backups need to be taken regularly and not just when you remember.
- Many people take backups at the end of a session of work.
- Not so many people bother to take backups of media such as music, images and video mainly because of the time it takes.

Organisations

- Organisations realise the importance of their data. They employ computer professionals who realise that the risk of losing data is real.
- Organisations are more systematic about backups.
- Backups are taken at the end of the day or more frequently depending on the volume of work.
- Large organisations normally take backups in the evening when the processing power of the computer is not needed for other tasks.
- Where continuity of service is crucial, the more expensive option of backing up continuously is taken.

How

How the data is backed up depends on the amount of storage capacity needed and if there is the requirement for the data to be recovered immediately, as in the case of on-line systems such as airline booking systems.

Backup storage devices and media

There is a huge range of backup devices and media that can be used for taking backup copies. The choice of backup device/media depends on:

- storage capacity needed
- portability of device/media (i.e., weight and size)
- speed of data transfer (the speed with which data can be written to or read from the device/media)
- speed of access (the time it takes for the device to find a specific piece of stored data)
- ability to be connected to different computers or other devices such as printers, cameras, etc.

Magnetic tape

Magnetic tape is an ideal backup medium – it is cheap and has a high storage capacity. Magnetic tapes are removable media which means they can be exchanged with any compatible drive.

Large organisations use tape libraries for their backup. These use lots of tapes and some even use robotic arms to load the tapes into the drives.

Summary of where to backup

Name of backup	Cost of backup	Storage capacity	Speed	Comments
3.5″ floppy	Cheap	1.44 Mb	slow	Very small storage capacity and not all computers have a drive to read them. Outdated now.
Flash/pen drives	Cheap	up to 4 Gb and rising	moderate	Very popular portable media. Has replaced the 3.5″ floppy.
CD-RW	Free comes with the computer	up to 700 Mb	moderate	Good backup media for PCs containing a small amount of data.
DVD-RW	Free as usually built in	up to 4.7 Gb	moderate	Greater storage capacity means that it is more suitable for backup of data on a home PC.
Hard drive (Fixed)	Free as built in	160 to 250 Gb and increasing all the time	fast	Huge amount of storage and some of the capacity could be used for backup but it would be on the same drive.
Hard drive (external or removable)	Moderate	up to 500 Gb and growing	fast	Great for fast backup. Needs to be disconnected and stored in a fireproof safe or stored off-site.
Magnetic tape drive	Expensive	Huge up to 8 Tb	fast	Good option where large amounts of data need to be backed up. Some tape systems have removable tapes.
ZIP-drive	Cheap	Up to 750 Mb and growing	slow	Disks can be removed and secured. Like a fatter removable floppy disk.
Internet backup	Cheap	Unlimited storage	slow	Charged according to amount of data stored. Has advantage that data is stored off-site.

Magnetic disk

The simplest form of magnetic disk backup simply takes the contents of one magnetic disk and copies it onto a different magnetic disk.

Optical media

This includes media such as CD-R, CD-RW, DVD-RW, etc. The main problem with optical storage for backup is that the transfer rate (i.e., the rate at which data is read to or copied from the media) is low, which means taking backups takes longer.

Pen/flash drives

These are very popular as they are small and portable and are ideal for backing up small amounts of work. They are easily lost or stolen.

EXAM TIP

In questions where you are asked to choose storage devices and/or storage media, always look to see if it mentions how much data is being backed up. This will determine the device and media. Many students put that you could back up a large amount of data on a floppy disk – clearly you can't. Floppy disks should no longer be mentioned as their storage capacity is too small for most uses.

Assigning responsibility for backup and recovery procedures and the need for continuity of service

▼ **You will find out**

▶ About responsibility for backup

▶ About responsibility for recovery procedures

▶ About the need for continuity of service

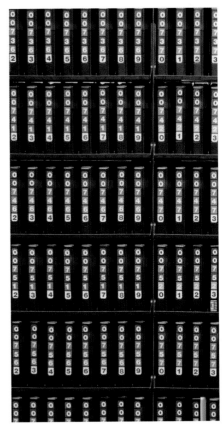

Introduction

Nearly all organisations use networks, so much of the data used is held centrally on a file server. This makes it easier for users as they do not have to worry about backing up their work on an individual basis, as all their work is backed up centrally.

In this section you will look at why responsibility for backups needs to be allocated to a person and also how the ICT services can be kept running should programs and data be lost.

The need for responsibility for taking backups

Backups should not be simply taken on an ad hoc basis (i.e., when people remember or can be bothered to take them). Leaving users to take regular backups is not a good idea, especially when critical company data is at stake.

Most organisations have a single person who is responsible for all aspects of backups. This means that backing up is taken seriously and not left to chance. It also allows the person who is responsible to create a backup strategy and also to check that the data can be recovered quickly from the backups.

Recovery procedures

Recovery procedures are those procedures that are put in place in order to get the ICT system working again should there be any loss of ICT

systems. There must be a tried and tested plan to get everything working again in the least possible time. Here are some things that would need to be considered in the recovery procedures:

- alternative accommodation should the building be destroyed
- availability of staff at short notice (usually 24/7) to help recover the backups
- availability of hardware to run the backups on
- training for staff to instruct them how to get things back to normal again
- availability of alternative communication lines in order to get network/Internet facilities back again.

The need for continuity of service

Some applications demand that the ICT systems are so critical to the business that their facilities cannot be lost even for a short period of time. This means the ICT systems must keep running, so a user would not even notice that anything had happened.

On-line booking and ordering systems are examples of systems where 24/7 reliability is essential. If a customer finds the system down, they will simply go to a competitor and may never return.

Systems for ensuring continuity of service

Backing up data is easier than it used to be because fast communication links between computers mean that the data can be transferred automatically to a backup copy. Some critical computer systems contain more than one processor and storage device located in different buildings, which can even be in different countries with high speed communication links between them. Any processing done by the computer is done in tandem and data backups are made automatically and transferred to the other computer. If one of the computers fails and the data is lost, the other one uses the copy of the data it has kept and continues the processing.

This system is used by airlines and banks where the loss of the computer just for a couple of hours could cost millions of pounds and cause a huge amount of disruption.

RAID systems

Many network systems use a RAID (redundant array of inexpensive disks) system for the backup of data. Basically they use a series of magnetic disks on which to store the data. There are different RAID systems and in one type the system will automatically take over if the original data is damaged or destroyed, ensuring the continuity of service.

Clustering

To improve network security a technique called clustering is used. Here files servers and storage devices are networked together so that the dependence on one file server and one storage device is eliminated.

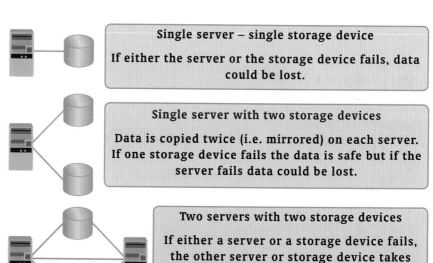

Single server – single storage device

If either the server or the storage device fails, data could be lost.

Single server with two storage devices

Data is copied twice (i.e. mirrored) on each server. If one storage device fails the data is safe but if the server fails data could be lost.

Two servers with two storage devices

If either a server or a storage device fails, the other server or storage device takes over. The middle line is a high speed data link between the servers.

Clustering is used with networks to avoid data loss.

Questions, Case studies and Activities

▶ **Questions 1** pp. 206–207

1 Threats to ICT systems can be internal or external. It is therefore necessary to protect against both types of threat.
   (a) Briefly explain, by giving an example of each, the difference between an internal and an external threat to an ICT system. (4 marks)
   (b) For each example you have given for part (a), describe a measure that can be taken to minimise or eliminate the threat. (2 marks)

2 The widespread use of laptops by company employees, especially in public places and at home, has caused an increase in the threats to company ICT systems.
   Describe **four** threats to ICT systems caused by employees using laptops. (4 marks)

3 The consequences of losing data and ICT systems can be very severe.
   Describe **three** consequences of a business losing data permanently. (6 marks)

▶ **Questions 2** pp. 210–211

1 An e-commerce business uses a database system to store customer and product information and to log the on-line payments made. Because the ICT systems are at the heart of their business, they need to have a backup strategy in place.
   (a) Give **two** reasons why it is essential for this business to have a backup strategy. (2 marks)
   (b) State **four** factors that should be considered when deciding on a back-up strategy, giving an example for each of the factors. (8 marks)

2 A company makes full backups every week and incremental backups each day between the full backups.
   (a) Explain what is meant by a full backup. (2 marks)
   (b) Explain what is meant by an incremental backup. (2 marks)
   (c) Give one reason why the company does not choose to make a full backup every day. (1 mark)

▶ **Questions 3** pp. 212–213

1 Explain the difference between backup and recovery procedures. (2 marks)

2 In order to ensure the security of its ICT systems, a company has procedures to back up all the data files on a regular basis. Explain why the company should also have recovery procedures in place. (3 marks)

3 An organisation is reviewing its backup procedures. Describe **three** items that should be included in a backup procedure. (3 marks)

4 A large supermarket chain has petrol stations and convenience stores as well as some of its larger stores open 24 hours a day. The network which runs all the point-of-sale terminals and the stock control system is essential to the smooth running of the business. Backup and recovery procedures are essential to this system. Describe **four** features the developers of these backup and recovery procedures should consider. (8 marks)

CDS Heating

CDS Heating is a small company that specialises in the installation and maintenance of central heating systems in homes and businesses in the Merseyside area.
CDS Heating has over 16,000 customers and a small computer network has been set up to keep track of orders, servicing, calls, stock, accounts and all the other day-to-day work.

The company has spent much of its time growing the business and getting the job done and has not given enough attention to the security aspects of the business. They decided to contract the services of a consultant to help them develop a security policy.

The consultant was horrified on her first visit to find that backup copies were only taken on an ad hoc basis and that the files and programs could easily be lost. No one person in the company was given responsibility for the taking of backup copies and they were only taken 'when we remember'.

The consultant told the management of the company that backup procedures need to be formalised and that they need to decide on the following:

- Responsibility for backups – one person needs to be responsible and others need to be able to take over if this person is absent.
- Backup medium – whether disks or tape are used or even whether an on-line service is used where the files can be stored on a remote server.
- The location of the backup – it is foolish to keep files near or on the actual computer. They should preferably be kept off-site.
- The type of backup – backups can be full, incremental or differential.
- Frequency of backup – this is how often the backups need to be made – this will depend on the volume of data.
- Testing of backup – there is no point in taking backup copies without testing that they would work in an emergency. Need to check that files can actually be recovered.
- Security of backups – backup files need to be kept safe.

1 Give **three** ways in which the data owned by CDS Heating could be lost. (3 marks)

2 The security consultant has advised that one person at CDS Heating should be given the responsibility for the backups. Give **two** reasons for this. (2 marks)

3 CDS Heating is connected to the Internet, which they use for communication with their customers and their suppliers. This, however, poses a threat to their data and programs.

(a) Threats to a computer system can be classed as internal or external. Describe what the difference is between internal and external threats to a computer system. (2 marks)

(b) Give **two** examples of an internal threat and **two** examples of an external threat to CDS Heating's files. (4 marks)

4 At present CDS Heating takes a copy of their data 'when they remember' and puts it on a CD which is placed in the top drawer of the desk the server is on.

(a) Describe **two** ways in which data on the server and on the CD could be lost together. (2 marks)

(b) Give **two** reasons why it is always best to keep backup data off-site. (2 marks)

(c) Backups can be full, incremental or differential. Explain the difference between each of these three types of backup. (3 marks)

5 Give **two** factors which CDS Heating need to take into account when deciding how frequently to take backup copies. (2 marks)

▶ Case study 2 | pp. 210–211

Microsoft Vista making taking backups easier

Microsoft Windows Vista is the latest operating system by Microsoft.

Microsoft Vista is the latest version of an operating system which makes use of the latest technology available. A new more up-to-date operating system was needed because of the demands placed on home and business users as they use video, music, gaming and other multimedia demands on a day-to-day basis.

The software contains many new security features designed to keep data and files safe. In particular there are new controls which make sure that users cannot make changes that make their system vulnerable.

Even if a computer is stolen, one new feature called BitLocker technology encrypts the hard drive and renders it useless to someone else. This means that they cannot access the data and programs on the hard drive. This is particularly

useful as more and more people use laptops in public places such as planes, trains, cafes, etc.

In Windows Vista backing up data is made much easier.

Other features of Vista include an easy to use Wizard which takes you though the steps of taking backups. It is easy to specify what files you want backing up, the device used to store the backup and the time to start the backup.

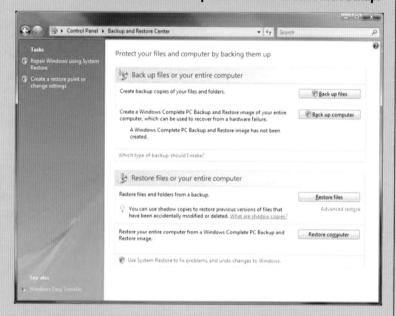

Read the above article carefully and then answer the following questions. You may need to do some research in order to answer these questions. Use books and on-line glossaries to help you. Good luck!

1   Vista is an operating system.
   (a) Write a brief description of the purpose of an operating system. (4 marks)
   (b) Describe two tasks an operating system would perform. (2 marks)
   (c) Microsoft Vista is an example of an operating system. Give the brand names of two other operating systems. (2 marks)

2 In the passage it says that 'there are new controls which make sure that users cannot make

changes that make their system vulnerable'. By giving an example, describe a change which could be made to the operating system that will make the ICT system more vulnerable. (2 marks)

3 Vista uses a Wizard to help users back up their data.
   (a) Describe what is meant by the term Wizard. (1 mark)
   (b) Explain why a Wizard is a helpful feature for a user. (2 marks)

4 When an ICT system is used in a business, the data stored is often much more valuable than the hardware or software.
   (a) State, by giving an example, why the above statement can often be true. (2 marks)

   (b) Explain two ways in which data can be lost from a computer. (2 marks)
   (c) Backups are taken so that files can be restored if lost or damaged. Give the names of two types of storage media that are appropriate for backup copies. (2 marks)

5 (a) Explain the meaning of the term encrypt. (3 marks)
   (b) Explain how encryption of data on the hard drive of the computer renders it useless to a thief who steals the computer. (2 marks)

6 Backups can be scheduled to take place at any time of the day. State, giving a reason, the time of the day when backups are best taken. (2 marks)

Case study 3 | pp. 212–213

Good planning keeps flooded businesses afloat

During the serious floods in June 2007 many businesses had their offices flooded. Some of the businesses were well covered and had plans in place to relocate staff to a disaster recovery centre where staff could use the ICT systems and their backup data to get their business up and running again.

Some firms had their computer systems flooded and completely destroyed. Others had problems with the electricity supply owing to water seeping into cables.

One member of the business community said that smaller less organised companies may not survive this, but larger companies will pull through because they have plans in place to keep their business running.

1 Describe **two** plans an organisation could put in place to keep a business running even though the ICT facilities in an office cannot be used and the data stored on the computers has been lost. **(6 marks)**

2 It is best to keep backup data off-site.
 (a) Give **one** reason why backup data should be kept off-site. **(1 mark)**
 (b) Describe **one** method for keeping backup data off-site. **(2 marks)**

▶ Activity 1 Presentation on backups

You have been asked to present a talk at a local computer club about the importance of taking backup copies and also how this should be done. As part of the talk you will be expected to show some slides using a presentation package such as PowerPoint.

In your talk you will be expected to cover the following:

- What the word backup means.
- How often backups should be taken.
- Where backup files should be kept.
- The best strategy for taking backups.
- What forms of backing storage media there are and the drives to go with them.
- A comparison of the speeds and transfer rates for different devices and some examples of the times taken to save different amounts of data.

▶ Activity 2 Producing a presentation on backup

You have been asked to give a presentation using presentation software on the importance of backup and the different types of backup available.

The firm you are presenting the information to has a very haphazard approach to backup at the moment and you will have to make a convincing argument that the time and effort in taking backups is absolutely essential.

The presentation is to last five minutes and during this time you will need to cover the following:

- The types of threat to data.
- The consequences to the organisation of losing their data.
- The need for regular taking of backups.
- The need for someone to be given overall responsibility for the taking of backups.
- The types of backup systems that are available.

Here is what you know about the organisation's procedures on backups at the moment:

- Someone has to remember to undertake the backup and if necessary take the backup off-site.
- Often the backup copies are not removed off-site.
- Everyone thinks it is someone else's job to take the backup.
- Backups are never tested so no-one knows whether the data could be recovered from them.

Your teacher/lecturer may ask you to produce this presentation on your own or they may ask a group of you to produce a group presentation.

Exam support

Worked example 1

1 A student is working on some ICT project work at school using the school's computers. They want to continue working on the project at home on their laptop computer.
   (a) Describe a suitable backup procedure that they could use. **(4 marks)**
   (b) The threats to laptop computers are often greater than those to desktop computers. Give **one** reason why. **(1 mark)**

Student answer 1

1 (a) Store the work on a disk and keep the disk in a safe place.
  (b) Laptop computers are lighter and so are easily concealed/stolen.

Examiner's comment

1 In part (a) there is no mention of the type of disk nor is there any mention that the disk is to be removed from the computer, so no mark.
   They do mention to keep the disk in a safe place but they have not said this should be away from the computer. It is still worth a mark.
   The student needed to look at the marks allocated. Four marks usually means 4 valid points or perhaps 3 with an extra mark for the clarity of the explanation.
   For part (b): laptop computers are lighter is a fact. But although it is obvious, the student has not been specific about the relevance of this. **(1 mark out of 5)**

Examiner's answers

1 (a) One mark up to a maximum of four for each of the following points:
   - Take a copy of the folder/files.
   - Store the copy onto removable media such as magnetic floppy disk, external magnetic hard disk, store on the server if students can access the server from the Internet.
   - Attach the file to an e-mail and send the e-mail to your home/school e-mail account.
   - Store the data on a removable pen/flash drive.
   - Store the copy onto an optical disk such as DVD-RW, CD-RW.
   - Files should be copied on a regular basis (e.g., at the end of a session).
   - Copies need to be stored in a safe place away from the computer.
   - It is essential that the backup copies are tested to make sure that the files can be recovered.
   (b) One reason for one mark such as:
   - Laptops are smaller and so are easier to steal.
   - Laptops are often used in public areas, so they are more likely to be stolen.
   - Wireless links to networks in public places may introduce viruses.
   - Laptops are more likely to be damaged (e.g., dropped, exposed to water, etc.).

Student answer 2

1 (a) Send an e-mail to their home e-mail address and browse for and attach the file or files they are working on to the e-mail. This means that the data will be sent off-site which is best for security and they can download the file or files when at home. There is the advantage in that there is no media to lose, such as pen drives, CD-RW, etc. They can also access the file on any computer connected to the Internet.
  (b) Laptops are portable and if you carry one along the road in a case then it is obvious you have one in the case and you could be attacked and the laptop stolen.

Examiner's comment

1 (a) Here the student has written four sentences and each one is relevant to the question and adds more information about the backup method chosen and the procedures that are adopted. Full marks for this part of the question.
  (b) Here the student has identified the threat which is theft, and has given a reason why this is more likely with a laptop. Full marks for this part of the question. **(5 marks out of 5)**

Worked example 2

2 All organisations should have a backup procedure so that their data can be recovered if it were lost due to a security breach. Give **five** items along with reasons that would need to be considered when deciding on backup procedures. **(10 marks)**

Student answer 1

2 Firewalls to prevent users hacking into the company's ICT systems.

Training to make sure that the users don't make mistakes and accidentally delete data.

The type of storage device such as pen drive or removable magnetic disk used to put the backup copy on.

Where to put the backup copy. It is best to store it away from the original data such as off-site.

How much data there is to store – if there is a large amount of data it would be best to store using magnetic tape as this has a very high storage capacity.

Examiner's comment

2 The first two answers the student has given show that the student has seen the word 'security breach' in the question and started to write about that. It is very common for students to answer the question they would like to have been asked. No marks for either of these two answers.

The next three answers are good. The student has now started to answer the question! **(6 marks out of 10)**

Student answer 2

2 How often to take backups. For example, with an on-line system where the data is changing by the minute, the backups need to be taken all the time. Other systems may only need backups once a day.

Where to keep the backups – off the premises is best, in case the backups are destroyed at the same time as the original data.

What medium to use to store the backups. This depends on how much data there is and how often it changes. Pen drives are good for small amounts and magnetic tape is good for backing up large amounts of data.

What type of backup to take – for example, there are incremental backups which only back up data that has changed since last backup.

Who takes the backup? It is best to give one person responsibility for taking backups.

Examiner's comment

2 This is a very good answer, and deserves full marks. **(10 marks out of 10)**

Examiner's answers

2 One mark for the name of the item and one mark for further expansion/explanation.

The type of backup that should be taken (1) such as full, incremental or differential (1).

How often the backups should be taken (1) such as continuously, every hour, every day (1), etc.

The backup medium/devices used (1) such as magnetic tape/disk (1), etc.

Where the backup is to be held/stored (1) – off-site, in fireproof safe, transferred using the Internet (1), etc.

Who should be responsible for the taking and storage of backups (1) – so that backups are treated as a high priority (1).

The need for regular and systematic backup

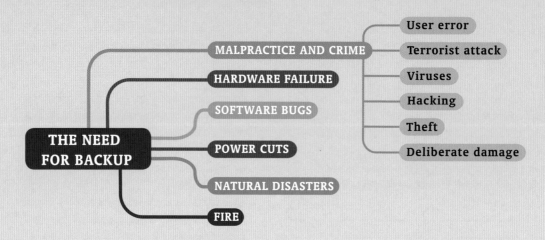

Backup strategy

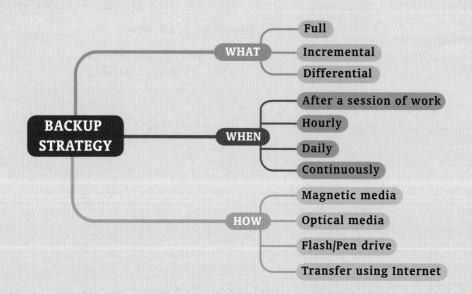

Backup and recovery procedures and the need for continuity of service

In this topic you will need to know about what ICT can provide. You will learn about what ICT offers to the solving of problems and what solutions it can provide. You will also look at the limitations of ICT systems and why their use is sometimes restricted. ICT systems provide processing and in this topic you will be spending time looking at the different types of processing, the characteristics of each type of processing and different applications for each type of processing.

▼ The key concepts covered in this topic are:

▶ What makes ICT so useful?

▶ Is the use of ICT systems always appropriate?

▶ Types of processing

CONTENTS

Unit 2 Living in the Digital World

What makes ICT so useful?

Introduction

In the early days of computers computing facilities were centralised but now computer systems can be accessed anywhere in the world using wireless links and satellites. The convergence of computers and telecommunications has provided a powerful combination and has opened up a whole new range of applications.

In this section you will be looking at those things that ICT can provide that are useful in business and our everyday lives.

What ICT can provide

What exactly makes ICT so useful? Let's take a look at the features of ICT that are used in ICT solutions.

Fast repetitive processing

Processes are so fast that there are not many tasks that challenge them. Many business transactions are simple, so the calculations, decisions, etc., performed by the processor of the computer are no problem at all. The main power of the processor is to complete huge numbers of these calculations each second. Fast repetitive processing is required in many applications such as billing systems for producing utility bills or credit card statements.

Vast storage capacity

The storage offered by ICT systems is now at the stage where it is almost limitless. Storage used to be very

Processing of credit card accounts

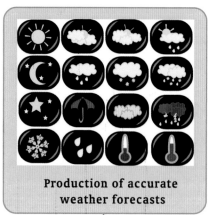

Production of accurate weather forecasts

Processing transactions in e-commerce systems

Production of utility bills

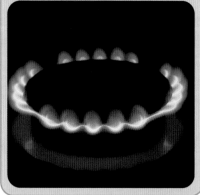

FAST REPETITIVE PROCESSING

Producing itemised phone bills

expensive but it is now very cheap and this has opened up many new applications. Vast storage capacity is available in the following forms:

- ROM and RAM – high storage allows many applications to be run together.
- Flash/pen drives – allows data to be moved easily from one computer to another. Also allows the insertion into portable devices such as digital cameras and photo printers.
- Optical media – such as DVD-RW are ideal for the storage of photographs, video and multimedia programs.

The facility to search and combine data in many different ways that would otherwise be impossible

Communications technologies such as networks and the Internet mean that data can be obtained quickly from different sources and combined together. For example, the police often have to solve crimes using information from a large number of sources such as the DVLA, CCTV footage, mobile phone and e-mail records, etc.

Improved presentation of information

It is now very easy to obtain images using digital cameras, copying them off the Internet or by using the many image libraries on the Internet. Video and audio files can be found and stored in a similar way. This means that this material can be incorporated into material such as documents, brochures, webpages and presentations.

It is also easy to create material such as graphs in one package and then load them into another package such

as a word-processing package, desktop publishing or a web-creation package.

Improved accessibility to information and services

Ability to shop for groceries and other items from home, using on-line stores – this is particularly helpful for the old or housebound as it allows them to keep their independence.

Using the Internet you have a global library at your disposal. Just think about the information you can access from your own home:

- latest news
- reviews of books, films, holidays, etc.
- opening times of stores and attractions
- road maps and routes
- the weather anywhere in the world
- timetable details of buses, trains and flights
- details of holidays and destinations
- content on every subject imaginable
- financial details – loans, savings, pensions, tax, mortgages, etc.

Improved security of data and processes

With a network, security is centralised by:

- someone being given responsibility for the taking of backup copies
- a single backup being taken to back up all files on the network.

Data kept in ICT systems can be more secure than data kept in other ways. For example, logs of who accesses the data can be kept and user permissions only allow certain people to access the information.

Biometric security can be used to check that only authorised people have access to ICT systems.

Processes such as the transfer of data can be secured by using encryption technology so that even if the data was illegally obtained, then no-one would be able to understand the data.

Is the use of ICT systems always appropriate?

Introduction

There is a tendency for thinking that there is not a problem that ICT cannot be used to solve but there are many situations where the use of ICT would be inappropriate. For example, no-one would like to hear about the death of someone or some bad news from a hospital as a text message or e-mail.

There are also limitations to ICT systems that are usually caused by hardware limitations, software limitations, communications limitations, current legislation, inappropriate design of systems or poor data control mechanisms.

The limitations of ICT systems in what they can be used for

The frontiers of ICT technology are being pushed back all the time as technology improves but there are still limitations for ICT systems and the main ones are shown here.

Hardware limitations

The hardware limitations include:

- Speed of processor – i.e., the speed with which the processor can process data (i.e., both data and instructions).
- Amount of main memory – the more memory, the more data that can be held for immediate access rather than having to access it from disk which takes time.

- Large amounts of memory are needed for multitasking. The more programs you are working on at the same time, the more demands you are placing on the memory.
- Limitations of peripherals – peripherals such as printers have a maximum speed and this could be a limitation in a bill processing and printing system.
- Printers have some memory, called buffer memory, where print jobs are kept so as to allow the computer to get on with other work while the printer prints previous jobs. Limitations on the buffer memory would restrict the user from being able to carry on working during large print sessions.
- Reliability – computer hardware is not completely reliable, so reliability is a limitation because it means that there is always the possibility that a vital part of the computer could break, meaning no access to programs or data.

Communications limitations

Most computers are now networked. There are two main communications limitations:

Network topology – the network topology is the way in which the computers are linked together. Certain topologies can only contain a certain maximum number of terminals.

Network has grown too big – if terminals keep getting added to a network without other changes, the whole network will start to run slow. File transfers will take a long time and frustrate users.

Bandwidth – bandwidth is often a limiting factor. As more demanding multimedia applications, such as video, are being run on networked computers then more bandwidth is needed. The maximum bandwidth can depend on whether the computers are wired to the network or whether they are using a wireless link. Availability of broadband – in this country we are now used to broadband but in many other countries they still have to use dial-up connections which take ages and limit many applications.

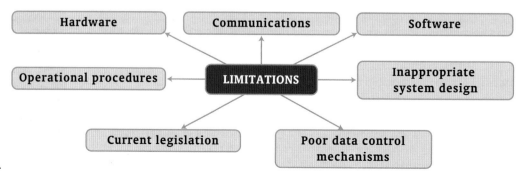

The limitations of ICT systems.

Software limitations

There are a number of software limitations:

- Ability to transfer data – data is frequently passed from one piece of software to another. If one piece of software could not read the data produced by a different piece of software, it would be a serious limitation.
- Bugs – software frequently contains bugs which cause the system to crash. Software needs to be thoroughly tried and tested before being passed to the user.
- Compatibility – you may not have an operating system capable of running the applications software. Also, you may not be able to pass the data from one piece of software to a different piece of software.
- Poor design of software – poorly designed software causes user frustration and stress and can also cause RSI if excess keyboard input is unnecessarily needed.

Fitting in with current legislation

There are many laws that concern the use of computers and these were covered earlier in the course.

The Data Protection Act 1998 covers the way personal data can be processed. This means that organisations cannot simply process this personal data in the way they would like. Instead they must obey the law.

An example of a limitation imposed by the Data Protection Act is the development of a huge database to be used by government and some private organisations. The idea is that they will be able to access the same set of personal information. However, the Data Protection Act makes it clear that data collected for one or specified purposes cannot be used for different purposes. Without a change in the law, this would limit the usefulness of the database.

Inappropriate system design

There are many projects that have been created that do not do what they set out to do. This is usually caused by:

- inexperienced development teams
- lack of project management
- lack of project control.

Operational procedures

Many organisations have set procedures by which they get a job done. When a new ICT system is developed, the developer has the choice of fitting in with the existing way of doing things or completely changing things.

Having to fit in with an existing system

If the owner of the business decides the ICT system will need to work around the same operational procedures, then this will limit the new system's effectiveness.

Poor or inappropriate data control mechanisms

Data control mechanisms should be put in place by individuals or organisations to protect the data. Here are some ways in which the data control mechanisms would be inadequate:

No proper verification or validation – data control mechanisms ensure that the data entered into and processed by the ICT system is correct and that human errors have been avoided. Appropriate verification and validation checks must be in place to prevent, as far as possible, introducing errors during the data input stage. A database containing incorrect information cannot be relied upon and places serious limitations on the system's usefulness.

No backup procedures – there may be no backup procedures in place and this can cause the loss of important data.

No proper limits to access – there may be no proper access controls in place to limit access to personal data, which may cause the Data Protection Act 1998 to be breached.

Limitations in the information they produce

If an ICT system is developed without proper analysis and consultation with the clients and users, then when it is first used the users will soon identify things that the system should have produced but doesn't.

The perfect ICT system is almost impossible to produce, because you would need infinite time and money and these are always restricted.

ICT systems do not always provide the most appropriate solutions

There are many different ways to solve a problem and some use ICT and some don't. An artist or designer may like to use an art package or computer aided design software to produce a drawing or design. Some artists may feel that they can be more creative simply by using pencil and paper for their initial designs.

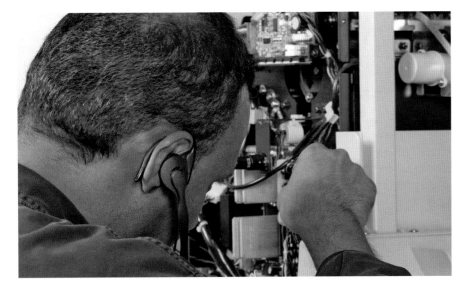

Types of processing

Introduction

ICT systems take data and process it to produce information.

Processing can be divided into the following three types:

- batch processing
- transaction processing
- real-time processing

The types of processing

Processing of data can take place as the transactions (i.e., items of business) occur, or the data can be batched up and processed in one go.

There are some systems where the processing needs to be immediate and even a small delay would result in danger. The type of processing chosen depends on the application.

Batch processing

With batch processing, the details of the transactions which need to be processed are collected or batched together over a period of time, after which they are all processed together.

The main features of batch processing are:

- No human intervention during processing – once the input data has been entered, the processing takes place automatically.
- Input data is batched – the input data, usually in the form of input forms (e.g., cheques, marked documents such as questionnaires, answers to multiple choice

questions), is all put into the reader in one go.
- There is a time gap between processing runs – data builds up over time and it is then processed periodically (e.g., every week, every month, etc.).
- Processing is done during a time when processing power is not needed for interactive applications – usually processing occurs at night or during the weekend when the computer is not being used for other applications.
- Used for large volumes of transactions – transactions need to be all of the same type.
- Transactions are processed as a group – transactions are not processed individually.
- Control/hash and batch totals are used – these totals help ensure that all the data on the forms has been read into the computer correctly.

Batch processing may seem dated, as the existing data goes out-of-date between the processing runs, but it is an ideal way of processing for certain applications. Ideal applications are those where the delay between processing runs is acceptable and there is a very large volume of processing done.

Examples of batch processing systems

Batch processing is ideal for repetitive high volume work that does not require human intervention. Typical applications for batch processing include:

- marking and processing of multiple choice examination/test papers
- cheque clearing in banks

KEY WORDS

Transaction – a piece of business (e.g., an order is made, cash is withdrawn from a bank, goods are paid for, an enrolment is made on a course, etc.)

- preparing a company's monthly payroll using input time data collected from time sheets/clock cards
- preparing utility bills (gas, electricity and water) using data collected by meter readers
- production of paper-based credit card statements
- the production and printing of monthly bank statements.

Transaction processing

Transaction processing processes each transaction as it arises. Examples of transactions include:

- an order being taken
- a customer making a payment
- a flight being booked
- a theatre seat being reserved.

Features of a transaction processing system include:

- It is an example of an interactive system. There is constant interaction between the user and the computer.
- A transaction is dealt with as soon as it occurs – transactions are processed almost immediately.
- Each transaction is completed before the next transaction is begun.
- Transaction processing is ideal for booking systems, since it will be impossible to book the same seat twice.

Examples of transaction processing

Examples of applications for transaction processing include:

- booking systems (plane, rail, holidays, theatre, concert, sports event, etc.)
- insurance quotes/renewals (car, house, contents, etc.)
- taking of orders for goods or services over the telephone.

Interactive processing

When data is entered into the computer by a user and it is processed immediately, then this is called interactive processing. The user is constantly interacting with the ICT system.

For example, when car insurance is renewed over the telephone, the insurance clerk types in the customer details to bring up their existing policy on the screen. They can then make any amendments and confirm the price details with the customer, who can then make payment using a card and the clerk can complete the transaction.

EXAM TIP

Many of the examination questions on types of processing will refer to a specific application or scenario given in the question. Do not give your answers in isolation of this. You should always refer to it in your answer.

The software for the interactive system will guide the clerk through the processes and instruct them what details need to be typed in.

Real-time processing

Real-time processing is the third method of processing and is the type of processing used when it is essential that the results of processing are obtained immediately. With real-time processing, the data received by the system is processed immediately without any delay. The system responds immediately and alters the external conditions in some way, which in turn affects the input.

The speed of real-time processing necessitates a computer devoted just to this type of processing.

Examples of real-time processing

- Process control – where a chemical process is controlled by computers using data from sensors as the input and motorised valves, heaters, pumps, etc., as the output.
- Flight control – automatic pilot or fly-by-wire where the computer takes over flying the plane using the input data such as from the computer containing the flight plan and data from sensors on the plane.
- Games – high speed action games where an immediate response is needed.

➡ KEY WORDS

Batch processing – all the inputs needed are collected, batched together, inputted and processed in one go

Interactive – where there is a constant dialogue between the user and the computer

Real-time processing – the input data is processed immediately as it arrives – the results have a direct effect on the next set of available data

Transaction processing – processing of each transaction as it arises

EXAM TIP

Real-time processing and transaction processing are often confused. In data processing systems (i.e., the type used by businesses) the processing is always batch or transaction. Real-time systems are used mainly for control.

Questions and Case studies

▶ **Questions 1** pp. 223–224

1 A large utility company sends electricity bills to all its customers. These bills are sent out over a couple of days every three months.
Describe **three** capabilities of ICT systems which make them ideal for the processing of the data needed to produce electricity bills. (6 marks)

2 In a newspaper article it said that one of the capabilities of ICT systems is that there is improved security of data and processes.
Give **two** reasons why the data in ICT systems is more likely to be secure compared to a manual system. (4 marks)

▶ **Questions 2** pp. 224–225

1 The Internet is an ICT system and your use of the Internet is limited by a number of factors. Name and describe **four** factors that limit your use of the Internet. (8 marks)

2 ICT systems are limited in what they can be used for. State **four** limitations of ICT systems. (4 marks)

▶ **Questions 3** pp. 226–227

1 (a) Give the names of **two** types of processing used in ICT systems. (2 marks)
(b) Which method of processing would be chosen for the processing of a large number of cheques in the cheque clearing process? (1 mark)
(c) Give **one** reason why the method of processing in part (b) is a suitable one. (1 mark)
2 Explain, by giving a suitable example, the meaning of the term interactive processing. (2 marks)
3 Name the type of processing that would be most suitable for each of the following ICT systems: (One word answers are acceptable for this question.)
(a) The monthly payroll for the staff employed by a large organisation. (1 mark)
(b) Controlling a chemical process. (1 mark)
(c) Processing the production of quarterly gas bills to be posted. (1 mark)
(d) Theatre ticket booking. (1 mark)
(e) Cruise control for a car which keeps it at constant speed unless the brakes are applied. (1 mark)

(f) Designing a new house using computer aided design software. (1 mark)
4 When an airline ticket is booked, the seat is held until the transaction is complete.
(a) Explain why this is done. (1 mark)
(b) This system is an example of a transaction processing system. Give one other example of a transaction processing system. (1 mark)
(c) Explain clearly why a transaction processing system cannot really be considered as a real-time system. (1 mark)
(d) Give **one** example of a real-time system. (1 mark)
5 Give the names of **two** types of processing that can be used with an ICT system.
Note: you only need to give the names. (2 marks)
6 A low-cost airline uses the Internet for the taking of bookings. The system uses interactive transaction processing. Explain what is meant by the terms:
(a) Transaction processing. (2 marks)
(b) Interactive processing. (2 marks)

▶ **Case study 1** p. 226

Case study Aberdeenshire Council: Paying catering and cleaning staff

Aberdeenshire Council had a problem to solve. They have to process 1800 timesheets every week to produce the payroll for their catering and cleaning staff.

Previously, the data was recorded by the employees on timesheets, which were then collected and the details they contained were typed into the payroll system. Because there were so many timesheets, the payroll clerks found it difficult to cope with the workload. The present system created a lot of problems – details on timesheets being illegible, missing information on forms, miskeying data, and so on.

They solved the problem using an automatic method of data capture which used both optical mark reading and optical character recognition. They used timesheet forms which could be completed by all abilities of staff.

The new system meant that all the completed forms could be batched together and then inputted into the computer where the hours could be calculated and the wage payments could be generated.

1 Give **two** advantages to Aberdeenshire Council in using the new batch processing system. (2 marks)

2 Explain the meaning of the term 'data capture'. (1 mark)

3 Give **one** reason why the forms which made use of OMR and OCR contained fewer mistakes than the original timesheets. (1 mark)

▶ Case study 2 | p. 227

ABS – a real-time system

Many cars are fitted with ABS. ABS allows drivers to control their car when braking hard. Using ABS, when you brake hard, you will stop faster and in a more controlled manner than if you were driving the same car without ABS. ABS prevents wheels from locking and going into an uncontrollable skid.

ABS works by detecting whether a particular wheel is about to lock and sending a message to the brake to relieve the pressure to stop the wheel locking. A real-time system is needed here because instant decisions need to be made based on the input data from the sensors. The processing therefore needs to be immediate.

1 Give **one** reason why batch processing would be unsuitable for a control system such as the ABS braking system used in some cars. (2 marks)

2 Real-time systems are used with control systems. Give **one** different example of a control system that would use real-time processing. (1 mark)

3 Many real-time systems make use of sensors. Give **one** reason why this is so. (1 mark)

▶ Case study 3 | pp. 226–227

Beating crime recording bureaucracy

Police forces are required to record crime in a standard way. One of the problems with recording crimes is that it needs to be done immediately. This is so that the new crime data can be searched and patterns noted between similar crimes. In the past the scene of crime officers would record the crime on paper at the location and then return to the police station where either they or skilled administrative staff would type the information into the database. Typing this large amount of data is both time consuming and error-prone. Additionally, it wastes time and prevents police officers focusing on 'real policing' instead of administration.

A form is filled in by the police officer which can be read automatically by a scanner. The data on the form is entered into a database automatically.

DRS, a company that specialises in the automatic capture of data contained on documents, have produced a solution for the Nottinghamshire Police.

They developed a form which could be filled in by the scene of crime officer and which is then returned along with all the other forms to the Police Station at the end of the day. The forms are batched together and read using a scanner which uses a combination of OCR and OMR to read the data and then processes it by putting it into a database structure.

The new system significantly reduced the time and cost associated with data entry by up to 90%. Plus the data was automatically cleansed using the validation rules in the software.

1 Give the name of the type of processing being used by the Nottinghamshire Police. (1 mark)
2 The passage mentions that a scanner uses a combination of OMR and OCR to read the data and then process it by putting it into a database structure.

(a) Explain the meaning of the terms OMR and OCR. (2 marks)
(b) Explain clearly what is meant by 'process it by putting it into a database structure'. (2 marks)

(c) Give **one** advantage in using OMR and OCR for the input of data compared to the alternative which is typing in the information. (1 mark)

Exam support

Worked example 1

1 Explain, with a reason, a suitable method of processing for each of the following applications:
   (a) Monthly payroll. (2 marks)
   (b) Cinema ticket booking. (2 marks)

Student answer 1

1 (a) Batch processing because all the data can be batched together for processing.
   (b) Real-time processing because it needs to be done instantly.

Examiner's comment

1 For part (a) batch processing is correct but the explanation does not display any understanding of the reasons for batch processing and this answer is what anyone could gain from the term batch processing. In part (b) there is often confusion between the terms real-time processing and transaction processing. Real-time processing is instant and is only used when the odd couple of seconds are crucial, such as for control systems such as aircraft auto-pilots and fast-moving action games. No marks for this part. **(1 mark out of 4)**

Student answer 2

1 (a) Batch processing because the data, such as time sheets, can be collected over the month and batched together. They can then all be processed in one go, producing the payslips in the process and paying money directly into the employees' banks.
   (b) Transaction processing because each transaction needs to be completed before the next transaction can commence. This will prevent two people booking the same seat.

Examiner's comment

Both of these answers are correct and in sufficient detail to gain the additional mark for each part. A very good answer which has clearly identified the correct processing for the situation. **(4 marks out of 4)**

Examiner's answers

1 (a) One mark for type of processing and one for the reason.
      Batch processing because the output (i.e., payslips, payments, etc.) is only required monthly.
   (b) One mark for type of processing and one for the reason.
      Transaction processing in order to prevent double booking.

Worked example 2

2 A college uses a computer-based batch processing system for the keeping of students' attendance records. Cards for each class containing class details and lists of students' names and numbers are given to lecturers. Marks are made on the form when a student attends class and every week the cards are collected into batches where they are used to update the master file. This occurs on a Friday afternoon as no classes occur on Friday afternoons.
   (a) Explain what is meant by a batch processing system. (3 marks)
   (b) (i) Give **one** advantage to the college in using a batch processing system. (1 mark)
      (ii) Give **one** disadvantage to the college in using a batch processing system. (1 mark)
   (c) The college intends to move away from batch processing and use instead a transaction processing system. As every room in the college contains at least one computer with access to the Internet, the college decided that each lecturer should enter the class details using this computer.
      (i) Explain the term transaction processing. (2 marks)
      (ii) Give **one** reason why the college has changed to a transaction processing system. (1 mark)

2 (a) A batch processing system puts all the input data together so that it can be processed in one go rather than a bit processed now and again.

(b) (i) More accurate.

(ii) Cheaper.

(c) (i) Each transaction is processed now and again.

(ii) Don't need to wait till all the data is batched before processing it.

Examiner's comment

2 There is a scenario given in this question and the aim of it is to help the students by giving them a context in which to answer the question. Students should be advised to refer to the scenario to help them with the explanations in their answers.

It is clear that this student has not paid much attention to the scenario.

Part (a) is for three marks so there needs to be three separate points. This answer warrants one mark for stating 'the data is processed in one go…'.

Part (b) answers are the superficial answers students should never give, so no marks here.

Part (c) answer is not a proper reason. The student needed to be specific and relate the answer to the scenario. No marks. **(1 mark out of 8)**

Examiner's answers

2 (a) Need three of the following for all three marks:
Cards containing the data are batched together.
Data is collected over a period of time – a week in this case.
Data is input by using a card read using OMR and OCR in one go.
Data is processed in one go.
Without any human intervention.
Ideal for processing large quantities of documents all of the same type.

(b) (i) One mark for one of the following:
Processing done at a quiet time so does not affect computer performance for other computers.
Do not have to pay people to input the details.
More accurate input than by typing.
Do not need lots of terminals.

(ii) One mark for one of the following:
Data is only up-to-date on Fridays. Gets progressively less accurate as the week goes on.

Student answer 2

2 (a) All the completed cards containing the attendance data are batched together and then input into the computer using a scanner, which reads the marks on the forms.

The marks for each class are processed automatically and without a person needing to be there.

(b) (i) It is cheaper because you do not have to pay someone to enter the attendance details into the computer using the keyboards. Also it is more accurate as there are no typing mistakes made.

(ii) If someone wants to know the attendance half-way through the week then the system will not tell them, and they will have to go and find the mark sheets.

(c) (i) The lecturer would have a terminal in each room and they would enter the attendance details for each student and when they have entered the details they would be processed.

(ii) They do not have to wait till the end of the week to get the attendance details for particular students as the data is constantly being updated.

Examiner's comment

2 Part (a) student has stated three valid points which are correct so three marks here.

Parts (b) are correct answers so two marks here.

Part (c) (i) The student has correctly identified that the processing occurs shortly after the details are entered for each student.

Part (c) (ii) is not clearly expressed – they needed to say that the data is continually being processed, so will represent the true attendance at any time during the week. No marks for this part. **(7 marks out of 8)**

Forms need to be collected and some may be missing.
Reject rate may be high due to damaged cards or cards not being completed properly.

(c) (i) An answer such as this for two marks:
Transaction processing is where the processing occurs as soon as or shortly after the event which triggers the need for processing occurs. So here the attendance would be entered during the lesson and the attendance details for each student would be updated.

(ii) One of the following for one mark:
Attendance is updated and it would be possible to identify particular students who were not in that day.
Data is more up-to-date compared to a batch processing system.

Unit 2 Living in the Digital World

Summary mind maps

What makes ICT so useful?

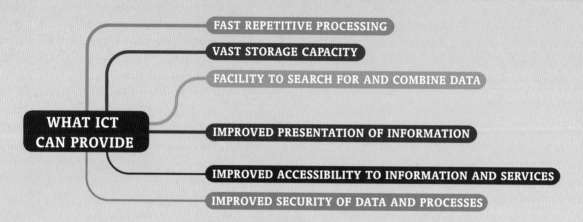

WHAT ICT CAN PROVIDE
- FAST REPETITIVE PROCESSING
- VAST STORAGE CAPACITY
- FACILITY TO SEARCH FOR AND COMBINE DATA
- IMPROVED PRESENTATION OF INFORMATION
- IMPROVED ACCESSIBILITY TO INFORMATION AND SERVICES
- IMPROVED SECURITY OF DATA AND PROCESSES

Is the use of ICT systems always appropriate?

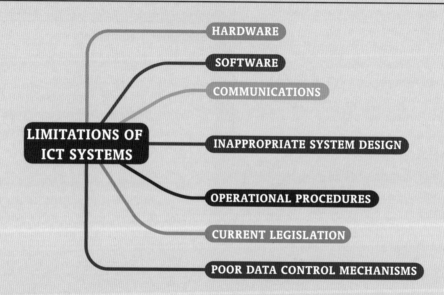

LIMITATIONS OF ICT SYSTEMS
- HARDWARE
- SOFTWARE
- COMMUNICATIONS
- INAPPROPRIATE SYSTEM DESIGN
- OPERATIONAL PROCEDURES
- CURRENT LEGISLATION
- POOR DATA CONTROL MECHANISMS

Types of processing

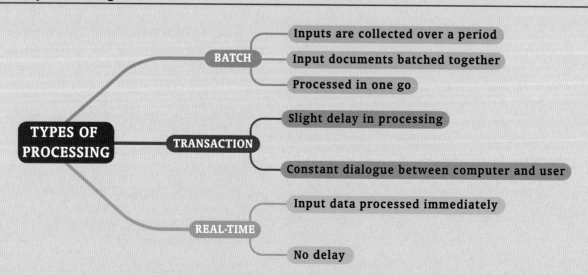

TYPES OF PROCESSING
- BATCH
  - Inputs are collected over a period
  - Input documents batched together
  - Processed in one go
- TRANSACTION
  - Slight delay in processing
  - Constant dialogue between computer and user
- REAL-TIME
  - Input data processed immediately
  - No delay

The UK is one of the most avid users of ICT but there are many countries in the world where the use of ICT systems is in its infancy. The growth of ICT systems is needed to cope with the complexity and demands of everyday living.

▼ The key concepts covered in this topic are:

▶ How the use of ICT is influenced by social factors

▶ How the use of ICT is influenced by cultural factors

▶ How the use of ICT is influenced by legal factors

▶ How the use of ICT is influenced by economic factors

▶ How the use of ICT is influenced by environmental factors

▶ How the use of ICT is influenced by ethical factors

CONTENTS

Unit 2 Living in the Digital World

Factors affecting the use of ICT

▼ You will find out

▶ About how the use of ICT is influenced by social factors

▶ About how the use of ICT is influenced by cultural factors

▶ About how the use of ICT is influenced by legal factors

▶ About how the use of ICT is influenced by economic factors

▶ About how the use of ICT is influenced by environmental factors

▶ About how the use of ICT is influenced by ethical factors

Introduction

In the section you will be looking at how certain factors influence the way in which ICT is used in a particular situation. In some cases a proposed system may encounter problems because there are legal or moral issues with it.

How the use of ICT is influenced by social factors

The widespread use of ICT has led to a lot of benefits to society but it does create a number of social problems such as:

- Reduces the number of manual jobs – those jobs where few skills are needed have been replaced by computers or robots.
- Changes in the way a job is done – ICT systems are constantly changing the way jobs are done and people have to be able to adapt to it. This places demands on people who have to learn to use the new ICT systems.
- Job loss – ICT systems are constantly evolving and are being used for new tasks.
- Widens the gap between the 'haves' and 'have-nots' – people who do not have a computer and Internet access pay more when paying for goods and services because on-line discounts are often offered.
- De-skills certain jobs – some ICT systems have de-skilled certain jobs. A typist was a skilled job but now anyone with a basic knowledge of word-processing software can produce professional-looking documents.
- Blurs the distinction between 'home' and 'work' – companies give staff laptops on which they can do work at home outside normal work hours which can cause family conflicts.

- Less security at work – there are many part-time and temporary posts owing to the fact that shops and businesses often have to trade 24 hours a day to remain competitive. This adds to employee stress.
- Reduced social interaction at work – more and more people are working from home using ICT systems, which sounds ideal. The downside is that it can be lonely and you miss the social interaction with your co-workers.
- ICT systems are less personal – e-mails, instant messages and chat room discussions can lock people into a cyber world where they are losing proper face-to-face interaction.
- Changes in leisure time – more people are working away from the old 9 to 5, Monday to Friday pattern and are working twilights, nights and weekends. This sometimes makes it hard for them to fit into family life.
- Addictions – many people are addicted to certain aspects of ICT, such as Internet gambling, pornography, chat rooms, playing on-line games, etc.

All of the above will need to be considered when ICT systems are being planned and developed. The trouble is that unless the development of the system is illegal, people will still go ahead with the systems if there are financial benefits.

How the use of ICT is influenced by cultural factors

In order to look at cultural factors you need to understand what culture is. Look at the following diagram which shows all the aspects of culture.

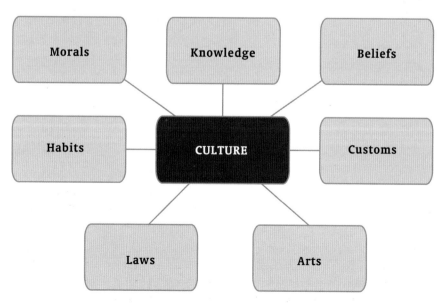

Changes in culture caused by ICT

Developments in ICT cause major changes in culture. Changes in any one or more of the items in the diagram represent a cultural change. For example, people are spending more time on the Internet and less time watching television than they used to. Here are some cultural changes brought about by the use of ICT:

- Many more people changing the custom of writing to each other by letter by sending a less formal e-mail.
- People changing their habits by texting each other rather than ringing.
- People having a more relaxed attitude to copyright issues.
- People being able to access information about the arts more easily, e.g. virtual art galleries, book reviews, book suggestions on on-line bookstores, etc.
- People taking a more relaxed view of issues such as pornography.
- People exploring new ideas such as new religions, complementary medicine, etc.

Faith on the web

Podcasting, Facebook, Myspace, blogs and online churches are all fast becoming the tools of faith for many religions. For example, someone in Leeds could listen to or watch a Friday service in a mosque in California. Gone are the days when you need to go to a mosque or church for spiritual advice. You can contact and talk to anyone around the world about your faith.

Podcasts are used by many churches to spread the message. Religion is about community and what better way than to use the Internet to create communities on the Web. Over five years ago a minister of the church would have been called on the phone to discuss a religious message but now it is much more common to receive an e-mail.

Many churches now have a website that allows their congregation and others to keep in touch and build a religious community. All the facilities of a website are used to enable effective communication, such as podcasts of services for people who are unable to attend church, message boards to keep in touch, e-mail facilities for getting in touch with the minister and so on.

Religion is such a big part of many people's lives around the world and ICT has been used to help spread the word. To see how much information there is on the web about God, Do a search for the word God. Today I did this and there were 355 million references.

St Pixels is an on-line church. Take a look at the website at www.stpixels. com to see the facilities it offers.

ICT and the arts

In the past if people wanted to listen to music they went into a shop on the High St and bought a CD. People wanted more flexible ways of selecting and listening to music. Here are some ways these users influenced the development of new ICT systems:

- Users wanted just to buy the tracks they liked and not necessarily the whole CD – hence the development of i-tunes.
- Users did not want to hunt down hard to find CDs on the High St – hence the development of on-line music stores such as CD-Wow and Amazon.
- Users wanted portability of music – they did not want to carry a load of CDs which could easily be scratched – hence the development of the MP3 player.
- Users wanted as many tunes stored as possible – hence the development of the compressed file format such as the MP3 format.

Bands who wanted to get known found it difficult to do this but with sites such as MySpace or YouTube they could get known for very little cost.

Cultural factors in other countries

Many developing countries have problems embracing ICT and this has led to a digital divide between the East and the West.

In the West we are able to access ICT with relative ease. In many developing countries this is not the case. Here are some reasons why:

- Low levels of education and literacy skills – make it hard for people to make use of ICT.
- Poor technology infrastructures – very few Internet service providers and an unreliable electricity supply and a patchy telecommunications system.
- Lack of money – the general population have very low incomes and cannot afford the new technology.
- Lack of ICT skills – there are few places to learn ICT skills that would be needed to set up ICT systems.
- Lack of fluency in English – about 80% of all information on the World Wide Web is in English.
- Distrust of Western values – in some Middle Eastern countries the Internet is viewed as a Western agent of moral and political subversion.
- Restricted access to the Internet – many leaders of countries do not want widespread access to the net in their country. You are restricted as to the sites you are allowed to visit.
- Lack of interest by foreign companies – foreign companies are unwilling to invest in certain countries because of the political situation there.

How the use of ICT is influenced by legal factors

The existing laws, such as the Data Protection Act 1998, may make it impossible for a system to be developed. For example, companies may want to create a large database with all the personal information held about us including our purchasing habits. This would not be allowed because the data from one company could not be passed over without our permission.

Copyright laws – prevent the free passage of music on peer-to-peer file sharing websites.

Selling devices which crack codes or copy protection – these would encourage people to break the law by copying software, music CDs and DVDs.

Mobile communication, such as the use of mobile phones whilst driving a car, is banned unless you have a hands-free kit. The ICT system (i.e., the mobile phone) had to be built in a way that would fit in with this.

How the use of ICT is influenced by economic factors

ICT systems have benefits which can sometimes be quantified in financial terms. In order for ICT systems to be developed it is often necessary to invest quite a lot of money in them and it is necessary for this investment to yield benefits usually by increased profits. If a system does not bring a benefit that is worth more than the cost of development of the system, then it is not worth pursuing.

The drive for cheaper and better products and services has led to organisations turning to ICT for help. The use of ICT can give a company an economic advantage until the other companies start using the same technology.

Remaining competitive is crucial for any business and many businesses are forced to change because of the changes which new ICT systems bring.

For example, a few years ago there were photo printing companies where you would send a roll of film for developing and printing. Sometimes they did this by post or you took them to a branch on the High St. In a matter of a few years, owing to the introduction of digital cameras, many people print copies out themselves or take the card or disk to a supermarket where they are printed.

Here are some economic factors that influence the use of ICT:

- Labour costs being cheaper elsewhere – many call centres are now located in India. As communication systems are so cheap and labour costs are lower, many companies now locate call centres in India.
- High labour costs – more uses for ICT have been sought that will reduce the wage bill in an organisation.
- Fuel costs – a lot of fuel is wasted if you get lost. If you are a delivery driver then not only are you wasting money, you are also wasting time. GPS systems and efficient routing systems, which work out the most economic route to take for a number of deliveries, are used by parcel and delivery firms.
- Availability of high speed Internet access – not everyone has broadband but the numbers are growing. The availability of fast Internet access is essential to a country's prosperity.
- Availability of skilled staff – for example, many ICT organisations will use programming and other development staff based in another country such as India.

How the use of ICT is influenced by environmental factors

There are a number of environmental factors that will influence the way in which ICT is used.

ICT systems such as portable players need to be used whilst on the move – the ICT systems need to have a high storage capacity in a small space (as is the case with portable players such as iPods).

ICT systems used in cars would need to have an interface that would not distract the driver too much. For example, global positioning systems make use of sound as well as output on a screen.

Thinking about the environment when creating and using ICT systems

ICT has been estimated to produce the same level of carbon dioxide emissions as the aircraft industry. The manufacture, distribution and use of ICT systems are responsible for approximately two percent of global carbon emissions.

You only have to feel the heat generated at the back of the computer to know that each computer generates quite a bit of heat when on. There are over 880 million computers worldwide, so this represents a huge amount of energy which has to be supplied as electricity.

The use of ICT systems contributes two percent of global emissions, which is the same as the aircraft industry.

When we use ICT systems or create ICT systems for others to use, we should be mindful of a number of environmental issues:

- Recycling of hardware – the fossil fuel required to make one PC is 240 kg, which is ten times the weight of the actual computer. This is much higher than most goods. Recycling reduces the carbon footprint.
- Print preview – by previewing your work before printing you can save by checking that you are printing exactly what you want.

Commuting to work is a major producer of greenhouse gases.

Recycling of printer cartridges

Where possible, rather than buying a new printer cartridge when the ink runs out and throwing the old cartridge away, it is better to have it refilled. There are many charity schemes where the money made goes to a charity.

Recycling of mobile phones

Like printer cartridges, mobile phones should not simply be thrown away. They should be recycled using one of the many charity schemes. There are many places in the world where any mobile phone, no matter what it looks like, would be really appreciated, so many of these schemes involve passing on the old mobiles to other countries.

Many ICT systems help the environment in some way. Here are some examples:

- Environmental control systems – here the heating can be controlled accurately in each room in a building. If a room is not being used, then the heating can be turned off. This helps reduce fuel bills as well as carbon dioxide emissions.
- Global positioning systems (GPS) save fuel and cut down on emissions by reducing journey time by helping you not to get lost or to avoid traffic black spots.

Mobile phones should be recycled and not just thrown away – you can give them away to charity or some will even give you some money back for them.

- Reduction in the number of printouts made – ICT systems should only produce printouts if absolutely essential.
- Recycle paper – printouts and other paper documents should not be thrown away with general rubbish. Instead it should be collected for recycling.
- Remembering to switch off computers and other equipment at the end of the day – equipment on stand-by still uses lots of power and wastes energy.
- Organisations may need to allow staff to work from home – this will reduce congestion and pollution and cut down on greenhouse gas emissions.

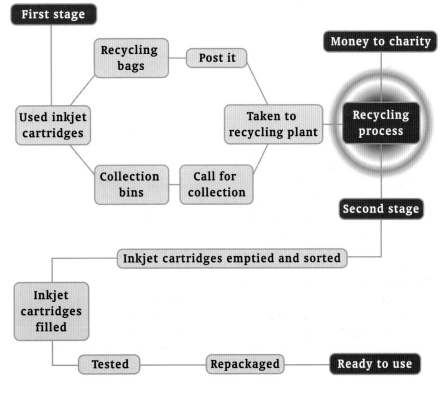

First stage → Recycling bags → Post it → Taken to recycling plant → Recycling process → Money to charity

Used inkjet cartridges

Collection bins → Call for collection

Second stage

Inkjet cartridges emptied and sorted

Inkjet cartridges filled

Tested → Repackaged → Ready to use

KEY WORDS

Carbon footprint – a measure of the impact human activities have on the environment in terms of the amount of greenhouse gases produced, measured in units of carbon dioxide

Flatscreens and the environment

Plasma and LCD (liquid crystal display) are the latest must have screens. The old style screen, consisting of a big bulky cathode ray tube, is rapidly becoming a thing of the past.

Flatscreens make up 80% of all screens sold but environmentalists are worried about their carbon footprint. Because they are lighter and cheaper to produce at larger sizes, flatscreens are 50% larger than traditional screens and this means that they use more electricity. In fact, by doubling the size of the screen, you quadruple the energy consumption and also quadruple the carbon footprint of running the screen.

If you do not want to get rid of your flatscreen you can do your bit by always turning it off when not in use rather than leaving it on standby.

How the use of ICT is influenced by ethical factors

If you are ethical, it means you are obeying a set of rules (but not necessarily laws) that govern the way you behave towards others. Often these rules need to be developed as situations change with the use of ICT.

Ethics are concerned with value judgements about what human behaviour is good or bad in a given situation. Ethics are the standards, values, morals and principles on which you base decisions. One of the main problems is that often there is no clear distinction between what is right and wrong.

Suppose you are in work and you send an e-mail to a friend about a night out you are planning. Suppose later on you decide to use the firm's computer, software and networks to work on a website for a friend, for which you are being paid.

Both of these are a misuse of the ICT systems and are unethical but to different degrees.

There are many ethical factors where some people might be put off an ICT project if it was unethical but many people will simply look at the financial rewards and go ahead with it.

Ethical factors include:

- Privacy – what privacy issues are there? Will people refuse to supply the information for the system because they are worried that their privacy may be eroded?
- Property – people who spent time developing ideas and products can have them copied. This is a real problem in some countries where fake products (e.g., computer software, music CDs and computer hardware) are the norm.
- Accuracy – mistakes can easily be made and can have serious consequences. A person could be refused credit because of a mistake made during data entry. Organisations have a duty to make sure the information is accurate and kept up-to-date.
- Accessibility – there needs to be proper security in place to ensure ICT systems cannot be accessed or hacked into by people not authorised to see the information.

How ICT can improve the economics of business

ICT can bring many economic benefits to businesses and organisations:

- Financial benefits – increased turnover, increased profits, lower overheads, etc.
- Lower wastage – makes the best use of the raw materials/resources.
- Better use of resources (people, equipment, buildings, etc.) – leads to lower operating costs.

- The need for more information – companies need to obtain more information about the characteristics and purchasing habits of their customers to market their products or services better.

The ethical and social problems social networking sites present

Social networking sites are websites for keeping in contact with old acquaintances and meeting new ones. Users can create their own webpage and post details about themselves: where they went to school, their favourite music, football team, etc., and their relationship status. They can link to friends on the same site, whose photos, names, and perhaps a brief description, will also appear on the webpage.

Social networking sites such as MySpace and Facebook are great fun but they do present a number of ethical and social problems.

Ethical problems

For example, many users of social networking sites reveal many truths about themselves that they may want their friends to know about but not their employers, tutors at university or authorities such as the police.

Many employers have learnt that applicants for jobs often use these sites and often reveal their true personalities on these sites. Employers, when looking for suitable employees, use these sites to vet applicants. Do you think it is ethical for potential employers to do this bearing in mind many people make material up on these sites?

Staff at one university use social networking sites to look for students who had trashed each other by covering others with drink and shaving foam. Great fun you might think but only if you are not the one having to pay to clear up the mess afterwards. The university knew that students take pictures of each other during these incidents and post them on social networking sites. University staff would look at the sites to find the culprits who could then be disciplined for their actions.

Many employers have banned their employees from using social networking sites because of the time employees spend using such sites when they should be working. You may feel that it is unethical to restrict employees in this way but you may also feel that from an employer's point of view it is unethical to waste time using these sites whilst an organisation is paying an employee for their time.

Social networking sites can be used to sell goods and services. For example, some companies who are marketing goods or services set up a profile. They then buy advertising tools which allow them to contact people most likely to be interested in the goods or services they are offering. Once a person has shown an interest in the goods or services, the tools will also target their friends and will even show a picture of you to help sell their goods or services. You may think that using your picture in this way is unethical.

Social problems

Social networking sites have brought about a number of social problems and these include:

- Paedophiles looking for young children can use these sites – there has been the problem of paedophiles looking for young children in chat rooms, but social networking sites present them with lots more information, such as photographs of the children and their friends. The more information about a child that these people have, the easier they find it to make friends with a view to arranging a meeting.
- They cause an erosion of privacy – social networking sites could be used by the authorities

> **KEY WORDS**

Social networking site – website for keeping in contact with old acquaintances and meeting new ones. Users can create their own webpage and post details about themselves: where they went to school, their favourite music, football team, etc., and their relationship status. They can link to friends on the same site, whose photos, names, and perhaps a brief description, will also appear on the webpage

and commercial organisations to find out a complete picture of people's lives. They can find out who your friends are and what their attributes are, and in doing this they learn a huge amount about you. It is not surprising that the security forces use such sites to investigate terrorist suspects. For example, by using such sites security forces can find out who their friends are because they could

also be terrorists. Other criminals could be similarly investigated.

- Use by identity thieves – the more an identity thief knows about their victim, the easier they will find it to commit fraud by pretending they are that person. Social networking sites can be used to glean more information such as mother's maiden name, e-mail addresses, names of pets, which are frequently used as passwords, etc.
- Can introduce malicious programs – suppose in your Facebook details you have said you like a certain band. You could be contacted by someone saying they have some information or music from the band which you then download. As well as the information and music, the download contains malicious code in a program that will collect your financial information such as account numbers, passwords, etc. This information can then be used to remove money from your accounts.

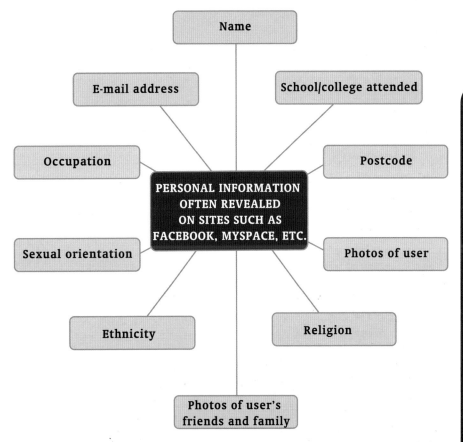

If a user has not changed the default privacy settings, social networking sites can reveal the personal information shown.

Questions and Case studies

Questions 1 pp. 234–235

1 Describe **one** example of a cultural factor affecting the way ICT is used in a developing country. (2 marks)
2 Many countries miss out on the opportunities provided by the use of ICT for economic reasons. Describe **one** economic factor that would influence the use of ICT in a certain country. (2 marks)
3 Language problems can hinder the introduction of ICT. Give **one** reason why this might be so. (1 mark)
4 Economic factors such as the need to be competitive often influence the way ICT is used in a business. Name a different economic factor and describe how it influences the way ICT is used. (2 marks)

Case study 1 pp. 238–239

A problem caused by an Internet message board

Around 500 Internet yobs trashed a 14 year olds birthday party at a church hall.

A teenager was about to celebrate her 14th birthday with family and friends when around 500 drunken youths turned up and gate-crashed the party.

Unbeknown to the young girl, a message about the party turned up on an Internet party message board.

The young girl and her friends and family were distraught as people smashed bottles, vomited, and smashed doors. The police were called and five patrol cars were needed to help quell the drunken youths. The police arrested four of the youths for being drunk and disorderly.

1 The example in the case study shows the problems caused by the free passage of information on the Internet.
   (a) Explain what is meant by an Internet message board. (2 marks)
   (b) Some message boards are moderated by the Internet service provider. Explain how this would have helped prevent this situation. (1 mark)
2 Free passage of information can create problems for society. Describe a different situation where problems for society have been created by the free passage of information using ICT systems such as the Internet. (3 marks)

Case study 2 pp. 238–239

On-line essay banks fail students

Students too busy or lazy to write their own essays, assignments or coursework may turn to the Internet for help.

Students have always been adept at cutting and pasting material from websites to cobble essays together and then pass it off as their own work. Luckily many education institutions have special software which can spot plagiarism and this software searches the Internet for sentences the same as the ones used.

Some students get around this by paying someone to produce an original piece of work for them. Buying custom work like this is clearly cheating. Apart from the ethical issues, there is the problem that the quality of the work bought is quite poor and unlikely to get anything like the grade promised.

One student who bought as essay which got an 'F' grade said, 'It was such as waste of money – I am never going to do that again'.

1 Give **two** reasons why essay banks could be considered to be unethical. (2 marks)
2 Describe **one** way in which the use of essay banks could affect society as a whole. (1 mark)
3 Do you think that essay banks should be made illegal? Give a reason for your answer. (2 marks)

Can you steal wireless?

Did you know that you can be arrested for connecting to an Internet service provider without permission?

The Communications Act 2003 states that a 'person who (a) dishonestly obtains an electronic communications service and (b) does so with the intent to avoid payment of a charge applicable to the provision of that service, is guilty of an offence'. It is also debatable whether a charge could be brought using the Computer Misuse Act.

This means that if you are wandering around with your laptop and find an open network which you can use to access the Internet, then you could be committing an offence.

Even if borrowing someone else's Internet connection is not illegal, is it unethical? If you watch someone else's firework display from inside your house, you wouldn't expect it to be illegal, nor would you consider it illegal reading a newspaper using someone else's light. So what is wrong with using their wireless Internet connection? You might argue that if they did not want someone else to use it, then it is easy to take steps to prevent them from doing so.

Some people argue that by using their wireless connection you are slowing down the service they have paid for. Others argue that there is too much 'yours' and 'mine' in society and what is wrong with sharing for a change. The communications companies do not like this idea as they would prefer everyone to pay.

1 Explain the steps you would take to log on to the Internet in a place where wireless Internet is available. (3 marks)

2 ICT systems can be used in many different environments and this affects the way ICT is used. Name and describe **three** different environments in which ICT is used. (3 marks)

3 Give **one** reason why it might be unethical to use someone else's wireless Internet connection without their permission. (1 mark)

VoIP and teleworking helping to save the planet

Many employees who work in jobs where people contact them, such as in call centres or help-desks, could easily work at home, provided cheap communication methods are available.

Many people work in contact centres where members of the public ring them to pay bills, place orders, query payments, ask for help, etc.

VoIP (Voice over Internet Protocol) is a system where voice calls can be made using a computer network such as the Internet. The system works by converting a voice signal into a digital signal, which then travels over the Internet and at the other end the digital signal is converted back into a voice signal.

The system can be implemented in several ways, one of which is to use software on the computer with a headset and microphone to make and receive calls. Another way is to use an ordinary phone or a special

VoIP phone which looks like an ordinary phone.

A headset consisting of earphones and a microphone is used so your hands are kept free for typing into the computer when taking calls.

The advantage of all this is that the calls are significantly cheaper than conventional phone calls and this can help companies keep costs low when they are allowing call centre staff to work from their own homes.

It is estimated that if contact centre workers (about 1 million of them) were all able to work from home, it would slash the carbon footprint by 1.3 million tonnes.

In order to offset this carbon footprint it would be necessary to plant around 1400 square miles of forest, which is nearly the entire area of the county of Kent.

In addition, the ability to telework would benefit new parents, older workers and the disabled, and free up the roads for workers with no other option but to commute.

1 (a) Explain what is meant by the term 'teleworking'. (1 mark)
  (b) Give **one** example of a job that is particularly suited for teleworking and explain the reasons why teleworking is suited. (3 marks)

2 Give **one** advantage that VoIP has over traditional telephone communication that will help encourage companies to allow some staff to telework. (2 marks)

3 (a) Teleworking reduces the carbon footprint of contact workers such as staff working in call centres. Give **one** reason why. (1 mark)

  (b) Give **one** advantage of teleworking to the employee and **one** advantage to the employer. (2 marks)
  (c) Other than reducing the carbon footprint describe **two** other environmental benefits of teleworking. (2 marks)

Unit 2 Living in the Digital World

Questions and Case studies continued

Case study 5 pp. 234–239

Rwanda has its sights on becoming the ICT centre of Africa

Rwanda, a country in Africa, is trying to become the centre of IT in Africa. This is despite the fact that it is a very poor country compared to its near, more wealthy neighbours that have wealth due to oil, diamonds and copper.

The government in Rwanda want to change from an agriculture-based economy to a knowledge-based economy. Two fibre optic rings circle the capital and another cable has been laid across the country.

Rwanda is one of the least-developed countries but its leaders see high-tech as the best way of trying to compete globally. Others, however, disagree and feel that the money should be spent more on necessities such as electricity for everybody in the country.

The future does look bright because nearly 70% of the population can read and they all speak the same language, which makes establishing a web presence easier.

Rwanda hopes to import cheap refurbished computers and since in some places there is little electricity, they intend to use low power computers with batteries that can be recharged using free solar power.

The aim is to have many of the computers in telecentres with broadband connections to the Internet. This would enable some Rwandans to find business opportunities, some to find jobs, and farmers to find out how to grow better crops. For the people who cannot read or write, ICT can be used to help them learn to read and write.

Some people inside the country think the whole idea is wrong, saying that you cannot build a school for a student to study at before you give them something to eat. Other people say that providing the infrastructure means the private sector will invest and this will benefit everyone.

1 Access the CIA website World Factbook using the following web address:
https://www.cia.gov/library/publications/the-world-factbook/index.html
Type in or select the country Rwanda.
Use the information contained on the webpages to fill in the details in the column for Rwanda.
Now obtain the figures for the UK and fill in the other column.
Write a short paragraph about the differences you have spotted between a poorly developed country, Rwanda, and the much more developed and technologically advanced UK. (5 marks)

Question	Rwanda	UK
Population		
Life expectancy (male)		
Life expectancy (female)		
Literacy of whole population		
Gross domestic product (GDP) per capita (i.e. per person)		
Telephone (main lines)		
Telephone (mobile)		
Internet hosts (i.e. ISPs)		
Number of Internet users		

2 (a) Describe **three** ways in which the use of the Internet would help some of Rwanda's population. (3 marks)
  (b) Give **one** reason why not all the population may benefit by access to the Internet. (1 mark)
3 Do you think this investment in ICT is good for Rwanda? Give a brief reason for your answer. (2 marks)

Exam support

Worked example 1

1 **The use of ICT is influenced by a number of factors.**
 Give the names of two such factors and for each one explain how each factor has had an effect on the use of ICT. (4 marks)

Student answer 1

1 Economic. A firm decides to relocate its call centre to India because the cost of the telecommunications is low and the wage costs in India are lower than they are in the UK. Environmental. ICT systems need to be used in many different places such as in planes, in hotels, on trains, etc. This means that the ICT system must be easily carried and have data on it that is scrambled so if it gets lost or is stolen, other cannot access the data. Ethical. ICT may be developed to help young students to do their coursework but such a system may be frowned upon by teachers as it encourages students to do little work.

Examiner's comment

1 This is an excellent answer to quite a difficult question. The student has clearly related the factor to the development of ICT systems by giving an example.
 Notice they have given three answers instead of two. You penalise yourself for time when you do this. Sometimes the examiner will only mark the first two answers. **(4 marks out of 4)**

Student answer 2

1 Social – a company may develop new ICT systems for use in the home to enable people to work from home to avoid travelling.
 Economic – if there is not enough money, then the ideal solution to an ICT problem may be a compromise.

Examiner's comment

1 The two answers are fine with a clear factor and reason. **(4 marks out of 4)**

Examiner's answers

1 One mark for the factor and a second mark for describing how this influences the use of ICT. Note that this could include an example. There are many examples and here are just a few of the possibilities.
 Legal – the law may forbid what an ICT does or the way that it does it.
 • The ICT system may harm the employee's health.
 • The system may be limited because the Data Protection Act does not allow the passage of personal data without the data subject's permission.
 • The government want to create a national database where all the information about people is collected in one place. Before this is done there would need to be a change in the law to allow personal data collected for one purpose to be used for another.

Economic – there may only be a certain budget allocated to a project, which will limit the ICT system built.
 • It may be necessary to conduct business in a way a competitor conducts business in order to remain competitive.
 • In the case of a public organisation, the budget from the government.
 Social – A proposed website wants to put known troublemakers' pictures on a community site so people can keep an eye on them. People are worried that this could cause people to take the law into their own hands.
 Cultural – An Internet search engine company wants to encourage the use of its search engine in all countries. The government does not want its citizens to view morally corrupt material such as porn sites, gambling sites, etc., so they want a filter on the search engines to filter out this material.
 Cultural – music CD companies decide to remove copy protection so people can copy CDs.

Unit 2 Living in the Digital World

Summary mind map

Factors affecting the use of ICT

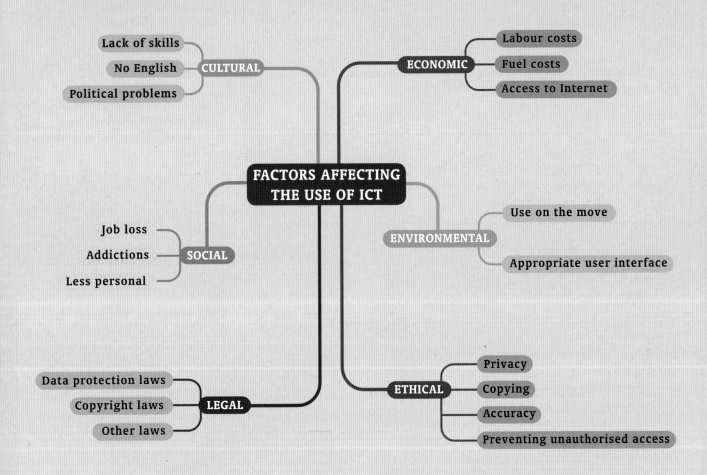

As societies become more reliant on computer networks, we become vulnerable to cybercrime as well as having our privacy eroded. Is this a price worth paying for the benefits that the technologies bring? Some people think not and that technology creates more problems than it solves. ICT can cause other social problems such as changes in jobs or worse still, unemployment. In this topic we will look at the effects of ICT systems on the individual and society.

▼ The key concepts covered in this topic are:

▶ The consequences of the use of ICT for individuals

▶ The consequences of the use of ICT for society

CONTENTS

Unit 2 Living in the Digital World

The benefits of working using ICT

▼ **You will find out**

▶ About the benefits for individuals

▶ About the benefits of teleworking

▶ About the benefits to different groups of people

Introduction

There are lots of ways in which the use of ICT affects individuals. One way is by changing the type of jobs and the patterns of work. Most jobs require some use of ICT, and ICT skills are just as important as literacy and numeracy skills.

ICT can have huge benefits to certain groups of individuals such as schoolchildren, the disabled and the elderly.

As well as providing many benefits to individuals and groups of individuals, ICT does present a number of problems.

Benefits to individuals

It is not hard to think of the benefits of ICT systems as there are so many of them. Benefits include:

Greater leisure time – ICT systems allow us to do more work in less time so it increases our productivity and can make the working week shorter.

Easy access to huge amounts of information – you are able to access huge amounts of information without leaving home. Via the Internet you have access to maps, encyclopaedias, opening hours of shops, bus and train timetables and so on.

Easy to exchange ideas – much easier to work in groups/teams using videoconferencing, e-mail, file attachments, etc.

Creation of new and more interesting jobs – many new skilled and interesting jobs have been created by the use of ICT, such as systems analysts, programmers, computer security experts, network specialists, help-desk staff and so on. Even jobs that are mainly clerical become more interesting as ICT takes over the more repetitive parts of the job.

Cheap methods of communication – cheap/free local and international phone calls made over the Internet using Skype means that it is easy for retired people to spend lots of time talking to friends and relatives who may live in this country or abroad.

You can even make video phone calls using Skype.

You can keep in touch with friends and relatives using websites such as Facebook, Friends Reunited, MSN, etc.

You can make savings for goods or services – it is very easy to search for the cheapest place to purchase a particular item using one of the many sites on the Internet. Sites like this can save you lots of money, particularly on large purchases such as cars, plasma TVs, white goods, etc.

There are many 'Internet only' offers which are only available if you buy certain goods or services on-line.

You can tailor-make your holiday – gives you the freedom to create your own holiday by booking flights, hotels and car hire separately.

Low cost airlines have revolutionised travel by the intensive use of ICT systems to reduce cost.

Ability to shop from home – home shopping enables people to order food, etc., and have it delivered straight to their home, which allows them to have more leisure time or time with their families. Home shopping is also very useful for people who cannot leave the house because they are ill, disabled, etc., as it allows them to retain their independence.

Opportunity to telework – makes it easier for people to live and work where they choose, as it is possible for some staff to work from home. It reduces traffic congestion and carbon dioxide emissions and is therefore 'greener'. This has an environmental benefit since there is no commuting to work. Also it helps support rural areas where people normally have to move away to get work.

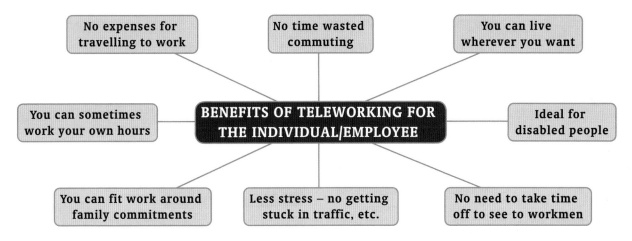

Working from home, called teleworking, is very popular with employees.

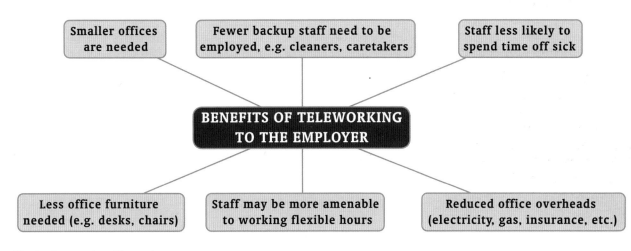

Teleworking is also popular with employers.

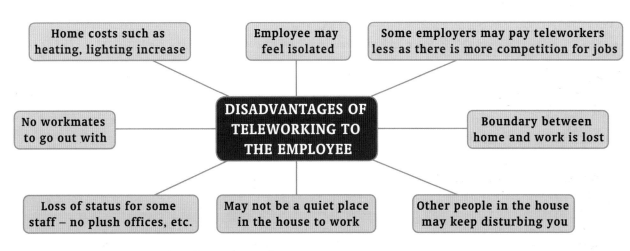

There are a number of disadvantages of teleworking to the employee.

The benefits of working using ICT
continued

Disadvantages of Teleworking to Employers
Change to organisational structure may be needed
Hard to determine how hard staff are working
Harder for managers to manage the work
More difficult to hold meetings
DISADVANTAGES OF TELEWORKING TO EMPLOYERS
Employers usually pay for the employees' ICT equipment
Increased number of sites for ICT equipment may cause more security risks

There are a number of disadvantages of teleworking to the employer.

The Benefits of Teleworking to Society
Reduced traffic congestion as fewer people travel to work
Fewer greenhouse gas emissions helps reduce global warming
Can help sustain rural communities as people can telework
THE BENEFITS OF TELEWORKING TO SOCIETY
Prosperity is spread around the UK rather than being mainly located in the cities
Less air pollution
Family relationships improve as there is more time in the home

There are many benefits of teleworking to society.

On-line banking – you can access important services without having to travel to a particular location. For example, it is possible to pay bills, check a bank balance, apply for loans and take out insurance all without leaving home.

Less control by repressive governments in some countries – it's easier for people to learn about oppressive regimes and abuses of human rights. If it occurs in their own country, they can let people in other countries know about what is going on.

Helps you with school/college work – allows students to access information to help with coursework, revision sites, etc. Can help individuals learn new skills such as ICT skills, language skills, etc. New technology enables students to learn at their own pace.

Access to media anyplace anytime – people used to only access media in one place but now media is accessible in many different places. Examples of this include:

- music can be played on the move using mobile phones and MP3 players
- video can be obtained on iPods
- video can be streamed and watched over the Internet

- you can listen to many radio programmes on demand (i.e., not necessarily when they were transmitted) using the Internet
- playback systems on TVs and satellite systems allow you to watch programmes you may have missed
- text messages, news, share prices, football results, etc., can be obtained on a whole range of portable devices from laptops to mobile phones.

ICT can help people with their personal problems – you can be anonymous on the Internet. You can go into chat rooms, seek medical information or counselling, put information up in blogs and remain anonymous.

You can freely discuss issues such as drugs, AIDS, abortion, gay rights and politics without anyone knowing who you are. Being able to discuss such topics openly is important.

Some countries do not have a free press and there is no freedom of expression, so anonymity is important if citizens want to let other countries know what is happening there.

Problems caused by ICT to individuals

There are a number of problems ICT brings to individuals. These include:

Information overload – individuals feel that with text messages, e-mails, instant messaging, voicemail, etc., there is too much information to sort through and they can find it stressful.

Hard to keep up with developments – the pace of change means that there are always new ICT systems, hardware and software to learn about. New skills need to be continually learnt and older people find this difficult.

Increased insecurity at work – new developments in ICT mean that certain jobs may not exist in the future. For example, if you worked for a travel agent, you may be worried that many people now can book holidays on-line.

Worries about children accessing the Internet – parents worry about their children having full access to the Internet as they could view pornographic websites accidentally, or talk to adults who could be paedophiles in chat rooms. Most Internet service providers have parental controls which parents can use to restrict access to certain parts of the Internet.

Health problems – continual use of ICT systems has given rise to a number of health problems such as RSI, eye strain, backache and stress. The use of mobile phones and WiFi systems may cause health problems but the problem is that they have not been around long enough to tell.

How ICT systems have benefited the disabled

ICT systems have benefited disabled people immensely and many systems allow them to be more independent and take up employment opportunities.

- Helps people with learning difficulties – some people find it hard to concentrate and have difficulty reading. Multimedia makes use of more than one sense to help reinforce learning.
- Helps people with unclear speech – if a person cannot speak or their speech is not clear, then to help them communicate with others there are ICT systems where they can type in a word and the word is turned into speech.
- Voice activation systems – these can be used to issue commands to lights or central heating controls.
- Helps people work – many disabled people are now able to telework from their home using ICT equipment.
- They can retain their independence – there is no need for people who cannot leave the house to use others to pay bills, do shopping, etc. All this can be done using the Internet.

How ICT systems have benefited older people

Many older people realise the benefits of using ICT and they use ICT systems to:

- Communicate with grandchildren, family members who may live in different parts of the country or even overseas using Internet telephony, e-mail, instant messaging, etc.
- Learn new skills using the computer such as how to edit photographs, create websites, etc.
- Manage their finances. Many retired people rely on money they have invested, so they use the Internet

▶ KEY WORDS

Podcasting – creating and publishing a digital radio broadcast using a microphone, computer and audio editing software. The resulting file is saved in MP3 format and then uploaded onto an Internet server. It can then be downloaded using a facility called RSS onto an MP3 player such as an iPod.

to get the best interest rate, the cheapest insurance, etc.
- Explore their family history (this is called genealogy).
- Gain access to the vast amounts of information on the Internet, from health to gardening.
- Form or join self-help groups to deal with similar problems such as health problems, caring for sick relatives, bereavement, etc.

How ICT systems have benefited students in school/college

ICT is now used in most lessons or lectures and all teachers are required to have a good knowledge of ICT systems. Here are some of the systems you will probably have seen being used.

Electronic whiteboards – enables lessons to be more interactive and to involve students more in the learning process.

PowerPoint presentations – makes subjects more interesting because video and sound can be used.

Facilitates group work – where students are working together on a project as they can keep in touch by text message or e-mail.

Students can work at their own pace – one problem in a class situation is that everyone has to work at the same pace. With educational software it is possible for students to progress at a speed that is suited to them.

Students can use podcasts for revision – there are many revision sites where podcasts can be downloaded onto your MP3 player and you can listen to them when travelling.

Students can access blogs, message boards and forums – so that they can chat about their learning and help each other.

Easy access to assessment material – specifications, exam papers and other materials can be downloaded from the examination board's website.

Access to massive amounts of information – students have access to a huge range of information and all from the comfort of their own home using the Internet.

Availability of revision sites – there are many revision sites aimed at helping you pass your exams. BBC Bitesize is an example of this.

Simulation software – can be used to simulate scientific experiments that would be too time consuming or dangerous to do in the lab.

Improved presentation of work – the use of word-processing, art software and DTP software means that students can produce very professional-looking work.

Personalised learning – students can learn at their own speed and at a level suited to their abilities using software which teaches them and then tests them on what they have learnt.

Students can help each other in message boards, download podcasts to play in their MP3 players, listen to revision lessons using their computer and read the scripts for the commentary as a PDF file.

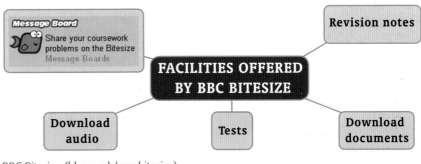

BBC Bitesize (bbc.co.uk/gcsebitesize)

The consequences of the use of ICT for society

Introduction

Some of the uses of ICT affect everyone in some way and alter the way things are done. Many of the uses of ICT benefit society but the widespread use of ICT has caused a number of problems such as misuses and loss of privacy.

Society has now become completely reliant on some ICT systems and when such systems fail to operate correctly, the general public is greatly affected. Examples of ICT systems which we depend on are the air traffic control systems and traffic management systems.

In this part of the topic you will look at the consequences of the use of ICT for different groups of individuals and society as a whole.

The problems of the use of ICT for society

In this section you will be looking at the problems created for society by ICT systems.

Problems with misuse

There is a whole range of misuse brought about by the use of ICT systems and these cause annoyance and frustration to individuals and society as a whole. Misuse includes:

- Identity theft – people gaining your credit card or banking details and then pretending to be you to buy goods or services.
- Hacking – people spying on what you have stored on your hard drive and perhaps altering files.
- Virus attack – causes software to malfunction or creates offensive messages or even deletes important files.
- Spam – wasting time opening and reading e-mails which are just useless advertising material for things you do not want.

Lack of privacy – with surveillance cameras, monitoring of e-mails and phone conversations, identity cards, large government databases, many people feel that they are continually being watched.

Lack of equality – people with ICT skills and access to the Internet can make big savings on goods and services compared to those people without the skills and access to the Internet.

De-skills or eliminates some jobs – many jobs that were performed by highly skilled people, such as typing or publishing, can be performed by anyone who takes the time to learn the software skills of word-processing or desktop publishing. Some jobs, such as filing clerks, have been completely eliminated.

Deserted city centres – as more and more people choose to shop on-line, shops in the city centres will close.

Cyberbullying – people have been bullied at school and at home using the Internet or by text messaging using mobile phones.

Access to pornography – unrestricted access to the Internet means that people can use their computers to access material that would be illegal in this country. There are many people that have gone on to commit crimes after viewing such material.

Illegal copying – the illegal copying of ICT hardware and software is bad for society, as much of the money is used to fund other illegal activities such as drug dealing, prostitution, etc.

Misinformation – there are many sites where users add comments to message boards or blogs or even add their own content to encyclopaedias. Some of this information is wrong as it is not supplied by experts on the subjects.

Using photo editing software to distort reality – by using photo/video editing software you can distort reality and you can no longer believe what you see in video, TV, newspapers, magazines and on websites.

ICT helping to spread rumours – news spreads very quickly using ICT, and rumours, even if they are false, can be spread. The trouble is that rumours

Society needs to censor certain offensive material on the Internet.

KEY WORDS

Cybercrime – crimes committed involving ICT systems as a major part

Spam – unsolicited bulk e-mail (i.e., e-mail from people you do not know sent to everyone in the hope that a small percentage may purchase the goods or services on offer)

and lies can be created on message boards or on blogs or in chat rooms and it is hard to determine who started them. This has caused many people a lot of distress.

Bogus sites – there are some bogus sites that are deliberately set up to deceive the users. Individuals may believe the information on such sites and add the information to coursework or project work for examinations.

Check out the website above where you can learn the benefits of, or even buy dehydrated water!

Globalisation – ICT systems have led to globalisation because it is so easy to conduct business between countries. Globalisation involves the breaking down of the economic, cultural and other barriers between countries making them less separate. Globalisation has led to:

- People listening to the same music and reading similar books.
- Jobs going abroad because people are more skilled and can do the job more cheaply.

EXAM TIP

Many of the examination questions on the consequences of ICT to individuals and society require lengthy almost essay-style answers where you have to discuss the issues. You need to have a plan when producing the answers. Remember you need to look closely at the mark scheme to work out how the examiner is likely to allocate the marks. In such questions you should not dwell on one point for too long. Make sure you have lots of points.

buydehydratedwater.com

| ► Home | ► Online Store | ► Franchise Op | ► Cool Jobs | ►Testimonials | ►Free Sample | ► FAQ | ► Media | ►Contact Info |

You've seen it on TV, heard it on the radio, and read it in your local newspapers, "Our Public Water Supply Is Polluted and Dangerous!"

Every year millions of gallons of crude oil and toxic waste materials are dumped into our oceans and water reservoirs. Many have heard of the Exxon Valdez oil spill. But what about all those other chemical spills that seemingly go undetected under the cover of night. No matter how much your city tries to cleanse their water system, traces of these dangerous chemicals still prevail all around. Cities across the United States and around the world have old, corroded, lead pipes that poison your water. More than ever before, people are turning to bottled water as a safety precaution against all these pollutants. But many of these bottled waters are even worse than public water supplies. Some bottling facilities do not change their filters frequently enough and thus inject hazardous substances into your water. Other bottling companies don't date their supplies and end up selling old water, which is equally dangerous.

It's time to stop the insanity and insist on a better quality of life. Stop drinking tap water. Stop drinking well water. Refuse to touch water from desalination plants. And remember that mountain spring water is a disaster waiting to happen. Do you know how many people and animals urinated in your spring water, upstream? Yes, it's disgusting to think about (perhaps even humorous), but it happens. So stop drinking it. Insist on only one natural substance... **Dehydrated water**.

It takes hundreds of years to form and only minutes to vaporize... Pure, refreshing, crystal clear, filtered, and compressed dehydrated water. No where on Earth will you find a more pure substance. Dehydrated water is compact, lightweight, easy to store, and perfect to take wherever you go. It's free of toxins, chemicals, lead, minerals, and almost every other dangerous substance you can think of. And best of all, it contains no calories nor any fat. Dehydrated water is the perfect addition to all high-fiber, protein, and carbohydrate diets. Try some today!

- A free marketplace where it is easy to trade with anyone anywhere in the world.
- The same shops and businesses in the high street (MacDonald's, Starbucks, etc.) anywhere in the world.
- A loss of the culture in certain countries.
- Alienation of those countries that do not wish to be part of it.
- Commercialism – where people are never happy with what they have and always want more.

Widens the gap between rich and poor countries – the use of ICT makes already rich countries richer. As many poorer countries do not have reliable electricity or telecommunications, they cannot take advantage of the financial benefits of ICT.

ICT and crime

Crime is a major problem in society and as well as creating a number of problems, ICT has been used by the police to prevent or detect crime.

ICT benefits society by helping police fight crime

There are many ICT systems that help the police solve crimes and these include:

- DNA databases where samples at the scene of crime are compared with DNA samples of convicted criminals or those suspected of a crime.
- Vehicle number plate recognition systems match number plates to owners of vehicles, which is useful in the detection of offenders (e.g., speeding, hit and runs, etc.).
- Fingerprint database – uses fingerprints from the scene of the crime to match against a database of fingerprints from known criminals.
- CCTV cameras help in the prevention and detection of crime.

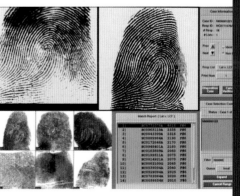

Fingerprints from the scene of crime can be matched against those held on a fingerprint database.

The consequences of the use of ICT for society
continued

KEY WORDS

Scams – setting up bogus companies with bogus websites and then making off with the money from customers' orders

ICT helps criminals to commit crimes

Cybercrime is one of the fastest growing areas of crime and it is a worldwide problem. Cybercrime covers a multitude of criminal activities such as financial scams, hacking, downloading illegal pornographic images, virus attacks, stalking by e-mail and producing websites that promote racial hatred.

Anonymity – it is possible to remain anonymous on the Internet. The downside of anonymity is that it can be exploited to aid undesirable computer activities such as:

- terrorism
- money laundering
- drug dealing
- preying on the vulnerable (e.g., paedophiles gaining access to children in chat rooms).

Benefits of the use of ICT for society

There are many benefits to society in using ICT and some are included here:

Greater democracy – E-voting systems allow the public to vote from the comfort of their own homes, which encourages more people to vote.

Greater productivity and less wastage – more efficient use of valuable resources.

Higher standard of living – countries that make the most use of ICT systems have the highest standards of living in the world.

Shorter working week – using ICT systems means organisations are more efficient and the same work can be completed in less time.

Helps disabled people to be more independent – teleworking makes it easier for disabled people to work. There are also ICT products and systems for disabled people to make their lives easier.

Makes life safer – there are many safety critical systems such as fly-by-wire aircraft systems, air traffic control systems, traffic management systems, etc., where human error is eliminated.

Videoconferencing helping society

Videoconferencing allows face-to-face meetings to be conducted without the participants being in the same room or even the same geographical area. In addition to sending the video and audio of the people taking part in the videoconference, videoconferencing can be used to share documents and presentations.

Because of the high bandwidth requirements for the video and audio, it is necessary to compress and decompress the signals in real time and this is done using a device or software called a codec (coder/decoder).

Videoconferencing systems consist of the following components:

Hardware

- High specification multimedia PC
- Video cameras or webcams – sometimes the cameras can be operated remotely so it is possible to zoom in on a particular speaker
- Microphones
- Screen (this can be a computer screen or it could be a large plasma display allowing many people to view the picture)
- Loudspeakers
- Sometimes the codec (to code/decode the signals) is hardware.

Some of the many crimes associated with ICT.

Some of the items needed for videoconferencing besides the computer and screen.

Software

- Sometimes the codec (to code/ decode the signals) is software.

Data communications

A connection to a high speed digital network.

Benefits of using videoconferencing

There are many benefits in using videoconferencing and these can be classified into benefits for different groups of people.

Benefits to the employee

- Less stress as employees do not have to experience delays at airports, accidents, road works, etc.
- Improved family life as less time spent away from home staying in hotels.
- They do not have to put in long working hours travelling to and from meetings.

Benefits to the organisation

- Much cheaper as they do not have to spend money on travelling expenses, hotel rooms, meals, etc.
- Improved productivity of employees as they are not wasting time travelling.

- Meetings can be called at very short notice without too much planning.
- Short meetings can be conducted where it would not be feasible for people to travel long distances for such short meetings.

Benefits to society

- Fewer people flying to meetings will cut down on the number of flights needed and hence reduce the amount of carbon dioxide emitted helping to reduce global warming.
- Roads will not be clogged up with traffic and this will cause less stress and cut down on pollution.

Disadvantages/limitations of videoconferencing

- The cost of the equipment – specialist videoconferencing equipment is expensive.
- Poor image and sound quality – image quality is seldom as good as you would get with a TV, owing to the need to compress and decompress signals sent over the communication links.
- People can feel very self-conscious when using videoconferencing and may fail to come across well.

- Although documents and diagrams in digital form can be passed around, an actual product or component cannot be passed around.
- Lack of face-to-face contact may mean a discussion may not be as effective.

Uses of videoconferencing

Education – some schools use videoconferencing for teaching A-levels where there are too few students to justify having a specialist teacher. One teacher can therefore be used to teach students in lots of different schools.

Medicine – busy doctors can use teleconferencing to hold meetings about patients, and X-rays, ultrasound images, laboratory analyses can be passed digitally to the participants.

Business – used extensively in business for conducting meetings at a distance.

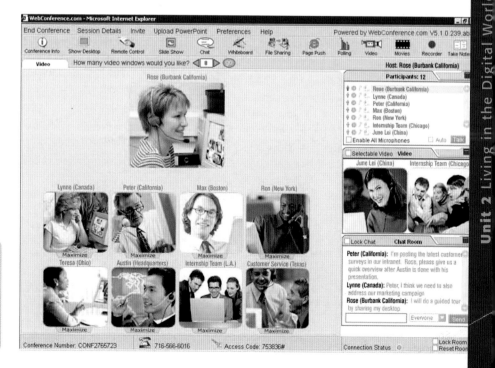

Case studies

▶ Case study 1 | p. 251

Automatic Number Plate Recognition systems helping police fight crime

Most police forces now use an Automatic Number Plate Recognition system. This system uses a van and several police traffic cars. The van contains a camera which reads the number plates of passing vehicles and the details are fed back to a computer system which checks them against a number of sources such as the Police National Computer (PNC), Driver Vehicle Licensing Agency (DVLA) and motor insurers' databases.

If a match is found, an alarm sounds and the intercept teams in the police traffic cars can then stop the vehicle. This really helps in the fight against crime, as vehicles used by criminals can be stopped. It can also be used to stop people who are driving without tax and/or insurance.

Police vans are used to house the digital video cameras.

1   The system uses digital video cameras to record the image. Special software is needed to interpret the image into letters and numbers. Give the name of this type of software. (1 mark)

2   Give **one** concern that an individual might have about such a system being used. (2 marks)

3   Describe **one** benefit to society of the use of this system. (2 marks)

▶ Case study 2 | pp. 252–253

Database bug delays UK salaries

Because of a software bug in a database program, over 400,000 monthly paid workers received their pay one day late in March 2007. The error occurred in a financial software system used by Bacs Payment Schemes Limited (Bacs), the organisation formerly known as the Bankers Automated Clearing System.

Bacs is used by employers to pay money directly into employees' accounts. On this particular day, a software bug caused the system to slow down, which resulted in the payments forming a 'traffic jam' and eventually caused the ICT system to fail.

A spokesperson said that the problem was not caused by virus activity or by human error, but they did not reveal the exact nature of the problem.

bacs

The problem for customers was that because they received their payments a day late, they may have had payments which were timed to go out on the day after they were paid. Without their wages going in, they could have gone overdrawn and potentially incurred bank charges. However, recognising this, the banking industry ensured customers were not left out of pocket and were reimbursed for any consequential charges incurred.

Bacs has only had one other problem and this occurred over 10 years ago when telecommunications equipment failed.

1   Explain what is meant by a software bug. (1 mark)

2   (a)   Explain the meaning of the term Bacs. (1 mark)
    (b)   Explain **one** task performed by the Bacs system. (1 mark)

3   ICT system failures can result in inconvenience to many people. Explain **one** inconvenience suffered by bank customers owing to failure of the Bacs system for a short period of time. (2 marks)

Bringing power to individuals

The British political system is based on old technology. We elect people to represent us by placing a cross on a paper ballot form and put it into a box. In many cases the votes are counted manually and the result is given by a person in a packed hall – about as low tech as you can get.

The person elected as an MP will then use their judgement to represent the people in the House of Commons.

With the use of ICT, this is all about to change.

On the E-petitions section of the Downing Street website you can view and add your name to petitions as well as start one yourself.

Political blogs or message boards are set up by individuals or newspapers to discuss and campaign on lots of issues that affect all of us, such as crime, health, education, unemployment, taxes, immigration, etc. The idea is that these will help politicians to keep in touch with public opinion.

E-petitions have been set up on the Downing Street website, which allows any individual to start up a petition on any topic and then encourage others to add their names to the petition to get politicians to take note. The politicians may then choose to take notice (or not) of what has been said and discuss the issues in the House of Commons.

Possible new developments

Anyone who had enough support from an e-petition could force the government to have a vote on the issue. This would mean more democracy and greater power to individuals. At present the government can choose to ignore these petitions, no matter how many people add their names to them.

Candidates in an election at the moment use methods such as visiting people or sending out leaflets to encourage people to vote for them. There is a move towards using social networking sites such as YouTube to encourage people to vote for them.

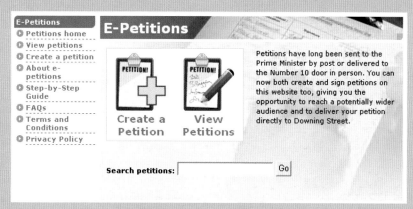

1 Explain the purpose of a blog and give an advantage in MPs using blogs to keep in touch with public opinion. (2 marks)

2 The case study mentions 'social networking sites'. Explain what social networking sites are and give the names of two such sites that you have encountered. (3 marks)

Chinese Web filtering

How would you feel if you were not allowed to access certain sites? In certain countries, such as China, the government use a firewall that filters out access to sites that they do not allow, which are usually sites that criticise the government or present the country in an undesirable way. The firewall blocks banned subjects, certain Web addresses and certain words.

Many people are worried that if they try to use these words or websites the government could identify who they are and then take action against them.

1 Web filtering is often done in schools or by the parents of young children. Give two reasons why this is necessary. (2 marks)

2 (a) Give one reason why Web filtering is performed by the Chinese authorities. (2 marks)

(b) Give the name of the device/ software that is used to block access to certain content using the Internet. (1 mark)

Questions and Activities

▶ Questions 1 | pp. 248–249

1 When you connect to the Internet there are a number of misuses that can occur.
Give the names of **two** misuses that an individual may encounter when connected to the Internet and for each misuse state one thing that can be done to prevent the misuse. (4 marks)

2 One of the misuses of ICT systems which affects the whole of society is identity theft.
(a) Explain what is meant by the term identity theft. (2 marks)
(b) Give **one** measure you can take to protect yourself from identity theft. (1 mark)

▶ Questions 2 | p. 248

1 The widespread use of ICT has led to a number of social problems. Describe two social problems that have been caused by the use of the Internet. (4 marks)

2 The use of ICT has enabled many staff to work from home.
Working from home has both advantages and disadvantages. Give **two** advantages and **two** disadvantages to an employee in working from home. (4 marks)

3 The way ICT systems are used can cause problems to individuals. Explain how each of the following affects the way an individual uses ICT systems.
(a) Viruses (2 marks)
(b) Hacking (2 marks)

▶ Questions 3 | p. 249

1 Write a short essay outlining how the use of ICT has benefited the disabled. (8 marks)

2 (a) Viruses are a problem for all computer users. Give **two** reasons why a user is likely to be worried about the introduction of viruses into their ICT system. (2 marks)
(b) Hacking is also a problem for anyone who connects their computer or network to the Internet. Give **two** reasons why a user is likely to be worried about others hacking into their ICT system. (2 marks)
(c) Explain why most users who use the Internet to conduct banking transactions and make purchases are worried about identity theft. (2 marks)

▶ Questions 4 | p. 251

1 (a) Explain what is meant by the term globalisation. (2 marks)
(b) ICT systems contribute to globalisation. Give **two** ways in which ICT systems contribute to globalisation. (4 marks)

2 (a) Explain the meaning of the term telework. (2 marks)
(b) Give **two** advantages to the employee of teleworking. (2 marks)
(c) Give the name of a job that is suitable for teleworking and give a reason why this job is particularly suited for teleworking. (2 marks)

3 As there has been a movement away from cash, criminals have turned to cybercrime. Cyber-criminals use ICT systems to commit crimes.
(a) Give **three** different examples of cybercrime. (3 marks)
(b) Give **three** steps that an individual can take to protect themselves from cybercrime. (3 marks)
(c) Many ICT systems are used by the police to help prevent or detect crime.
Describe **one** such system and explain how the ICT system helps. (3 marks)

4 Developments in ICT have had significant effects on society, individuals and organisations. By referring to examples of your own choice, discuss this statement including in your discussion the following:
The effects of ICT on society at large
The effects of ICT on employment and work methods
The effects of ICT on individuals (15 marks)

Research activity Useful websites

Here are some particularly useful websites. Access each of these sites in turn and take a good look at them and then write a short paragraph about each one explaining why they are so useful for an individual.

Site 1 Kelkoo
http://www.kelkoo.co.uk/

Site 2 Faceparty
www.faceparty.com

Site 3 MySpace
www.myspace.com

Site 4 Multimap
www.multimap.com

Research activity E-petitions

Log onto the Internet and access the Downing Street website using the following address: http://petitions.pm.gov.uk/
   Write a short paragraph to explain how e-petitions can help an individual have more power over the way the country is run.

Activity PowerPoint presentation preparation

This activity is best undertaken as a small team. You will need to divide up the work and agree on some things before you start.
   You have been asked to give a PowerPoint presentation on how the police use ICT to prevent, detect and solve crime. Luckily someone has done some preliminary research and found some key words which you need to find further information about.

- **CCTV**
- **Automatic Number Place Recognition systems**
- **Speed cameras**
- **Face recognition systems**
- **Police National Computer**
- **National Fingerprint Collection**
- **The national DNA database**
   Feel free to extend your search for information beyond the systems in the above list and also in the list of websites shown below. Some useful websites:
   http://www.thamesvalley.police.uk/news_info/departments/anpr/index.htm
   http://www.suffolk.police.uk
   http://en.wikipedia.org/wiki/Police_National_Computer
   http://www.alcester.net/AS/it01resources/itpolice/pnc1.htm
   http://www.spsa-forensics.police.uk/about/faq/fingerprints_faqs
   http://www.npia.police.uk/en/5971.htm
   http://www.homeoffice.gov.uk/science-research/using-science/dna-database/

Exam support

Worked example 1

1   The use of ICT systems has benefited children tremendously. There is, however, a downside in allowing children to use some ICT systems. By giving an example of each, explain **two** different problems caused by children using ICT systems. **(4 marks)**

Student answer 1

1   Children could have health problems caused by sitting at the computer too long.
    They could get tricked into meeting paedophiles pretending to be children their own age. They could get sexually assaulted, raped or even murdered by these people.

Student answer 2

1   There are bogus sites with completely wrong information. For example, there is one that explains how Velcro grows on plants. The pupils could accidentally access pornographic sites and this could cause problems.

Examiner's comment

1   The first answer does not identify a particular health problem – if anyone sat doing anything for too long it would cause a health problem so no marks here.
    They need to say what it is specifically that causes the health problem such as incorrect posture, repeated mouse movements and give more detail on the health problems.
    The second answer is better. However they have not mentioned that it is the Internet that is used and that this would probably occur in a chat room. The example gives details of the potential problem. Only one of the two marks here. **(1 mark out of 4)**

Examiner's comment

1   By looking at the question carefully the student needed to identify or explain the problem and then give an example.
    The first part of the answer identifies what the problem is but they have not given an example such as 'the pupil could repeat the information as an answer to an examination question and get it marked wrong'.
    Similar problems occur with the second part of the answer. They have given the problem but no example. **(2 marks out of 4)**

Examiner's answers

1   One mark for the name or brief description of the ICT system and one mark for an example that explains the problem x 2.
    Chat rooms – adults could entice children to meet them without their parents' knowledge and with the obvious dangers.
    Continual/obsessive playing of computer games:
    – wastes time when they could be getting on with school work
    – does not encourage children to adopt a healthy lifestyle as they could be getting exercise by playing games such as football, netball, etc.
    Health problems
    – repeatedly typing at a computer/using a mouse/using a joystick can cause repetitive strain injury (RSI).
    – can cause backache if child slouches in their seat whilst using the computer.
    Some sites contain bogus information – set up to deceive people, and children will believe them and use the material for homework or project work at school.

Worked example 2

2   Many companies (multinational companies) have offices in many different parts of the world. This makes it hard for staff to feel they all belong to the same organisation.
    (a) Explain how the organisation can use ICT to enable staff working in different places around the globe to communicate effectively. **(8 marks)**
    (b) There are a number of problems in communicating using ICT.
         Describe **three** disadvantages of using ICT for communicating. **(6 marks)**

Student answer 1

2 (a) They can use text messaging as texts are cheaper than phone calls made abroad. It also means they can read them at a time to suit.

They can send e-mails. E-mails are good because they are stored automatically and they can arrive almost instantly. Replies can be written quickly and you do not have to waste time explaining what you are replying to.

You can use chat rooms where you can meet and chat to your colleagues in a chat room if you get lonely.

(b) If the equipment breaks down then you cannot communicate. People like to chat face to face. It is harder to tell if someone is lying or how they feel about what you are saying by simply looking at their face.

E-mail is no good for bringing bad news – no-one wants to be sacked from a job by e-mail as this should be done personally.

Examiner's comment

2 Eight marks are available for part (a) so there need to be eight relevant facts.

Text messaging, although an important communication method, is only suitable for short messages and is not a method by which people in organisations communicate, so no marks for this answer.

The answer about e-mail makes three relevant points so three marks here.

Most companies would not want staff discussing organisation business in a chat room, especially if it were open to the public. No marks here.

Students should be referring to business methods of communication and not the way they communicate on a personal level with their friends. **(3 marks out of 8)**

Part (b) has six marks available so there need to be six valid points.

There are two answers here – each with a statement and further explanation which are both correct so four marks here. **(4 marks out of 6)**

Student answer 2

2 (a) Staff can use e-mail to communicate with colleagues. This is faster than ordinary mail which can take weeks to arrive in some countries.

Replies are easy to make because you only have to click on reply and type your message to the original e-mail.

You do not have to wait for the post or queue for stamps, etc.

The organisation could set up a blog which allows all staff to post their comments. This allows people to air problems or grievances they have.

The company managers could choose to do something about them or not.

Staff can use videoconferencing to organise virtual meetings where everyone can see each other and they can pass around electronic documents and watch presentations. No time is wasted travelling to meetings, and the costs are much lower as the management do not have to pay for travel, meals, hotel costs, etc.

(b) People sometimes like a change away from the office and they like to socialise with others. Videoconferencing takes this away.

It is hard for people to act naturally in a videoconferencing situation and many people like proper face-to-face contact.

E-mail is useful for quick communication but it can appear quite abrupt.

People may not feel it is a good idea to post up material on blogs and message boards as they feel the comments could be easily traced back to them

Examiner's comment

2 Part (a) has been well answered and includes all relevant points and is clearly expressed. There are eight separate points here which are correct for this answer, so full marks for this section. **(8 marks out of 8)**

Part (b) is also a very good answer where five valid points are made. **(5 marks out of 6)**

Examiner's answers

2 (a) One mark for a statement of a suitable communication method that must be appropriate for a business. Then one mark for each explanation about how the communication method can be used.

E-mail to be used to communicate with colleagues (1). Provides fast communication as there is no wait for post (1). Cheap method as e-mails are almost free (1). Good because original e-mail and reply can be kept together so no time wasted searching for original e-mail (1). Can attach files and other documents to e-mails for comments (1). Videoconferencing can be used for virtual meetings (1). It saves employees having to travel to a real meeting (1). Saves the company money by not having to pay for venue, travel costs, hotel costs, meals etc. (1). Meetings can be called at short notice on an ad hoc basis (1). Forums/blogs/message boards allow staff to communicate with each other (1). They can set up discussions and ask others for comments (1).

(b) One mark for the disadvantage and one mark for an explanation of the consequences that the disadvantage would have.

Lack of face-to-face contact (1). It is important to see people's faces and read their body language (1). Relies on technology which may not always be reliable (e.g., satellite links) (1). Equipment may break down and cause no communications at all (1). Sometimes more sensitive when giving bad news to communicate in person (1). Sometimes e-mails are too brief and can cause misunderstandings (1).

Summary mind maps

The consequences of the use of ICT for individuals

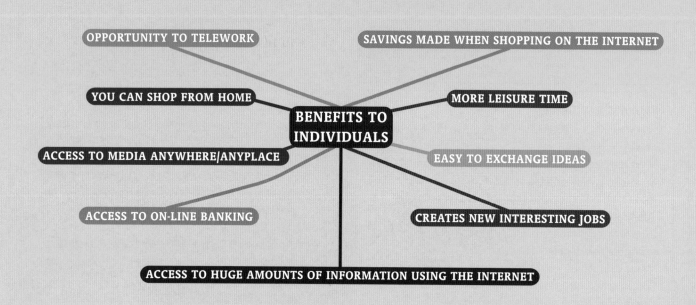

OPPORTUNITY TO TELEWORK

SAVINGS MADE WHEN SHOPPING ON THE INTERNET

YOU CAN SHOP FROM HOME

MORE LEISURE TIME

BENEFITS TO INDIVIDUALS

ACCESS TO MEDIA ANYWHERE/ANYPLACE

EASY TO EXCHANGE IDEAS

ACCESS TO ON-LINE BANKING

CREATES NEW INTERESTING JOBS

ACCESS TO HUGE AMOUNTS OF INFORMATION USING THE INTERNET

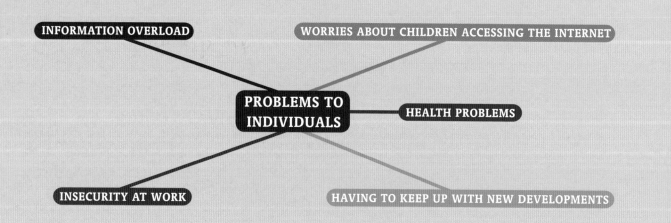

INFORMATION OVERLOAD

WORRIES ABOUT CHILDREN ACCESSING THE INTERNET

PROBLEMS TO INDIVIDUALS

HEALTH PROBLEMS

INSECURITY AT WORK

HAVING TO KEEP UP WITH NEW DEVELOPMENTS

The consequences of the use of ICT for society

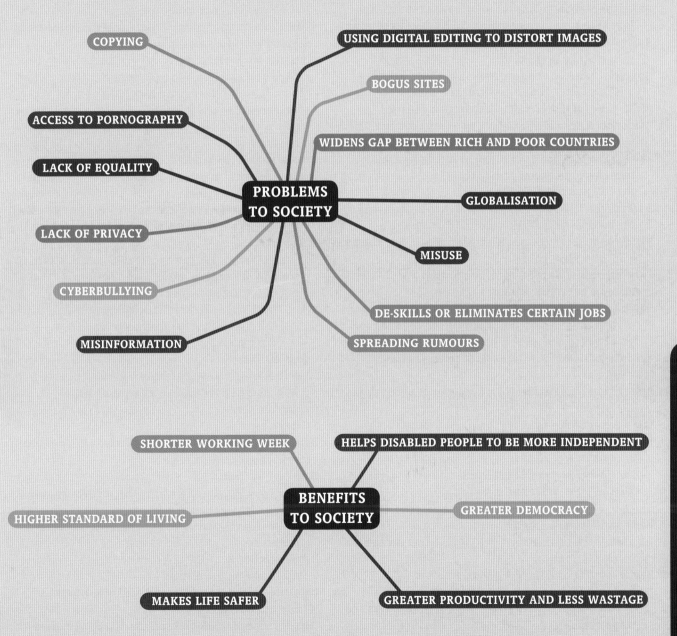

COPYING

USING DIGITAL EDITING TO DISTORT IMAGES

BOGUS SITES

ACCESS TO PORNOGRAPHY

WIDENS GAP BETWEEN RICH AND POOR COUNTRIES

LACK OF EQUALITY

PROBLEMS TO SOCIETY

GLOBALISATION

LACK OF PRIVACY

MISUSE

CYBERBULLYING

DE-SKILLS OR ELIMINATES CERTAIN JOBS

MISINFORMATION

SPREADING RUMOURS

SHORTER WORKING WEEK

HELPS DISABLED PEOPLE TO BE MORE INDEPENDENT

BENEFITS TO SOCIETY

GREATER DEMOCRACY

HIGHER STANDARD OF LIVING

MAKES LIFE SAFER

GREATER PRODUCTIVITY AND LESS WASTAGE

Glossary

Acceptable use policy Document making it clear to all employees or users what is acceptable use of ICT systems and what isn't.

Access rights Restrictions to a user's access to only those files they need in order to perform their job.

Address book In the address book are the names and e-mail addresses of all the people to whom you are likely to send e-mail.

American Standard Code for Information Interchange (ASCII) A code for representing characters in binary.

Analysis Breaking a problem down so that it is easier to understand and solve.

Append Users can add new records but they will be unable to alter or delete existing records.

ASCII Code for representing characters in binary.

Audience A person who will only view the content. They will not alter inputs or change content in any way.

Backup Keeping copies of software and data so that the data can be recovered should there be a total loss of the ICT system.

Backup file A copy of a file which is used in the event of the original file being corrupted (damaged).

Bandwidth A measure of the amount of data that can be transferred using a data transfer medium.

Bar code reader Input device used to scan a series of lines (called a bar code).

Batch processing Type of processing where all the inputs needed are collected, batched together, inputted and processed in one go.

Bespoke software Software specially written for a particular user.

Binary code Code made up from a series of binary digits – 0 or 1.

Bit Binary digit 0 or 1.

Blog A website providing commentary, personal thoughts or news on a particular subject. It is written in chronological order and can include text, images and links to other blogs and websites.

Blogger A person who posts their comments to a blog.

Bookmark Storage area where the URL (i.e. the web address) of a website can be stored so that it can be accessed later using a link.

Bug A mistake or error in a program.

Bullet point A block or paragraph of text that has a symbol placed in front to make the section of text stand out.

CAD (Computer Aided Design) A method of using the computer to produce technical drawings.

CCITT (The International Committee for Data Communication) Popular standard used for electronic communication.

Character Any symbol (letter, number, punctuation mark, etc.) that you can type from the keyboard.

Check digits Numbers placed at the end of the block of numbers used to check that the numbers have been entered correctly into the computer.

Client The person who needs the solution to an ICT problem that they have identified.

Client-server A network where several computers are connected to one or more servers.

Coding Producing a shorter version of the data to aid typing in and to aid validation of the data.

Computer Misuse Act 1990 An Act which makes illegal a number of activities such as deliberately planting viruses, hacking, using ICT equipment for fraud, etc.

Continuous stationery Stationery that is all joined up to be used with a printer. It may be pre-printed with company logos, etc.

Control total A meaningful total (e.g., the total of a batch of invoices) which is entered to check that all the data has been entered/processed.

Cookie A small text file downloaded to your computer, used by websites to collect information about how you use the website.

Copyright, Designs and Patents Act 1988 An act, which amongst other things, makes it an offence to be caught copying or stealing software.

CPU (Central Processing Unit) The computer's brain. It stores and processes data. It has three parts: the ALU, the control unit and the memory.

Crime An illegal act.

Cross field checks Checking the data in more than one field with other fields to make sure they make sense.

Cybercrime Crime committed involving ICT systems as a major part.

Data Raw facts and figures or a set of values, measurements or records of transactions.

Data capture Term for the various methods by which data can be entered into the computer so that it can be processed.

Data controller The person whose responsibility it is in an organisation to control the way that personal data is processed.

Data Protection Act 1998 Law to protect the individual against the misuse of data.

Data subject The living individual whom the personal information is about.

Data type check Check to ensure the data being entered is the same type as the data type specified for the field.

Design techniques The ways you use the design tools to solve problems.

Design tools The software you use to provide a solution to an ICT problem.

Desktop The working area of the GUI and where all the icons are situated.

Double entry of data Two people use the same data source to enter the details into the ICT system and only if the two sets of data are identical, will they be accepted for processing.

Dpi (dots per inch) A measure of the resolution of images. The more dots per inch in an image, the higher the resolution.

Drag and drop Allows you to select objects (icons, folders, files, etc.) and drag them so that you can perform certain operations on them such as drag to the recycle bin to discard, add a file to a folder, copy files to a folder and so on.

Driver A short specially written program that understands the operation of the device it controls/operates. It is needed to allow the systems or applications software to use the connected device properly.

Encoding Process of putting information/data (e.g., text, numbers, symbols, images, sound and video) into a specified format that allows effective transmission or storage by an ICT system.

Encryption Coding data whilst it is being sent over a network so that only the true recipient is able to decode it. Should the data be intercepted by a hacker, then the data will be in code and totally meaningless.

Ergonomics An applied science concerned with designing and arranging things people use so that the people and things interact most efficiently and safely.

Erroneous data Data that is ridiculous or totally unsuitable.

Evaluation The act of reviewing what has been achieved, how it was achieved and how well the solution works.

External threat A threat to an ICT system that comes from outside the organisation.

Extranet An external network that can be used by the customers, suppliers and partners of an organisation as well as the organisation itself.

Favourites Storage area where the URL (i.e. the web address) of a website can be stored so that it can be accessed later using a link.

Federation Against Software Theft An anti-piracy organisation who work to protect the work of software publishers.

File attachments Files that are transferred along with an e-mail.

File compression Used to compress files before storing or before being sent over a network.

File management software Part of systems software used to create folders, copy folders/files, rename folders/files, delete folders/files, move files/folders, etc.

File/Table lookups Used to make sure that codes being used are the same as those used in a table or file of codes.

Firewall Either hardware and/or software that work in a network to prevent communication that is not allowed from one network to another.

Flash/Pen drives Popular storage media which offer cheap and large storage capacities and are ideal media for photographs, music and other data files. They consist of printed circuit boards enclosed in a plastic case.

Footer Text placed at the bottom of a document.

Format checks Checks performed on codes to make sure that they conform to the correct combinations of characters.

Forward If you are sent an e-mail that you think others should see, you can forward it to them.

Freedom of Information Act 2000 Act giving the right of access to information held by public authorities.

Generic software Applications package that is appropriate for a wide range of tasks and can be used in lots of areas of work.

GIGO Abbreviation for garbage in garbage out. It means that if you put rubbish into the computer then you get rubbish out.

Grammar checker Used to check the grammar in a sentence and to highlight problems and suggest alternatives.

Graph plotter A device which draws by moving a pen. Useful for scale drawings and is used mainly with CAD packages.

Graphics tablet An input device which makes use of a large tablet containing many shapes and commands which may be selected by the user by moving a cursor and clicking. Basically it moves the toolbars onto the tablet rather than clutter up the screen when doing large technical drawings using CAD software.

Groups Lists of people and their e-mail addresses.

GUI (Graphical User Interface) An interface that allows users to communicate with ICT equipment by making use of icons and pull-down menus.

Hacker A person who tries to or succeeds in breaking into a secure ICT system.

Hacking The process of trying to break into a secure computer system.

Hard copy Printed output on a computer which may be taken away and studied.

Hardware The physical components of a computer system.

Hash total Meaningless total of numbers used to check that all the numbers have been entered into the computer.

Header Text placed at the top of a document.

Health & Safety (Display Screen Equipment) Regulations 1992 Regulations making it law for employers to take certain measures to protect the health and safety of their employees who use ICT equipment.

Health and Safety at Work Act 1974 Law making sure that employees have safe working conditions and methods.

Hot spot A region where the Internet can be accessed wirelessly.

Icons Small pictures used to represent commands, files or windows.

ICT systems Hardware and software working together with people and procedures to do a job.

Identity theft/fraud Using your banking/credit card/personal details in order to commit fraud.

Implementation The process of producing the working version of the solution to the problem as identified by the client.

Indexing Allows words to be highlighted so that they can be used to form an index.

Information Output from an ICT system or data that has been processed and gives us knowledge.

Information Commissioner The person responsible for enforcing the Data Protection Act. They also promote good practice and make everyone aware of the implications of the Act.

Ink-jet printer A printer that works by spraying ink through nozzles onto the paper.

Input Act of entering data into an ICT system.

Input device The hardware device used to feed the input data into an ICT system such as a keyboard or a scanner.

Input media The material on which the data is encoded so that it can be read by an input device and digitised so that it can be input, processed and turned into information by the ICT system.

Input message A message which when the field or cell is selected, gives the user some advice on the kind of data that should be entered.

Integrated software An application package consisting of software for several distinct applications. There will always be two or more applications packages in integrated software.

Interactive Where there is a constant dialogue between the user and the computer.

Interface The point where two objects meet. In ICT this is usually between a device such as a computer, printer, scanner, etc., and a human.

Internal threat A threat to an ICT system that comes from inside an organisation.

Internet A huge group of networks joined together.

Internet service provider (ISP) The organisation that provides your Internet connection.

Intranet A private network used within an organisation that makes uses of Internet technology.

Laser printer A printer which uses a laser beam to form characters on the paper.

Length check Checks to make sure that the data being entered has the correct number of characters in it.

Macro Used to record a series of keystrokes so that, for example, your name and address can be added to the top of the page simply by pressing a single key or clicking on the mouse.

Magnetic Ink Character Recognition Input method making use of numbers printed onto a document such as a cheque in a special magnetic ink which can be read by the magnetic ink character reader at very high speed.

Magnetic media Media such as tape and disk where the data is stored as a magnetic pattern.

Magnetic strip Data is encoded in the magnetic strip and when the card is swiped the data from the card is used to record the transaction.

Magnetic strip reader Hardware device that reads the data contained in magnetic strips such as those on the back of credit cards.

Mail merge Combining a list of names and addresses with a standard letter so that a series of letters is produced with each letter being addressed to a different person.

Malpractice Improper or careless use or misconduct.

Memory cards Thin cards you see in digital cameras used to store photographs and can be used for other data.

Menus Allow a user to make selections from a list.

MIDI (Musical Instrument Digital Interface) Used mainly to communicate between electronic keyboards, synthesisers and computers. MIDI files are compressed and the files are quite small.

Mind map A hierarchical diagram with a central idea, or image, at the centre of the map surrounded by branches that extend from the central idea.

MP3 Music file format that uses compression to reduce the file size considerably and this is why the MP3 file format is so popular with portable music playing devices such as iPods.

Multimedia A means of communication that combines more than one medium for presentation purposes, such as sound, graphics and video.

Natural language interface An interface that allows the user to interact using natural written or spoken language (e.g., English) as opposed to computer language and commands.

Network A group of computers which are able to communicate with each other.

Network A group of ICT devices (computers, printers, scanners, etc.) which are able to communicate with each other.

Networking software Systems software which allows computers connected together to function as a network.

Non-volatile memory Memory stored on a chip which does not lose data when the power is turned off.

Normal data Entering data that should be acceptable to the solution.

Notification The process of letting the Information Commissioner's Office know that an organisation is storing and processing personal data.

OCR Optical Character Recognition. This is a combination of software and a scanner which is able to read characters into the computer.

Off-the-shelf software Software that has not been developed for a particular use.

OMR Optical Mark Reader/Recognition. Reader that detects marks on a piece of paper. Shaded areas are detected and the computer can understand the information contained in them.

Operating system Software that controls the hardware of a computer and is used to run the applications software. Operating systems control the handling of input, output, interrupts, etc.

Optical Character Recognition (OCR) Input method using a scanner as the input device along with special software which looks at the shape of each character so that it can be recognised separately.

Optical Mark Recognition (OMR) Input method using paper-based forms or cards with marks on them that are read automatically by a device called an optical mark reader.

Output The results from processing data.

Package software A bundle of files necessary for a particular program to run along with some form of documentation to help a user get the program started.

Password A series of characters which need to be typed in before access to the ICT system is allowed.

Peer-to-peer Network arrangement where each computer is of equal status.

Peripheral A device connected to and under the control of the central processing unit (CPU).

Personal data Data about a living identifiable person, which is specific to that person.

Personal skills Those skills a person possesses and which are transferable to any job or task.

Phishing Tricking people into revealing their banking or credit card details.

Piracy The process of illegally copying software.

Pixel The smallest dot of light on the computer screen which can be individually controlled.

Podcasting Creating and publishing a digital radio broadcast using a microphone, computer and audio editing software. The resulting file is saved in MP3 format and then uploaded onto an Internet server. It can then be downloaded using a facility called RSS onto an MP3 player such as an iPod.

Pointer This is the little arrow that appears when using Windows.

Presence checks Check to make sure that data had been entered into a field.

Primary storage Storage in chips inside the computer.

Print preview Feature that comes with most software used to produce documents. It allows users to view the page or pages of a document to see exactly how they will be printed. If necessary, the documents can be corrected.

Printer driver Software that converts commands from the systems or applications software into a form that a particular printer can understand.

Privacy Being able to choose to keep certain aspects of your life private.

Process Any operation that transfers data into information.

Processing Performing calculations or arranging the data into a meaningful order.

Programmer A person who writes computer programs.

Proof reading Carefully reading what has been typed in and comparing it with what is on the data source (order forms, application forms, invoices, etc.) for any errors, which can then be corrected.

Protocol A set of standards that allows the transfer of data between computers on a network.

RAID (Redundant array of inexpensive disks) A system used by networks to keep backups.

RAM (Random access memory) Used to hold the data temporarily whilst the computer is working on it. Contents are lost when the computer is switched off.

Range check Data validation technique which checks that the data input into the computer is within a certain range.

Read only A user can only read the contents of the file. They cannot alter or delete the data.

Read/Write A user can read the data held in the file and can alter the data.

Real-time processing The input data is processed immediately as it arrives. The results have a direct effect on the next set of available data.

Relational database management system (RDMS) Database system where the data is held in tables with relationships established between them. The software is used to set up and hold the data as well as to extract and manipulate the stored data.

Relationship The way tables are related to each other. Relationships can be one-to-one, one-to-many or many-to-many.

Reply Allows you to read an e-mail and then write the reply without having to enter the recipient's e-mail address.

Resolution The sharpness or clarity of an image.

ROM (Read only memory) Memory stored on a chip which does not lose data when the power is turned off.

Router Hardware device which is able to make the decision about the path that an individual packet of data should take so that it arrives in the shortest possible time.

RSI Repetitive strain injury. A painful muscular condition caused by repeatedly using certain muscles in the same way.

Scams Setting up bogus companies with bogus websites and then making off with the money from customers' orders.

Scanner Input device that can be used to capture an image and is useful for digitising old non-digital photographs, paper documents or pictures in books.

Search engine Program which searches for required information on the Internet.

Secondary (or backup storage) Storage outside the computer.

Security Making sure that the hardware, software and data of an ICT system does not come to any harm.

Shockwave audio Format used for very high quality sound with very small file size.

Software Programs which supply the instructions to the hardware.

Software licence Document (digital or paper) which sets out the terms by which the software can be used. It will refer to the number of computers on which it can be run simultaneously.

Sorting Putting data into ascending or descending order.

Spam Unsolicited bulk e-mail (i.e., e-mail from people you do not know, sent to everyone in the hope that a small percentage may purchase the goods or services on offer).

Specific software Software that only performs one task.

Spellchecker Facility offered by software where there is a dictionary against which all words typed in are checked.

Spyware Software which collects information about the user of a computer connected to the Internet without their consent.

Storage capacity How much data can the storage device/media hold? Usually measured in Mb or Gb.

Systems software Any computer software that manages and controls the hardware thus allowing the applications software to do a useful job. Systems software consists of a group of programs.

Taskbar Shows the programs that are open. This facility is handy when working on several programs together.

Technical skills Those skills necessary to complete a specific job in ICT.

Telecommunications The field of technology concerned with communicating at a distance (e.g., telephones, radio, cable, etc.).

Templates Used to specify the structure of a document such as fonts, page layout, formatting and styles.

Test plan The approach that will be used to test the whole solution and consists of a suite of tests.

Thesaurus Allows a word to be chosen and the word processor will list synonyms (i.e., words with similar meanings).

Toner Black plastic particles used by laser printers as the 'ink'.

Topology The way a particular network is arranged. Examples include ring, star, mesh and bus.

Touch screen Screen that allows a person to make selections by simply touching the screen.

Transaction A piece of business, e.g. an order, purchase, return, delivery, transfer of money, etc.

Transaction processing Processing of each transaction as it arises.

Transcription error Error made when typing data in using a document as the source of the data.

Transmission medium The material which forms the connection between the computers in a network (e.g., air in the case of wireless, metal wire, optical fibre).

Transmission rate The speed of data flow in bits per second (bps) through transmission media.

Transposition error Error made when characters are swapped around so they are in the wrong order.

Trojans Lines of computer code stored in your PC without you knowing.

Uninstallers Software used to remove all the files put onto the computer when a piece of software was installed.

UPS (Uninterruptible power supply) A backup power supply (generator and battery) which will keep the computer running should the mains power supply fail.

URL (Uniform Resource Locator) The web address used to locate a webpage.

User A person who makes active use of an ICT solution to solve an ICT problem.

Username A way of identifying who is using the ICT system in order to allocate network resources.

Utility Part of the systems software that performs a specific task.

Utility programs Software which helps the user perform tasks such as virus checking, file compression, etc.

Validation checks Checks a developer of a solution creates, using the software, in order to restrict the data that a user can enter so as to reduce errors.

Validation expression/rule Command that a developer must type in order to set up the validation for a particular field/cell.

Validation message A message which appears if the validation rule is breached.

Verification Checking that the data being entered into the ICT system perfectly matches the source of the data.

Videoconferencing ICT system that allows face-to-face meetings to be conducted without the participants being in the same room or even the same geographical area.

Virus A program that replicates (i.e. copies) itself automatically and usually carries with it some payload which causes damage.

Voice recognition Voice recognition systems allow you to enter data via a microphone directly into a computer.

Volatile memory Memory which loses data when the power is turned off.

WAV Used with Windows for storing sounds. Files in this format are not highly compressed.

Web browser The software program you use to access the Internet. Microsoft Internet Explorer is an example of a web browser.

Webcam A small video camera used as an input device to send a moving image over an intranet or the Internet.

Webpage Single document on the World Wide Web.

Wi-Fi A trademark for the certification of products that meet certain standards for transmitting data over wireless networks.

WIMP (Windows Icons Menus Pointing devices) The graphical user interface (GUI) way of using a computer rather than typing in commands at the command line.

World Wide Web A means of accessing information contained on the Internet. It is an information sharing model that is built on top of the Internet.

Worm A program that keeps replicating itself automatically, and as it does so it takes more and more disk space and also uses a greater proportion of the system's resources for each copy.

Index

Acknowledgements

Folens Limited would like to thank the following for giving permission to use copyright material.

p.2, © Adam Borkowski/Fotolia; p.2, © Panagiotis Parthenios/Fotolia; p.3, Glasbergen; p.3, © Radu Razvan/Fotolia; p.3, © Mark Aplet/Fotolia; p.4, GreenGate Publishing; p.5, Connect Systems; p.5, Ergoption; p.5, Glasbergen; p.5, KB Covers; p.6, © Alexey Khlobystov/Fotolia; p.6, © Doug Olson/Fotolia; p.6, © Tomasz Trojanowski/Fotolia; p.7, © Anneke Schram/Fotolia; p.7, © Stasys Eidiejus/Fotolia; p.14, © Philip Date/Fotolia; p.15, © Kelly Young/Fotolia; p.22, © Andres Rodriguez/Fotolia; p.23, © Aloysius Patrimonio/Fotolia; p.25, © Big Daddy/Fotolia; p.28, © Tadija Savic/Fotolia; p.46, © This image is a copyright of SnappyStock, Inc./Fotolia; p.46, GreenGate Publishing; p.47, © Anatoly Vartanov/Fotolia; p.47, Datamatic Ltd; p.47, Epson (UK) Ltd; p.47, © Michael Pettigrew/Fotolia p.47, © Victoria Alexandrova/Fotolia p.48, DRS Data Services Ltd; p.48, © Karen Roach/Fotolia; p.48, Scanning Pens Limited; p.49, © Leticia Wilson/Fotolia; p.49, Magtek; p.50, © Kevin Penhallow/Fotolia; p.50, © PhilEddies/Fotolia; p.50, © philippe Devanne/Fotolia; p.51, © Bube /Fotolia; p.51, © Alexey Khromushin/Fotolia; p.51, © Anette Linnea Rasmussen/Fotolia; p.51, © Gudellaphoto/Fotolia; p.51, © Kirsty Pargeter/Fotolia; p.51, © kmit/Fotolia; p.51, © Tinka/Fotolia; p.51, GreenGate Publishing; p.58, © Harris Shiffman/Fotolia; p.58, © Tan Kian Khoon/Fotolia; p.59, Jellyhead360/Fotolia; p.59, © Anette Linnea Rasmussen/Fotolia; p.59, © Slawomir Jastrzebski/Fotolia; p.59, © Andrew Williamson/Fotolia; p.60, © Andrzej Tokarski/Fotolia; p.61, © Aron Hsiao/Fotolia; p.61, GreenGate Publishing; p.61, © Labrador/Fotolia; p.62, © Kirsty Pargeter/Fotolia; p.62, © PhilEddies/Fotolia; p.62, © Podfoto/Fotolia; p.63, © Andy Mac/Fotolia; p.63, GreenGate Publishing; p.63, © Yong Hian Lim/Fotolia; p.71, Epson (UK) Ltd; p.72, © Bryan Kuntz/Fotolia; p.72, Glasbergen; p.73, © GraAa Victoria/Fotolia; p.73, © Tan Kian Khoon/Fotolia; p.75, © Gilles Parnalland/Fotolia; p.75, Protouch; p.81, Larry Ewing, Simon Budig and Anja Gerwinski; p.81, GreenGate Publishing; p.83, Thompson; p.85, Que Tek Consulting Corporation; p.85, © Nikolai Sorokin/Fotolia; p.87, Glasbergen; p.93, AOL; p.94, Adobe; p.95, Adobe; p.105, © Forgiss/Fotolia; p.111, © Ivana Korab/Fotolia; p.119, © Ewa Walicka/Fotolia; p.124, © Marek Slusarczyk/Fotolia; p.133, © Paul Herbert/Fotolia; p.138, © Lisa F. Young/Fotolia; p.138, © Ron Chapple/Fotolia; p.139, © Andres Rodriguez/Fotolia; p.139, © Arkna/Fotolia; p.139, © Ramona Heim/Fotolia; p.140, © Feng Yu/Fotolia; p.140, © Nenad Djedovic/Fotolia; p.141, © Sean Gladwell/Fotolia; p.143, Glasbergen; p.144, Glasbergen; p.144, © Jaimie Duplass/Fotolia; p.145, © Endostock/Fotolia; p.145, Glasbergen; p.152, © Marc Dietrich/Fotolia; p.152, © Stephen Coburn/Fotolia; p.153, © 2005 Sean MacLeay/Fotolia; p.153, GreenGate Publishing; p.154, © 2005 Sean MacLeay/Fotolia; p.154, © Nathalie Dulex/Fotolia; p.154, © dechefbloke/Fotolia; p.154, © Dominique Luzy/Fotolia; p.154, © Com Evolution/Fotolia; p.154, © Jeff Gynane/Fotolia; p.154, © Galyna Andrushko/Fotolia; p.155, © Stephen Finn/Fotolia; p.155, © Godfer/Fotolia; p.157, KaZaA; p.169, Glasbergen; p.169, Lloyds TSB; p.170, McAfee; p.170, © Samuray/Fotolia; p.171, © Cristina Fumi/Fotolia; p.171, J. Sainsbury plc; p.171, © Feng Yu/Fotolia; p.172, Lloyds TSB; p.172, © Darko Novakovic/Fotolia; p.172, © Mark Stout/Fotolia; p.173, © Paul Preneau/Fotolia; p.173, © Thorsten Rust/Fotolia; p.174, © 2006 Ron Hudson /Fotolia; p.174, © ewerest/Fotolia; p.174, © James Steidl/Fotolia; p.174, © NorthShoreSurfPhotos/Fotolia; p.174, © Pattie/Fotolia; p.174, © Robert Paul van Beets/Fotolia; p.175, GreenGate Publishing; p.178, Glasbergen; p.179, Glasbergen; p.180, © Dimitrios Kaisaris/Fotolia; p.180, © Dominique Luzy/Fotolia; p.181 Glasbergen; p.181, © rgbdigital.co.uk/Fotolia; p.182, © Carsten Reisinger/Fotolia; p.182, © Slavoljub Petrovic/Fotolia; p.182, © Stephen Coburn/Fotolia; p.183, © Aloysius Patrimonio/Fotolia; p.183, © Kirsty Pargeter/Fotolia; p.183, © Sally Wallis/Fotolia; p.183, © Sean Gladwell/Fotolia; p.183, © Zen2000/Fotolia; p.184, © Julien Eichinger/Fotolia; p.185, © Peter Baxter/Fotolia; p.186, © Kirsty Pargeter/Fotolia; p.186, © Yong Hian Lim/Fotolia; p.187, © Moïse Parienti/Fotolia; p.187, © Aurelio/Fotolia; p.188, © Feng Yu/Fotolia; p.188, © Tomislav/Fotolia; p.189, © Dana Bartekoske/Fotolia; p.190, Reproduced with kind permission from The Co-operative Financial Services; p.193, Experian; p.198, Voice in a Crowd; p.207, © Clivia/Fotolia; p.208, © Ana Vasileva/Fotolia; p.208, © Andy Mac/Fotolia; p.208, © Nikolai Sorokin/Fotolia; p.208, © Paul Lockwood/Fotolia; p.208, © Paul Maguire/Fotolia; p.209, © Andrew Khritin/Fotolia; p.209, © Glenn Jenkinson/Fotolia; p.209, © Sean Gladwell/Fotolia; p.211, © James Blacklock/Fotolia; p.211, © Yong Hian Lim/Fotolia; p.212, © HinelineDesign/Fotolia; p.212, © Murat Baysan/Fotolia; p.213, © Norman p.213, © Peter Galbraith/Fotolia; p.213, © Willem169/Fotolia; p.222, © david hughes/Fotolia; p.222, © Valery Potapova/Fotolia; p.222, © 3DWeave, all rights reserveda/Fotolia; p.222, © Stolbtsov Alexandre/Fotolia; p.222, © Ivan Kmit/Fotolia; p.222, © Aloysius Patrimonio /Fotolia; p.223, © Bobby Deal/Fotolia; p.223,© Edward White/Fotolia; p.223,© Press Boy/Fotolia; p.224,© naskybabe/Fotolia; p.225,© Eric Simard/Fotolia; p.227,© Dmitry Ersler/Fotolia; p.227, Sony; p.235, St Pixels online church, http://www.stpixels.com; p.237, © Dylan J Burrill/Fotolia; p.237, © Santa Maria/Fotolia; p.237, © steven Husk/Fotolia; p.246, Friends Re-united; p.246, Skype; p.246, © www.c-foto.dk - Lars K. Christensen/Fotolia; p.249, BBC (bbc.co.uk/gcsebitesize); p.250, © Douglas Stevens/Fotolia; p.250, © Feng Yu/Fotolia; p.251, © Kevin Chesson/Fotolia; p.252, © Andres Rodriguez/Fotolia; p.252, © Kirill Zdorov/Fotolia; p.253, GreenGate Publishing; p.253, © Norman Chan/Fotolia; p.254, Bacs; p.254, Suffolk Police; p.255, Ergoption.

Adobe product screen shot(s) reprinted with permission from Adobe Systems Incorporated.

Microsoft product screenshots reprinted with permission from Microsoft Corporation.

Every effort has been made to contact copyright holders of material used in this publication. If any copyright holder has been overlooked, we should be pleased to make any necessary arrangements.